Understanding the Edwardian and Inter-War House

Understanding the Edwardian and Inter-War House

Alan Johnson

A Historical, Architectural and Practical Guide

The Crowood Press

First published in 2006 by
The Crowood Press Ltd
Ramsbury, Marlborough
Wiltshire SN8 2HR

www.crowood.com

British Library Cataloguing-in-Publication Data
A catalogue record for this book is available from the British Library.

ISBN 1 86126 834 3
EAN 978 1 86126 834 1

Disclaimer
The author and the publisher do not accept responsibility in any manner whatsoever for any error or omission, nor any loss, damage, injury, or adverse outcome, or liability of any kind incurred as a result of the use of the information contained in this book, or reliance upon it. Readers are advised to seek specific professional advice relating to their particular house, project and circumstances before embarking on any installation or building work.

Dedication
For Heather and Neil

Acknowledgements
I am very grateful to Richard Kay for providing many of the drawn illustrations and to Robin Bishop whose prolific slide photography made an important contribution to the collection from which I have drawn many of the photographs; to Ian Dungavell for very kindly contributing the foreword and to Roy Brook, Robert Eastleigh and Jim Joyce for the loan of photographs illustrating the historical connection between provision of public transport and housing development.

For much of the information setting the socio-cultural context for the inter-war house building campaign in Britain, I am particularly indebted to Alan A. Jackson's magisterial *Semi-detached London* and *Dunroamin: The Suburban Semi and its Enemies* (Oliver, Davis and Bentley).

I also owe my thanks to The Crowood Press for encouraging me to review and recast material long-dormant, and last, but by no means least, to my wife Liz for her stoical toleration of the additional domestic pressures resulting from my decision to return to this project.

All photographs are by the author unless otherwise stated.

Designed and typeset by Focus Publishing,
11a St Botolph's Road, Sevenoaks, Kent TN13 3AJ

Printed and bound in Great Britain by
The Cromwell Press, Trowbridge

Contents

Foreword

The tide of architectural taste has shifted enormously in the past sixty years. As post-war planners surveyed the country's stock of dilapidated houses badly in need of maintenance that had been deferred by the war, it seemed to them that the future lay not in individual brick houses and terraces, but with industrialised building methods using steel and concrete. Government policy was to demolish – councils got big grants to put up new houses, but not to bring 'obsolete' old ones up to scratch.

We're now familiar with the results, and we can only be thankful that lack of money put paid to many of the more ambitious rebuilding schemes. Remarkably, houses that were then thought of as outmoded, are still going strong, while many of their replacements have been condemned and are being demolished in their turn. Traditional buildings have proved more adaptable to modern requirements and to have a lower long-term cost of ownership than new ones. Now, in more energy-conscious days, we also understand that it's more sensible to bring old buildings up to scratch than to demolish them and start again.

Buyers have voted strongly with their feet. Surveys tell us that Edwardian and inter-war houses are tremendously popular. Even speculatively built homes boast individual touches and a level of craftsmanship that is not so easily achieved today. Large windows and high ceilings, great assets in the days of gas lighting, now provide the bright, airy interiors that suit us even better in the days of central heating. Painted inside in light colours, they adapt to modern styles of decor remarkably well, while also offering a desirable canvas for those who want to recreate a period look.

Of course, Edwardian and inter-war houses come in great variety. Some Edwardian houses could be mistaken for those built thirty or forty years earlier, just as some inter-war houses look Edwardian. Innovations in plan and decor were taken up with greater or lesser enthusiasm depending on the builders' understanding of the market. But others are very much of their time.

What they all share is that their structure and materials are different, or used differently from houses being built today. This means that some special knowledge will be invaluable to anyone who owns or lives in an Edwardian or inter-war building. Through understanding the particular characteristics of these houses, costly or damaging mistakes can be avoided. But the right information can be difficult to come by. Ordinary builders, not necessarily trained in traditional ways, cannot be expected to know; neither can all architects. And there are many firms who have nothing to lose by selling you an 'improvement' you do not need and which may ultimately reduce the value of your house.

The Victorian Society has for a long time provided information and guidance to owners of Victorian houses, culminating in our book, *The Victorian Society Book of the Victorian House*. Confusingly, 'the long Edwardian period' (from the death of Queen Victoria in 1901 to the First World War) has always been within the Society's remit, though our founders presumably found the 'Victorian and Edwardian Society' too much of a mouthful. Edwardian and inter-war dwellings share many of the same characteristics as their predecessors and there has been a demand for a special book devoted to such houses. This is it.

Dr Ian Dungavell
Director, The Victorian Society
www.victoriansociety.org.uk

Preface

Due mainly to the preferences of the literary intelligentsia of the last century, the story of the semi-detached house and suburban estate development is largely untold. Yet millions have benefited from the facilities and amenities they offered as an improvement over the regimented urban housing that had swelled the sprawl of nineteenth-century towns and cities. This book aims to redress this imbalance by explaining the cultural origins and constructional anatomy of cottage-style houses of the Edwardian and inter-war periods.

A main aim of my earlier book *How to Restore and Improve Your Victorian House* (1984) was to counteract the tendency of contemporary DIY handbooks to recommend the removal of distinctive features of Victorian houses in the name of 'modernisation'. Thankfully, that phase has itself become part of history and the intervening years have witnessed enhancement of the treatment of modest Victorian houses, in extreme cases, almost to the level of museum artefacts. There is now a range of publications giving sound advice on the conservation and repair of these dwellings. However, almost nothing has been done to extend the study to cover the constructional form of inter-war houses, four million of which were added to the national stock of dwellings during the period 1919–39.

This book has been written in the conviction that these buildings deserve an understanding of their anatomy and the forces that brought them into being. It is my hope that this book will assist and enthuse householders seeking to conserve and enhance the cherished qualities of these characterful dwellings.

Alan Johnson
Hampton Wick
Spring 2006

Author's note: Where terms in the text appear in italics, definitions will be found in the Glossary of Terms on pages 215–19.

FIG. 1. Bedford Park, Chiswick, west London: a typical house of this 1870s estate.

CHAPTER 1

Historical Background 1870–1939

At first sight, it might be thought strange to couple Edwardian houses with inter-war dwellings and stranger still to link the latter to nineteenth-century housing. Yet today's older generations will confirm the view that some 'Victorian values' in British society endured into the early 1960s and it is certainly the case that the mode of interior decoration in speculatively-built inter-war houses had its roots firmly in mid-Victorian taste. Today's visitor to an untouched semi-detached house of the 1920s or 30s will be struck by the overwhelming darkness of the interior. This reality stands in stark contrast to the image presented in modern TV and film productions which portray carefully coordinated schemes of interior design, often dominated by light or radiant colours, stuffed with Art Deco furniture and furnishings. Such integrated schemes of interior design were rarely, if ever, achieved in speculatively built houses, if only because their occupants generally lacked the means to purchase these 'ultra-modern', craftsman-made – and therefore expensive – fittings and furniture.

Although society *was* changing between the 1870s and 1939, many of the staple features of life remained the same. A preference for gloomy interiors prevailed from the middle of the nineteenth century and was not easily changed, and in a nation in which the open coal fire remained the principal source of room heating (as late as the 1960s in most small suburban houses) there was certainly a practical reason for adopting schemes of interior decoration favouring dark colours, as anyone who has had to handle the ash and dust resulting from open fires will confirm.

However, acknowledging that there are distinctions between the form of Edwardian and inter-war houses and the urban and suburban houses that preceded them, it is necessary to trace the origins of these differences.

Social historians have noted that from the 1860s some of the tensions in mid-Victorian society began to ease. The expanding middle classes were in need of a new lifestyle, different from the relentless industry of their parents' generation and more in tune with the gentlemanly virtues recommended in the novels of W. M. Thackeray. In 1869 the poet and critic Matthew Arnold had written an essay, *Culture and Anarchy*, which gently criticised the sometimes mindless energy of mid-Victorian society and pleaded for a more general appreciation of beauty and enlightenment in contrast to the contemporary preoccupation with expansion of industry and commerce.

This appeal had its first impact on the design of suburban dwellings in a new development at Chiswick, west London, called Bedford Park, which, from 1875, was established as an enclave for these newly enlightened folk of 'artistic temperament'. Located only thirty minutes' journey away from the City of London via the District Railway, Bedford Park was the brainchild of Jonathan Carr, the landowner, who wished to develop the land not merely as a housing estate but as a new community for artistic people, including a church, shops, art school and social club. To establish the architectural style for the new houses, Carr employed two of the most fashionable architects of the time – Edward Godwin and Richard Norman Shaw. The success of Bedford Park meant that its architectural details –

'Dutch' gables of red brickwork, tile-hanging and multi-paned white-painted wooden windows, were subsequently copied all over suburbia (Fig. 1). Even more influential was its general atmosphere. Compared with later developments, it is too cramped to qualify as a true 'garden suburb' but it is conspicuously leafy, and the fairly wide freedom accorded to designers of individual houses, which caused a considerable variety of designs to be erected, as well as the slightly irregular road layout (dictated by the policy of preserving existing trees) creates a 'cosy' environment which was to become characteristic of the Garden City Movement and a quality sought in most of twentieth-century suburbia.

Unfortunately, the picturesque values embodied in the forms and layout of Bedford Park were not typical of late nineteenth-century residential estate development. Grid-iron plan estates composed of monotonous, straight, parallel 'by-law streets' as prescribed by local building by-laws developed from the Public Health Act of 1875 continued to be built in many towns and cities until the start of the First World War and the house type which populated each such street was rather different from the villas developed by Jonathan Carr. The late-Victorian terraced house differed from its mid-century forebear only in incorporating adaptations forced on the builder by the terms of the model by-laws – a defined minimum distance across streets between front elevations of facing houses, prescribed minimum zones of open space at the rear of each dwelling etc. Builders were devoted to the aim of producing a saleable product and saw no advantage in dispensing with the traditional back extension. Consequently, the dimly lit rear rooms of the 'tunnel-back' dwelling continued to be erected until new predilections forced builders to create a product which would sell in a changed market.

This change in taste resulted from changes in the preferences of the architectural *avant garde*. The Queen Anne Revival style which characterised Bedford Park proved to be very durable – some of its features were still appearing in speculative dwellings into the early 1920s – but *avant-garde* architects had long since tired of its relative fussiness. The calm qualities of the traditional 'vernacular' houses of the English countryside were beginning to be rediscovered by the most advanced architects as early as the 1860s. Initially, features noted in sketches of old cottages were 'inflated' for use in the large houses commissioned by the rich clients of architects such as R. N. Shaw (Fig. 2) but the history of the late nineteenth century is also the story of an enlarging middle class and soon clients of more modest means could afford to commission architects to design smaller houses of appropriate specification.

FIG. 2. *The Old English style: half-timbering on a mansion, 'Grim's Dyke' Harrow Weald, Middlesex (1872) designed by Richard Norman Shaw (1831–1912). (Robin Bishop.)*

FIG. 3. 'Moor Crag', Windermere (1899); architect C. F. A. Voysey (1857–1941). (Paul Renouf.)

Many architects, who had shunned the ornateness and over-elaboration characteristic of mid-nineteenth century taste in favour of the simpler palette of materials and forms of traditional rural buildings and the 'Old English' style which sprang from it, were only too glad to recreate these features and forms in new houses for these new clients. The leading architect of this movement was C. F. A. Voysey (1857–1941) who drew inspiration not only from the pioneers of the Old English style such as Shaw, Nesfield, Champneys and Devey (his one-time employer) but also from the simple forms and ground-hugging profiles of English yeoman houses of the seventeenth century (Fig. 3).

Several problems resulted from the desire to apply the style of this new architecture to the typical form of suburban house derived from close attention to the standards of the model by-laws of 1877. First, estate developers tended to crowd both sides of new streets with terraced dwellings at a density of up to thirty houses per acre in order to maximise the income from their development. Open space between neighbouring dwellings was not thought to pay as well as the maximum internal accommodation created in a continuous terrace of houses. The resultant proportions of individual houses (successors of the terraced type lining the streets of eighteenth-century towns) were high and narrow and therefore unsympathetic to the low-level horizontality that characterised traditional rural dwellings.

Secondly, the apparently indispensable back extension of the typical terraced house, in producing an L-shaped plan, also militated against application of a 'vernacular' treatment to its form; replication of the small rural house required a simple plan-form – ideally a single rectangle – admitting the possibility of capping the accommodation with a single pitched and hipped roof. As this craving for a style more reminiscent of rural dwellings became more pronounced, so the speculative builders were forced into changing their standard formula for the saleable or lettable suburban house.

From Regency times, the semi-detached house had been a legitimate type, even for erection by speculative builders, and by the late 1880s architects had shown that the features of vernacular architecture could be grafted on to this plan-form to produce a suitably convincing result. So a plan-form neither so

11

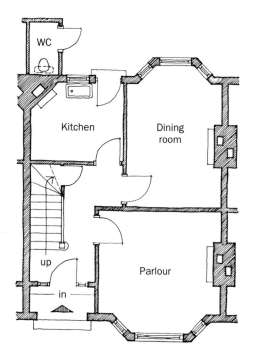

FIG. 4. Ground-floor plan of a double-fronted Edwardian house showing the back extension reduced to an outside WC.

extravagant in land use as the detached house nor so unsympathetic to 'vernacular' treatment as the terraced type had been developed and, although in 1911 terraced houses represented almost 90 per cent of the housing stock and were to remain the dominant house type in speculative development until the First World War, their primacy was beginning to be threatened by the increasing number of semi-detached houses. Yet, in view of its popularity among builders, the convincing 'vernacularisation' of the terraced type was an equally important issue. The difficulty of applying an overall vernacular treatment to terraced dwellings was eventually solved either by entirely omitting the back extension or by reducing it to a vestigial single-storey outshot (Fig. 4). Condensing virtually all of the accommodation into a simple rectangular plan allowed the vernacular style to be applied to the entire exterior of the house, but only at the price of widening the plan into 'double-fronted' accommodation (Fig. 5). However, this

change also assisted the adoption of the cottage style by creating more horizontal proportions in the front and rear elevations, which therefore more readily accepted the forms and details of the vernacular treatment.

Of course, changes in fashion and related changes in architectural style were not the only forces moulding the Edwardian and inter-war houses that are familiar to us today. Builders had to satisfy changing functional requirements. Certainly the typical family of the inter-war years was different from the family of the mid-Victorian era. The birth rate had been declining from the 1870s and the average number of children per family fell from 5.8 in 1871 to 2.2 in the 1930s. Even in Edwardian times family size had reduced considerably from the mid-Victorian norm. The population of the UK rose from 41.5m in 1901 to 45.2m in 1911 largely because people began to live longer and by the Edwardian period the upper and middle classes in particular were raising smaller families than their forebears. Improvements in medicine, hygiene and housing cut the infant mortality rate and raised life expectancy.

Another child of the late-Victorian enlightenment encouraged by Matthew Arnold was London's International Health Exhibition of 1884 which symbolised the move away from 'Trust in God' to better knowledge and practice of hygiene, and in some ways the demand for healthier conditions in new houses was the keynote of much Edwardian residential development. This desire to 'get the house right all round' (that is, kitchens and bathrooms were almost as deserving of careful design as the main living rooms) dovetailed neatly with the appeal for aesthetic consistency made by the architects of the Arts and Crafts Movement and probably contributed to much of the ornamentation which had embellished front elevations of Victorian houses being omitted after the turn of the century. Certainly, contemporary writers on Edwardian interior design frequently commented adversely on furnishings that created dust traps and there was much praise for the inclusion of fitted (and therefore less dust-generating) furniture in new houses.

Yet all these preferences would have been insignificant socially in the absence of a mass market for

Edwardian, and later, inter-war, speculatively built houses. In relation to the terms for occupation of a house, even until the outbreak of the First World War in 1914, almost 90 per cent of the housing stock was rented and, though it is hard to believe in an age dominated by owner-occupation, for the middle classes of Edwardian Britain, renting was the more respectable form of tenure. Nevertheless, diversity and experimentation in forms of tenure increased in the Edwardian period as new housing cooperatives were set up and developers increasingly encouraged freehold and leasehold purchase of houses. The influence and resources of the building societies were growing and it was beginning to be considered legitimate to take out mortgages. By the inter-war years this had become the favoured mode of procurement of a new house. None of this would have been possible without the promise of a steady income into typical families and certainly many people were able to contemplate far more secure conditions of trade or employment by the late 1930s than had applied fifty years earlier.

Before the First World War, indeed right up to its outbreak in 1914, the gap between rich and poor remained very wide. In 1911 a High Court judge might earn £5,000 whilst a charwoman's annual earnings were just £30. In 1891, 16.1 per cent of the working population of England and Wales was employed in domestic service, with the generally poor terms and volatile conditions of employment that such occupations imply. Compared to the years 1880–1896 when wages had risen by 40 per cent working people were worse off in the Edwardian years because prices had risen while wages remained the same. Yet the proportion of people in secure employment was rising and these folk provided the mass market for the new houses. In all the large cities, but particularly in the capital, the number of white-collar workers who were essential to the expanding public services and the growth of commerce grew rapidly. Central and local government staffs more than doubled between the years 1891–1911 and in commerce the development of joint-stock companies, the boom in trade, shipping and overseas investment as well as the expansion of retail outlets in Britain all required supporting office workers. The emergence of a great number of clerks mirrored an increase in the number of directors, managers and senior officials.

The collectivist policy necessitated by waging the

FIG. 5. The terrace as a row of cottages: double-fronted houses at Gravesend, Kent.

First World War spilled over into the inter-war decades, leading to further growth of the public services. Incomes from salaries, which had formed 10.5 per cent of the total national income in 1911 increased to 24 per cent by 1938. The plethora of new, smaller families tended to find their housing needs satisfied through products offered by the speculative house builders.

In the mass market, speculative development of small and medium-size houses remained the general formula for the satisfaction of housing needs. This is a form of development in which the builder has no specific tenant or purchaser in mind when construction commences. Of course, a proportion of houses continued to be created on the 'bespoke' basis – individual clients commissioning purpose-designed houses – but these dwellings represented an insignificant proportion of production, particularly in the inter-war years. Naturally, speculative development for renting could not have proceeded on the massive scale that applied in the nineteenth and early twentieth centuries without large-scale investment (the many small building companies which created Victorian and Edwardian suburbia rarely provided the finance for development). A multitude of small investors saw housing as a comparatively safe form of investment in a time of periodic economic boom and slump ('as safe as houses'). Property appeared permanent and performed reliably by comparison with stocks and shares, which could suddenly become worthless. Also, suburban housing was the most attractive kind of property for this type of small investor. The small suburban house was sought after as a long-term permanent home by the self-respecting and thrifty Edwardian clerk or official. Benefiting from the comparative security of a white-collar occupation, he was less likely than the tradesman to default on rent payments because of an unreliable income or unemployment. The accompanying status and self-esteem would cause him to be scrupulously law-abiding and respectful of other people's property as well as his own, and he would treat the house carefully.

Despite these propitious conditions, life in the unregulated market of Edwardian housing was far from perfect for many of the participants. Throughout the nineteenth century, up to 10 per

cent of houses had stood empty and when the supply of houses significantly exceeded demand, rents had to be lowered. However, rather in contrast to the condition of trade in the rest of the economy, from 1905 the building industry suffered a downturn that lasted into the war years. Thus, despite the completion of almost a million new dwellings in the period 1901–11, by 1914 there was a housing shortage. From the point of view of modern owners of Edwardian houses, the depressed state of Edwardian house building may be thought advantageous. With international trade booming, good-quality building materials could be imported at comparatively low cost, and, in historical terms, skilled labour might be bought cheaply too. With an excess of supply over demand, competition for employment in building was intense, even cut-throat, as is recorded in Robert Tressell's 1906 novel set in the context of the English house building trade, *The Ragged Trousered Philanthropists*.

At best, artisans had seen their wages increase fractionally while the cost of living increased markedly; the average weekly earnings of labourers in 1907, at less than £1, had risen by 3 per cent over the preceding ten years, but in the same period the cost of living had risen by 10 per cent. The consequence of these conditions on the form and anatomy of Edwardian houses was the general use of good-quality materials and suitably skilled labour in their execution; factors that would not have been guaranteed in the speculatively built Victorian villas that preceded them.

The First World War effectively closed down civil construction as building workers drained away into the fighting forces or emergency work, and materials became scarce or unobtainable. The freeze in construction, higher wages and the concentration of workers in areas of war production forced up rents to a level that introduced the threat of general civil disorder. In 1915, central government responded by fixing both the rents of smaller houses and mortgage interest at pre-war levels. In London, apart from one or two special projects of state-sponsored housing for munitions workers, there was no new residential construction from the middle of 1915 for nearly five years. At the end of the war, with materials and labour still in short supply, and with bank interest rates at a high level, it cost about four times as much to build a small house as it had in 1914 (by the autumn of 1920 wholesale prices of building materials were three times their 1913 level). The housing shortage that applied in 1914 remained; by a conservative estimate there was a shortage of between 600,000–800,000 dwellings in England and Wales in the immediate post-war years. It was apparent that repeal of the wartime rent controls would lead to extortionate rents, threatening civil unrest. Rents were therefore kept artificially low (the restrictions being due to end in 1923). This caused the economic rent for a new small dwelling to be not only beyond the reach of those for whom it was designed, but to compare unfavourably with the controlled rents still charged for existing properties, much reducing its appeal to prospective tenants. Consequently, the multitude of small-scale investors who had funded the massive pre-war provision of private, rented housing, deserted the housing market. Builders tended to prefer to build larger houses for rent, competing with the existing larger houses whose rents were not controlled, or houses for sale. Although, in 1922, with the removal of rent controls, the Health Minister hoped that '...future state intervention will not be required and that the building industry will return to its pre-war economic basis...' private investors were not attracted to invest again in rented housing, fearful that state intervention in the working of the housing market might return. The future provision of houses through the endeavours of private enterprise was to be almost exclusively houses for sale.

This is not to say that government, anxious about the consequences of a housing shortage, did not take action to provide small houses for rent. If, in the context of rent controls, private enterprise would not gear up to satisfy demand, government had to act. Fearful of post-war revolutions as had occurred in Russia and Germany, they recognised that the shortage of housing (particularly for working-class people) would at least have to be eased if there was not to be trouble at home as the combatants returned from the war. For some years, provisions had existed to allow local authorities to develop housing for rent and the most energetic authority in this respect was the London County Council, formed in 1888, which

FIG. 6. At the Totterdown Fields Estate, Tooting, south-west London, the architects of the London County Council enlivened utilitarian terraced houses of 1903–11 with tile-hung gables. (Robin Bishop.)

had erected both 'green field' and inner-city housing (following slum clearance) from before the turn of the century (Figs 6 and 7).

Other large cities followed similar initiatives. Manchester completed at least one municipal tenement block towards the end of the century, soon after the power to build had been granted by the Housing of the Working Classes Act (1890), and Liverpool was similarly active. The government recognised that this form of housing development might act as a palliative to revolutionary sentiments and in July 1917 set up a committee under the chairmanship of Sir Tudor Walters MP, which reported in 1919. Its report was largely the work of Raymond Unwin, a pioneer town planner and champion of garden cities. In a speech made by the Prime Minister, David Lloyd George, in Wolverhampton in November 1918, the question and answer, 'What is our task? To make Britain a fit country for heroes to live in,' acknowledged the importance of housing as a political issue and was quickly converted into an election slogan, 'Homes fit for Heroes'. In a public pronouncement of 1919, King George V observed; '...If 'unrest' is to be converted into contentment, the provision of good houses may prove one of the most potent agents in that conversion...' and in that same year Dr Christopher Addison, Minister of Health in the new coalition government, introduced a Housing and Town Planning Act which placed the responsibility for supplying low-rent housing squarely on the shoulders of the local authorities, who received a guarantee that any loss incurred above the income generated by a penny rate would be made good by the Treasury. Rents were to be fixed according to capacity to pay (and hence at an uneconomic level) and adoption of the standards recommended in the Tudor Walters Report was obligatory. Standards in this new post-war local authority housing were significantly higher than those of municipal dwellings erected in the pre-war years and, for almost all the tenants, represented a great advance on what they had known before.

The threat of revolution soon faded, however, and the largesse of the Treasury ended when it became apparent that the huge subsidy to the local authorities resulting from application of the Addison Act could not be sustained. In June 1921 the government's decision to limit the number of houses subsidised to only a few more than had been built or approved at that time stalled the local authorities' mass house-building campaign with only 214,000 houses built out of a projected 500,000, forcing some councils to curtail the development of a host of 'garden city' estates. By 1923 local authority building had almost dried up, although, even in Greater London, 34,330 houses had been erected under the 1919 legislation, of which almost 27,500 were 'council' houses. The local authorities had built more than ten times as much housing over the years 1919–22 than they had in an identical period before the First World War.

In stark contrast to the crowded, grid-iron streets of terraced dwellings typical of much Edwardian suburbia, the 'Tudor Walters' standards to which the local authority estates were built suggested a maximum of twelve houses per acre and such low-density development necessitated the use of cheap land at the very outer limits of cities. Although seemingly nothing more than a relentless swathe of virtually identical brick-built houses existed on most of these estates for many years, officials in the town halls harboured the aspiration to create fully functional

FIG. 7. Gambrel roofs and slate-hanging graft a rural character on to another a range of terraced council houses at Totterdown Fields. (Robin Bishop.)

FIG. 8. *An electric tramcar glides past similarly new terraced houses in this Edwardian view of Erith, south-east London. (Robert L. Eastleigh.)*

communities having their own shops, libraries and so on, and in times before private car ownership was within the grasp of everyman, it was clear that provision of good public transport was more than desirable.

From the import to London from Paris in 1829 of Shillibeer's omnibus, the facility of public transport had acted to stimulate suburban development. For much of the nineteenth century, this process had been intensified by the expansion of the railways, particularly after the early 1880s when some railway companies accepted the statutory obligation to offer cheap fares. Even earlier, from the 1860s, much of north-east London had witnessed the creation of a terraced-street suburbia stretching out many miles from the Liverpool Street terminus of the Great Eastern Railway after that company pioneered workman's fares and half-fare travel on certain early trains. From this time onwards, suburban living was no longer exclusive to the middle class. Along some lines, for example the Great Northern Railway's main line through north London, ribbons of housing had spread as far as the current 'green belt' by 1914.

The advent of street-running electric tramways from around 1900 stimulated more suburban growth. The services of the Metropolitan Electric Tramways Company in north London (from 1904) led to significant development at Palmers Green, Southgate, Winchmore Hill and Enfield, the population of the last growing by 32 per cent between 1900 and 1911. Finchley, which was served by trams from the Golders Green terminus of the Northern Line underground railway, increased in population by 78 per cent between 1901 and 1911. Similar growth was promoted in west and south-west London by the activities of the London United Tramways Company after 1901; Hounslow, Twickenham, Teddington, New Malden, Raynes Park and Surbiton all expanded. In London, the tramways acted as feeders to the main suburban railway stations sited on the network radiating outwards from the city centre, and the linking tram routes created 'tramway suburbia'. In almost all of the outer districts served by the new tramways during the years 1900–14, new houses appeared at a rate which cannot be entirely explained by contemporary improvements in local rail services.

In north-east, east and south-east London electric tramways were developed by municipal enterprise, either by conversion of existing horse-drawn tramways or by new construction (Fig. 8). This was

17

FIG. 9. Manchester City Council's Old Moat Estate of 1927 was served from its inception by a reserved-track tramway along Princess Road. (Roy Brook.)

the general condition outside the capital, even comparatively small towns such as Camborne, Glossop, Rothesay and Wrexham developing tramway systems during the 'tramway mania' of the Edwardian period. In the inter-war years many of the councils of provincial cities which had made a heavy investment in an electric tramway network chose to extend existing systems to serve further housing development; Birmingham, Leeds, Liverpool and Manchester (Fig. 9) all acted in this way and the London County Council's network was extended in fulfilment of the aspiration to provide, from the outset, the facility of good public transport for the new post-war municipal housing estates of south-east London.

However, the 'writing was on the wall' for the comparatively inflexible street-running tramways, particularly with the growth of motor traffic and the obstacle trams provided to its free circulation. In London, 1923 was the year when, for the first time, motorbuses carried more passengers than trams and the long-term threat of private car ownership to the existence of a comprehensive public transport system of any type was first acknowledged in the 1936

annual report of the London Passenger Transport Board. In the capital, the inter-war years saw no significant growth in mainline railway or tramway services. The main developments in public transport were the rise of the motorbus and the extension of existing lines of the underground railway to up to ten miles from the city centre. Although the ascendancy of the motorbus was also witnessed in countless other towns and cities, London was unique in developing a 'tube' network and the effect of expansion of this latter mode of transport on estate development was much more important.

In 1921, Edgware was a small village in north-west Middlesex. By the early 1930s, following the completion of the Northern Line extension from Golders Green, it was a suburb thirty-five minutes by tube from central London with a train leaving the northern terminus every five minutes. By the mid-1930s, the line was the busiest in London and Edgware's population rose by 1,167 per cent between 1921 and 1939. Served by an intermediate station *en route* to Edgware from Golders Green, Hendon's population rose from less than 58,000 in 1921 to 146,000 in 1939. Due north of the city centre, similar spectacular suburban sprawl was stimulated by the building of the Cockfosters extension of the Piccadilly Line, northwards from Finsbury Park, in the early 1930s. As in the case of the Edgware line, some of this area had already been developed but much new building was a direct result of the arrival of the tube. A map of London in 1920 shows considerable tracts of open land in north London; it is clear that a vast quantity of new building was stimulated by both the Edgware and Cockfosters extensions. South of the Thames, electrification of the Southern Railway's extensive network of suburban lines, bringing faster, more frequent services, similarly assisted large-scale residential estate development in south, south-east and south-west London.

Just as the changing preferences of investors had brought about the demise of large-scale private house building for rent immediately after the First World War, so this circumstance stimulated development of housing for sale. Before World War I, the building societies (the earliest of which were founded in the late eighteenth century) had concentrated on providing funds for large-scale estate development of mainly rented houses. Post-war uncertainties over the return on such investment caused institutional investors like the building societies to seek alternative forms of income generation, particularly as the small-scale investors who had also withdrawn from rented housing were increasingly placing their funds in the societies as a more secure form of investment. The societies had to adapt to these changed circumstances or fold up and so the financing of owner-occupation (the original function of the terminating societies of a century earlier) became once again their main concern.

Several factors combined to make it practicable for the building societies to change direction in this way. First, the incomes of wage-earners in the inter-war years (unless they were among the 10–20 per cent who were unemployed during the Great Depression) rose substantially and it became easier for prospective homeowners to find the means to make mortgage repayments. Secondly, government intervened by providing tax relief on mortgage interest payments and thirdly, by the 1930s, through arrangements with the builders (who were naturally keen to widen the market for home ownership) the cash deposit

required from mortgagees was significantly reduced below the 20–25 per cent of house purchase price which had been normal. All these factors acted to increase the societies' business in providing loans to house purchasers and thereby offering attractive rates of interest to investors. Over the nation as a whole, the building societies' total lending increased from £66m in 1914 to £700m in 1938; they advanced £32m to mortgagees in 1923, more than £103m in 1933 and, in 1936, the peak year of the inter-war period, lending totalled £140.3m. Borrowers in 1928 numbered just over half a million but by 1936 the total had grown to 1.3m. By the mid 1930s the house builders could see the approach of market saturation. So general had been the conversion of the middle classes to the concept of home ownership that virtually everybody who could afford a speculative house had already bought one (during the period 1919–1939 an average of more than 17,500 houses of all types were completed each month – a total of more than 4m homes in twenty-one years). This realisation had three main effects: first, it encouraged the builders to cheapen their conventional family houses to appeal to a wider market. This could only be done by reducing costs, primarily by simplifying the form and construction of each house. Secondly, it encouraged the building of a wider range of dwelling types designed to appeal to special groups such as the elderly (the building of bungalows expanded), single people (construction of blocks of flats in suburban locations increased) and the newly married (note that the typical customer for the suburban 'semi' was the mature married man, established in a secure job, who had accumulated enough savings to allow him to make the required deposit). Finally, this circumstance stimulated changes in the building societies' attitude towards the financing of houses for the less well off as was evidenced by their willingness to enter into arrangements with the large speculative house builders to reduce the cash deposits required from purchasers.

From about 1932, in the trough of the Great Depression, with mortgage interest rates coming down and building costs at their lowest since 1914, a meaningful number of houses appeared on the market in Greater London in the price range £350–£550; this opened up the possibility of house ownership to those earning between £3.50 and £4.50 a week, for the first time offering the status of 'owner-occupier' to the better-paid manual worker.

One may imagine that this massive campaign of outer-suburban low-density private house building was not without its critics (to suggest standards superior to the high-quality, post-war council houses, developers tended to construct only detached and semi-detached houses). As early as 1921, W. R. Davidge had complained of '...a steadily creeping paralysis of 2-storey villadom, mile after mile of brick and mortar, slowly eating up the countryside'. Although there had been town planning legislation since 1909, it was fairly toothless and the presumption remained that all land in the UK was available for development, without the need to first obtain any official permission. Naturally, the house builders seized whatever opportunity presented itself to expand British towns and cities with the popular detached and semi-detached house types. Owing to its proximity to the towns and cities, the land they used was invariably high-quality agricultural land. And when the inter-war campaign to improve trunk roads for the better flow of motor traffic initiated the building of by-passes for the more congested towns, the builders were naturally happy to populate the sides of by-passes with ribbons of new housing. It was this gratuitous sprawl into the countryside, corroding its traditional character, which so enraged contemporary commentators like the architect Clough Williams-Ellis when he wrote his diatribe *England and the Octopus* in 1928. Realising the mistake it had made in not banning development from the edges of the new Kingston by-pass at the end of the twenties, Surrey County Council sponsored a special act of Parliament forbidding such ribbon development (and thus preserving the function of the by-passes) and this move achieved national application with the passing of the Ribbon Development Act of 1935.

Now it seems strange that many actually preferred to live on main roads and would pay extra for the privilege, but the volume of motor vehicle traffic in the thirties was not what it is today. Of course, it was not merely ribbon development and its extravagant use of land which outraged informed opinion; the 'sameness' of suburban houses, manifesting the ubiquity of the semi-detached type, was also a cause for complaint, as it was felt to blot out the 'local' character (both in form and building materials) represented in traditional houses. Certainly many of the new suburbs must have seemed very raw before the new trees grew to maturity to give the leafy image of much middle-aged suburbia as we appreciate it today.

Acknowledging anxieties over the squandering of good-quality agricultural land and the possible disappearance of prized rural landscapes on the doorsteps of the towns, the government acted in 1938 by introducing the Green Belt Act, requiring the towns and cities of England to place a limit on their expansion. Suburban growth had eliminated vast tracts of countryside previously accessible to town dwellers – devouring land at a rate of 70,000 hectares per year.

After 1939 the demands of wartime once again called a halt to civil construction, and when peace was restored in 1945, the *laissez-faire* approach of the inter-war years to house building was considered inadequate. The wartime techniques of planning appeared to have worked so well that they were continued into the administration of peacetime affairs. This development paved the way for the Town and Country Planning Act of 1947, finally achieving Raymond Unwin's goal of reversing the presumption of right to build to one of 'no right to build' in the absence of official *planning permission*. The seemingly endless tracts of inter-war suburbia that surround many of Britain's towns and cities were to remain a hallmark of residential development of the 1920s and thirties, never to be repeated.

CHAPTER 2

Edwardian and Inter-War House Types and Estate Development

If the increasing appeal of the Old English style in the late nineteenth century caused a change both to the treatment of the most common house type – the terraced house – and the increasing adoption of the semi-detached house as a type more readily treated in this way to achieve a convincing result, this is not to say that the conspicuous domination of pseudo-Tudor went unchallenged, particularly during the inter-war period.

Looking first at the house type that was the building-block of the earliest mass suburban house building – the terraced house of late Victorian or Edwardian times – it is clear that there is often nothing to distinguish a terraced house of 1890 from its descendant of 1905. Admittedly, changing fashions in the visual arts affected the design of decorative features such as stained glass fanlights and door glazing so that patterns seen in coloured glass panels in houses of 1905 are likely to show the influence of art nouveau motifs in contrast to the more 'mechanical' patterning which would have applied twenty years earlier, but in the treatment of joinery 'trim'; skirting boards, picture rails, door and window architraves, there is virtually nothing to distinguish the anatomy of the Edwardian speculatively built house from that of its late-Victorian forebear. In terms of the plan and sectional arrangement, the back extension survived as a feature of many new terraced houses until the First World War and the mezzanine relationship of rooms in the back extension to those of the main block remained popular, notably in London houses (Figs 10 and 11).

In south-east England, a concession to the appeal of cottage prototypes was the substitution of red brick for the buff stock brick which had been the standard construction material, though this revision tended to be reserved for the street elevations, the less visible side and rear elevations continuing to be constructed from stock brick. Similarly, the somewhat 'machine-made' regularity of slated roofslopes was sometimes shunned in favour of the tweedier rustic texture achievable through use of clay plain tiles although, again, this modification was often restricted to roofslopes capping street elevations and Welsh slate continued to be the finish for rear roofslopes. Fenestration, too, was affected by the desire to replicate cottage prototypes, even in urban terraces, as the front elevation windows set in a field of red brick came to be of casement type, contrasting with the vertically sliding sashes retained on back elevations, or sashes subdivided into a multi-paned format which attempted to simulate rural window types more closely than the standard sheet-glazed sash window.

Other aspects of the detailed treatment of the million dwellings constructed between 1901 and 1911 reflected the increasing mechanisation of production of building materials and the abundance of cheap labour. These circumstances allowed an increasingly elaborate treatment of trim both inside and outside houses. So it is that even quite modest Edwardian terraced houses often display a good deal of painted woodwork framing porches and complex patterns of glazing bars to windows, whilst larger

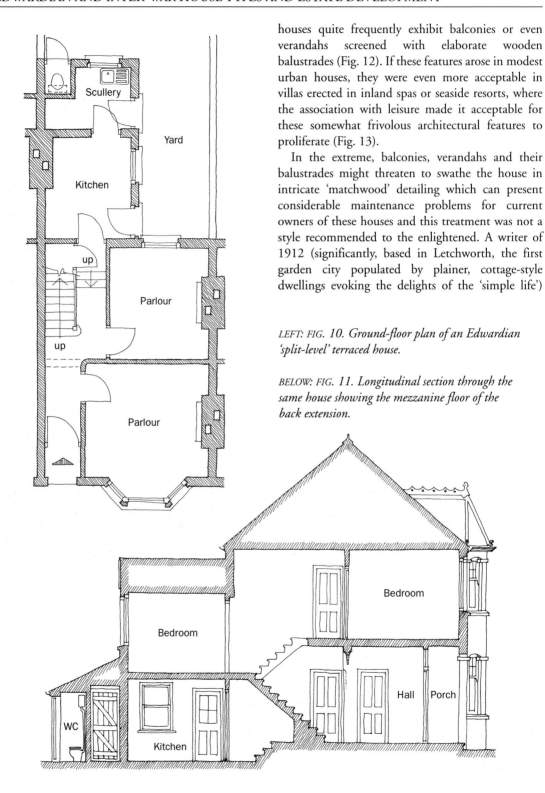

houses quite frequently exhibit balconies or even verandahs screened with elaborate wooden balustrades (Fig. 12). If these features arose in modest urban houses, they were even more acceptable in villas erected in inland spas or seaside resorts, where the association with leisure made it acceptable for these somewhat frivolous architectural features to proliferate (Fig. 13).

In the extreme, balconies, verandahs and their balustrades might threaten to swathe the house in intricate 'matchwood' detailing which can present considerable maintenance problems for current owners of these houses and this treatment was not a style recommended to the enlightened. A writer of 1912 (significantly, based in Letchworth, the first garden city populated by plainer, cottage-style dwellings evoking the delights of the 'simple life')

LEFT: FIG. 10. Ground-floor plan of an Edwardian 'split-level' terraced house.

BELOW: FIG. 11. Longitudinal section through the same house showing the mezzanine floor of the back extension.

FIG. 12. Elaborate turned and fretted woodwork in a suburban setting: Teddington, south-west London.

FIG. 13. Turrets, dormers and balconies on show in villas at Lynton, north Devon.

counselled '...it is well to avoid anything of brittle construction, and to steer clear of the amazing and uncomfortable looking fretwood treatment affected by some speculative builders...'. Clearly, there was more opportunity for a convincing reproduction of the features of traditional rural dwellings in detached and semi-detached houses, and, to some extent, bungalows.

Unfortunately, the aspirations of leading Arts and Crafts Movement architects such as C. F. A. Voysey in this connection were often frustrated by the offi-cial control of constructional standards established by the 1877 Model By-laws. Although these regulations related primarily to urban districts, these could include what we would still consider to be suburban locations and the creation of Urban and Rural District Councils in 1894 resulted in many new local authorities that were keen to outlaw anarchic or hazardous construction practices. They therefore adopted either the Model By-laws developed for application in the inner city or later codes (such as the Rural Model By-laws of 1901). This policy gave

FIG. 14. A low-ceiling bay window of a house by the architect C. F. A. Voysey. (Robin Bishop.)

particular problems for the leading domestic architects of the time, whose style the builders followed. An essential feature of the rural or suburban houses of Voysey and his admirers was the lowness and horizontality seen in the rural yeoman's house of Tudor England and these qualities demanded low-ceilinged rooms (Fig. 14). However, concerns about the potentially harmful effects of stale air in domestic interiors had caused an 1890 revision to the Model By-laws (under the Public Health Amendment Act of that year) to require a minimum internal room height of 8ft (2.44m), some local authorities demanding a dimension of at least 8ft 6in (2.6m). This stipulation contrasted starkly with the 7ft (2.2m) room height advocated by Voysey and others. The existence of this legal requirement provoked two distinct responses from these architects: first, design ingenuity in

making houses containing rooms of 8ft minimum (2.44m) internal height look, to the outside world, as if they contained low rooms (by setting windows low in the walls and bringing down the eaves level so that upper-storey rooms projected partly into the roof space) and secondly, campaigning (entirely unsuccessfully, it seems) for the amendment or abolition of the regulations so that low rooms would again be legal. The existence of these mandatory official standards explains why, in the hands of less talented architects and builders, many rural-style dwellings of the Edwardian or inter-war periods do not convincingly replicate the ancient prototypes.

The story of the Edwardian phase – that speculative builders attempted to copy the example of the most fashionable designers of bespoke houses – continued into the inter-war years. It is hard to find details to distinguish a speculative semi-detached house of 1920 from one of 1913, but the 1920s and 1930s did witness considerable changes in the pattern of patronage of the designers of bespoke houses, their workload and the fashions in architectural style to which they were susceptible. Before World War I it had been possible for well-connected and talented architects to practise successfully by designing large country houses for rich clients, but the war brought about some radical changes in British society. The middle classes emerged from the war both greater in number and poorer in income than they had been in 1914. Their ranks had been swollen by the lower-paid, white-collar workers in new administrative and commercial occupations, whilst the traditional, wealthy middle class suffered a reduction in their incomes through increased taxation and war-induced inflation. Almost all architects found it was no longer possible to practise by designing elaborate country houses for large families and armies of servants. Instead, the leading designers of inter-war domestic architecture catered for the affluent commuters who inhabited the private estates and high-class suburbs on the fringes of the conurbations and in their work an insipid version of the High Victorian 'Battle of the Styles' tended to continue as 'Old English' (or 'Stockbroker Tudor' as it came to be termed in the 1930s) vied with the newly fashionable neo-Georgian. The speculative builders followed suit by dressing up their brick-structured products with low-cost versions of the features adopted by the leading domestic architects.

No doubt the British architectural establishment was complacent in believing it had found a style of domestic architecture appropriate to the twentieth century by developing an expression conceived in the nineteenth because in the more volatile social context of the inter-war years, this smugness could not go unchallenged. In the post-war social ferment of central Europe, and particularly in Germany, still reeling from her defeat by the allies, experiments to originate an architecture expressive of the new circumstances were well under way by the early 1920s, and Britain was not immune from these developments. British architectural magazines began to illustrate the flat-roofed creations of continental 'modern movement' architects from the mid-1920s and in 1928 the annual *Ideal Home Exhibition* at Olympia, west London, featured both a 'concrete house' and a remarkable cubistic *House of the Future* by the architect R. A. Duncan which attracted much scorn from the architectural establishment.

Indigenous architects remained very sceptical of both the functional performance and revolutionary symbolism of modernism but among the clientele for bespoke houses some middle-class professionals who were apprised of European developments began to generate a demand for this type of dwelling. The first was W. J. Bassett-Lowke, a manufacturer of engineering models, who commissioned the German architect Peter Behrens to design a flat-roofed cubical villa, 'New Ways' at Northampton in 1925. So resistant was the architectural establishment to the forms and ideals of continental modernism that almost all the subsequent bespoke modern-movement houses erected in Britain in the inter-war years were designed either by immigrant European architects or English-speaking designers born, not in the UK, but in the Dominions. Thus the next prominent house, 'High and Over' of 1928 at Amersham, Buckinghamshire, for Professor Bernard Ashmole, was designed by a New Zealander, Amyas Connell.

More palatable to established UK architects than the stark forms of European modernism (and enthusiastically taken up by some of the graduates of the recently established schools of architecture) was the new style which dominated the 1925 Paris *Exposition*

Internationale des Arts Decoratifs et Industriels Modernes – subsequently termed *art deco*. This style shared some features with modernism, for example, a taste for large, bare expanses of wall in external elevations, but in *art deco* this 'breadth of treatment' was always contrasted with richly ornamented details, often reflecting contemporary interest in newly discovered buildings or artefacts from the ancient civilisations of Egypt or south and central America. It may have been recognition of a lack of intellectual rigour – in contrast with the principles clearly underlying the modern movement – as well as the feeling that the style was less extreme than modernism, that caused this treatment to be termed 'modernistic' even in the 1930s. Streamlined and stylised forms, which readily found their way into designs for furniture and light fittings, also made an appearance in architecture, though they were often more acceptable when used on commercial, industrial and entertainment buildings (for example, the 'super-cinemas' of the 1930s) than when applied to houses. Forms and details too redolent of the efficiency and productivity of modern industry were not thought appropriate for the decoration of dwellings by most clients or house purchasers. Perhaps the most enduring result of enthusiasm for this style in modest speculative houses was the 'sunrise' motif which was a pattern frequently employed in coloured glass fanlights and on garden gates.

If adoption of the modern and modernistic styles was to remain a minority interest among clients for bespoke houses, it was even less likely to impact upon the architectural treatment adopted by the speculative builders. That is, until changing circumstances forced the builders to assess the potential advantages of modernism. With the prospect of market saturation in the early 1930s engendering the need to widen the market for their products, mainly by lowering prices through a reduction in building costs, some speculative builders realised that houses of modern-movement design offered opportunities for simplifying the general building form and, perhaps, construction methods. The simple forms of the experimental 'international style' houses, which had been erected for *avant-garde* patrons seemed potentially cheap to build. The result was that, from 1932 onwards, house builders in a number of London areas offered speculative versions of these dwellings, at the cheaper end of their ranges. Despite extensive advertising on the theme of the contemporary cult of the sun and low prices, the earliest examples of these boxy, flat-roofed houses proved extremely difficult to sell.

Nevertheless, the 1934 *Ideal Home Exhibition* (itself an invention of Edwardian times) saw a determined effort to promote this kind of house, all the show houses being of this type, grouped into a 'Village of Tomorrow'. A Surrey builder, astute enough to recognise that simple elevations meant reduced building costs, offered small semi-detached houses at the Upper Farm Estate, West Molesey, from March 1934 for £395 (Fig. 15). In the spring and summer of that year all the larger house-building firms had jumped on the bandwagon, advertising their versions of the modern style. However, the vision of a modern movement dwelling for everyman soon evaporated as the public again proved reluctant to embrace the new values and lifestyle symbolised, and to some extent required, by occupation of these houses. House buyers were generally conservative in their tastes, did not welcome designs which advanced beyond their concept of what a house should look like, and which smacked of the dehumanising influ-ence of either big business or strong government. By April 1935, the Surrey builder was advertising new development at the Upper Farm Estate with drawings of pitched-roof houses and no mention of the outdoor lifestyle. Prices had risen to £425–£495. By the end of 1935 the fashion for flat roofs and 'suntrap' houses was almost over as far as London speculative builders were concerned, though the tradition of toleration of unconventional, even whimsical architecture at British resorts allowed the 'international style' to continue to exert a grip on seaside housing development until World War II.

Nonetheless, some benefit flowed from these experiments. Following an unsuccessful foray into full-blown modernism on an estate at Hendon, north London, in 1931–1932, an enterprising architect named Herbert Welch realised that some of the forms of modernism might be integrated into the general format of the typical hipped-roof 'semi' to produce an acceptable compromise. His practice of Welch, Cachemaille-Day and Lander first achieved this modernistic result in speculative housing at Old Rectory Gardens, Edgware for the builder Roger Malcolm, in 1932. This new type of house employed white-painted, cement-rendered walls and horizon-tally stressed steel-framed windows within 'suntrap'

FIG. 15. Flat-roofed, semi-detached houses on Upper Farm Road, West Molesey, Surrey (1934).

FIG. 16. A well-preserved example of the pioneer modernistic, semi-detached house of 1932 with its 'suntrap' steel-framed windows: Rectory Gardens, Edgware, Middlesex.

bays under conventional hipped roofs (Fig. 16). It is clear that the type was successful because soon other local firms were building very similar houses. The builders had discovered that simple modernistic elevations would sell well enough if set below the familiar, reassuring pitched and hipped roof and an increasing number of these compromise designs appeared from early 1933, sometimes with roofs of bright green or blue-glazed pantiles instead of the usual pink clay-plain tiles. The 'old English' format remained durable, however, and enthusiasm for sham half-timbering, pebbledash and leaded lights continued to the end of the inter-war period.

Of course, functional pressures were also changing the form of houses and one of the most potent influences on the external form was increasing ownership of the motor car. Semi-detached houses of the Edwardian years were rarely sited so as to allow vehicle drives to be installed between adjoining pairs of houses and this arrangement continued to apply in the earliest post-war dwellings. Yet car ownership was growing; in 1913, 338,000 private cars were bought in Britain at an average price of £340 – more than twice the price of

a small suburban dwelling – and builders were having to think about the action they should take to cater for the new need to house the family car. Even from Edwardian times there were isolated examples of speculative houses being built in such a way that a car could be accommodated. In his book *Semi-detached London*, Alan A. Jackson notes that the space demands of the car were acknowledged in an incipient suburb as early as 1906 when new houses on an estate in Edgware were advertised as having 'room for motor'. Garages were generally described as 'motor houses' into the inter-war years and were included in a few speculatively built London houses from about 1912, but the majority of 1920s houses still lacked this feature. Many builders began to acknowledge the changing circumstances by including enough space for garage drives between pairs of semi-detached houses from the mid 1920s. By the early 1930s builders were willing to construct brick-built garages alongside their houses for £30–£60. In this decade an increasing number of the more expensive speculative detached and semi-detached houses (that is, exceeding a purchase price of £850) were designed with integral garages though

27

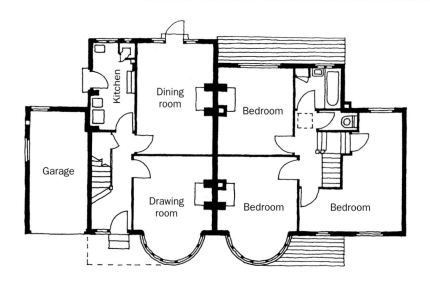

FIG. 17. Ground and first-floor plans (left and right) of semi-detached houses with integral garages.

these would rarely accommodate anything but the smallest mass-produced cars (Figs 17 and 18).

The housing of cars was not an essential consideration in the design of modest speculative houses in Britain by 1939 because there was still only one private car to every twenty-five people – approximately two million vehicles. The massive growth of private car ownership has been a phenomenon of the post-World War II years as the period to the early 1960s produced a more than threefold increase and

we have witnessed a further acceleration in growth to a total today of more than 27 million vehicles.

The internal arrangement of the house was also being affected by social and technological developments. At the end of the First World War the newly impoverished traditional middle class were no longer able to afford to employ the many domestic servants conventional in their households before the war. The large houses which had accommodated these big households were thus less in demand and cheaper

FIG. 18. An integral garage gave scope for an extra bedroom on the upper floor of the larger 'semi'.

means had to be found to manage even the more modest houses.

Technology came to the rescue in the form of domestic appliances that made the running of the household less labour-intensive. The electrically powered vacuum cleaner had come into use in Edwardian times but was thought to be something of a curiosity when the services of housemaids might be bought cheaply. The radically changed circumstances of the post-war period greatly increased its appeal, along with that of the freestanding gas cooker and the electric iron. The performance of the gas cooker was much improved after 1923 with the introduction of the 'Regulo', a thermostatic control which meant that constant supervision of the oven and its contents was no longer necessary. The merits of the electric iron, the cheapest and most popular of the new domestic appliances, were quickly appreciated and gas and electric water-heating, superseding the solid fuel-fired back-boiler, also grew in popularity. Changed social, economic and domestic circumstances suggested the simplification of house plans and the reduction in number of rooms to the maximum manageable by the one person occupying the family home for the larger part of each weekday and in the absence of any servants – the housewife. With the help of the new domestic appliances, the servantless housewife played the key role in creating the new 'ideal home'. The 'servant problem' was a popular cause for complaint in the 1920s and 1930s and the scarcity of domestic help led builders to realise the idea of 'the servantless home', expounded in women's magazines of the time, by building very few houses with accommodation for servants. Like her Edwardian counterpart, the mistress of the inter-war suburban house was responsible for creating a homely atmosphere for her family and providing a peaceful haven for the commuting husband to return to after a hard day's work.

In 1904, official reports on the poor state of health of the British forces in the Boer War had highlighted the shortcomings of the homes of the recruits. This discovery forced a new emphasis on improving the home, and schools began to teach domestic science. As it was the schoolchildren of this period who became the adults of the 1920s and 1930s, it is not surprising that an obsession for hygiene and cleanli-ness found its fullest expression in the inter-war years, with the responsibility for the health of the nation lying chiefly with wives and mothers.

The most important development facilitating the management of the servantless house by the house-wife was the introduction of domestic electric power. Throughout the inter-war years, gas and electricity companies fought each other fiercely to win the favour of the housewife, with electricity's main disad-vantage being its high price. However, the establish-ment of the Central Electricity Board in 1926 brought some order to the pricing policies and supply arrangements of the many electricity companies, and the cost of electricity fell steadily through the inter-war years whilst the real prices of coal and gas hardly changed.

The availability of labour-saving appliances and the increase in the amount of housework which had to be done by the housewife in the absence of servants, caused changes not only to the general configuration of the house plan but also to the design of individual rooms. Now that the lady of the house was obliged to spend more time in the kitchen, there was greater reason to ensure that the keynotes of its design were lightness, cleanliness and convenience. The cooker, sink and worktops were more likely to be arranged in one room to improve efficiency in food preparation and the built-in, open-shelved dresser of Edwardian times was replaced by the more hygienic fitted cupboard. Owners of unmodified semi-detached houses built in the 1920s and 1930s will be familiar with the 'kitchenette': a room often as small as 3 × 1.8m (10 × 6ft) – hardly more than a broad passage between entrance hall and side or rear door – which was commonly promoted as a labour-saving arrangement, but also satisfied the desire of builders to erect the maximum number of houses with the minimum acceptable floor space on almost every estate.

In relation to the stove or cooker as a staple feature of the kitchen, it is clear that in the inter-war years, the emphasis moved from providing a durable item fabricated by iron founders to a lighter, freestanding appliance of modern design and affordable price, fuelled by gas or electricity rather than coal, and thus easier to operate and clean. The new cookers were made of pressed-steel panels, finished in an easy-to-clean enamel of black, white or mottled grey. The cheapest of all electrical appliances – the electric iron – was affordable by most households, and in 1939, 77 per cent of all homes wired for electricity owned an electric iron. The vacuum cleaner provides the best example of the commercialisation of cleanliness in the 1930s. Its price fell as the use of lighter and cheaper materials in its construction became possible. It became easier to use and allowed effective cleaning with much less work, whilst ownership of the appliance also acted as a status symbol. To stimulate sales, manufacturers promoted the idea that housework was something to enjoy and women's magazines began to depict the role of the housewife as a profession. This redefinition of her role meant that the housewife was now obliged to spend more time than ever before on efficient housework.

The hygienic revolution also caused the bathroom to be remodelled on simple, easy-to-clean lines. A factor in the reappraisal of the design potential of bathrooms may have been the recognition that all post-1919 council houses incorporated this facility, so that houses for sale had to 'go one better' by at least suggesting a luxury treatment of the bathroom in contrast to municipal utilitarianism. Suites of matching sanitary ware; bath, wash-hand basin and WC, were installed in contrast to the formerly unco-ordinated items, and the aesthetic potential of hygienic half-height tiling and the 'boxing-in' of the bathtub allowed colour and pattern to find a place in the bathroom to almost the same extent as applied in living rooms and bedrooms.

The relationship of rooms in speculative semi-detached houses was fairly fixed. The smallest type of 'semi' and the larger type, incorporating a garage, shared the same basic layout and arrangement of rooms, but some builders did vary this format in the interests of economy, by adopting what was termed the 'chalet' type of house, a form which proved cheaper to build because some of the upper-storey accommodation was contained in the roof space (Figs 19 and 20). The price of this reconfiguration of rooms was to assign one of the three bedrooms to the ground floor. The dominant 'catslide' extended roofslope that resulted, as well as being cheaper to build than the consistent two-storey brickwork shell that would otherwise have been necessary, granted a reassuringly

domestic ground-hugging profile to each block of paired houses (all too easily destroyed by additions to the upper-storey rooms – see Chapter 11).

Wider variations from the standard semi-detached house plan were found in the layouts of bungalows. These houses were more expensive in terms of land used and for this reason were often sited on low-cost, poor-quality land where a substantial bearing capacity for new structures could not be guaranteed. The name is a corruption of the Indian word *bangla*, referring to that area of the sub-continent now known as Bangladesh. The first British single-storey dwelling inspired by the Indian prototype was built in the 1830s, and an estate of expensive seaside bungalows at Birchington, Kent, followed in the early 1880s. Initially they were viewed as suitable dwellings for affluent bachelors who wished to live in the countryside, or as short-life dwellings for holiday use and hence were largely of 'temporary' timber construction. The potential ease with which such timber-framed houses might be erected by unskilled labour increased their appeal to the DIY-minded in the years of housing shortage immediately following the First World War and many virtually unplanned estates of timber-framed bungalows grew up in the inter-war period, particularly on seaside and rural riverside sites (Peacehaven, Sussex, originally named New Anzac-on-Sea was a prime example). In the tradition of Edwardian houses, a characteristic of these early bungalows was a good deal of turned, fretted and painted external woodwork.

As the market for 'stock' semi-detached houses began to approach saturation point, large-scale, speculative house builders began to see some advantage in building bungalows. If marginal sites could be purchased cheaply to yield the larger plot sizes required for bungalows, these dwellings might appeal to elderly or disabled house buyers, and an increasing number of bungalow estates appeared from the mid-twenties in outer-suburban locations as well as at the seaside. Like conventional two-storey houses, bungalows were developed in detached and semi-detached versions (Fig. 21).

Looking at the way the inter-war estates were laid out, it is clear that the values of the Garden City pioneers had considerable influence, even if they were not as pervasive in private development

FIG. 19. Chalet style, semi-detached houses in south-west London.

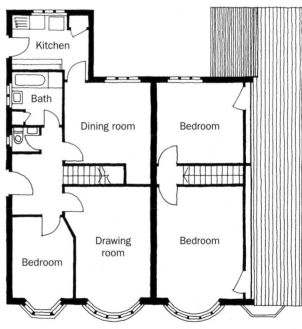

FIG. 20. Ground and first-floor plans (left and right) of chalet-style, semi-detached houses.

FIG. 21. Ground-floor plan of a two-bedroom bungalow.

as they were in the council estates. The lesson of Bedford Park had its first impact in the corporate realm in the later industrial model villages. Enlightened industrialists from the time of Robert Owen's initiative at New Lanark, Scotland, in the early nineteenth century, had sought to improve the living conditions of their employees. This tradition came to be influenced by the atmosphere of the pioneering west London garden suburb, as is seen in the treatment of Port Sunlight, Cheshire, which was developed over a long period between the early 1880s and the start of the First World War. The workers' housing, much of it owing a good deal to the Cheshire vernacular (Fig. 22), was sited on the doorstep of the soap factory which was the main enterprise of its creator, W. H. Lever, but it was arranged tastefully around greens and broad avenues in an attempt to create a synthesis of good-quality urban housing and a traditional village environment.

This sort of conspicuously 'designed' industrial model village was the most potent contemporary prototype for the earliest town planning projects, the first of which was Letchworth Garden City, established in 1903. It is therefore no surprise to find that Letchworth's designers, Raymond Unwin and Barry Parker, were also engaged at that time in creating a garden village for the Rowntrees of York, for the purpose of housing the workers employed in that family's confectionery factory. Despite an element of formality conferred by the simple geometry of the central area (absorbed from the contemporary American 'City Beautiful' movement) Parker and Unwin's layout of Letchworth, like that of New Earswick, the model village at York, tended to follow the informal lines first seen at Bedford Park, in which existing trees were retained and landscape features dictated layout. As protagonists of Arts and Crafts principles, Parker and Unwin, in their designs for new houses in Letchworth, attempted to simulate the forms of rural vernacular architecture – they were very much 'cottages' displaying dominant roof surfaces, composed from a palette of traditional features and materials. Raymond Unwin disliked the 'spotty' effect on landscape of developing residential areas with only detached and semi-detached houses (Fig. 23) and much of the Edwardian housing at Letchworth is in the form of short terraces (these were to be a potent prototype for the composition of the later, inter-war council estates comprising dwellings of 'Tudor Walters' standards). The work of other architects who contributed to Letchworth tends to be of the same general format, achieving a pleasing scale and stylistic coherence which may continue to look somewhat stark where mature trees are absent (Fig. 24).

FIG. 22. A short terrace of workers' houses at the industrial 'model village' of Port Sunlight, Cheshire.

In the layout of Letchworth it is easy to see the prototype for many later municipal estates erected even as late as 1960, but other stylistic influences came into play, particularly after the First World War. The neo-Georgian style, a logical development of architects' earlier enthusiasm for the neo-baroque and 'English Renaissance' expressions as revivalism advanced through historical periods, first surfaced in the smartest and most expensive bespoke houses created just before and after the First World War. The increasing involvement of fashion-conscious architects in the design of council housing soon stimulated the realisation that this was a style which might be more appropriate to municipal dwellings than the 'neo-vernacular' first adopted in Edwardian times and which retained a monopoly into the 1920s (Fig. 25). Naturally, it was easier to apply to the vertical-format, balcony-access, multi-storey blocks of flats which authorities such as the London County Council were erecting in the 1920s and 1930s than to two-storey houses capped by pitched roofs, but it offered the appeal of a 'corporate image' seen as desirable in these initiatives of municipal enterprise. Generally shunned by the builders of estates of speculative semi-detached houses, the neo-Georgian gave the public sector architects (and their employers) the opportunity to distinguish their creations from the products of the speculative builder, a distinction that

FIG. 23. The 'spotty' effect resulting from developing landscape with detached and semi-detached houses (Minehead, Somerset).

FIG. 24. Letchworth Garden City, Hertfordshire: a short terrace of houses designed by Geoffrey Lucas.

FIG. 25. *Gambrel-roofed terraced houses continued to be built in Manchester's garden city, Wythenshawe, into the 1930s.*

could be further emphasised by the grouping of dwellings and the layout of the estate. To project a corporate image, obtain best value for money and create a scale in harmony with retained landscape features as recommended by Raymond Unwin, council houses tended to be grouped in short terraces rather than being semi-detached. Whether in short terraces or semi-detached, great care was also taken to give interest in the design of end elevations in corner locations so that the raw end gables of terraced spec-ulative dwellings were avoided and houses could be seen to 'turn the corner' to give an integrated com-position (Fig. 26). Conversion to neo-Georgianism was also encouraged by the popular success of the first inter-war garden city, Welwyn Garden City, Hertfordshire, built in 1920 and uniformly neo-Georgian in its composition, consisting of rectilinear brick-built houses patterned with vertically stressed sliding sash windows.

The garden suburb for private housing had not died with Bedford Park and the protagonists of garden cities were equally active in advancing the concept of the garden suburb. In the wake of their success in the competition for their design of

Letchworth, Parker and Unwin were retained to plan Hampstead Garden Suburb, a development in north-west London that was under construction from 1907. In consequence of his dislike of the rigid lines of 'by-law street' layouts and their lack of sympathy with the form and features of the natural landscape, Raymond Unwin had by 1905 managed to arrange an Act of Parliament approving a radically different layout for Hampstead Garden Suburb and to nego-tiate, with the nascent Hendon Urban District Council, a set of building by-laws which were more liberal than those based on the 1877 Model By-laws. The special Act of Parliament granted exemption from such matters as street widths, dispensing with the rigid controls laid down in the 'New Streets' section of the Model By-laws. The Hendon By-laws, which were in the process of being drawn up at the same time the Hampstead Garden Suburb Trust were purchasing their estate, were modified in such a way as to please Voysey and other critics of official controls by allowing half-timbering to be used in houses without the brick backing normally demanded by the regulations. Timber framing, tile and slate hanging of walls, the use of reinforced concrete and concrete blocks and the concealment of pipework behind render in chases in the external walls were also permitted. Replication of the vernacular cottage in a semi-urban context was officially approved for the first time.

However, the relaxation of the conventional building codes and the scrupulous attention to preservation and enhancement of natural features that applied at Hampstead Garden Suburb were to be the exceptions rather than the rule in later private estate development. Contemporary developments in Ilford, Walthamstow, and Southfields, south-west London, as well as the myriad complexes of terraced streets created in provincial towns and cities throughout this period were much more characteristic of the Edwardian suburb's slavish conformity to grid-iron layouts of by-law streets. It was this unimaginative sprawl away from city centres that provoked the ire of the Archbishop of Canterbury; speaking in a House of Lords debate in 1907 he noted that, '... nothing could be more deplorable either aesthetically or from the point of view of health than the miserable monotonous rows of long, ugly, mean streets which are growing up all around London ...'. Despite an increasing vogue for semi-detached houses, this form of estate development continued until World War I and it was only in the post-war years in which the speculative builder was

First floor

Ground floor

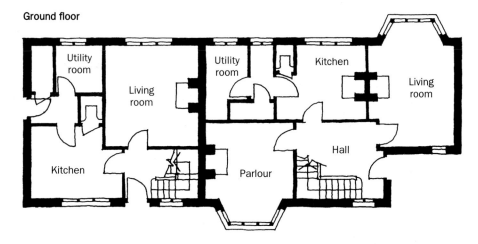

FIG. 26. Ground and upper-floor plans of two and four-bedroom council houses.

forced to outdo the councils in suggesting a suburban environment more spacious and differentiated than the council estates, that some of the monotony of private development began to reduce. Sinuous roads and cul-de-sacs (beloved of Raymond Unwin and employed in countless inter-war council estates) began to replace straight and parallel by-law streets. Even in these seemingly more spacious layouts, builders were keen to minimise costs and roads were often of gravel, flint or granite chips laid over hardcore, with kerbs of creosoted timber beams. Footways were similarly of slag, clinker or hardcore, producing dusty wastes in summer and rutted quagmires in winter until the local authority chose to adopt these thoroughfares and 'make them up'. Sometimes this did not take place until many years after the estate had been completed. The installation of permanent concrete roads in advance of house construction was not practised widely until the early 1930s.

Whether they realised it or not, many of the urban dwellers dreaming of a new house in the suburbs were seeking to renew contact with the rural environment which their forebears had deserted in the hope of attaining a better standard of living in the towns and cities. Thus it is reasonable to suppose that they were glad to find at least a suggestion of the country

cottage in most new suburban houses. In relation to house types, terraced houses, even if erected in short rows, were too reminiscent of the urban environment and, for most, the detached ideal was too greedy of land to be generally available at an acceptable price. Therefore the semi-detached represented a suitable and very popular compromise. Recognition of this thinking explains why very few of the semi-detached houses erected in the inter-war years are planned on the preferred 'halls together' arrangement in which noise from the adjoining dwelling is buffered by the adjacent entrance halls and staircases. In order to give to owner-occupiers of adjacent dwellings the maximum feeling of independence it was necessary to site entrance doors as far apart as possible and thus the entrance hall of the typical 'semi' is sited at the front corner of the ground floor, well away from that serving the neighbouring house (Figs 27 and 28).

The private developer was happy to follow Raymond Unwin's pre-war prescription for estate development – as practised in the layout of the first post-war council estates – by filling his land with semi-detached houses at ten or twelve per acre. The 'semi' imparted an illusion of privacy and offered a basis for snobbery with its suggestion of the detached privacy that had so long been the prerogative of the

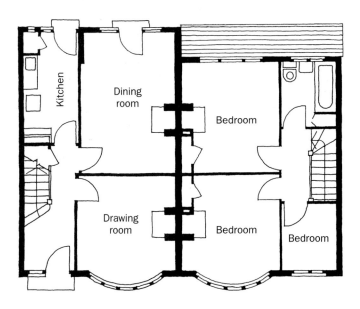

FIG. 27. Ground and upper-floor plans (left and right) of three-bedroom, semi-detached houses.

traditional middle class. Recognising the dangers of creating dwellings too like the council houses developed to an identical density (the biggest fear was inability to sell their products) many builders placed great stress on the wide variety of designs or individuality of each design offered. 'Semi-detached but each pair of a different design' was the ideal and, indeed, the reality offered by various builders.

Yet despite all the attention devoted to superficial features and variety of detail, monotony was not avoided. The basic size, shape and plan of the semi-detached house was virtually the same everywhere; in Glasgow, Plymouth, Manchester or Cardiff. Nor was imagination much in evidence in estate layouts, and most speculative building was rightly considered unattractive, even ugly, by those who could afford to employ their own architect. Throughout the inter-war years, and, indeed, for the entire post-war period, the style of the inter-war suburbs and the petty snobberies they might house have been targets for the literary intelligentsia. It is true that many inter-war suburban estates are vast and unrelieved and there are some that are dull and lacking in stimulation, failing to evoke a sense of community or belonging. It is possible, too, that the uniformity of some may have acted to inhibit individual expression, streets being sometimes long and monotonous, whilst others are painfully narrow, tortuous or confined. Yet it is also true that many inter-war suburbs granted their occupants a quality of life far superior to that available in the slums of the inner city, or for that matter, in some of the more intensive housing developments that have been created since (for example, low-rise, high-density or tower block municipal housing).

Nature, time and, since the 1960s, the increasing popularity of DIY, have done much to modify the results of the massive house building campaign of the inter-war years. Athough there remain places where the effect is as stark and alienating as when

FIG. 28. The front entrance door of the inter-war, semi-detached house was almost always placed at the front corner, well away from that of the neighbour.

the buildings were new, testifying still to the baleful effects of large-scale private residential development where unregulated by an official planning policy balancing all land uses, there are also many examples of well-loved 'semis' in countless suburbs which have not only demonstrated the intrinsic responsiveness of the type to changing family needs, but which also continue to contribute to an attractive and distinctive residential environment.

CHAPTER 3

Foundations, Basements and Ground Floors

FOUNDATIONS

The first part of any building to be built is the foundation. This is achieved by excavating the ground to a level believed to be sufficiently firm to accept the load imposed by the complete construction of the building: walls, floors and roof. In ancient, timber-framed rural buildings this often meant simply digging a shallow trench in the alignment of the walls, laying a few courses of roughly hewn stone and building the wooden frame off the approximately level top surface of the masonry. With the adoption of brick construction this change of materials close to ground level was dispensed with because the brickwork used for the superstructure functioned equally well as the material for a satisfactory foundation. A simple, stepped-brick footing sufficed as the foundation for innumerable houses, even to the end of the nineteenth century, but the inclusion of concrete in foundations began to be accepted practice around 1900. Even seemingly stone-built houses of the nineteenth and twentieth centuries are likely to be founded on brick footings because they are usually not of solid stone construction; a stone outer skin faces a brick backing in the external walls and where the stonework cannot be seen (below ground) walls generally revert to solid brickwork.

The brickwork being carried down to a suitable bearing stratum, it is clear that the stability of the building is improved if the foundation is widened at its base. In the simplest Edwardian constructions this was achieved by widening the brick footing to up as much as 680mm (27in) in the case of a 215mm (9in) one-brick-thick external wall, up to six bricks being laid side-by-side across the bottom of the foundation trench. Through four or five courses of superincumbent brickwork 'stepping-in' above, the footing narrows to the thickness of the external wall. In speculative housing, the depth of the underside of the footing from external ground level might be as little as 375mm (15in) and was commonly 450mm (18in), though poor ground sometimes forced the builder to dig deeper.

With the beginning of the twentieth century, it became common to first place in the foundation trench a strip of concrete not less than 600mm (24in) wide and up to 215mm (9in) thick, off which the walls would be built (Fig. 29). Even in this arrangement, a stepped-profile brick footing would be superimposed upon the concrete in order to satisfy local regulations that commonly stipulated a 57mm (2¼in) recession of each course from the lowest level and a width of underside of footing at least twice the thickness of the external wall. This stepped brickwork has been dispensed with in modern construction because a simple mass concrete strip foundation adequately distributes the load.

Subsidence

It should be clear that the policy of digging only a shallow trench to accommodate foundations is likely to cause subsidence and encourage the structural distress that is seen in many older houses. In houses in Greater London, subsidence was clearly revealed during the drought of 1976. The bearing stratum for the foundations of many houses built in the London area is, or is close to, a shrinkable clay substratum. The hot summer of 1976 dried out the clay and shrinkage resulted, so that many shallow foundations were left partly unsupported and sections of the footings collapsed in consequence, causing damage to the superstructures.

The converse condition obtains when the ground is subjected to severe frost. Previously saturated clay soil becomes frozen and the clay expands, pushing parts of the foundations upwards and causing cracking of the masonry. It is clear that the dangers of clay shrinkage and expansion are reduced by digging the foundations deeper to a subsoil whose moisture content is more stable under all climatic conditions, and this is a remedy to which local authority building control officers have turned in their consideration of plans for new work. It is worth noting that in southern England, frost rarely penetrates more than 450mm (18in) below ground level, though 600mm (2ft) is the vulnerable zone in northern Scotland.

A further threat to the integrity of foundations is the proximity of mature trees. Tree roots quite often breach brick footings in their search for moisture and distress to superstructures may result either from the existence or removal of mature trees. The fact that a large tree is not cheek-by-jowl with a house may not reduce the risk. The roots of the Lombardy Poplar, for example, travel a great deal further horizontally than the height of the tree at maturity, the fine roots reaching out several hundred yards, although close to the ground surface. The only effective treatment for tree roots that are causing problems for foundations is to dig out the affected ground and eradicate the roots. Where there is no evidence of structural distress in a building founded on shrinkable clay that adjoins mature trees, it is often a mistake to cut down the trees. They have been efficiently draining moisture from the clay and with their removal this moisture is retained, causing the clay to swell and inviting disturbance of footings by 'ground heave'.

Underpinning

A well-known technique for arresting structural distress resulting from subsidence is underpinning, which may be used to form deeper or wider founda-

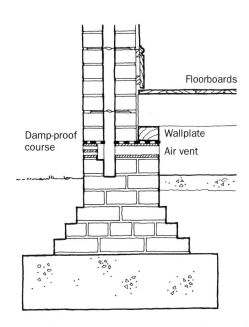

FIG. 29. Stepped-brickwork and concrete strip foundation showing an air duct venting the void below the suspended timber ground floor.

tions. Its execution relies on adjacent excavations that need to be shored up and are generous enough to allow access for concreting. It is installed by excavating short sections of ground below the footing in a sequence that ensures that adjoining sections are not excavated consecutively. Each excavation should expose no more than a 1.4m (4.5ft) length of wall, which must be capable of arching over the excavation. Where the quality of the brickwork is in question, this length of excavation may need to be halved and account should be taken of the locations of door and window openings, piers and crossbeams so that sections of the structure carrying heavy loads are not left unsupported. The progression of underpinning along a wall is normally in groups of five short lengths which are excavated in the order 3, 1, 4, 2, 5 then 3, 1, 4 and so on, where the first excavation is not at a sensitive part of the building. The first section of trench having been dug beneath the existing foundation, the underside of the footing is cleaned. Shoring up the sides of the excavation should prevent collapse of the soil on any side of the

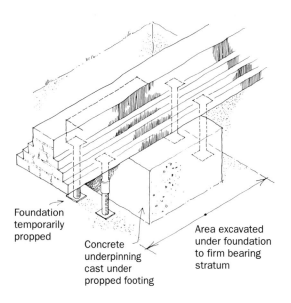

FIG. 30. Installation of a concrete 'pin' beneath a stepped-brickwork footing.

footing. Any temporary shoring, which for practicality must be left permanently in place, should not decay to leave voids in the ground. When the desired bearing stratum is reached, the concrete 'pin' is poured to within about 75mm (3in) of the underside of the footing. When this new base has hardened, the gap between the concrete and the footing is then packed with 'dry-pack' mortar (Fig. 30). This material is usually a 3:1 mixture of sand and cement mixed to a dry consistency, which is well rammed into the void to limit further movement. On completion of each sequence of excavations, the ground around is reinstated and it is hoped that the subsidence has been arrested.

The calculation of the size of the pins and extent of underpinning is a specialised task best undertaken by a structural engineer because an over-strong or over-large sub-foundation may induce subsidence elsewhere. Clearly, underpinning is usually an expensive operation as it may involve not only a large amount of excavation and reinstatement of external ground, but also the possible excavation and reinstatement of the lowest internal floor, as the foundation may need to be underpinned from both sides.

BASEMENTS

Edwardian houses often incorporate basements or cellars, though they are fairly rare in inter-war dwellings. The walls of these rooms were generally constructed in the same way as those of the upper storeys, although a thickening of solid brick walls to at least 327mm (13in) instead of the 215mm (9in) usually adopted above was common. Solid stone basement walls are conventionally at least 500mm (20in) thick and are usually of the most easily constructed rubble masonry. On completion of the basement walls, it was good practice to backfill the excavation in which the wall had been erected with gravel or sand, allowing groundwater soaking through this permeable material to drain away freely, improving the chances of achieving a dry basement (Fig. 31). The damp-proofing of cellar walls and floors was a subject which preoccupied the Edwardians at least as much as the attention it is given by today's owners of these houses. A favoured

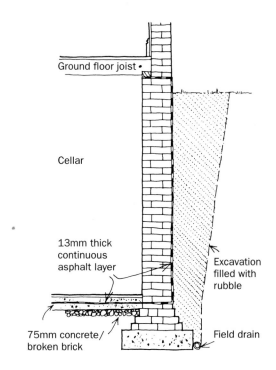

FIG. 31. The enclosing wall of a basement showing waterproofing asphalt 'tanking'.

method for excluding damp from the basements of new houses involved laying 75–100mm of broken brick or stone over the newly excavated ground. The whole area was then covered with a 75mm (3in) thick layer of concrete. When the concrete was dry it was covered with a 13mm (½in) layer of asphalt which was carried through the enclosing walls, then up the outside of the wall, against the earth and back through the wall to form a damp-proof course above the external ground level. Where good quality rock asphalt was applied this form of construction may continue to grant dry conditions for many years. However, this is quite a sophisticated constructional form and most Edwardian basements relied only on the concrete or an equally thin layer of stone slabs as protection against dampness from the ground. It was hoped that external walls at least one-and-a-half bricks thick would resist water incursion around the sides, but it will be appreciated that without the impervious asphalt membrane layer there can be no guarantee of watertightness and it is wise to accept that most basements are damp, a circumstance due to the normal, damp condition of the surrounding earth where leaking rainwater or foul drains are not the source of the problem. Another cause of dampness in basement walls is the absorption of groundwater from below by capillary attraction. Stone walls are particularly prone to this problem, which usually results from the lack of a damp-proof course.

The damp condition of thin basement walls is often worsened by the paint finish of their internal surfaces. Limewash was a favourite treatment for cellar walls and often compounds – or even causes – the problem of dampness because lime is hygroscopic (it attracts moisture to itself both from the air and the brickwork). If the internal surface of brickwork is damp, the application of gloss paints in substitution for the limewash produces disfiguring rashes of discoloration where the brickwork is unable to 'breathe' and allow the dampness to evaporate. Permeable, water-based emulsion paints should always be applied to such raw masonry surfaces where decoration is desired and appropriate, and if mould growth is feared, an emulsion paint containing a fungicidal additive should complete the process of decoration, preceded by application of a proprietary mould inhibitor. Where brickwork has been previously treated with a traditional distemper finish, a great deal of preparatory work is usually necessary to ensure that the new emulsion paint finish will continue to adhere to the distempered surfaces.

Good ventilation of cellars reduces the risk of damp conditions and consequent decay; the dry rot fungus flourishes in warm, damp basements where there is little air movement. It can infest damp brickwork and is often only eradicated by cutting out all of the affected material and replacing it with new construction.

Retaining Walls

The basement walls described above are examples of retaining walls – walls erected to prevent the collapse of surrounding earth into the lowest storey of the building as well as providing support to the external walls of the superstructure. Retaining walls not fulfilling this latter purpose are often found in terraced gardens, or act as flank walls to external areas adjoining basements and external basement-access staircases. Such ancillary walls were often cheaply made, the thin masonry failing to provide durable earth-retaining structures and they are often subject to bulging from subsidence of the retained earth, or

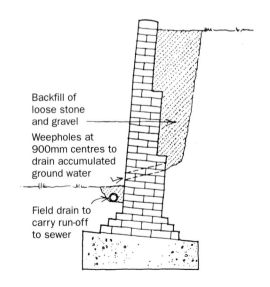

Backfill of loose stone and gravel

Weepholes at 900mm centres to drain accumulated ground water

Field drain to carry run-off to sewer

FIG. 32. Cross-section through a garden retaining wall.

overturning, in which case the foot of the wall is pushed out by settlement and its top moves backwards. A common cause of failure of retaining walls is the omission of drainage at low level in the form of built-in pipes or *weephole* (open vertical joints in the brickwork) which allow water to drain away from the retained earth behind. If the structure is not drained in this way, water percolating through the retained earth will eventually threaten the stability of the retaining wall (Fig. 32).

GROUND FLOORS

The difficulty of damp-proofing floors next to the ground was acknowledged in traditional construction by the almost universal adoption of timber for the structure of a suspended floor which, in the best work, is positioned over a thin concrete ground layer, a continuous airspace being left between the concrete and the joisted timber floor. In practice, where this form of construction was adopted in speculative houses, this 'oversite' concrete was often omitted, leaving an irregular surface of dry, compacted earth at least 250mm (10in) below the floorboards. The most durable version of this construction placed a concrete ground layer 150mm (6in) thick across the site and granted a zone at least 300mm deep from its top surface to the underside of the ground-floor joists. This depth of void was often necessary to ensure that the damp-proof course, located below the timber *wallplates* supporting the floor joists, would be at least 150mm above the external ground level – a stipulation of the building by-laws intended to prevent the external wall from being saturated by rising damp or splashes from rainwater hitting the external ground surface. Because the airspace between the floor joists and the oversite slab must be ventilated to prevent a damp and stagnant atmosphere congenial to dry rot, the ventilation ducts in the external walls were located close to the timber wallplate supporting the ends of the floor joists (Fig. 33). The wallplate was commonly sited on a ledge on the inner face of the external wall, causing the wall construction at this low level to be a half-brick – 112mm (4½in) – thicker than upper sections of the wall. Below floors of large rooms it was necessary to install intermediate supports for the joists at not more than 3m (10ft)

intervals. These could be in the form of square brickwork piers, a pier supporting each joint between joists, though by the end of the nineteenth century the advantages of the single-skin honeycomb brickwork *sleeper* wall as the means of intermediate support for suspended ground floors were widely recognised. Gaps were left between the individual half-bricks of such walls, giving a honeycomb appearance, to allow air movement throughout the whole of the underfloor void and the walls were capped with timber wallplates that support the joists. In cheaply constructed houses where the concrete ground layer was omitted, sleeper walls were founded either on well-compacted dry earth or brick rubble.

The suspended timber ground floor can introduce problems additional to the hazard of propagation of dry rot induced by inadequate ventilation. The void below the floorboards is a favourite nesting place and route for rodents invading the premises from gardens or neighbouring properties. The airspace is also a source of draughts because a stratum of cold air is continually present below heated rooms and the cold air is exchanged for the warm air through gaps between floorboards and skirtings. In a thorough renovation of a house with a suspended boarded ground floor, it is worth considering the upgrading of the scant insulation afforded by the boards by taking them up and stapling tough PVC garden netting on to the sides of the floor joists so that a mesh layer is obtained across the entire floor area of each room below the boards. A glass-fibre or mineral wool quilt is then unrolled to be supported by, and completely cover, the netting and, finally, the floorboards are re-laid on top of the joists. As this exercise often entails the removal and refixing of skirtings, it is worthwhile wedging a foam polyurethane sealing strip between the boards and the underside of the skirting to further discourage draughts (Fig. 34).

Implementation of this improvement may not be feasible where the floorboards are of the tongue-and-groove type which is more difficult to lift than plain-edge boards without causing significant damage (for the constructional detail of this type of floor see Chapter 6). In these circumstances it may be possible, in some cases, to insert the fine blade of a portable jigsaw into the joints, detaching the tongues

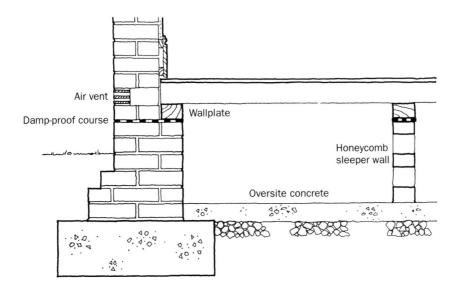

FIG. 33. *Suspended timber ground-floor construction showing a sleeper wall supporting an intermediate wallplate.*

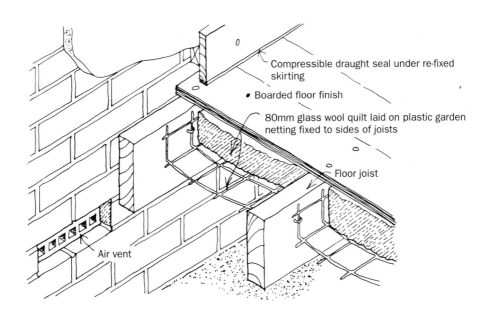

FIG. 34. *Installation of glass-wool quilt thermal insulation between the joists of a suspended timber floor.*

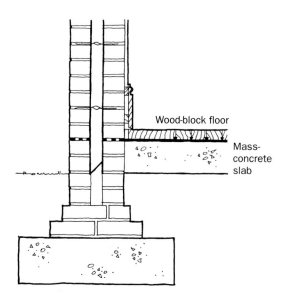

Wood-block floor

Mass-
concrete
slab

FIG. 35. *Cavity wall construction above a stepped-brickwork and concrete-strip foundation and adjacent to a mass concrete ground-floor slab.*

from particular boards so that panels of boarding may be lifted to the extent that it is practicable to fix the insulation support netting. However, it is not likely to be possible to treat all the tongued-and-grooved boards of a room in this way, nor is it advisable in view of the strength gained from the interlocking of the boards,

If fungi or insect attack (perpetrated most often by the common furniture beetle or 'woodworm') has ravaged the majority of the timber structure it may be better to consider wholesale replacement of the wooden construction with a solid concrete ground floor, laid on a continuous damp-proof membrane

that must connect with the damp-proof course built into the external walls.

By the beginning of the twentieth century it had become clear to some designers of bespoke houses that there was little merit in complicated suspended ground-floor construction when a solid floor of concrete which obviates draughts could be laid directly on to the ground, its top surface being waterproofed with asphalt before timber boarding or a sand/cement screed to accept a tiled floor finish was laid. In food preparation or circulation spaces, slate slabs or marble or ceramic tiles granted surfaces more resistant to spillages, wet boots and heavy traffic than that of wooden boarding. By the inter-war period, this type of solid construction had largely superseded the suspended ground floor in small speculative houses without basements, though the damp-proof membrane was usually omitted, damp resistance being sought from the concrete slab which was conventionally 150mm (6in) thick. In the absence of an impervious damp-proof membrane, long-term resistance of this form of construction to rising damp cannot be guaranteed. A more durable compromise construction was often achieved where floors of interlocking wood-block parquet were installed over the concrete, because the blocks of this floor finish were almost invariably bedded in hot bitumen, an impervious material which offers better damp resistance than the simple concrete slab (Fig. 35). In time, the bitumen bedding becomes brittle and shrinkage of the timber further encourages individual blocks to become loose. Correction of this condition frequently requires the lifting of the panel of affected blocks, renewal of the related area of exposed bitumen bedding and installation of new wood blocks replicating the form and material of the original components.

CHAPTER 4

External Walls

In Edwardian and inter-war houses, as in the architecture of almost every other historical period, it is the external elevations that offer the designer the greatest scope to express architectural style. Therefore, the treatment of external walls was at least as much affected by changes in fashion as it was by technical developments offering new or improved ways of achieving a weatherproof construction.

BRICKWORK

Millions of Edwardian and inter-war houses are essentially of brick construction. The colour and physical properties of the bricks themselves varied widely according to their composition (partly dependent on the geology at the source of the constituent clays) and method of manufacture. In London and south-east England, the yellow London stock bricks are very familiar, although the preference for red 'wealden' bricks which arose out of the taste of architects practising the Old English style in the last decades of the nineteenth century caused yellow stock bricks to be viewed as an inferior material, suitable only for side and rear elevations, even in speculative houses. In north-west England, a hard, almost shiny red brick which originates from Accrington in Lancashire is commonly seen in association with a blotchy pink *common brick* (sometimes termed a 'Cheshire stock') used in side and rear elevations, whilst many southern houses contain whitish facing bricks ('gaults' and other varieties) that are almost as common as the yellow stocks. The north-west Midlands is home to many buildings incorporating the famous Staffordshire blue bricks. These colour

differences are largely accounted for by the varying constituents of different brick-making clays.

Types of Brick

Common bricks were made from local or readily available brick clays and little attention was given to evenness of firing or regularity of form in the product. Such bricks were often unsuitable for use as facing bricks but were strong and hard enough for general purposes. In the inter-war period in southern England this description came to refer to the plain *Fletton* bricks which are often used in work concealed by decorative finishes. They are named after the village near Peterborough where they were first made in the 1880s and are machine-made bricks moulded from the Oxford clay of the Bedford, Buckingham and Northampton districts. Their normal colour is pink – usually patched where the bricks have been stacked on top of one another inside the kiln.

Stock brick is a term that usually refers to bricks moulded by hand from southern English clay mixed with chimney ash, which were burnt in a 'clamp' to produce the yellow-brown bricks that are a familiar sight in many of the older buildings of London and south-east England. A clamp is a large, elongated, flat-topped 'pyramid' of dried, unburnt bricks below which lies a shallow bed of coke that is ignited and allowed to burn for a period of ten to twelve weeks. When the fire has died out, the clamp is dismantled and the fully burnt stock bricks are removed from its core. Stock bricks produced in this way were often used externally, and being more durable, were more suitable for this purpose than common bricks.

Place bricks. Bricks which, having been furthest from the fire in the clamp or kiln, did not receive enough heat to burn them thoroughly. They are soft, uneven in texture and red-pink in colour. At best, they were suitable for use only in non load-bearing partitions. They deteriorate readily if exposed to the weather.

Rubbers, cutters or red builders. Bricks that are lightly burnt to be soft enough to cut or rub down very evenly and uniformly. They have no 'frog' (indentation in the top surface) and they were usually made oversize to allow for rubbing.

Engineering bricks. These are strong, dense and smooth-faced. They are obtained by burning dried bricks to vitrification. Staffordshire blue bricks are the best-known bricks of this type, although stronger red varieties were made at Accrington, Bristol, Ruabon (North Wales) and in parts of Yorkshire. Similar, though less strong 'pressed' bricks were made in Leicestershire and are termed *Leicestershire reds.* The use of all types developed from civil engineering applications in the nineteenth century, particularly the construction of railway viaducts and overbridges.

Gault bricks. Hard, close-textured, pale buff bricks manufactured from the chalky clay of the same name in Cambridgeshire, Bedfordshire, Essex and parts of Kent. Gaults were among the first bricks to be mass-produced by machine and dense, precisely shaped varieties were available from the 1850s though new bricks of this composition and with these qualities are unobtainable today.

Concrete bricks. Cast in moulds, they differ from the other forms of brick in that the aggregate is physically bound by cement rather than chemically combined with the other constituents, as occurs in firing. Concrete bricks were only produced in quantity after 1920 so that though they may be found in some inter-war houses, they are unlikely to be original to the anatomy of Edwardian houses.

Even into the inter-war period, it was common for quite small towns to boast their own brickworks and so it is feasible only to describe a few of the more common types that are found in houses of the Edwardian years, and the 1920s and 1930s. It is also important to recognise that the bricks used in many buildings erected as late as the early twentieth century were often of varying quality. Sound and regularly shaped bricks were more expensive than 'commons' but were necessary to achieve a durable finish on the weathering faces of buildings. However, the inner, concealed body of a solid external wall (or the inner leaf of a cavity wall where this construction was adopted) usually consisted of the softer and cheaper place bricks. Rubbers were frequently used to form arches and decorative band courses, particularly in Edwardian work. Party walls between terraced or semi-detached houses are often entirely of place bricks, as are panels of external walls coated with stucco, pebbledash or roughcast rendering.

In addition to bricks of standard format (approx. 215mm (9in) long, 102mm (4in) wide and 65mm (2.5in deep), many types of brick, purpose-made to particular shapes, were used to create sloping sills, cornices, arches and jamb mouldings as well as copings to freestanding walls and other features of 'hard' landscaping, in gardens, and although the high period for such elaborate brickwork had already passed by the start of the Edwardian era, speculative builders continued to embellish houses with showy detailing up to the First World War (Fig. 36).

Types of Mortar

The principal reason for laying bricks or stones in mortar is that bedding in mortar encourages a uniform transfer of load through elements whose irregularity or distorted form might invite fractures, even under quite light pressure. The use of mortar also allows irregularities to be absorbed, removing the need to accommodate variations in the coursing; it acts as a gap filler to exclude the weather and, particularly in the case of cement mortar, its adhesive properties bond together the units from which the wall is made. Friction and adhesion between mortar and brick or stone prevent dislocation of individual components and enhance the load-bearing properties of the wall. Almost all mortars used in nineteenth-century house construction were lime based, but in the early decades of the twentieth century these were increasingly giving way to cement-based mortars.

Lime-based mortars. Chalk, which is a form of lime-stone, is the raw material for the production of pure or 'fat' limes. These are readily 'slaked' with water, generating considerable heat and a doubling of volume. The resultant slaked lime sets or hardens by absorbing carbon dioxide from the atmosphere to form a soft crystalline carbonate of lime and its slow gain in strength makes mortars based on such limes unsuitable for use in high-strength masonry or structures where speed of construction is the chief concern. Consequently, the white 'lime putty' which is the product of slaking fat limes was often reserved for non-structural, semi-decorative work such as the pointing of 'red rubber' brick arches.

Limestones containing clay impurities can be burnt to produce calcium silicates and aluminates. With the addition of water, these so-called 'hydraulic' limes set and harden mainly by independent internal crystallisation. Any free lime present hardens by absorbing carbon dioxide. Generally speaking the greater the clay impurity, the faster the setting time and the less carbon dioxide is required. Hydraulic limes are generally stronger than fat limes and they were used extensively in load-bearing masonry. Indigenous resources of hydraulic lime are largely worked out, but similar materials are imported from mainland Europe and the past fifteen years have witnessed a revival of interest among architects and surveyors engaged in building conservation work in the use of this material in preference to the cement-based mortars which have become the industry standard. Limes used in building structure were normally mixed with sand (around 1:3 by volume) to increase the bulk of the material, to assist setting and to reduce drying shrinkage.

In performing one of the principal functions of a mortar – the role of joint filler – lime mortars were found to be adequate because an external weathering surface to joints – pointing – was provided. Whereas it was acceptable to formulate the joint-filling mortar with regular fat (or 'hydrated') limes, in order to be durable it was necessary for the lime used in pointing to be hydraulic lime and a clear distinction was made between the mixes used for these separate purposes. One of the chief advantages of any lime mortar – and particularly the material used in bedding bricks or stones – is that, being generally plastic rather than

FIG. 36. Showy brickwork details in evidence on semi-detached house of 1908.

brittle, it is able to accept some deformation before any opening of bed joints or splitting of bricks occurs. This explains why any expansion of new bricks in older buildings caused little visible cracking in contrast to the effects that are seen in modern masonry.

Portland cement mortar. The manufacture of Portland cement in its modern form dates from the middle of the nineteenth century although it was many years before its usefulness to general building construction, and particularly to house building, was generally recognised. Its basic ingredients are limestone and clay in the proportion 2:1. These materials are ground together and the resulting powder is burnt in a kiln at a high temperature to incipient vitrification to form clinkers. These clinkers are then ground to a fine powder, which is the finished cement. The addition of water triggers a series of chemical reactions resulting in a dense and solid crystalline formation, which seemed so similar to Portland stone that its inventor named the product 'Portland' cement.

After 1900, use of lime mortars in masonry slowly gave way to cement mortar and by the 1930s cement mortar had become the predominant material. Very often such mortar contained a small proportion of lime to improve workability during construction (for example, 1:1:6 cement/lime/sand).

Cement mortars are comparatively hard and brittle and they have higher crushing strengths than lime mortars. Consequently, walls built with cement mortars have a greater tendency to crack when subjected to distortion – either by brittle fracture of the mortar or, if the brick is the weaker material, by the snapping of bricks. Relatively small distortions may cause visible cracking. Lime mortars, being more plastic, accommodate long-term movement better.

Brick Bonding

To ensure solid and permanent construction, good adhesion of brick to brick through the mortar is obtained through the bond. As early as the eighteenth century the art of bricklaying was well developed and the properties of different brick bonds were understood. In traditional buildings, the most popular bonds were the *English* and *Flemish* bonds, the latter being the most widely used in eighteenth, nineteenth and early twentieth-century house construction. In *Flemish bond*, each course comprises alternate 'header' bricks (ends of bricks showing) and 'stretcher' bricks overlapping with alternate headers and stretchers in the course below (Fig. 37). The headers were intended as full bricks to bond the facing skin into the backing work, the latter usually being constructed from place bricks. Flemish bond was considered to give a more attractive appearance than the other main form of solid construction, *English bond*. This applied because it is composed of alternating courses of headers and stretchers, producing a distinct, regular 'striping' (Fig. 38).

Forms of densely bonded construction that are quicker to construct than either Flemish or English bond are the garden-wall bonds which were often used in external works as their names suggest.

Flemish garden wall bond. This is similar to Flemish bond, except that three stretchers are placed between each header in each course (Fig. 39). It is thus a weaker bond than the full Flemish bond.

English garden wall bond. This economises on headers by alternating either three or five courses of stretchers with one of headers and is consequently weaker than the full English (Fig. 40). Nevertheless, it was one of

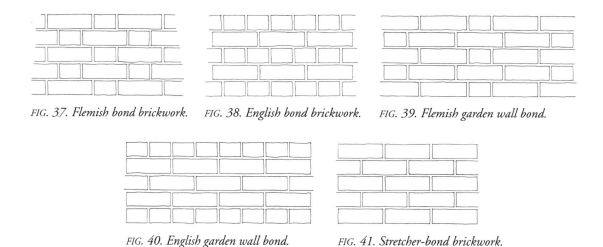

FIG. 37. Flemish bond brickwork.　　FIG. 38. English bond brickwork.　　FIG. 39. Flemish garden wall bond.

FIG. 40. English garden wall bond.　　FIG. 41. Stretcher-bond brickwork.

the most popular of all brickwork bonds, particularly in the north of England and Midlands.

The existence of these apparently solid types of brick bonding in external walls does not necessarily testify to the presence of solid (more than half-brick thick) construction. Flemish or English bonds have often been used purely for decorative reasons, the bonded look being obtained in an external brick skin by building 'snap' headers or 'half bats' (cut bricks) into the work in the header positions. This was sometimes done for decorative effect in the outer leaf of a cavity wall, but even seemingly solid external walls were often constructed as almost independent weathering and backing skins, the weathering skin containing more than a sensible proportion of snap headers rather than full bonding bricks, thus posing problems for the long-term integrity of the wall, as will be seen later.

With the increasing popularity of cavity-wall construction in the later inter-war period, the desire to drive down construction costs suggested that there was no advantage in continuing to incorporate 'sham solid' construction in the outer leaves of cavity walls by continuing the expensive technique of installing snap headers. It was essential only to achieve the most basic, and thereby cheapest, form of brick bond, and the treatment with which we are most familiar today as the standard product in new buildings is *stretcher bond* (Fig. 41) in which header bricks only make an appearance where it is necessary to terminate panels of brickwork at corners or window or door apertures.

Brick Jointing

The way the mortar joints between the bricks are formed may be as important for the appearance of the wall as the pattern of the bond. The completion of the partly filled joints of a new brick wall to give a neat mortar joint on, or close to, the face of the brickwork is termed *pointing*. The eventual replacement of this mortar surface is called *repointing*.

A variety of types of brick jointing, practised in the eighteenth and nineteenth centuries, continued to be used by the Edwardians and an awareness of the different types is essential if proficient restoration of an old facing or the blending of new work with old, is to be managed.

In the *flush* joint, the mortar is finished on the same face as the brickwork and this treatment can produce a very flat, undifferentiated surface, particularly where the bricks are of regular and precise shape (Fig. 42A). This type of joint is rarely suitable for repointing old brickwork because the process of raking out the old mortar damages the edges of soft bricks and the very wide joints that result from flush-pointing such damaged brickwork dominate the repointed surface in an unattractive way.

Much more suitable for this purpose is the *keyed* joint which is achieved by running a short section of hosepipe or iron bucket-handle along the wet mortar to give a slightly recessed joint (Fig. 42B). However, even this treatment is to be deprecated where the desire for authenticity and the existence of a substantial budget allow repointing to be executed with a pointing iron to fully pack and finish the joint to a slightly recessed profile.

The *struck* or *weathered* joint is an alternative profile which is formed with the bricklayer's diamond trowel (Fig. 42C). It makes the brickwork appear stratified because its sloping profile introduces horizontal shadows, causing these joints to dominate the surface, and the pleasant irregularities of old, oddly shaped bricks are thereby obscured. Nevertheless, it is an efficient shape for throwing rainwater off the wall and, although it was not favoured in brickwork erected before the late nineteenth century, its popularity with today's bricklayers does not automatically disqualify it for use in the repointing of Edwardian or inter-war houses because it is clear that it was employed in the construction of a substantial and increasing number of ordinary houses from the end of the nineteenth century.

The most elaborate joint is produced by *tuck pointing*, which is an old-fashioned way of making ancient brickwork look new, precise and regular, or of making new brickwork of partly decorative features such as arches, plaques or sub-sill spandrel panels which are formed from irregular, low quality bricks, look like the best fine-tolerance construction. In old work, the original mortar having been raked out, the open joint is pointed up flush with a mortar coloured to match the general brickwork surface. Into this flush joint is inserted a thin, projecting and continuous square-section bead of white lime putty which

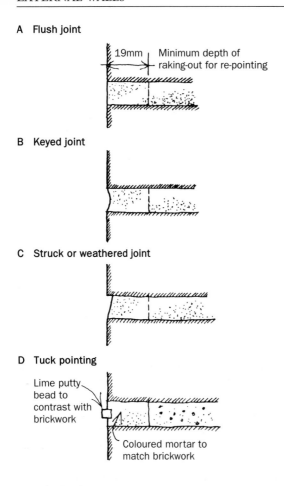

A   Flush joint

19mm | Minimum depth of
raking-out for re-pointing

B   Keyed joint

C   Struck or weathered joint

D   Tuck pointing

Lime putty
bead to
contrast with
brickwork

Coloured mortar to
match brickwork

FIG. 42 Brick jointing.

contrasts strongly with the brick colour to suggest that the wall has been erected to close tolerances (Fig. 42D). The thin putty bead of tuck pointing is easily explained: traditionally, thin mortar joints were equated with top-quality construction and, in times when labour costs were low, tuck pointing was a low-cost way of making a surface look better built than it was. Although commonplace Edwardian brickwork (and almost all brickwork of ordinary inter-war houses) displays the approximately 10mm (⅜in) wide joints that are conventional in modern work, the facing brickwork of the front elevations of Edwardian houses formed from precise, pressed bricks such as the 'Accrington red' may show joints of only half this thickness.

Repointing

The first general principle to be followed where repointing of brickwork or stonework is contemplated is that it should only be undertaken where the mortar has been scoured or washed out by the action of wind and rain, leaving open or deeply recessed joints vulnerable to water penetration, or where the mortar is very soft or loose. Thus it is clear that overall repointing of a house is rarely necessary. The parts most exposed to the weather are likely to be those most in need of attention and even in these areas deterioration of mortar joints may not be uniform, encouraging the retention of even quite small sections of sound old pointing. From the foregoing account, it will be appreciated that pointing makes a significant contribution to the character of a house and it should not be renewed unnecessarily. Defective repointing is one of the most common causes of damage to the character of old houses *and* of damage to the masonry from which they are built. Even where some repointing is essential, the mortar should not be removed with a powered disc cutter as this is likely to cause damage to the edges (*arrises*) of bricks, and, if used on the vertical joints (*perpends*) the faces of bricks above and below each joint are in danger of being grooved by the action of such a tool.

The second principle to observe is the matching of the new work to a sound example of the original pointing found at a sheltered part of the building. In some cases it may not be possible to match the original mortar, in which case a mix should be chosen which is both compatible with the porosity and strength of the bricks or stones constituting the wall and which is suitable to the degree of exposure to the weather of the particular location. Normally the mortar should be slightly weaker than the masonry. A mortar that is harder than the general walling material prevents moisture from evaporating out through the joints, causing it to come out only through the stones or bricks and thus both accelerating their rate of decay and leaving the mortar joints standing proud of the wall surface. Naturally, the new pointing should also be finished in accordance with the original form of joint where evidence of this treatment has survived. It is never correct to spread mortar beyond the joint on to the faces of bricks or stones.

Decorative Brickwork

Many Edwardian houses incorporate areas of decorative brickwork in their external walls, and even the plainest brick-built, inter-war 'semi' is unlikely to lack some feature relieving the uniformity of wall surfaces composed of continuous stretcher-bond brickwork. Arches over window and entrance door apertures were favourite candidates for execution in bricks contrasting with the body of the construction either in colour or form (or both). In the south of England red bricks (or whitish malm bricks) often contrast with the yellow stocks which are the main construction as the quoins sited at corners of external walls. Also, projecting horizontal string courses or cornices formed from moulded bricks into quite complicated classical profiles often grace main elevations of the more expensive houses. A simplified version of this treatment, which was widely employed in speculative houses, particularly to terminate the pebbledash or roughcast rendered finish of an upper storey at the head of a ground-storey brickwork plinth, was the projecting *string course* composed of two courses of brickwork simulating the lower part of a classical 'dentil' cornice: alternately projecting headers supporting an equally projecting continuous course of headers (Fig. 43). A variation on this form set the lower course of bricks at the diagonal, giving a 'sawtooth' profile to this course (see Fig. 36 above). Bull-nosed brick mouldings or quarter-brick recessions or projections in brickwork were quite often used near to window openings in Edwardian houses in continuation of a fashion founded in late-Victorian times. However, the increasing desire to simulate the characteristics of cottages in suburban houses meant a reduction in the use of such ornamentation in the work of all but the most conservative speculative builders.

Damp-proof Courses

Depending on local building by-laws, from the late 1870s new houses had to incorporate a damp-proof course in their external walls. The function of the damp-proof course is to prevent saturation of the masonry by groundwater and the resultant deterioration of internal finishes. This was achieved by incorporating a horizontal layer of impervious material (asphalt, bituminous felt, lead or slate) in the external

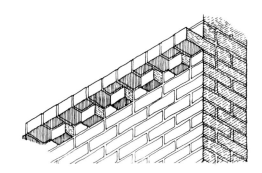

FIG. 43. Brickwork dentil cornice.

wall below the ground-floor construction. In most British houses of the early twentieth century this was easy to arrange because ground floors were almost invariably of timber boards laid on timber joists (suspended ground-floor construction). The joists themselves were either supported on timber beams, themselves supported on low piers of solid brickwork, or directly on low brickwork 'sleeper' walls built on a shallow concrete ground layer or a level area of firm ground. This deep form of composite construction enabled a damp-proof course to be incorporated in the external walls at a suitable height above the external ground level to resist damp penetration (see Fig. 33 in Chapter 3) but on a sloping site the underside of the timber ground-floor construction might well be below the general external ground level, and consequently below the level of the damp-proof course. This difficulty could be overcome either by excavating the foot of the earth bank abutting the wall to provide a gangway guaranteeing no breaching of the damp-proof course by adjoining ground, or by adopting a profile at the foot of the wall which would allow the damp-proof to change level without discontinuity. This could be done by forming a cant-brick plinth at the foot of the wall (a feature quite popular in conventional conditions in Edwardian houses in any case), concealing two continuous horizontal damp-proof courses linked by a vertical damp-proof course at the rear of the external half-brick 'skin', thus ensuring continuity of the damp-proofing (Fig. 44). The increased thickness of the wall at its base also allowed the incorporation of vertical ducts in the brickwork, linking the under-floor space with the outside air. Similar ducts were incorporated even in the standard arrangement of a ground floor sited above external ground level because the main danger of not ventilating the under-floor void is the encouragement of a dry rot outbreak in the timbers. Cast-iron or terracotta gratings, which may be seen, sited at regular intervals, on the outside surface of the external walls of many older houses, close to ground level, testify to the existence of these ducts.

Reduction in Thickness

Even if not providing support to suspended timber ground floors, the external walls always provide support for timber floors at upper levels. In multistorey construction it was usual to reduce the wall thickness on the internal face at the level of each principal floor above the ground floor by a half-brick thickness to provide a ledge accommodating a plate that bears the ends of the floor joists. This policy might mean installing very thick walls at the base of

the building (Fig. 45). A more economical construction was obtained by housing the floor joists in sling-like metal joist hangers hooked into the horizontal mortar joints of the wall, or by corbelling two or three courses of brickwork immediately below upper floors to provide a bearing for the joists, but in low-cost construction it was normal simply to house the joists in small pockets left in the brickwork. In the 215mm-thick solid brickwork which is commonly found in early twentieth-century houses, this arrangement leaves only a half-brick thickness separating the joist ends from outside air and in the long term this could lead to rotting of the joist ends from damp penetration through this single-skin brickwork, particularly if the external mortar joints are in need of repointing. It is a detail which should not be adopted where joists are being replaced. New joists should be located on galvanised or stainless steel joist hangers built into the brickwork. Plainly, an advantage of the cavity wall, which was increasingly adopted even by speculative builders as the twentieth

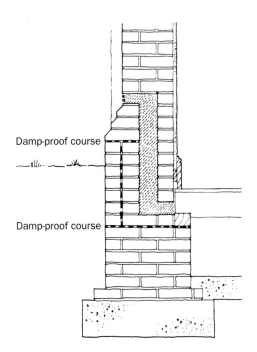

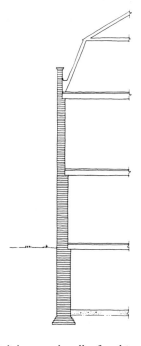

FIG. 44. A cant-brickwork plinth may incorporate cranked ducts venting the underfloor void where external ground level is higher.

FIG. 45. Solid external walls of multi-storey houses often reduce in thickness with height.

century progressed (largely for its superior performance in securing dry conditions inside houses), was the fact that joist ends were entirely isolated from the outer skin of brickwork (see Fig. 29 in Chapter 3).

Disfigured Facing Brickwork

The bricks of a brickwork external wall are much less likely to break down as a result of constant exposure to the weather than are the mortar joints which bind them together. Bricks darker than their neighbours in the wall surface are likely to have been over burnt, harder than the rest and therefore less liable to decay, and by the same logic, under burnt bricks, which may not prove as durable, are often recognisable by their lighter colour. Such bricks are particularly prone to early deterioration where close to external ground level or where used as copings of garden walls or party wall parapets projecting above roof surfaces. In these exposed or vulnerable locations, the bricks are easily saturated by driving rain even if the mortar joints are complete, and a subsequent frost will cause the bricks to 'burst' or delaminate as the entrapped water expands upon freezing. Bricks that lose their durable outer surface in this way will quite quickly deteriorate as their softer clay cores are exposed to the elements. The only satisfactory long-term remedy is to cut out the affected bricks and replace them with new or good-quality salvaged bricks. Other apparent defects in external brickwork include efflorescence and 'rust staining', two problems that detract from the appearance of the brickwork rather than its structural stability.

In efflorescence a damp white powder appears across the surface of the bricks and the mortar joints. This occurs when soluble salts are washed out of the brick clay and the mortar, or because of the chemical reaction of the two with rainwater. When the brick surface dries out, the salts are deposited. Efflorescence is most often encountered in new brickwork in exposed positions (such as boundary walls), though it may emerge on newly repointed old brickwork. In the course of time it will disappear.

Rust staining, which produces patches of brown discolouration on external brick surfaces, is caused by the reaction with rainwater of iron compounds contained in the brickwork. Like efflorescence, this discolouration will diminish gradually.

STONE EXTERNAL WALLS

In various areas of Britain, even as late as the Second World War, it was conventional to build good-quality houses of all sizes with external walls of natural stone. Stonework continued to be regarded as superior to brick because of its renowned solidity and its association with permanence. Also, the erection of stone masonry requires greater skill than building in brickwork. Bricks, being all of the same size, are laid according to a regular pattern, whereas with each stone, considerable judgement is required so that it may be laid in the best way.

The appearance of solid stonework was often achieved in *compound* construction (that is, stone facing with a brickwork or rubble backing) and the facing of such walls in *ashlars* (precisely shaped rectangular blocks) was rare in house construction, although external corners formed from natural stone were almost always achieved in this way.

Types of Building Stone

The majority of building stones used in the British Isles falls into the two distinct categories of limestones and sandstones. Although other types of building stone are found, notably *granite*, which is prevalent at two extremities of mainland Britain – Cornwall and north-east Scotland – it is unusual to find such hard and dense stones as the main material for the construction of modest houses. The *Millstone Grit* of west Yorkshire, east Cheshire and north Derbyshire is a famous sandstone, as is Derbyshire's *Darley Dale* stone, Yorkshire's *Bolton Wood*, Edinburgh's *Craigleith*, the red sandstones of west Cheshire (such as *Runcorn* stone) and Nottinghamshire (*Mansfield* stone, which should not be confused with the whitish magnesian limestone also quarried in that area) and the famous *York* stone which was favoured for doorsteps and from which many older city pavements are made.

British limestones commonly used in building construction include the famous buff-coloured *Bath* stone from which that city is almost exclusively built, the equally celebrated whitish *Portland* stone from Dorset's Isle of Portland and the indigenous yellow-brown stones of the Cotswold region. Lesser-known limestones, which nevertheless found favour among

Edwardian architects, include *Ketton* stone (from Leicestershire) and *Hopton Wood*, a drab-coloured carboniferous limestone from Derbyshire. *Bolsover Moor* limestone also originates from this district. It was favoured because its light brown tones were only slowly affected by sooty city atmospheres and it is easy to carve.

Slate, too, is of course a building stone, and as well as being used as a roofing material it was sometimes used as an internal floor finish because it provides a smooth and level surface which is virtually impervious to spillages. Accordingly, it was often used for kitchen and larder floors in good-quality houses, a treatment which is enjoying something of a revival in the present day. Larder shelves, chimneypieces and steps might also be formed from thick slabs of slate.

Much building stone had been imported from mainland Europe throughout the Victorian period, a process that continued over the first four decades of the twentieth century, but its consequently high cost prohibited its use in external walls. 'Sicilian' marble and similar metamorphic stones were usually reserved for use in expensive chimneypieces or in conjunction with sanitary ware.

Defects in Stonework

It would be comforting to believe that the density and apparent solidity of building stone guarantees it against decay and deterioration. Unfortunately, this is not so. As applies with all other building materials, the chemical constituents of stone react with chemicals present in the atmosphere, resulting in the eventual breakdown of the material. This process was particularly acute before the introduction of 'smokeless zones' in British towns and cities created by the Clean Air Act of 1956. In the decades preceding the Second World War, the atmosphere was often loaded with the products of soot from domestic coal fires, producing 'smog', particularly in winter. In the case of central London in the mid 1930s, solid impurities in the air fell at the rate of 475 tons per square mile per year. The City of Westminster was covered by a heavy smoke haze for a third of the year, a condition borne out by the images in old newsreel films featuring the capital. One ingredient of this soot was a mild sulphuric acid formed from the combination of sulphur produced by domestic coal fires and water

vapour. Sulphuric acid acts on limestones and calcareous sandstones, converting the normally insoluble calcium carbonate constituent of these stones into calcium sulphate, which eventually becomes soluble, causing erosion of the stone. Carbonic acid, which is present in rain containing dissolved soot, also reacts with calcium carbonate, turning it into soluble calcium bicarbonate with the same results. Hence, limestone sills and lintels, which are often elements of suburban Edwardian houses, may display sooty and decayed stone surfaces on their undersides which are almost entirely composed of calcium sulphate, rainwater not having had a chance to wash soot deposits from these surfaces. Any limestone string courses (or cornices, rarer in modest Edwardian houses than their Victorian predecessors) will be similarly affected.

The chemical compounds that polluted the air of pre-war British cities are less pervasive today, but motor vehicles are increasingly the cause of atmospheric pollution that has a destructive effect upon natural stonework, particularly magnesian limestones. Many of the ancient buildings of the Oxford colleges have lost much of their elaborate carved stone ornament in the space of a few years because of the action upon their magnesian limestone of an atmosphere polluted by traffic fumes.

A further cause of decay in limestones is the use of limestone and sandstone in juxtaposition, where the former is subject to attack and the formation of soluble salts. If these salts are washed on to the sandstone, its rapid decay will ensue.

Solid Stone External Walls

In house construction it is unusual to find forms of stone external walling other than the different forms of rubble, because the use of fully 'dressed' (shaped) ashlar stonework throughout was very expensive and gave a severe appearance which was regarded as inappropriate for dwellings, particularly at a time of enthusiasm for the replication of cottage prototypes.

Rubble walls are not easily built if they are less than 450mm (18in) thick, and like all forms of solid masonry they should contain bond – or throughstones – extending at least two-thirds of the way through the thickness of the wall to obtain an integrated construction. Rubblework is a general term for

FIG. 46. Random rubble stonework.

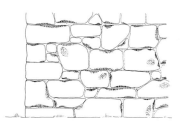

FIG. 47. Rubble wall of roughly squared stones.

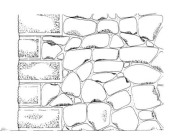

FIG. 48. Random rubble with ashlar quoins.

FIG. 49. Random rubble built in courses.

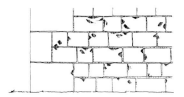

FIG. 50. Regular coursed rubble.

masonry in which the stones are of various and irregular sizes, and, in most cases, quite small. The bed joints and vertical joints in rubblework vary in thickness and the strength of the walling depends greatly on the mortar. *Random rubble* walls were much used in country districts for centuries before design became the self-conscious activity into which it developed in modern industrial society and therefore they were thus favoured for evoking the desired associations when used in early twentieth-century cottage-style dwellings (Fig. 46). *Kentish rag*, a type of limestone found in Kent, is particularly suitable for this form of construction because individual stones are small, hard, irregularly shaped and difficult to dress. Good quality, random-rubble walling was quite expensive because of the large amount of labour involved in dressing the beds and joints of the stones to fit close. If the joints exceed 13mm (½in) in thickness, the work is not of the best quality.

A superior type of rubble wall attempts to arrange the stones in more nearly horizontal courses, the stones having been roughly squared so as to achieve this, and the wall being bonded through every 1200–1500mm (4–5ft) (Fig. 47). It was thought

appropriate for stone-built houses sited in towns to attempt some degree of formality and more geometrically regular forms of rubble walling were adopted for these locations. The most informal of these treatments was the combination of random rubble walls with precisely squared quoins (corner stones) of the same stone (Fig. 48).

Random rubble built in courses was a common treatment in some parts of the country, the aim being to obtain a true horizontal bed every 300–450mm (12–18in), these bed levels corresponding with the top and bottom surfaces of each corner stone (Fig. 49). *Regular coursed rubble* gives the most uniform appearance of all, the courses being of identical height, causing the main difference between its appearance and that of conventional, stratified brickwork to be the slightly irregular configuration of vertical joints, which results from using stones of differing lengths (Fig. 50).

A hybrid form of construction that is encountered in some regions is the stone wall with brick quoins. Red brick is most commonly used for this treatment, the brick quoins being usually three to six courses deep, with plinths, dressings and arches to door and

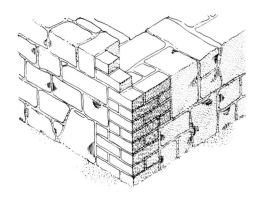

FIG. 51. *Rubble walling with brick quoins.*

window apertures and band courses (at the head of each storey) also being formed in brickwork. In this form, in order to bond with the regular strata dictated by the brickwork quoins, all the top and bottom joints of the rubble courses have level beds. Such walls were built cheaply if the local stone split readily when worked, could be laid on its natural bed without the need for laborious dressing, and when stone suitable for shaping for quoins was too costly or difficult to obtain (Fig. 51).

A variation on this type of composite construction is *flint work* often found in Sussex, Kent, and the downland of Surrey, Hampshire and East Anglia; districts where large quantities of flints are found below the beds of chalk. The walls might be built throughout in flints and faced with small uncut stones, or the flints might be used simply as a facing. Larger flints used for the facing were usually *knapped* or *polled* (split so as to show a vertical face rather than a pointed profile) and in the best work they were roughly squared and laid in regular courses. Quoins, window and door dressings were always built in stone or brick and 'lacing' courses of stone, brick or tile were introduced at intervals of about 1800mm (6ft) vertically to bind together a potentially weak construction and to introduce some visual order into the composition (Fig. 52). An effective wall decoration was sometimes achieved using panels of flints let flush into stonework in 'chequerboard' pattern. The dark colour and smooth texture of the flints often contrasts beautifully with the stone or brick dressings to produce this chequered effect, otherwise known as *diapering*. These treatments were rarer in speculative houses than in bespoke dwellings but the enthusiasm of the architects of the Arts and Crafts Movement for reviving the traditional building crafts of the districts in which they worked, ensured that some spectacular examples of flint, pebble or cobble wall construction in rural houses were created in the twenty years preceding the First World War.

Lintels and Sills

In all types of stone construction, the stones surrounding door and window openings are

FIG. 52. *Flintwork walling with brickwork quoins and lacing courses.*

necessarily regular because the walling material at these positions has to be compatible with such precisely made features as wooden doors and window frames. Therefore, stone lintels and sills (respectively above and below door and window openings) are always precisely shaped for their specific locations. In order to support the superincumbent masonry and to remain in place, lintels must have a *bearing* or piece of wall in which each end of this component sits. Today, lintels are almost always of reinforced concrete or steel, but until the Second World War, lintels expressed externally in house construction were commonly of stone (lintels spanning internal openings were often timber). Generally, the lintel is a single stone with 150–220mm (6–9in) bearing at each end into the supporting masonry. Where the span of the lintel was quite long – say 2.4m (8ft) over a range of windows – increasing the lintel in depth to achieve stability would result in a clumsy appearance, so a *relieving arch* was sometimes installed over the lintel to transfer most of the load away from the window head. In thick brickwork walls, or compound construction of brickwork faced with stone, a rough-ring brickwork segmental arch was sometimes built within the inner skin of the wall, thus relieving some of the load from the lintel without affecting the external appearance (Fig. 53). If this form of construction is encountered, it is important to remember that the arch and the lintel are interdependent and that both perform the function of supporting the wall, so that neither should be removed, replaced or modified without first obtaining the advice of a structural engineer.

Similar in shape to the lintel but sited at the foot of window and door openings is the *sill*. In solid brick or masonry external walls sills are generally of stone. Sills are usually arranged to project in front of the wall surface, though in some cases they were left flush with the wall. *Lug* sills are formed with lugs or *stoolings* which are flat-faced for ease of building into the wall, in contrast to the general top surface of the sill which is sloped or *weathered* to throw off rainwater (Fig. 54).

In addition to the sloping top surface of the sill, rainwater is encouraged to drain away from the profile by projecting the front surface of the sill in

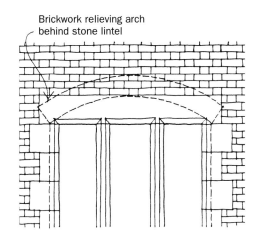

FIG. 53. An unseen segmental arch often relieves load from an external stone lintel.

front of the general wall surface and providing a drip groove or *throating* in the underside of this projection, causing rainwater running backwards into the joint of the sill and masonry to drip off before reaching this joint. In good-quality construction, a groove to accept a continuous metal water bar was also incorporated in the sill's top surface to prevent water being drawn through the fine joint between the stone sill and the wooden window sill.

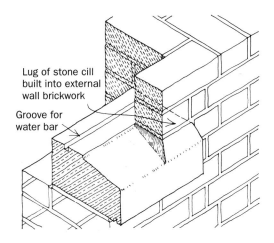

FIG. 54. Junction of moulded stone sill and brickwork external wall.

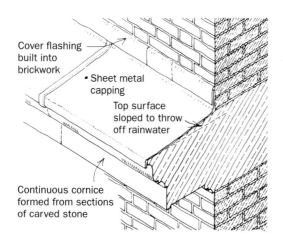

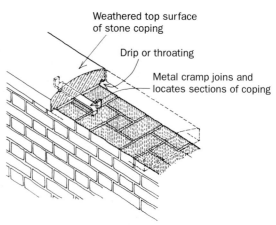

FIG. 55. Junction of moulded stone cornice and brickwork external wall.

FIG. 56. Brickwork parapet capped with moulded coping stones.

String Courses, Cornices and Copings

Continuous horizontal bands of stone – often moulded – projecting slightly from a building's elevation are termed *string courses*. Moulded bands, considerably deeper and more prominent than strings, are called *cornices*. The top surfaces of all strings and cornices should incorporate an outward and downward slope away from the wall (the *weathering*, as in a sill), for obvious reasons. Similarly, a *throating* or drip mould should be incorporated on the underside to prevent rainwater from flowing down and discolouring the face of the wall below by partial washing of its surface. Cornices which project out in excess of 150mm (6in) should have their top surfaces protected by a sheet metal capping of lead, zinc or copper if gradual deterioration of the exposed stonework is to be prevented (Fig. 55).

The final stone constructional component commonly found in modest houses is the stone wall coping. To prevent rainwater from washing out the joints between bricks or stones at the top of parapet walls, the construction is capped with a wide stone coping (Fig. 56). It should be of non-absorbent stone about 75–100mm (3–4in) wider than the wall below with its upper surface weathered and with a drip groove on its underside where it projects in front of the wall surface. Coping stones were commonly cramped or dowelled together (sometimes with

rather ineffective slate cramps) to prevent them becoming displaced in high winds or through mechanical damage. Where the party walls of terraced dwellings project up above roof surfaces (as in the London area, Fig. 57), or a gable similarly projects above the roof profile, gable coping stones were sometimes employed to cap the walls. Individual gable copings could be as long as 1800mm (6ft) in order to minimise the number of vulnerable butt joints between stones; for a whole range of these components to be secure against sliding off it was necessary for the undersides of some of them to incorporate short wedge-shaped sections which would act as bond-stones into the supporting masonry or brickwork. Because they slope, gable copings do not need to be weathered on top, though they must project and incorporate drip grooves to shed the rainwater. At the top of the gable the apex stone is of triangular form, bedded on a horizontal joint of the supporting brickwork or masonry. Rather than relying only on its self-weight for stability, the apex stone was often tied to the wall below with iron straps concealed in the wall thickness. The incorporation of a decorative finial, which adds to the weight, reduces the chance of the apex stone being dislodged.

In London house construction, where the local building acts insisted upon party walls being carried up above roof surfaces, the weather-tight coping of

FIG. 57. Party wall parapets project above the roof surfaces of an Edwardian terrace, south London.

these walls was more commonly achieved by building a course or two of fireclay *creasing tiles* into the party wall parapet, the tiles projecting out to either side in front of the brickwork to form a drip for rainwater. A brick-on-edge course was then added on top of these tiles to secure them in place and give a neat finish to the walltop. (Fig. 58.)

Compound Construction

Compound construction in stonework refers to brickwork or rubble with a dressed-stone facing. In good-quality work the thickness of the stone facing

would be not less than 175mm (7in) with about a quarter of the stones exposed on the external face being built into the backing by a further 125mm (5in). As applies in solid masonry, the facework was always bedded in lime mortar, though where a brick backing was used, the bricks were laid in cement mortar to avoid shrinkage and de-bonding of the facing and backing skins. Brick was used more extensively than stone as a backing because it is the cheaper material and the backing needed to be at least as robust as the facing – a minimum thickness of 200mm (8in). Modern textbooks on compound

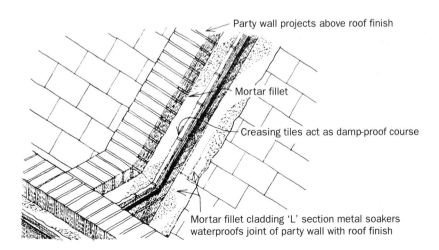

Party wall projects above roof finish

Mortar fillet

Creasing tiles act as damp-proof course

Mortar fillet cladding 'L' section metal soakers waterproofs joint of party wall with roof finish

FIG. 58. Brickwork party-wall parapet construction.

construction emphasise that the outside surface of brickwork bonded to the stone facing should be painted with a bituminous coating to obtain a vertical damp-proof course. In old construction this damp-proof membrane is likely to have been omitted and porous stone or open joints between the stones could admit moisture to the inner skin of brickwork or rubble, causing damp staining and deterioration of internal finishes.

Sometimes compound construction comprised a facing skin of ashlars or coursed rubble masonry and a parallel backing skin of brickwork or rubble bonded together across an intervening cavity. This cavity was often filled with small loose stone chippings and broken blocks, frequently with little or no binding mortar. A variation of this method aimed to overcome bonding problems by building the facing work independently of the backing but tied in with iron cramps or dowels located in slots in the individual stones which were sealed with lead or mortar. The lack of homogeneity resulting from use of these methods is likely to endanger the structural integrity of the wall in the long term (see later section: Defects in Masonry External Walls).

Preservation and Repair of Stonework

As it is the external surfaces of stonework not washed by rain which decay most rapidly in polluted air, it should be clear that regular, careful washing with clean water is the best form of maintenance for large areas of stonework. Where decay is causing conspicuous erosion, it may be necessary to apply special treatments to better preserve and repair the surviving stonework.

Much controversy surrounds the application of silicone compounds, otherwise known as silanes, to stonework, though this has been a traditional method of stone preservation. The hardening of the outer layer of stone caused by coating the material with silicone is believed by some to accelerate deterioration of the stonework when it is saturated by rain or delaminated by a sudden frost, because lumps of silicone-hardened stone are likely to fall off the still soft core. Nevertheless, the refinement of silane preparations by experiment and observation of test applications on historic buildings (such as the statues

of the west elevation of Wells cathedral) seems to offer the best hope for developing a treatment that will significantly delay the decay of eroding stonework. Various epoxy-based adhesives are now available for reassembling broken stone details or resurfacing small areas of decayed stonework (such resurfacing or reconstitution of damaged masonry is termed *plastic repair*). In circumstances where complete sections of stone have worn away or are fractured in a way that makes them impossible to mend either by plastic repair or by 'stitching' with stainless steel bars set in epoxy resin in drilled sockets, it may be necessary to contemplate replacement of individual building stones. Such careful 'dentistry' repairs demand the attention of a skilful mason.

TERRACOTTA

Terracotta had been an important substitute for brick or stone throughout the final decades of the nineteenth century and it continued to be an important material, particularly in city centre buildings erected throughout the inter-war period. Its chief advantage was its impervious finish, which made it an ideal facing for new buildings in sooty industrial towns where stonework was likely to be quickly impregnated with dirt. For this reason, terracotta was often referred to as 'self-cleansing'. The scope to effectively create identical intricately detailed components by semi mass-production methods and to save weight in comparison to masonry construction were additional advantages of terracotta. It was not widely used in house construction except to embellish front elevations of terraced suburban houses of conservative design (Fig. 59) and to cap parapet and garden walls, in which case moulded coping blocks of 'saddleback', 'ogee' or segmental section were used.

The material is of almost the same composition as clay brickwork, but for the manufacture of terracotta only good-quality fireclays were used. Manufacture of the material is very similar to brickmaking, the 'grog' mixture, which constitutes part of the terracotta (a mixture of fine sand, pulverized brick or burnt clay) being mixed with water and the ground-up fireclay before being formed into cakes prior to moulding. Complex shapes or elaborate ornamentation were achieved more easily in terracotta than in brickwork – one of the properties that endeared it to designers of flashy Edwardian public houses – and manufacture of these pieces necessitated construction of full-size clay models from which plaster casts were taken. Into this mould the tempered clay was pressed by hand to form a hollow block of clay with a shell of uniform thickness whose outside surface was a perfect impression of the mould's form. The clay in the mould was allowed to become partly dry before being removed, after which thorough drying was carried out elsewhere in the factory. Finally the moulded block was fired in a kiln over several days. In the burning of certain clay mixtures a chemical reaction occurs which produces a hard, vitreous glaze on the surface of the terracotta, rendering the material more durable. Imperfections in, or damage to this surface impair the durability of the material.

A property of terracotta, which has led to its general abandonment in favour of ceramic tiles, is shrinkage of the constituent clay during firing. The unfired clay components were made one-twelfth larger than the desired finished size to account for this shrinkage and some small loss of precision in the finished product resulted from this. However, these small irregularities grant a 'hand-wrought' quality to the material, very rare in modern building products, which causes it to be valued today.

By the Edwardian period, terracotta was available in a wide range of colours including red, buff, pink, tawny and grey. Other colours were produced by the addition of chemicals, but a more reliable material resulted if the colours were restricted to those natural to the original clays. Three varieties of terracotta were manufactured – *ordinary*, with a plain, unglazed surface (porous and therefore unsuitable for external use), *vitreous*, covered with a very slightly glassy glaze and hence impervious to moisture and *full-glazed* or *matt-glazed* terracotta which is normally referred to as *faience* and is recognisable by its smooth and shiny surface, achieved through the firing of a glaze or enamel on to the already burnt material. Faience was not often used externally on houses (a remarkable exception is Ernest Debenham's house on Addison Road, West Kensington, designed by the architect Halsey Ricardo, which was completed in 1907) but Edwardian city pubs continued the late-Victorian policy of facing street elevations with bright green,

peacock blue, turquoise or maroon-glazed terracotta and the 'super cinemas' serving the new estates of suburban housing of the 1930s made extensive use of black and cream-coloured faience.

Although moulded terracotta is generally viewed as obsolete, its function having been taken over by sheet-metal cladding or ceramic tiles, at least one UK firm continues to manufacture the material to order, primarily for the purpose of repair or adaptation of terracotta-clad buildings. Repairs to the material should be thought of in the same way as repairs to stone masonry – significant damage or deterioration will require the replacement of complete blocks, but smaller flaws can be corrected by plastic repair in mortars coloured to match the original fabric.

FIG. 59. A terraced house with elaborate terracotta ornament.

PEBBLEDASH AND ROUGHCAST RENDERS

Towards the end of the nineteenth century, external wall renderings other than the smooth stucco favoured previously became popular, again as part of the fashion for replicating the constructional composition of traditional rural houses. The most common 'textured' finishes were *roughcast* and *pebbledash*.

Roughcast is minimum two-coat work, the first *straightening* coat being composed of 1:1:6 cement/lime/sand. It was normal for this layer to contain animal hair as a binding agent. After application this coat was combed out to provide a 'key' and then left to dry out. A wet plastic mix of one-and-a-half parts of cement, half a part of lime, two parts of shingle or crushed stone and three parts of sand was then made up and thrown on to the wall with a hand scoop or laying-on trowel. This produces a finish of 'coated' pebble texture and it was commonly used to waterproof 215mm (9in) solid brickwork external walls.

FIG. 60. Bands of fishscale tiles alternate with plain tiles to clad a gable.

Light-coloured distemper paintwork was usually applied across the entire surface of the finishing coat because the use of Portland cement in the mix resulted in a drab grey colour that was not liked. Amongst Edwardian architects, the main advocate for roughcast rendering as an external wall finish was C. F. A. Voysey who used it in almost all the rural and suburban houses he designed, the details and general treatment of which were widely copied by speculative builders.

Pebbledash differs from roughcast in that a selected coarse aggregate such as spar or pea shingle, graded from 6–20mm (¼–¾in) in size, is thrown on with a hand scoop when the top coat of render is still soft. Care is necessary in choosing the colour of the aggregate because, unlike roughcast, in pebbledash the self-colour of the stones remains exposed unless the material is painted over.

It is clear that a good appearance and durability in both of these external render finishes relies very much on the skill of the tradesman. Poor adhesion of the render to its backing (usually brickwork, but not uncommonly wooden laths on timber framing) in the long term causes cracking which will invite water penetration. The rainwater is drawn into the cracks by capillary action, causing neighbouring areas of render to be dislodged as well as saturating the backing. In this circumstance, there is no alternative to hacking off the affected area of render to the line of sound material and patching-in a panel of matching render.

TILE HANGING AND SLATE HANGING

Tile hanging attained popularity for the same reason that textured render finishes were revived – its earlier use in traditional rural buildings. Slate hanging in the ubiquitous Welsh slate was less well regarded because its use in antique structures was much rarer and the size of the units could not contribute to the diminutive scale desired in new cottage-style dwellings. Hence there were few examples of use of slate hanging for decorative purposes, but it was sometimes adopted as a weatherproof skin for walls insufficiently resistant to rainwater penetration, including the external surfaces of many gables.

Adoption of tile hanging for its 'rustic' effect usually meant commencing this treatment at first-floor level and continuing it up to the eaves of the house. In the rare multi-storied dwellings that were clad overall in this way and in single-storey structures so treated, it might commence at plinth level, about 450mm (18in) above the ground. The tiles could be the plain rectangular type as used in roofing, or of more complicated 'fish-scale', dogtooth, scallop or toothed-edge shape, or the plain and profiled types might be interspersed in bands to produce patterning (Fig. 60). Red-orange, sand-faced tiles were most often used, fixed in various ways to the backing construction. Where the first-floor walling is of timber framing, tiling battens identical to those used to locate and fix tile-type roof coverings were simply nailed horizontally across the wooden posts to provide fixing 'rails' for the tiles. Because such tile hanging is either vertical or near vertical, a 38mm (1½in) lap of tiles (overlap) was sufficient to prevent rain driving in – That is, considerably less than the lap of tiles on roofs pitched, conventionally at around 40 degrees to the horizontal. In new construction or the renovation of existing work of this type, a continuous vertical layer of bituminous felt or building paper should be installed across the timber posts before the battens are reinstated as a further check against rainwater penetration.

Tiles might also be used to clad solid brickwork external walls and the incompatibility of the brick coursing with the tiling gauge (spacing of tile courses) prohibited direct nailing of the battens into mortar joints. This condition led some builders to set vertical wooden pads into brickwork joints as 'grounds' for fixing the battens. Such construction may have suffered badly from decay of the timber grounds because these fixings were not adequate to take the load imposed by the construction. A better method was to build bricks of coke breeze into every course at about 900mm (3ft) centres, staggered vertically, thus providing an open-textured material to which the 50 × 19mm (2 × ¾in) battens would be nailed. The thickness of the brick backing to such a cladding was usually 215mm (9in) but if 327mm (13½in) brickwork formed the backing, it was feasible (though not recommended) to lay the external skin of bricks on edge, thus obtaining bed joints at around

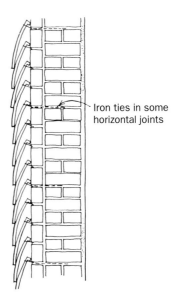

Iron ties in some horizontal joints

FIG. 61. Battens supporting tile hanging were sometimes obviated by nailing tile courses into bed joints of an outer skin of bricks laid on edge.

110mm (4½in) centres to which the battens (or possibly just the tiles without battens) could be fixed (Fig. 61).

Junctions of window and door openings with such constructions were sealed by the application of timber mouldings to bring their frames flush with the tiling. Lead flashings and cement fillets were used liberally at heads and sills to guarantee the draining out from the tile hanging of trapped water, which might otherwise attack window joinery. An alternative treatment was to set back the window frame 110mm (4½in) from the tiled face, and then to apply render to the edge of the tiles and any brickwork forming the window and door reveal. This treatment was defective, inviting problems through the admission of water into the window/wall junction via cracks in the render. A timber *scotia* moulding was commonly used to cloak the junction of the head of the wall tiling with the soffit board of the roof eaves, obviating precise fitting of the top of the tile-hanging to the soffit (Fig. 62).

Where tile hanging that clads an upper storey terminates at first-floor level, it was common

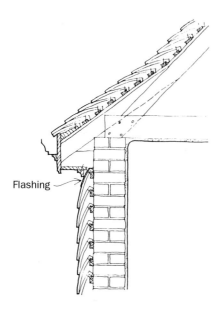

Flashing

FIG. 62. *Junction of tile-hanging on battens with sprocket-eaves soffit board.*

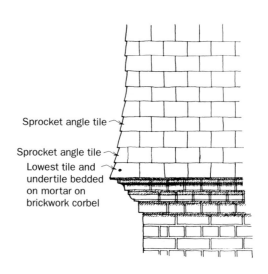

Sprocket angle tile

Sprocket angle tile

Lowest tile and undertile bedded on mortar on brickwork corbel

FIG. 63. *Junction of tile-hung upper storey with brickwork lower storey.*

to adopt a 'bellmouth' profile for the foot of the tiling to throw the rainwater off the elevation more effectively with a pronounced 'drip' over the brickwork or render below. This was usually achieved by corbelling out the supporting brickwork with plain or moulded bricks to give the desired projection (Fig. 63).

Slate hanging was installed in the same way, but the unit size of slates being generally larger than tiles,

they were applied at a wider gauge. In the condition in which slates were applied to a gable to ensure weather resistance, one improvement to the appearance of the slating that was sometimes made, was its completion at the roof verges with 'Winchester cut' slates. In this treatment the underside of each slating course is 'turned up' to meet the verge and a neat junction of the verge with the slated gable results (Fig. 64).

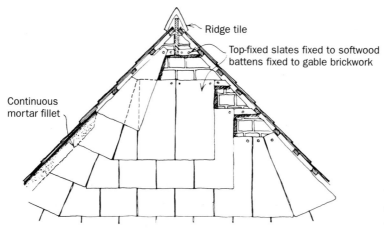

Ridge tile

Top-fixed slates fixed to softwood battens fixed to gable brickwork

Continuous mortar fillet

FIG. 64. *Slate hanging on a gable with 'Winchester-cut' slates at the verge.*

DEFECTS IN MASONRY EXTERNAL WALLS

In the preceding sections, something has been said about building defects that can arise in individual materials. It is plain, however, that problems also arise from over-optimistic assessments of the strength or durability of materials, particular structural forms (for example, physical limitations on use of load-bearing masonry external walls in multi-storey construction), use of unsuitable combinations of materials, or defective construction methods. It is therefore essential to describe common structural defects affecting external walls to provide a 'spotter's guide' to potential problems as well as identifying appropriate remedial measures.

In structural terms, most traditional buildings (including all houses lacking a discrete structural frame, which represents the vast majority of dwellings erected down to the present day) rely on gravity and friction to hold themselves together and have little tensile capacity. Thus, with thermal or ground movement they can come to lack 'togetherness'. It is also important to recognise that the building type most variable in terms of constructional quality was the speculatively-built house of the eighteenth, nineteenth and early twentieth centuries. In these buildings, lack of care in brick-bonding was widespread and external rendering was often used to hide a poor-quality building shell.

Defects in one building are often observable in contemporary structures or neighbouring buildings. Builders were often optimistic about the bearing capacity of foundations and settlement often took place after construction. This is the principal cause of in-plane deformation of walls and most often arises from inadequate size of footings or moisture changes in the soil. 'Ground heave' may also be a problem, particularly in clay subsoil where mature trees and their roots have been removed, causing the subsoil to expand and soften as the moisture content increases. Settlement cracking should not be confused with cracking resulting from thermal movement such as expansion and shrinkage. In-plane distortions are less serious than out-of-plane movement and they are often evidenced by opening-up of diagonal cracks suggesting sliding of panels of masonry. From a fairly

quick visual analysis it can often be seen that vertical loads retain a clear 'load path' down to the ground and the existence of even quite large cracks, though detrimental to appearance and weather resistance, need not be structurally significant. In structural engineering parlance, crack widths of less than 1mm (¹⁄₁₆in) are termed 'very slight' and those less than 5mm (¼in) are termed 'slight'. However, these classifications relate to the degree of damage and whether or not the movements are active.

The first step in assessing whether a wall that shows out-of-plane deformations can be retained is to measure its deformation by physical survey. Wall deformations can be extremely deceptive to the eye and a visual assessment made from ground or roof level is often incorrect. The simplest technique is the plumb-line survey and in surveying an entire wall surface not less than three plumb lines should be dropped, one at the centre and one close to each end of the elevation. Offset readings should be taken at and between floor levels, clearly related to a horizontal baseline or 'datum', which must intersect with all plumb-line locations. Structural movements in buildings are usually better understood if they can be monitored over a period of time. Out-of-plumb walls and cracking are natural candidates for such attention. It is important to understand how any defects arose and whether they have reached a stable state. Most structurally defective old buildings exhibit warning signs before they become dangerous, and even buildings that appear to be unsafe may continue to resist load without apparent distress.

As a general rule for remedial work, it is important to recognise that many structural shortcomings respond best to a 'helping hand' rather than brutal surgery, which can generate further problems. The need to supply some tensile capacity to help to hold the building together can often be satisfied by quite simple means, such as anchoring the floor structures more firmly to the walls with local ties. Stone masonry and brickwork are often weak and new steel ties are very strong, so it is preferable to provide wall restraint in small sections rather than in concentrated areas.

Improper Bonding of Brickwork
Where front elevations were faced with rubbed bricks laid in thin 'putty' joints, the depth of the facing

courses was less than in the backing of common brickwork. Thus, only occasionally could the wall be bonded by the projection of header bricks from the facing skin into the backing where the courses happened to coincide. The same weakness arises in the more common condition in which the facing and backing skins were laid in courses of nominally identical height, but the appearance of a solid bond (most often Flemish bond) was achieved in the facing skin largely through the use of 'snap' headers. This arose because the backing skin was often erected first by apprentices in order quickly to achieve rooms shielded against the weather, pockets being left in the backing skin to accept some of the headers of the succeeding facework. In practice, coursing the facing skin to suit the inaccurately built backing would have given an unacceptable appearance and so snap headers were incorporated in the facework to give the appearance of a solid bond. This inner skin of poorer bricks, often containing built-in timbers, was likely to be carrying loads from the intermediate floors which were also often the only elements restraining the external walls. Any compression or contraction of this inner brickwork can cause shearing of the few bonding headers, causing delamination of the outer skin, which is then unrestrained.

Another example of lack of homogeneity in the masonry shell of a house may be found where external walls and the party wall are improperly bonded together. In terraced and semi-detached houses, the party walls were often erected in advance of the more visible and therefore neatly constructed front elevation, using the only nominally skilled tradesmen who were also deployed to construct the backing skin of the front elevation. The party wall might be toothed to unite with the subsequent external wall construction, but the coursing of the two walls was rarely lined through so that most of the toothing was abandoned and the larger part of the junction was left unbonded. Sometimes a vertical slot was formed to house the end of the party wall or no attempt at bonding resulted in a plain butt joint. In both cases no effective restraint is given to the external wall between floor levels and vertical or toothed cracks in wall finishes cladding such junctions are common. Where the party wall and the outside wall are reasonably plumb at their junction

and do not need to be rebuilt, the incorporation of stainless-steel wire ties may be a practical means of preventing their further dislocation. If the junction is allowed to remain unbonded, the building will continue to lack the stability that may be needed to resist the action of extraordinarily high winds. The 'hairpin' ties are installed by drilling pairs of small holes through the bed joints of the external wall brickwork at vertical intervals not more than twice the thickness of that wall, each hole of each pair being roughly 20mm (¾in) inboard of both faces of the party wall. The short sections of joints between these holes are then raked out to a depth of 20mm (three-quarters of an inch) and grooves of identical depth are cut into the faces of the party wall to a length four times its thickness. Small-diameter 75mm (3in) deep holes are then drilled into both faces of the party wall at the end of each groove. 3mm (⅛in) diameter stainless steel wire bent into a 'U' shape is threaded through the outside wall and the legs of this 'hairpin' are laid in the party wall grooves, the ends of these legs being tucked into the party wall (Fig. 65). To complete the installation, mortar pointing is applied over the wire, and the gap that necessitated the work is dry-packed with 1:3 cement/sand mortar.

Faults and failures related to bonding within and between brick walls can equally well occur in stone

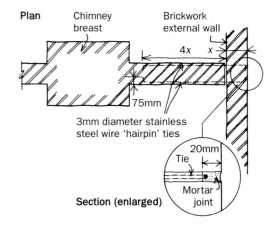

FIG. 65. Brickwork external wall tied to internal wall with 'hairpin' stainless-steel ties in bed joint.

construction. Where the masonry consists of an ashlar, or coursed rubble facing, bonded back into poorer quality rubble or common brickwork, the coarser and more numerous joints in the backing may be more susceptible to compression than the fewer and finer joints in the facing, resulting in differential settlement or bulging. Localised bulging of walls constructed in a different but equally common way – where a facing skin of ashlar and a parallel backing skin of brickwork are bonded together across an intervening rubble-filled cavity – may indicate the emergence of a very serious problem because it suggests delamination of the compound construction is occurring and that the deformation is accelerating towards collapse under the surcharge imposed by the loose filling.

Unfortunately, the twentieth-century enthusiasm for adopting cavity walls as the main means of ensuring dry conditions inside houses has not eliminated the susceptibility to defects that might be thought to be unique to solid external wall construction; rather it has served to introduce a new range of building defects. Where the original construction was not carried out carefully and the central cavity of brickwork external cavity wall construction was not kept clean of mortar droppings as construction proceeded, mortar may have accumulated on the metal wall-ties which were used to connect the two leaves of masonry so that wind-blown rain, which quickly saturates the external leaf, is conveyed to the internal leaf through this porous material, causing damp patches on internal finishes. The only remedy for this defect is the removal of the offending wall-ties and their replacement with new fittings.

More significant as a generic defect of the conventional cavity wall construction that has dominated housebuilding in load-bearing brickwork since the 1920s is the loss of integrity owed to the corrosion and snapping of cavity wall-ties. The form of cavity wall that was recommended from the mid-nineteenth century relied upon various patented types of stepped ceramic bonding bricks to tie the inner leaf of the wall to the outer skin. When the inevitable differential movement between the two skins occurs, it is common for the bonding bricks to shear because they are brittle and weak, usually being of perforated form

to facilitate good drainage of the cavity. Differential movement of the facing and backing brickwork can be better accommodated by the tolerance of bending or rotation which is a property of the metal ties that were universally adopted when the shortcomings of bonding bricks became apparent. However, the type of tie which was almost invariably used – namely the galvanised steel-wire 'butterfly' tie – is flimsy and lacks the long-term corrosion resistance promised by its galvanised finish. In practice, it has been found that ties, which it was believed would last for sixty years, have rusted through and snapped after only twenty years. The consequent freeing of the facing skin is the worst defect that may be encountered in cavity construction. Fortunately, various manufacturers of metal masonry fixings have recognised the potentially large market for simply installed and low-cost remedial devices which will rectify this condition and several types of supplementary cavity wall-ties are available for insertion into holes drilled into the bed joints of the facing brickwork. Tightening captive nuts on the shanks of these fixings expands metal anchors in the wall's inner leaf and causes the ties to grip the outer leaf close to the external wall plane. The ends of these new metallic connections may then be concealed behind local repointing of the affected bed joints.

Structural Problems from Use of Defective Materials

It has been noted that the practice in speculative development was use of the best bricks where good appearance was the chief concern and employment of poorer and cheaper material where the work was concealed. From this policy arises the paradox that the backing brickwork, which tends to carry most of the load from floors and roofs, was constructed from the poorer bricks. It is logical that greater deformation under stress should be expected in these softer, under-fired bricks. Also, the wall being eccentrically loaded by upper floors and the roof, stresses on the inner face may be considerably greater than those on the outer face. Weakness of the inner-skin bricks is further compounded by greater consolidation of any 'lean' mortar (mortar with inadequate cement content) more likely to have been used in the construction of this part of the wall. Combination of

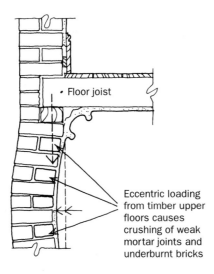

- Floor joist

Eccentric loading
from timber upper
floors causes
crushing of weak
mortar joints and
underburnt bricks

FIG. 66. Bulging of brickwork external wall owed to defective materials.

all these factors can lead to bulging of the wall's outer face (Fig. 66).

Before Portland cement was cheaply and readily available, other materials with cementing qualities were used to make mortars with strengths greater than lime mortar. One of the principal alternative materials was ash from coal-burning operations in industry. This 'flyash' was very variable in quality and because of its high sulphur content it was acidic – in contrast to alkaline lime. Thus, metallic items tend to corrode in flyash mortar, which is usually distinguished by its dark appearance. Termed 'compo' by bricklayers in the north of England, it was often employed where appearance demanded a dark mortar. In some industrial areas, it was a standard construction material throughout the 1930s and owing to its widespread use in South Wales, the corrosion of metal wall-ties in cavity wall constructions in that region continues to be a serious problem.

A common cause of deterioration of Portland cement mortar leading to structural instability is the presence of soluble sulphates in the brickwork or in groundwater. These salts slowly attack the cement under continuously wet conditions, resulting in expansion or softening of the mortar. In severe cases,

complete disintegration of the mortar can occur. It follows that external rendering and other finishes that contain Portland cement are also susceptible to sulphate attack. This defect is most likely to materialise in the superstructure brickwork when driving rain or moisture trapped under rendering saturates the bricks and transports soluble sulphates from the bricks to the mortar joints. With expansion of these joints, rendered surfaces crack horizontally and vertically in a pattern reflecting the brickwork bond behind. Chimney stacks which have been built or repointed in cement mortar may begin to lean because their windward faces are more prone than are the leeward faces to sulphate action and consequent expansion of mortar. Thus, bulging walls, curving chimney stacks, cracked and loose rendering and brickwork joints exhibiting friable cement mortar may all be owed to sulphate attack. The risks of this damage resulting are higher if Fletton bricks were used behind rendering (for example, roughcast or pebbledash) in the original construction or any subsequent alteration, because this type of brick often has a high sulphate content and if sulphate resisting cement was not used in the construction, any breakdown in the render skin which admits rainwater will cause soluble sulphates to migrate into the brickwork joints and render, leading to deterioration of the cement content of both.

Mortar deterioration under sulphate action is an irreversible process that can only be stopped by eliminating the sources of water. In cases of severe damage where water cannot be prevented from saturating the walls and the brickwork or adjacent soil has a high sulphate content, demolition and rebuilding of walls with bricks of special quality and mortar containing sulphate-resisting cement may be the only solution.

Paradoxically, Edwardian houses, the oldest buildings dealt with in this book, are less likely than interwar dwellings to suffer from this problem because lime mortar was almost invariably used in the construction of their walls. The sulphate-susceptible compounds, which are relatively abundant in Portland cement, are scarce in building limes, so that sulphate attack is less of a problem in lime mortar. Therefore it is often a mistake to attribute bulging of exposed walls bedded in lime mortar to sulphate action. Such deformations are more likely to relate to premature loading of the brickwork when it was new, lack of lateral restraint or non-uniform construction of the wall in cross-section (as in use of 'snap headers' described earlier).

Deformation of Untied Flank Walls

Perceptible bulging of an entire wall plane, where the largest deformation is at mid-height and there are gaps between the external wall and adjoining floors and partitions, may be as attributable to an original lack of 'togetherness' in the structure as to shortcomings in the materials or particular combinations of materials. This judgement applies particularly to flank walls that run parallel to the joists of upper floors.

The condition is most common in detached and semi-detached houses in which the timber floors span from front to rear and do not restrain the external flank walls because they do not bear on them. Even when the floors do span on to the flank wall, in the typical inter-war, semi-detached house, there is usually a staircase running up inside the wall which eliminates floor restraint over a significant section of the wall. Over many years, this effectively free-standing wall bulges outwards in the vertical plane between the restraint afforded by the ground floor and the roof structure, and in the horizontal plane between the front and rear corners (Fig. 67). This bulging is caused by the imposition of load from the

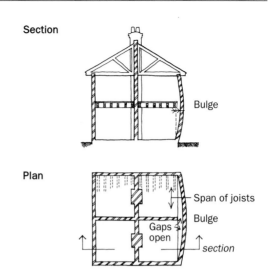

FIG. 67. *Deformation of an untied flank wall.*

roof construction, wind suction, thermal movement and so on.

Provided the wall has not bulged outwards by more than one-sixth of its thickness, it can be restrained against further deformation by the insertion of stainless steel straps at each floor level and by bracing the floors with plywood decking to deliver the restraining force back to load-bearing walls at right angles (Fig. 68). If the wall is not restrained, the

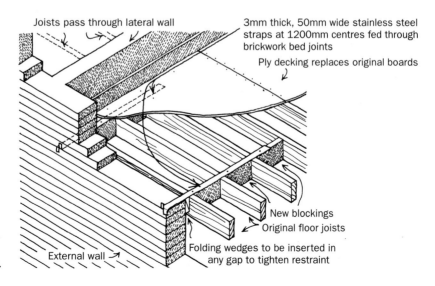

FIG. 68. *External wall restrained by stainless steel straps added to upper floor construction.*

out-of-plumb forces of the bulged wall will cause it to bulge further until it collapses. The stainless steel straps used to reinforce the construction consist of 30 × 5mm (1¼in × ¼in) bars 1200mm (4ft) long with one end bent over. They are fed through a bed joint of the brickwork from outside and then fixed on to the notched top surfaces of the first three floor-joists with three No. 12 countersunk-head woodscrews. Either 50 × 50mm (2 × 2in) herringbone strutting or full-depth solid blocking is fitted between these three joists before the straps are fixed and the whole assembly is tightened against the inside face of the external wall with folding wedges before large sheets of ply decking are installed in lieu of the original floorboards.

Sometimes there have been previous attempts to restrain bulging walls and the existence of cast-iron bosses, cruciform or S-shaped steel plates on external wall surfaces provides evidence of built-in tie rods which may simply anchor back a bowing external wall to the opposite wall. If these connections are insufficient to restrain the wall, in time they pull the opposite wall out-of-plumb. To obtain stability, all forces must be opposed by equal and opposite forces. As the object of restraining a bulging wall is to stop it moving further, tie bars must be anchored to something stiff like a wall corner. Hence it may be possible to rearrange restraint straps so that they are anchored to masonry walls running at right-angles to the bulged walls. This can be achieved either by creating a 'diaphragm floor' with plywood sheets screwed to

the joists, or by running steel straps diagonally across the tops of the joists, anchored to the corners of the opposite wall (Fig. 69). This latter rearrangement depends upon side walls not being weakened too much by window openings. Alternatively, it may be possible for existing ties to be replaced with the less conspicuous stainless steel straps described earlier.

Built-in Timbers

Deformations in masonry may be exacerbated by the presence of built-in timber. 'Bonding' or 'coursing' timbers were often used behind the stone or brickwork facing skin of external walls, or in internal walls, as a means of obtaining some bond between otherwise almost independent masonry elements and to spread out loads from higher panels of brickwork on the slow-setting weak lime mortar of the earlier construction. Sometimes such timbers were built-in to provide joinery fixings and wallplates set into the brickwork were used to support the floor joists. Natural cross-grain shrinkage or compression of bonding timbers can result in wall movement, particularly bulges in external walls.

More serious is the risk of timber decay from rot or insect attack which can cause serious structural problems, particularly in narrow and heavily loaded panels as are found between closely spaced window openings. Not only is the effective section of the brickwork reduced, it is also subject to eccentric loading (Fig. 70). This type of masonry pier, located between sash windows in an Edwardian house, may

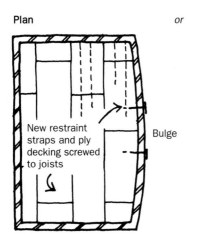

Plan   *or*

New restraint straps and ply decking screwed to joists

Bulge

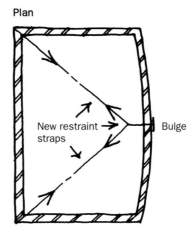

Plan

New restraint straps

Bulge

FIG. 69. Bulging of flank wall restrained by added steel straps/ plywood decking on upper floor.

have a substantial part of its area taken up by the weights boxes of the windows. It may also have built into it the ends of some floor joists as well as wallplates and bonding timbers holding poor-quality masonry together. Once the facing skin has started to move away from the backing, there is little that can be done to save it. The use of drilled-in replacement cavity-wall ties is not effective because most walls were built with lime mortar that has lost its adhesive properties by becoming dry and friable. Stripping and rebuilding the facing skin is not likely to be successful because the backing skin is so weak that it may collapse as the outer skin is removed. The only cost-effective remedy may be to demolish and rebuild the wall.

Where rotting of bonding timbers can be deduced from the interior following stripping of corroded plaster, but this defect has not yet affected the verticality of external wall surfaces, it is possible to prop the superincumbent brickwork temporarily and to remove the timber, filling the masonry void with new brickwork and dense mortar dry-pack to replace the decaying wood. Where the former timber members provided a bearing for floor joists, this can be restored by installing a continuous steel angle support, fixed to the face of the wall with chemical anchors and providing a ledge on which bear the joist ends (Fig. 71).

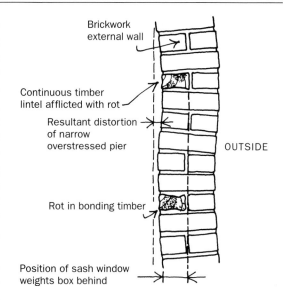

FIG. 70. *Deformation of external wall owed to structural weakness and defective materials.*

Another problem that may result from the combination of timber with masonry is the deformation of brick arches owed to the failure of their wooden backing lintels. This condition may be deduced from diagonal cracks in the facing brickwork above the arched opening and sagging in the centre of the arch

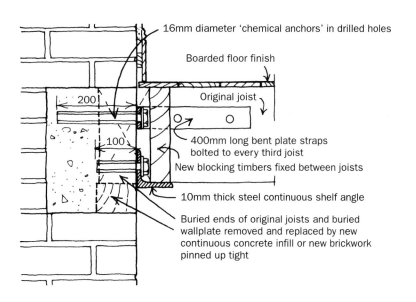

FIG. 71. Replacement bearing for suspended floor where joist-ends penetrating external wall have rotted.

or the arch bulging outwards. In contrast, loose arch bricks and vertical cracks in the brickwork above and below the opening are likely to be signs of failure of the surrounding structure rather than the arch itself. The former types of deformation are brought about by sagging of the backing lintel due to rotting. Thus, more load is thrown on to the slender 'soldier course' brick arch and it may be induced to buckle and bulge outwards. Alternatively, the top of the arch compresses and sags, allowing the superincumbent brickwork to crack and drop. This condition can be rectified by propping the structure, 'needling' the wall above the opening and carefully numbering and dismantling the arch bricks for re-use. The timber backing lintel is removed and the arch is re-set in mortar on temporary timber centring with stainless-steel butterfly wall-ties projecting from the rear of its radial joints. While the mortar is still 'green', the centring is eased down to allow the arch to tighten under its own weight and a reinforced concrete-backing lintel is cast in situ against the ties and brickwork (Fig. 72). Finally, the joint of the head of the arch and lintel with the supported brickwork is packed tightly with dry mortar and slates and the needles and props are removed.

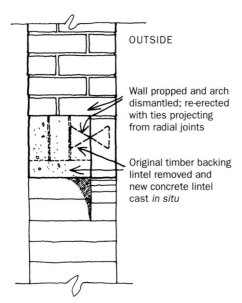

OUTSIDE

Wall propped and arch dismantled; re-erected with ties projecting from radial joints

Original timber backing lintel removed and new concrete lintel cast *in situ*

FIG. 72. *Concrete backing lintel replacing rotted timber to rear of segmental arch.*

WOODEN EXTERNAL WALLS

The incorporation of bonding timbers into otherwise solid masonry construction can be regarded as a vestigial feature of the fully timber-framed structures which dominated English house construction until at least the seventeenth century and it is clear that, other than for temporary use, later houses constructed entirely of wood above the foundations are quite rare in Britain. However, from the late nineteenth century, the growing appreciation of traditional building techniques stimulated interest in timber-framed and timber-clad buildings, causing these treatments to enjoy a revival as they were reintroduced to form at least part of the format of the 'vernacular-revival' dwellings which represent the greater part of all houses erected between the start of the twentieth century and the outbreak of the Second World War (Figs. 73 and 74). Also, in the countries formerly constituting the British Empire, tropical countries and North America, wooden-walled houses have been continuously erected throughout the last two hundred years. They can be divided into two general types; *braced frame* and *balloon frame* structures.

A braced-frame building is one in which each piece of the framing is carefully joined with mortise and tenon joints, the corners being held rigidly with diagonal pieces. In this way the whole skeleton is made secure and stiff in itself before any covering is applied and this form of framing is more characteristic of UK practice than the balloon frame in which the structural timbers are simply butt-jointed and nailed together and the structure depends greatly on the sheathing (outer covering) for its strength and stiffness.

Carpentry work in a framed building commenced when the foundation was complete. The first operation was to lay a horizontal timber (the sill) in mortar on top of the foundation wall as the base for the wooden superstructure. In braced-frame buildings sills might vary in size between 200 × 150mm (8 × 6in) and 250 × 200mm (10 × 8in), though balloon-frame structures called for a slighter member, perhaps 200 or 150 × 100mm (8 or 6 × 4in). It was laid 25mm (1in) inboard from the outer face of the foundation wall. Corners of this sill were halved (half the

ABOVE: FIG. 73. An Arts & Crafts Movement house clad entirely in tarred weatherboarding.

ABOVE RIGHT: FIG. 74. Rustic weatherboarding clads the gable of 'Folly Farm', Sulhamstead, Berkshire (Edwin Lutyens, 1912).

thickness of both meeting pieces is removed, allowing the timbers to sit on top of each other without enlarging the sill's thickness) and when the wall was longer than could be accomplished in a single piece of timber, a bevelled joint was generally used to prevent pieces of the sill from pulling apart.

Corner posts were then erected at the angles of the house (up to 250 × 200mm [10 × 8in] in braced frames; 200 × 150mm [8 × 6in] in balloon frames) and in braced frames these were mortised into the sill at the halved corner and into the wallplate at the eaves of the house. In the simpler balloon-framed work, the corner posts were butt-jointed to the sill (that is, allowed to 'rest' on it) before being nailed (or *spiked* in carpenter's parlance) to it and the eaves-level wallplate. Internal angles were formed by simply spiking a regular *stud* to each face of the corner post (Fig. 75).

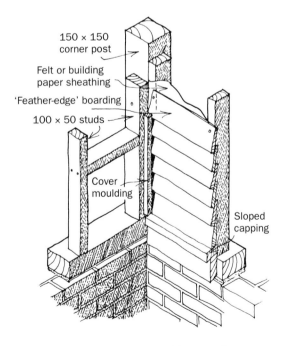

FIG. 75. Internal corner of braced-frame timber construction.

73

The studs (regular timber posts) were sometimes mortised into the sill, into the *girt* or *intertie* (the horizontal bracing timber at intermediate-floor level) and into the eaves-level wallplate. The drive to reduce the skill content in house building led to the practice of simply butt-jointing them into position except where double-thickness studs had to be installed to flank window and door openings. However, it is a principle of balloon-frame construction that the studs must extend from the sill to the wallplate in one piece if possible. Where this height was too great for single timbers, separate sections were spliced together by nailing long wooden fishplates to both broad faces of the composite stud across the butt joint. To carry the joists of the first or second floor of a balloon frame, a *ledger board* is notched into the studs, each joist being spiked to the adjacent stud. In braced frames, the upper-floor joists rest on the intertie already described. The external surface of such timber-framed houses was commonly of horizontal *feather-edge* boarding. In the case of the balloon frame the boarding acts as bracing and is therefore an essential element of the structure. Before the introduction of plasterboard or expanded metal lath, a smooth and continuous internal surface was achieved by applying lime plaster over wooden laths (see Chapter 6).

Decorative Half-timbering

As part of the new appreciation of traditional buildings that developed in the late nineteenth century, a fashion emerged for reproducing the appearance of Tudor or Elizabethan half-timbering on the outsides of houses. It will be appreciated that in ancient timber-framed buildings the timbers exposed externally were structural members often equal to the full thickness of the outside wall. By the sixteenth century, in contrast to the 'wattle and daub' infill used previously, the gaps between these stout posts and braces were frequently filled with brickwork whose outside face was either rendered or painted with limewash to contrast with the timbers which came to be tarred in later times in an attempt to improve their durability. However, in the Victorian, Edwardian and inter-war reproduction of this treatment, the usual aim was to obtain the half-timbered 'look' at low cost and this precluded use of the massive timbers of earlier periods. One means of obtaining the desired effect was the adoption of a timber-framed construction similar to the balloon frame, studs being placed at about 450mm (18in) intervals, with the externally exposed timber being nailed to the face of each stud. These 'cosmetic' sections were about 50mm (2in) thick and between 200–250mm (8–10in) wide on the face. Small

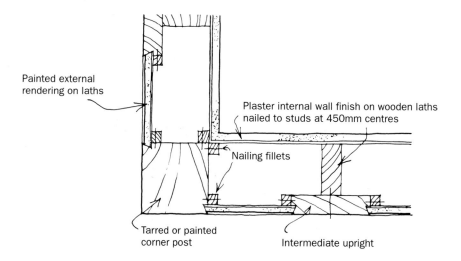

Painted external rendering on laths

Plaster internal wall finish on wooden laths nailed to studs at 450mm centres

Nailing fillets

Tarred or painted corner post

Intermediate upright

FIG. 76. Decorative half-timbering on timber framing.

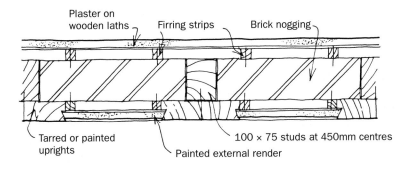

Plaster on wooden laths — Firring strips — Brick nogging

Tarred or painted uprights — 100 × 75 studs at 450mm centres — Painted external render

FIG. 77. Decorative half-timbering on brickwork.

battens were nailed to the vertical edges of these timbers to accept thin wooden laths on which the external render was applied (Fig. 76).

An alternative and certainly more robust and weatherproof form of sham half-timber construction incorporated panels of brickwork at the core of the wall, between the studs. The appearance of wide, tarred timbers was obtained by fixing 50mm (2in) thick planks to the studs, and it was conventional for the laths supporting the external render infill to be nailed to thin vertical battens flanking these planks. The render was often directly applied to the brickwork surface, with the consequent risk of water entering the structure at cracks caused by shrinkage of the timber. Similarly, the internal plaster surface might be applied directly to the brickwork, though here too it was not unusual for *firring strips* or battens to be nailed to the brickwork before timber laths were laid across them and the plaster finish then applied (Fig. 77). The entrapped air which resulted, granted some thermal insulation to the wall, but this form of construction would not obtain official approval today because it is neither thermally adequate nor constructionally secure, its long-term weather tightness and durability being dependent on the use of high-quality materials and the exercise of great skill by the original tradesmen. Modern repairs to such construction which rely upon kiln-dried timber and sand/cement render, lacking respectively the durability and flexibility of the Edwardian materials, are unlikely to endure, and care should be taken to apply materials that are physically identical to those used in the original construction.

A third, and the simplest means of obtaining the half-timbered 'look' was to nail or screw 50mm (2in) thick planks of wood to the brickwork backing wall, infilling the interstices with plain, roughcast or pebbledash render applied to the brickwork's outer face. This form of construction was often forced upon builders by a building by-law, adopted by many local authorities, which demanded the provision of 215mm (9in) thick solid brickwork at the rear of any half-timbering, whether decorative or structural. It can be seen that this treatment shares the potential for early deterioration of materials with the forms of construction first described.

Following the precedent of historic buildings whose jettied-out upper storeys most prominently display their half-timbered construction, sham half-timbering in Edwardian and inter-war houses was almost always restricted to upper storeys, rarely commencing below first-floor level.

75

FIG. 78. The dominant roof of 'Spade House', Sandgate, Kent (1899–1903) by C. F. A. Voysey.

CHAPTER 5

Roofs

It is clear that roofs are employed to cover buildings to protect them from the effects of weather. What is not so apparent is the function of roof structures in tying-in the external walls.

Nineteenth-century houses employed a wide range of roof forms, including flat roofs, which were often used to cover small projections from the main block such as bay windows. However, the most common form was the pitched roof covered with small-size overlapping units of slate or tile. This formula continued to be applied to most houses erected in Britain in the twentieth century. For reasons of fashion, by the beginning of the twentieth century, clay plain tiles were displacing Welsh slate as the most popular covering for pitched roofs. Increasing respect for traditional buildings of the English countryside and enthusiasm for adoption of the Old English style engendered by this interest caused the expression of roofs to be once again an acceptable element of domestic architecture and in the work of the leading house architects of the Edwardian years roofs often became the dominant feature (Fig. 78). In speculative building, such an extreme expression of roof surfaces was rare, but nevertheless roofslopes were given greater prominence and the arrangement of pitched roofs of terraced houses shielded by a parapet above the street elevation had effectively died out, even in conservative London building practice, by the 1880s. The Edwardian years continued the wide range of roof forms employed in the nineteenth century, though the inter-war period witnessed some rationalisation of this diversity as house building became a larger-scale activity of a smaller number of

bigger companies, and municipal authorities who were seeking economies from simplified building construction.

ROOF STRUCTURES

The structures of pitched roofs of Edwardian and inter-war houses differ from those capping modern houses. Today such roofs are usually constructed from 'trussed rafters'; light, prefabricated timber trusses, mass-produced to predefined spans. They are erected on timber wallplates at the head of the external walls of the house and are sited at close centres to accept the battens on which the roof covering is laid. This practice was established only after the Second World War and until 1939, the pitched roofs of all small and middle-sized houses were carried on *purlin* construction, in which a longitudinal timber member spanning between gables, hip rafters or party walls supports the regular sloping timbers or *common rafters*.

By the Edwardian period, inclusion of some form of rudimentary trussing in the main roofs of houses was prudent, if only to secure official approval for development (from 1875 the 158th section of the Public Health Act required drawings of proposed buildings to be submitted to the local authority for their approval). The simplest truss-form likely to be encountered is the *couple-close roof* in which the ceiling joists act to restrain the feet of the common rafters which are simply leaned against, and nailed to, the ridgeboard at quite close centres. A version of this roof which is found where top-storey rooms extend partly into the roof space is the *collar* roof in which

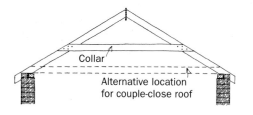

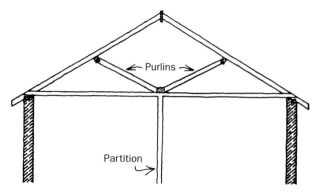

ABOVE: FIG. 79. Collar and couple-close roof structures.

RIGHT: FIG. 80. Strutted-purlin roof structure.

the ceiling joists have been moved up to form a shorter 'collar' – obviously this is a weaker form (Fig. 79). At smaller spans, neither of these forms incorporated purlins, but where spans of rafters exceeded approximately 3m (10ft) – and this applied in all but the smallest roofs – purlins had to be introduced to reduce the span. Thus a roof formed over 'double-pile' accommodation (that is, with separate rooms in the main block facing to both front and rear) would be structured, with ceiling joists meeting over a plate sited on a central transverse wall.

Although acceptable where purlins span a short distance between party walls, this structure is unsatisfactory where the distance between party walls exceeds about 5m (16ft). In the case of double-fronted terraced houses where party walls are at least 6m (20ft) apart, semi-detached houses of identical width or detached and semi-detached houses with pitched and hipped roofs, additional support is needed to prop the purlins. So emerged the strutted-purlin roof which is one of the most common forms in houses of the Edwardian and inter-war periods (Fig. 80). In this case, the struts propping the purlins bear on a plate sited at the head of a transverse wall or partition. Plainly, the existence of these struts tends to constrain the options for use of the roof space in any loft-conversion project as their removal leads to a significant weakening of the roof structure with potentially disastrous results. If it is proposed to use such a 'wasted' roof space for additional living accommodation, it is essential to replace the strength lost in removing the struts by reconfiguring the roof

structure so as to maintain consistent propping of the purlins or the common rafters.

In large houses, these fairly primitive structural arrangements were seldom adequate to cope with the loads imposed. The designer's approach tended to be more 'scientific', accepting that walls flanking large rooms require adequate tying-in at the head and a stiff truss-form to obviate any deflection of roof surfaces. These demands were met by installing a primary structure of *principal rafters* which formed the top members of purpose-made prefabricated trusses, located at wide centres. The most common type of such a principal is the *kingpost truss* (Fig. 81). In this construction, the common rafters occupy a zone above the principals and bear on the stout purlins that link the trusses. A variant on the Kingpost truss, which allows use of the continuous roof space, is the Queenpost truss in which two vertical posts replace the central post of the Kingpost truss. In France, this form was developed at an early stage into the *mansard truss*, in which useful space in the roof is maximised and the structure is pushed right out to the edge of the roof's cross-section (Fig. 82). This form is sometimes seen capping Edwardian houses and flats located over terraced shops, as well as in a significant number of 2-storey council houses of the inter-war period (see Fig. 25 in Chapter 2). In these houses, construction costs were substantially reduced by restricting brick masonry to the shell of the ground storey and cladding the entire timber-framed upper storey in tiles or slate hanging. In the case of all prefabricated roof trusses, a good deal of metal was used to guarantee the integrity of the structure in the form of wrought-iron straps, clamps and wedges which were variously bolted, screwed or driven into the timber members to obtain sound connections. Though they may have obtained a patina of rust since they were installed, such components are likely to be equally effective today because cast and wrought-iron fittings are not so subject to serious deterioration from rusting as is modern mild steel and the removal of straps, bolts or ties (or other seemingly advantageous modifications of timber structures) should not be attempted before the advice of an architect, structural engineer or building surveyor has been obtained.

More common in inter-war houses than the simple gabled, pitched roof (and growing in popularity in the late Victorian and Edwardian periods) was the hipped roof, the purest version of which is a pyramid.

In this variant, the basic components of the pitched-roof structure – rafters and ridge board – are supplemented by the pieces which form the hip, namely the *hip rafter* which links the corner junction of the wallplates with the end of the ridge board and the *jack rafters*, so called because they span between the wallplate and the hip rafter and are thus shorter than the common rafters (Fig. 83).

Apart from its clearly rural associations, the hipped roof was favoured by speculative builders because, within the vocabulary of traditional construction, it was the cheapest way of roofing the generally square plan of the semi-detached house. The volume of the hipped roof was less than that contained by the 'saddleback' or gable roof; consequently the amount of constructional timber was reduced and the building of an expensive masonry gable was obviated,

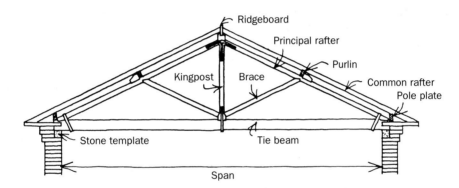

FIG. 81. Kingpost truss.

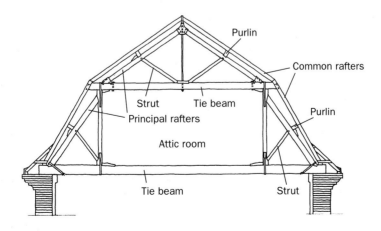

FIG. 82. Mansard roof structure.

the substitute sloping-surfaced hip being achieved in cheaper timber and tiling. Although the hipped-roof form is almost universal in detached and semi-detached houses and there are many examples of roofs of houses at the ends of terraces which are treated in this way, even in modest houses in the middle of terraces it is common for some form of hipped-roof construction to exist, if only as the covering to a square or splayed bay window. In Edwardian terraces, as in late Victorian examples, often a small hipped roof, ancillary to the slope of the main roof and structurally dependent on it, caps a projecting bay of semi-polygonal plan below, so that four hip rafters rather than the two which a square shape would necessitate, are required (Fig. 84).

This junction of a main and secondary roofs also gives rise to a feature (which is dealt with in detail in the later section entitled Roof Coverings): the *valley*,

which occurs wherever two pitched-roof surfaces meet at an internal angle.

In addition to these main types of simple pitched roofs, larger Edwardian houses often exhibit roofs of special form such as conical, pyramidal, ogee (bell-shaped) and domed roofs of turrets, towers or bays. Cones and pyramids, if of sufficient size, can be covered with small slates, clay tiles or timber shingles, but the curvature of small hemispherical domes or ogee roofs generally precludes the use of tile-type coverings and the sheet-metal cladding which is normally applied to these shapes is also dealt with in the later section on roof coverings.

In a conical roof, the rafters are notched over the timber wallplate in the same way that a couple-close roof is structured, but the way the upper ends of the rafters are mitred at the apex is necessarily different. To create the true conical form, the first four rafters

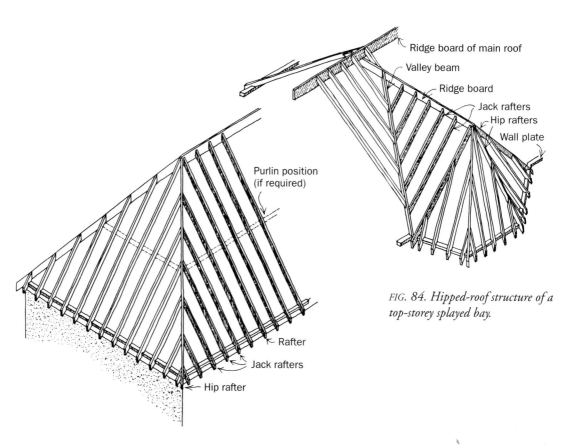

FIG. 84. *Hipped-roof structure of a top-storey splayed bay.*

FIG. 83. *Hipped roof structure.*

to be erected (at right angles to each other) are simply butted squarely together, but the top ends of the infilling rafters of each quadrant are shaped to ensure that the top surfaces of all the sloping timbers lie in the same cone-shaped plane in order to accept the battens in preparation for tiling.

Flat Roofs

Though they are usually associated with mid-twentieth century buildings, flat roofs may be found in Edwardian and inter-war houses, especially where it was impracticable to span an awkwardly shaped or irregular plan with a pitched-roof form. Except where brick vaults roofing cellars provide support for terraces or gardens, the type of flat-roof structure adopted in almost all Edwardian houses was indistinguishable from the most common type of floor construction; namely, boarding on timber joists spanning between wallplates sited on top of the supporting walls. A weatherproof finish was generally achieved by laying rock asphalt or sheet metal on top of the boarding. A roof of up to about 12 degrees pitch (approximately 1 in 4) was defined as a flat roof, steeper slopes being generally covered with a finish of overlapping units (for example, tiles or slates) which is unsuitable for pitches below 22½ degrees. Flat roofs of houses were never finished completely level because some slope was essential for the drainage of rainwater. It is unusual to find any surface exposed to the weather sloped at less than 1 in 60.

In houses of the inter-war period, the use of flat roofs to cap *all* of the accommodation enjoyed a brief period of popularity in the mid 1930s. In most cases these larger-span roofs were of reinforced concrete construction and they can pose problems for durability and sustaining an equable internal environment. Because they pose problems particular to one building type, they are dealt with in Chapter 10, which concentrates on the anatomy of 'Modern Movement' dwellings.

Roof Windows

There are several means of providing natural light in attic or loft spaces contained within pitched roofs, but the most common way of fulfilling this requirement in Edwardian or inter-war houses was the

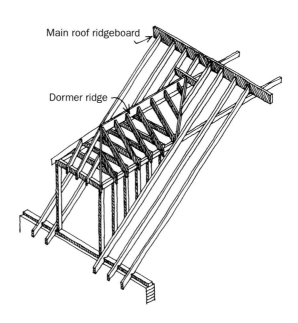

FIG. 85. Hipped-roof structure of a dormer window.

dormer window. Dormers project up from the roof surface and are framed up when the roof structure is erected. The structure of a dormer is formed from components very similar to those of the main roof structure. The common rafters of the main roof are 'trimmed' above the opening which accommodates the dormer construction with timbers generally at least 13mm (½in) thicker than the common rafters. Timber uprights or studs are then erected at 300–450mm (12–18in) centres on the floor joists to form the structure of the flanks or *cheeks* of the dormer. Where the dormer was due to be clad in sheet metal, boarding was applied to the cheeks and any flat roof, capping the structure before the lead, copper or zinc cladding was applied.

Perhaps the commonest form of dormer in Edwardian houses was the type that displays a pitched roof terminating in a miniature gable or hip. This form is constructed in exactly the same way as the main roof – with ceiling joists and rafters (Figs 85 and 86). On steeply pitched main roofs, dormers were sometimes roofed with a structure consisting of common rafters sloped at a lesser angle than those of the main roof, terminating on a timber lintel sited

FIG. 86. Stone-slated, hipped-roof dormers.

over the window aperture, giving a dormer projection that is wedge-shaped in cross-section. This form simplified the construction and eliminated potentially troublesome valleys at the junction of the roof surface of the dormer and the main roof surface. Dormer windows were often used in traditional rural houses to increase the headroom of parts of an upper storey, the external walls of which projected only slightly above the attic floor level. Thus only the upper parts of the dormers projected above the main house eaves. Useful attic bedrooms were often obtained in this way and the appearance of the roof was enriched by breaking the often excessively regular eaves line and introducing the interest of the faceted dormer projections. Naturally, these features appealed to the Arts and Crafts Movement architects who wished to simulate the qualities of traditional rural dwellings in new houses of the new century.

This was also the only form of dormer that was compatible with the use of thatch for the roof covering (see below). Similarly, there are many examples of attractive tiled, pitched and hipped roofs on dormers, particularly on country buildings. Where a dormer was capped with a flat roof, this was generally covered with sheet metal, laid to a minimal fall. Although the sheet metal could also be used to clad the cheeks, these triangular areas were as commonly waterproofed with tile hanging or slate hanging, and in some cases they were glazed to admit further light into attic rooms.

Where a simpler means than a dormer was required for illuminating attic rooms, *skylights* or *rooflights* were incorporated parallel to the plane of the roof surface. A void was formed in the structure by terminating a series of rafters on trimmers sited at the top and bottom of the required opening. On top of the horizontal trimmers and the rafters (or additional sloping trimmers) forming the sides of the opening, a continuous timber kerb was constructed to carry the sash of the skylight, which was proud of the roof surface. This sash was framed in the same way as a normal window sash – though usually made of thicker timber – and it was located so as to overhang the kerb, to which it was fixed with a tenoned joint on the main sides. The top rail was thicker than the sill rail so that the skylight glass could be grooved or rebated into it. The glass was allowed to run over the sill rail to ensure quick drainage of rainwater, and at the sides it was rebated into the stiles and any intermediate glazing bars (Fig. 87). The most durable finish for such a skylight was secured by installing a continuous lead sheet covering of the sash frame surface. Ideally, on the top and side rails, this covering was dressed over the putty on to the glass, so that any water running from the lead capping would not affect the putty joint. A groove was worked into the underside of the sash's head rail at its junction with the kerb so that any water finding its way past the lead drip would not run into the skylight void via the tenoned joint of the timber members.

Condensation inevitably forms on the underside of the glass of any single-glazed roof light, and to prevent it dripping into the room or roof space below, a channel was often formed in the lead covering the sill rail. The moisture then runs down the underside of the glass and into this channel, from which it is conveyed away on to the roof below via holes or grooves in the sill rail. The lead forming a protection to the sill lapped the tiled surface below as a flashing to exclude rainwater. Above the head of the rooflight, a small triangular fillet eased the junction of any roof boarding with the kerb so that the lead sheet in this location could be dressed to form a gutter, enabling rainwater running over the edge of the tiles above the skylight to find its way down the sides of the kerbs flanking the rooflight aperture, and thence down the slope of the roof. The tiling above the skylight terminated on a tilting fillet in the same way that it would at the main roof eaves. Opening skylights were constructed in a very similar way, the opening mechanism normally being as simple as a pair of strong hinges fixed to the sash head and the kerb below it, the skylight being held open by means of a conventional casement stay screw-fixed to the inside face of the sill rail and engaging on a lug fixed to the sill of the fixed frame.

When it is necessary to entirely renew such a skylight because it has proved to be defective, and there is no requirement for a facsimile reproduction of the original feature (as might apply in repairs to a 'listed' building, in which case a cast-metal 'conservation' roof light, produced in a range of standard sizes, is available) or it is appropriate to install new windows in an existing roof, the simplest policy is to purchase proprietary prefabricated roof windows of similar size (where an exact match cannot be made) from a local builders' merchant and to fit them into the existing voids. These products are supplied with flashings suiting the type of roof covering – i.e. with profiles compatible with slates, tiles or pantiles – and matching the metal cladding of the sash frame. The windows are normally supplied with sealed double-glazing already fitted, which obviates condensation on the underside of the glass. Designed to open fully, they incorporate a vent in the window head, which can be left open yet will not admit rainwater even in storm conditions. The metal cladding of the sash frame is a dark, colour-coated aluminium that complements the tone of slated roofs and a 'low-profile' version of this type of window may be employed where there is objection to even the shallow upstand (lower than the projection resulting from the traditional opening rooflight detail) needed for the standard product.

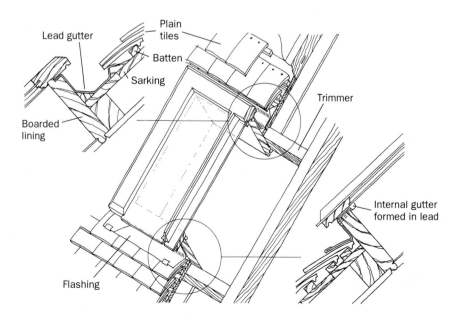

FIG. 87. Rooflight construction.

ROOF COVERINGS

Pitched Roofs

Tiling

Clay tiles have a long history as a roofing material in Britain. A fireclay product, like brick, clay tiles have been in use in some areas of the country for more than four hundred years. Even in the late nineteenth century, at the height of its popularity, Welsh slate roofing failed to unseat clay tiles as the conventional roof covering in those areas of the country noted for the production of fireclay building materials. Thus, in Victorian East Anglia it remained cheaper to use local clay tiles or pantiles than it was to import Welsh slate and many terraced houses in Norwich bear witness to this fact, differing from their contemporaries in London and the industrial towns of the Midlands and north mainly in the colour and texture of their roof surfaces.

Clay plain tiles are fairly thin plates of brick earth of a standard size between 250 × 150mm (10 × 6in) and 280 × 175mm (11 × 7in) and of thickness 10–24mm (⅜–1in). During manufacture, each tile is formed with two nail holes in the 'hanging' end and normally two or more 'nibs' or lugs project from this upper edge as well. Tiles are an artificial product manufactured in a plastic condition and can be moulded to any simple shape during manufacture. Once fixed, they should be cut as little as possible because the fired clay cannot be precisely shaped with much success, unless a powered disc cutter is used with great care. However, it is a simple matter for the manufacturer to make tiles for special situations and a smooth appearance in a clay-tiled roof of complicated shape is always attributable to varieties of special tile being used in conjunction with the plain type. Moulding of the clay during manufacture also allows a camber to be incorporated in the plain tile which causes the tiles to lie close on the roof whilst preserving an airspace underneath, allowing air movement and thus safeguarding the timber fixing battens against rotting.

Although, in the nineteenth century, in districts where tiles predominated as a roofing material, there were local tile works, by the inter-war period many of these factories had fallen prey to takeover,

amalgamation or bankruptcy, leaving particular sites or towns as places noteworthy for the manufacture of roof tiles: Bridgwater, Somerset; Broseley, Worcestershire; Knowl Hill near Reading and Keymer, East Sussex, all produced the red-pink clay plain tiles common to most inter-war suburban housing of southern England before a cheaper product, in the form of cast concrete tiles, began to be widely employed by speculative builders (clay tiles of darker hues were produced by various Staffordshire tile makers and were much used in the Midlands and north). From these factories, tiles were increasingly distributed to all parts of Britain and in this context of growing free trade, specialised types of roofing tile were also imported from northern Europe. Concentration of tile making into a few centres was also encouraged by the appeal of increasing production through adoption of machine manufacture in preference to retaining 'handmade' methods.

The use of machines did not change the essential character of the traditional sand-faced tiles (in which the mould is sanded to prevent adhesion of the clay and to give a granular top surface to the tile) and smooth-faced tiles could also be produced quickly and to much more uniform size, shape and colour, in large quantities.

When faced with the need to repair a roof of handmade tiles, householders should not discount the scope to obtain matching material. Several manufacturers continue to produce handmade tiles and this type of tile tends to be tougher, if more absorbent, than the machine-made type. It is also less liable than the mass-produced product to delaminate when attacked by frost (Fig. 88). Although there are examples of tiled roofs which have endured for perhaps 70–80 years without significant loss of tiles through decay, delamination or fracture as effects of rain penetration and 'bursting' by subsequent frosts, most manufacturers are reluctant to guarantee a lifespan of more than 30 years for clay plain tiling.

The chief principle of setting out tiling is that the head of any course (except the top course of a roof-slope adjoining the ridge) should be covered by the tail of the course next-but-one above it; that is, there are three thicknesses of tile at this point and a minimum of two thicknesses anywhere on the roof – a 'double-lap' system of roof covering). The depth by which the head of a course is covered by the tails of the tiles two courses above is called the *lap*. In plain tiling, the depth of lap is not less than 65mm (2½in). It is necessary for the tail of a tile to overlap the head of the tile two courses below, because rainwater running down the roof and entering the joints between adjacent tiles will fan out on the tiles of the undertiling course and on a low-pitched roof the rainwater will drop into the joints of this lower course too (Fig. 89). If the lap of the tiles is not sufficiently deep to ensure a further layer of tiling below these joints at the point of drainage, the rainwater will enter the roof.

The need to preserve the property of resistance to breakage of the fired clay in manufacture, transport and fixing places clear limits on the maximum size of unit, related to the conventional thickness of not more than 24mm (1in). To achieve a reliable product, plain tiles (in the tile-and-a-half format for use at verges) cannot be made to a size larger than 280 × 230mm (11 × 9in) and so the opportunity to increase size of unit and therefore lap to allow the material to be applied to quite shallow-pitched roofs which exists where slates are employed as the roof covering does not apply to tiles. Therefore, in situations of average exposure to wind and rain (in other words, *not* rural hilltop or coastal locations where a steeper pitch should be adopted) it is not advisable to lay plain tiles on roofs pitched at less than 35 degrees.

FIG. 88. *Roof surfaces of handmade clay plain tiles. (Redland Roof Tiles.)*

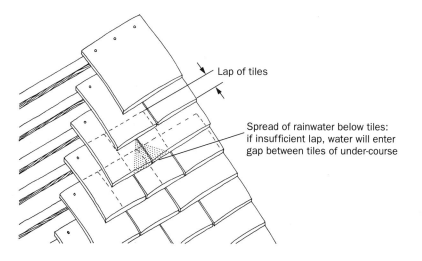

Lap of tiles

Spread of rainwater below tiles: if insufficient lap, water will enter gap between tiles of under-course

FIG. 89. *Spread of rainwater under clay plain roof tiles.*

85

At this pitch it is necessary to nail only every fifth course, but the heavy weight of clay tiling makes it essential to nail every course of tiles on roofs pitched steeper than 60 degrees. At verges, hips and other exposed locations on roofs of shallower slope, courses should in any case be nailed at closer intervals.

In overhauling older roofs of some bespoke Edwardian houses (this treatment is unlikely to be encountered in inter-war houses, other than those in which antique construction was simulated), tiles without nibs, hung with wooden pegs driven into holes at the head and lodging on the battens, may be found. These tiles, either 'peg tiles' or 'Kent peg tiles' (originating in that English county and of a slightly smaller size than the other 'peg' type) are quite common in older buildings in south-east England. A handmade product, they are still produced today by several manufacturers and new units should be hung either on the traditional split oak pegs or wedge-shaped metal pegs of aluminium alloy.

As it is less liable than slating to conduct heat or cold, the fixing of tiling to an *open-batten roof* (in which the fixing battens are laid directly on to the rafters and there is no boarding) is a suitable form of construction, though bituminous under-tiling felt must first be laid over the rafters before the battens are fixed to provide a second line of defence against

rain or snow penetration, particularly in consequence of loss or fracture of tiles.

The principles of laying clay plain tiles apply equally to concrete plain tiles – an invention of the 1920s which rapidly displaced clay tiles in speculative suburban houses and which remains one of the most common forms of pitched-roof covering today.

Laying Tiles
Ridges. The half-round tile for the roof ridge is widely used and is thought by many to give the best appearance at the apex of a tiled roof. Special under-ridge tiles 215mm (9in) long are used to form a course below the ridge and to preserve the gauge (that is, uniform spacing of the courses and their fixing battens), the battens normally being spaced at 100mm (4in) centres. In many Edwardian houses, special finials or stop-end ridge tiles were often used to terminate tiled ridges above hips or gables, although an ordinary ridge tile with the open end filled in with mortar and tile-slips or even the base of a black glass bottle was common and simpler treatments aping cottage prototypes were certainly preferred by the start of the 1930s.

Hips. The half-round ridge tile is sometimes continued down the hips to cap the otherwise open joint at the junction of tiled roofslopes, but the use of half-cone-shaped or *bonnet hip tiles* grants a smoother hip finish to a tiled roof. The bonnet hip readily fits the range of roof pitches that are appropriate for plain tiles. An alternative, which requires great care in laying to give a neat appearance, is the *arris hip* of specially made hip tiles incorporating a right-angled external corner. Where half-round ridge tiles are used to cap the narrow gap between roof surfaces at the hip, it is essential to secure the lowest hip tile with a shaped iron hook to prevent it from sliding off if it becomes loose (Fig. 90).

Valleys. A sheet-metal-lined valley gutter in a tiled roof is often an unattractive feature and is not normally necessary because most tile manufacturers produce specially shaped valley tiles to course and bond with plain tiling. However, the rounded valley tile is often less successful in complementing the general tiled finish than is the bonnet hip because the

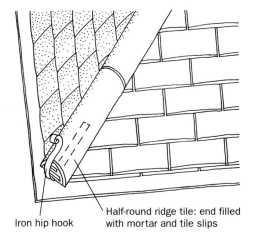

Iron hip hook

Half-round ridge tile: end filled with mortar and tile slips

FIG. 90. *Decorative hip-hook retaining half-round tiles capping junction of clay plain tiles at the hip.*

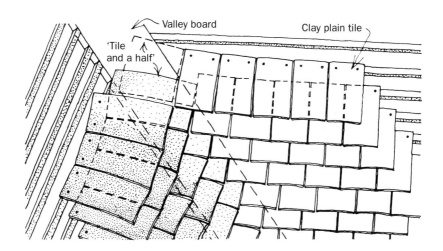

FIG. 91. 'Swept' (or 'laced') valley in clay plain tiling.

concentration of water resulting from a narrow valley and the fact that the awkwardly shaped valley tiles are often less well-burnt than the plain tiles (to restrict warping in the kiln) together cause the valley to weather darker than the rest of the roof. The traditional *swept* or *laced valley* avoids this defect by achieving a broader valley profile and employing plain tiles. It is achieved by installing a broad board (about 220mm [9in] wide) up the valley, its top surface roughly corresponding to the top surfaces of the tiling battens. On to this valley board the tiling courses of the intersecting roofslopes are turned, each rising up its own roofslope and increasing its tilt until opposite courses interlace along the centre of the valley (Fig. 91). Alternately, the courses from each slope are taken over and under each other, the last tile of each course (of which only the corner shows) being a 'tile-and-a-half'. The real difficulty for the tiler in forming such valleys is the starting and finishing where some cutting and packing is entailed. Also, the swept valley cannot be properly formed where two ridges intersect at the same level; one must be lower, otherwise the ridge lines must either rise in a point or one must be humped over the other.

Verges. A close verge in tiling usually projects 50–70mm (2–3in) beyond the gable and should be given a slight tilt inwards to direct the flow of rainwater back across the roof surface and away from the edge. This detail is often achieved by bedding a course of tiles on the wall against the end rafter and projecting it to the same extent as the verge, thereby tilting up the tile-fixing battens which terminate about 75mm (3in) from the verge. The ends of the battens are covered by the pointing between this undercloak and the roof tiling (Figs 92 and 93). As well as holding the pointing, this arrangement gives a thick verge characteristic of the old rural buildings, which the builders of residential suburbia normally wished to simulate. The inward tilt of the tiles dictates an equal tilt in the ridge tile that gives a 'finished' appearance.

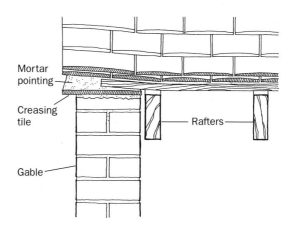

FIG. 92. Close-clipped verge in clay plain tiling.

FIG. 93. A roof covering of machine-made clay plain tiles appears more 'mechanical' than one clad with the handmade type.

For the purpose of preserving bond at the verge and obviating the use of half tiles, which often prove to be difficult to fix, *tile-and-a-half* tiles are made. A sophisticated job by a skilled tiler will omit these 'specials' which tend to weather differently from the plain tiles because their clay composition may be distinct from that of the standard product to ensure proper firing in the kiln and their finished colour and texture are consequently different. Instead, some tiles in each course are cut to achieve a properly bonded arrangement of apparently standard tiles.

Tiling at the verge may also be terminated over a wooden bargeboard, the top surface of which lies in the plane of the fixing battens. Thus, the bargeboard supports the edge of the tiles, protects the end grain of the battens from rot and grants the opportunity for a decorative treatment of the top of the gable. However, this option was not nearly so often exploited in Edwardian or inter-war houses as it was in Victorian houses.

Eaves. As the tiles at the verge may end over a barge-board, so the eaves tiles are often terminated over a continuous wooden fascia, the ends of which may be exposed where there are no bargeboards to cloak the end grain. Alternatively, the ends of the fascia may be closed off by two or three courses of corbelled brickwork or jettied carved stone end-blocks built into the gables. The edge of the tiles should project about 50mm (2in) in front of the fascia, over the eaves gutter; a lesser projection may allow the rainwater to be blown back below the tiles and to run down the fascia behind the gutter which will have a detrimental effect on fascia and walling alike. The under-tiling felt should always be run into the gutter below the projection of the tiles. The minimum two thicknesses of tile are achieved at the eaves by incorporating a plain tile undercloak or *doubling course* of tiles of lesser length (approximately 175mm (7in)) than the standard tile. In traditional construction where no fresh-air ventilation was incorporated at the eaves (a requirement of the current Building Regulations in relation to new work), it was customary to bed the eaves course on mortar on top of the wall to ensure a secure fixing.

Sprocket eaves. This is often seen on Edwardian houses and was employed in many of the more expensive houses of the inter-war years. In this treatment, the roof pitch is slightly flattened close to the eaves by projecting short rafters at a shallower slope than the main timbers from positions adjacent to them. This construction pleasantly softens the silhouette of the roof and slows the flow of water off its surface at the point where it is important for the accumulated run-off to drain into the eaves gutter. Unfortunately, this slight flattening of the roof pitch renders an already vulnerable area more prone to rainwater penetration. It is clear from the surviving hybrid roof coverings of tiles that give way to slates in the eaves courses that this problem was recognised by the old rural builders. Therefore, an essential rule for the re-covering or restoration of a sprocket eaves in a plain tiled roof must be to ensure that the pitch of the sprocketed section is not less than 35 degrees.

Pantiles. Pantiles and the various related forms of tile are moulded fireclay products that are laid according to a principle different from that which applies to plain tiling. They are laid to a single lap and the majority of the roof surface is covered with only a single thickness of tile. There is no bond, the principle being that the tiles, when laid, form a series of channels from ridge to eaves, confining the rainwater to a straight course and preventing spreading.

The ordinary pantile is of wave section and is 220–250mm (9–10in) wide. From head to tail it is about 350mm (14in) long. In manufacture it is first moulded flat and then bent to shape before being fired. The thickness of the clay is usually about 19mm (¾in), but owing to the single-lap arrangement, a square of pantiling weighs only about half as much as an identical area of clay plain tiling. Partly for this reason, pantiles were a common finish for the cheaply made and lightly structured roofs of ancillary buildings such as the stables and outhouses attached to large urban and rural houses. For roofs of houses in Norfolk, Lincolnshire and north Nottinghamshire they are a particularly prevalent finish, though Bridgwater, Somerset, which produced several types of patented pantile in addition to the plain tiles for which it is more noted, also boasts many pantiled roofs. In addition to tiles of the natural fireclay colour, the local manufacturer also produced pantiles finished in green, blue and black glazes, although where this finish is seen on a roof it is much more likely to be the result of use of imported interlocking tiles (see below).

Pantiles should be hung on stout timber battens by the single nib integral to the head of each unit. Particularly where roof pitches are steeper than 45 degrees they are additionally secured with 50mm (2in) copper nails. It is worth noting that because rainwater is quickly discharged from a pantiled roof via the corrugations, a very steep pitch may cause the rainwater to overshoot the gutter. At the other extreme, pantiles may be laid safely to a pitch as low as 30 degrees. The headlap of pantiling is from 75–87mm (3–3½in), the sidelap being 50mm. To resist the penetration of windblown rain, the sidelap of each tile must always be pointed up with mortar.

Study of roofs covered in pantiles quickly shows that, owing to its quite bold scale and rigid lines, the method is really suitable only for covering roofs of simple shape. It does not lend itself to a roof cut up

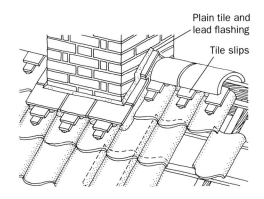

Plain tile and
lead flashing

Tile slips

FIG. 94. Junction of pantiles with roof ridge and chimney stack.

by numerous projections necessitating valleys that are awkward to form. Hips, too, are not easily formed and pantiling is most compatible with gables capped by parapets. The conventional half-round ridge tile commonly used with plain tiling perfectly complements pantiles. Owing to the wavy line of the pantiling, the ridge tiles rest only on the rolls, leaving a hollow at each 'furrow' that has to be filled. The traditional means of achieving this is to bed graded strips of plain tile in mortar, more of which is used to seal each hollow completely (Fig. 94). No eaves doubling course is required in a pantiled roof and because of the bold profile of the tiles, flashings of the roof covering against parapets or chimney stacks are better formed with mortar fillets – supplemented with plain tiles and pieces of waste tile – than with sheet metal.

Other forms of profiled clay tiles are the so-called Roman, Spanish and French tiles. Roman-tiled roofs are made up of trough-section *undertiles* and half-cone-shaped *overtiles* which taper from tail to head so that under and overtiles interlock along their side edges and the courses overlap. The undertiles are usually nailed on to boarding crossing the roofslope and the overtiles are nailed to battens sited between the rows of undertiles running up the roof slope, at right-angles to the boarding. Spanish tiles (or 'mission' tiles from their use in traditional church buildings of the south-western states of the USA) employ the same principle as the Roman type, the main difference being that the undertiles are concave. These units are nailed sideways into the vertical battens on each side and the overtiles are single-nailed to the top of the battens.

The term 'French tile' relates to the many forms of machine-made interlocking tiles that were widely used in the inter-war period. Many of these tiles were of foreign manufacture, although they were usually imported from Belgium or Holland rather than France. The town of Courtrai in Belgium was the point of origin for many of these tiles which were available either in their natural terracotta colour or glazed to give bright green, turquoise or deep blue roof surfaces. Hung, like conventional pantiles, on wooden battens laid horizontally, they were rarely fixed with nails because their interlocking profiles helped to keep them in place. These types of interlocking tile continue to be made and imported and many small changes to tile size and the interlocking system have been made within an unaltered basic format. In cases where the modern product is slightly larger than the original, preventing easy patching of small areas with new material, repairs to the roof covering usually necessitate stripping of the affected roofslope for wholesale replacement with new tiles, the salvaged original tiles being used to repair other areas. It is often possible to match the glazed finish of the original tiles in the glaze applied to modern tiles of very similar profile.

Slating

Although by the early years of the twentieth century changing fashions had caused natural slate to lose its place as the favoured roof covering for houses, in places such as North Wales and Cumbria where this material was a local resource and could continue to compete with cheap clay or concrete plain tiles shipped from other areas, slate continued to be used as the standard pitched-roof covering for the whole of the inter-war period. The use of a slate roof covering on the roofs of semi-detached houses of the 1930s in these areas may supply the only evidence of adherence to local building practices in a design which is otherwise a 'standard kit-of-parts' used apparently indiscriminately throughout Britain. Therefore, owners of these houses need to know the principles underlying the form and details of a natural slate

roof, not only to understand the anatomy of the original construction for diagnosis of faults and appreciation of prospective problems, but also to be able to specify and monitor repairs and to order wholesale replacement of outworn slate roof surfaces with authentic material and details, when necessary.

British natural slates are quarried from a type of sedimentary rock, which is not divisible along its planes of bedding but instead, along 'planes of cleavage' which may be at any angle to the bedding. For building purposes, British slates fall into two main categories. In the first are those slates that have a relatively smooth face. These are quarried mainly in North Wales and are traditionally known as Bangor and Portmadoc slates. At the quarry or slate mine they are trimmed to standard sizes and are as thin as possible, often not exceeding 3mm (⅛in) thick. In colour they are blue-grey, purple or greenish-grey. In the second category are slates that have a granular cleavage and these are quarried in Cumbria (that is, Cumberland, Westmorland and north Lancashire according to the county boundaries that applied until 1973). These 'Lakeland' slates are dressed to random sizes and are thicker than the typical Welsh roofing slate. In colour they are pale green, blue-grey or blue-black.

In addition to these two main types, slates that originated in Cornwall (Delabole) or South Wales (Prescelly) were also used in those areas and other parts of west and south-west England, though buildings of the inter-war period that are roofed with these materials are rare. Dressed, like the Cumbrian product, to random sizes, they are intermediate in character between North Wales and Lakeland slates. In colour they are greenish-grey to rusty brown.

Extreme 'mechanical' neatness is associated with roofs covered in North Wales slates, a quality thought to be unattractive by all but the most conservative architects of the Edwardian period. Speculative builders consequently adopted these values, employing clay plain tiles in preference to Welsh slates, although even in south-east England, distant from the slate quarries, there are many Edwardian terraced houses in which clay plain tiles appeared only over the prestigious street elevation and rear roofslopes continued to be covered with the ubiquitous Welsh slates. In northern England, slate retained its dominance until after the First World War. Where Edwardian architects thought slate to be appropriate (usually as a tribute to local, traditional building techniques), the tweedier texture of Lakeland slate roofing, executed in diminishing courses, was preferred to the uniformity of Welsh slate.

It is worth noting that a neat and orderly appearance in a slated roof is no guarantee of watertight construction, for it is found in practice that the rougher texture and thicker edges of Lakeland slates exclude the weather better than smoother and thinner slates which lie close together. This is partly due to the fact that the air contained between the uneven surfaces of the slates reduces capillary attraction, and partly due to the tendency of each slate's thick edges to deflect the wind, thus preventing water from being blown over the lap. These properties are possessed even more clearly by English stone slates, which are described later in this chapter. Delabole and Prescelly slates are laid in almost the same way as Lakeland slate and they share many of its advantages in terms of weathertightness and durability.

Laying Slates
The principles of lap and bond essential to plain tiling apply equally to slate roof coverings, although the wide range of sizes available in slates (in contrast to the fairly standard format of the clay plain tile) grants the opportunity to reduce or increase the lap from a standard dimension of 75mm (3in) to suit the degree of exposure to the elements and pitch of the roofslope (for example, a building in an elevated coastal location is much more at risk of water penetration by windblown rain than one in a low-lying inland valley). In relation to roof pitch, in a low-pitched roof (say 25 degrees), the lap should be longer than that which applies on a steeply-pitched roof (say 50 degrees). On the more steeply pitched roofs, the spread of water over each slate is less as gravity assists the rain to run off more quickly and the lap of the slates can be reduced. The *margin* is the area at the tail of each slate exposed to view, and corresponds to the *gauge* or spacing of the courses and their fixing battens.

Correct bond is also critical for ensuring weathertightness in a slated roof. Even if they are laid with an adequate lap, the use of narrow slates poses the same problem of water penetration that results from adoption of an inadequate lap.

The risk of water penetration is most pronounced at the eaves of a long roofslope where the pitch of the roof has been slightly flattened by a sprocket-eaves profile and where the volume of water passing over the roof is at its greatest. With the use of regularly sized slates at this location, an even bond will reliably exclude rainwater from the roof space or wall top, but with the random sizes that occur in Lakeland, Cornish, South Wales slates and stone slates, the skill and judgement of the slater determines the watertightness of the roof.

A slate is fixed with nails driven through two holes punched either 25mm (1in) below the head of each slate or a distance above the tail equal to gauge and lap plus 13mm (½in) clearance. In either case, the nail holes are about 32mm (1¼in) from the long sides of the slate. The former technique is called *head-nailing* and the latter *centre-nailing*. Head-nailed slates always have two thicknesses of the material over the nail holes and the actual lap is 25mm (1in) greater than the nominal lap, which is measured from the nail holes. Head nailing requires more slates than centre nailing to cover a given area and is therefore more expensive. Apart from its more economical use of slates, centre nailing offers the further advantage that it shortens the lever arm between tail of slate and fixing which is acted on by the wind and thus reduces the risk of the roof being stripped in a gale. Centre-nailing largely replaced head-nailing as the favoured method from the middle of the nineteenth century and it was rarely used to secure slate roof coverings on early twentieth-century buildings.

Copper, stainless steel or aluminium alloy nails provide enduring fixings for natural or fibre-cement slates (see later section: Restoring Pitched Roofs with New Materials). Ungalvanized steel nails quickly corrode and may not last twenty years, whilst natural slate will easily last eighty years or more.

Today, there are two customary methods for providing a fixing surface for slates above the rafters of a conventional pitched roof. The first, which is also the simpler and cheaper, is the open-batten roof found under tiled roof coverings, in which rough-sawn, rot-proofed timber battens approximately 25mm deep × 50mm wide (1 × 2in) are fixed to the rafters at the appropriate gauge, a bituminous under-slating felt having first been loosely fixed over the rafters. In this way, any water penetrating the slates is allowed to run away into the eaves profile on top of this *sarking felt* and below the slates. Superior to this construction and also much more expensive, is a totally boarded covering of the rafters. The felt is tacked to this continuous wooden surface (or sarking) before counterbattens running up the slope at about 600mm (2ft) intervals are applied, followed by the slate-fixing battens themselves (Fig. 95). The omission of the counterbattens is a false economy, for in their absence, water penetrating defective slates and running down the felt lodges on the battens and finds its way into the batten fixings to cause eventual rotting of the sarking.

Victorian and Edwardian builders were fond of yet another form of construction which, in the long term, leads to the problem posed by omission of counterbattens. Slates were sometimes fixed directly to the sarking, the battens, too, being omitted. Where the roof surface is weathertight, the boarded substrate is protected, but a small chink in the slating caused by a cracked or broken slate will invite water into the shallow cavity below the slates and on to the boarding, threatening the timber with wet rot from the outside and dry rot from within, the latter condition being encouraged by poor ventilation of the related roof space.

Slates eventually decay because of their reaction with weak acids formed from sulphur and other pollutants dissolved in rainwater. They exfoliate and begin to absorb moisture with the efficiency of blotting paper. Slated city roofs are likely to have reached this state after about eighty years' exposure to a polluted atmosphere. Clearly, the 'grip' of a slate on its fixing nails is not assisted by this softening of the material and the dislodged slates often seen on old roofslopes may have slipped because decay has affected those parts of each slate closest to the fixing holes. A much more common reason for slipped slates is the rusting of the original iron fixing nails. The weight of a slate will eventually sever the corroded shanks of iron nails and high winds encourage dislodged slates to slip further out of place (Fig. 96). A slate roof afflicted in this way is said to be 'nail sick'. Damage to people and property are possible consequences of slipped slates in the absence of timely repair.

Slipped slates are resited by extracting the remains of the corroded fixings from beneath the overlapping course with a slater's ripper. The head of a strip of lead, zinc or copper which will form a clip or *tingle* is then fixed to the sliver of batten accessible through the joint exposed by the missing slate and the slate is slid back into place over this strip and secured by folding the free end of metal over the lower edge of the slate (Fig. 97). This clip-fixing of dislodged slates

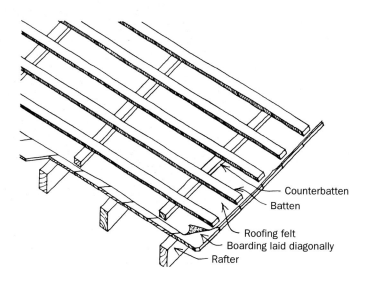

Counterbatten
Batten
Roofing felt
Boarding laid diagonally
Rafter

FIG. 95. Boarded, counterbattened and battened underslating construction.

is merely an expedient that cannot forever put off the day when the permanent refixing or renewal of the entire roof covering is necessary. Roofslopes that display a forest of slowly unfolding metal clips clearly indicate that they are due for renewal (Fig. 98).

Sizes of Slate

The supply of Lakeland slates in random sizes demands sorting of the stock by the slater in order to obtain consistent courses. Welsh slates, by contrast, are available in a range of standard and quite precise sizes boasting attractive titles. *Ladies* are among the smaller slates, measuring 350mm long by 300mm wide (14 × 12in), but the conventional sizes for covering most main roofslopes are *Countess* slates at approximately 500 × 250mm (20 × 10in) and *Duchess* slates which are slightly larger at around 600 × 300mm (24 × 12in).

Slate Roof Details

Ridge. In common with pitched roofs covered in clay tiles, the feature most vulnerable to damage by high winds is the capping to the apex of the roof, or ridge. The normal method of shielding the junction of slated pitched roof surfaces at the ridge from rain is that adopted for tiled roofs – namely, installation of an unbroken row of fireclay ridge tiles. As applies in association with plain tiling, the ridge tiles may be half-round in section or pre-formed to an inverted 'V' to an equal or lesser angle than the junction of the roofslopes. They are bedded on mortar and lap the topmost course of the double-skin slate covering which abuts both sides of the ridgeboard. Ignoring the half-round pattern, which is of a scale and profile that better complements a tiled roof, the 'weaving shed' double-pitched ridge tile is the plainest type. Almost equally common is a tile that incorporates a raised rim at one end so that it overlaps its neighbour, shielding the mortar joints between the tiles from rain penetration. More decorative varieties of ridge tiles incorporating elaborate crests and finials may be seen on urban and suburban houses of the Edwardian years (particularly in areas such as north Staffordshire, renowned for the manufacture of fireclay products), but the craving for this form of 'mechanical' ornateness soon faded in the early years of the inter-war period.

FIG. 96. The shanks of iron nails formerly used to fix slates eventually rust through. High winds dislodge slates and ultimately they slide off the roof. (Redland Roof Tiles.)

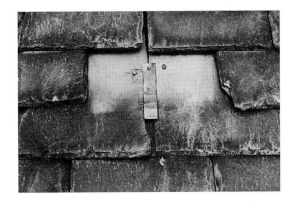

FIG. 97. The site of a slipped slate previously fixed on a zinc clip illustrates the normal method of patch repair of a slated roof. (Redland Roof Tiles.)

FIG. 98. A deformed chimney flashing and a host of dislodged and delaminating slates on metal clips are signs of an outworn roof covering. (Redland Roof Tiles.)

Though most readily available in the reddish colour natural to most earthenware products, ridge tiles were also produced in a blue-black finish resulting from the firing of dark Staffordshire clays and this colour is much more in harmony with the colour of Welsh slate roofs than the red-orange cast of unglazed earthenware which was the accepted finish for chimney pots. New weaving-shed-profile ridge tiles sporting a blue-black finish are still obtainable from two or three Midlands tile makers.

The lime mortar used by Edwardian builders to bed and point up fireclay ridge tiles is eventually washed out by rainwater and a high wind easily dislodges a loose ridge tile overhanging a gable. In original roofs lacking the second line of defence of roofing felt, the missing ridge tile reveals a gap that allows rainwater to saturate the apex of the roof structure. Where such slipped ridge tiles are being refixed or replaced, it is essential that the work is carried out carefully, the void between the underside of each tile and the top of the ridgeboard being fully packed with mortar and the flanges of each tile being seated in a thick mortar bed.

Hips. As applies with tiled roofs, the types of ridge tiles used at the apex of the roof can also be used to waterproof the joint between slated roofslopes at the hip of a pyramidal roof. However, this treatment can look clumsy where the thick tiles have to be cut to meet at the junction of the hips and the ridge. This criticism applies most obviously to the poor finish often seen at this junction where several hip cappings meet the end ridge tile as occurs in roofs capping projecting semi-polygonal bays. A neater, if more expensive detail is the *hip roll* in which a length of timber, similar in cross-section to a broom handle is run down on top of the hip rafter and is clad in lead, copper or zinc, with 'wings' of the metal extending out from this capped batten to mask the joint with the slates and thus exclude the rain. This treatment can be equally well applied to the ridge so that all external junctions of the slated surfaces are protected by strips of sheet metal (identical to the shingled roof ridge shown in Fig. 106 below).

It is also possible to waterproof the joint of slates at the hip 'invisibly' (that is, without any form of capping) by interleaving thin sheet-lead soakers

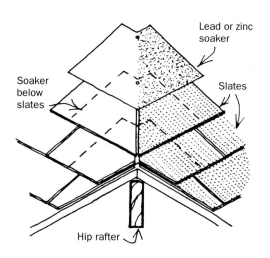

FIG. 99. Slates meeting at a mitred joint over sheet-lead soakers at the roof hip.

between succeeding courses of slates, individual slates being mitred to fit close at the hip (Fig. 99). This is a particularly suitable detail for the thicker slates of Cornwall or Cumbria. Hips are more susceptible to early decay than ridges because heavy ridge tiles are more easily dislodged from the slope of a hip than from a level ridge. Where ridge tiles are used to cap a hip, it is essential that the lowest tile is restrained against slipping by a hip iron fixed at the foot of the slope, in the same way as applies with the tiled-roof detail (see Fig. 90 above). Where the hip is 'secretly' waterproofed with zinc soakers, corrosion of the metal by the weak acids contained in rainwater and city atmospheres is a common cause of leaks; in this circumstance replacement of the zinc fittings with lead soakers is the best prescription for a durable repair.

Valleys. In roofs covered with thick slates, valleys may be treated in the same way as hips – the slates being close-mitred at this junction of roof surfaces with sheet metal soakers interleaved between the courses. A less attractive treatment is the sheet-metal-lined open valley in which a which a wide wooden valley board at, or below, the level of the slate-fixing battens, is covered in sheet metal, lapped by the slates to either side (Fig. 100). This detail produces an ugly gash at the junction of roof surfaces and ought not to be substituted for an original close-mitred valley in any re-roofing project (though its use may be unavoidable at the junction of roof surfaces of different pitch or where the thicker tile-type materials such as clay pantiles or interlocking concrete tiles are employed). The third and most satisfactory arrangement, which may be found on expensive bespoke houses of the Edwardian and inter-war periods which were detailed in deference to traditional, local building techniques, is the *swept valley*, similar to that often adopted in Cotswold stone slating which is described in the following section. *Skew* and *bottom* slates are run alternately up the 215mm wide valley board, preserving the line of each slating course across the valley. In any restoration of this detail, bituminous underslating felt should be laid below the valley board, which is sited in the plane of the slate-fixing battens.

It will be appreciated that the internal junction of roofslopes is often the area most prone to rainwater penetration because it acts as a channel draining rainwater from parts of two roofslopes. In extending the treatment applied across plain roof surfaces to this zone, the swept valley provides the most secure valley cladding. Close mitreing of the slates over zinc soakers is an arrangement as susceptible to early decay as the identical treatment of the hip, and where over-long lead sheets have been used to line an open valley gutter, the metal can become corrugated laterally, inducing splits in its surface which draw in rainwater. This common defect arises in addition to the normal erosion of the metal gutter lining caused by chemical reactions with rainwater and air carrying pollutants. Where a roof is to be re-covered with a tiling system that does not include purpose-made valley tiles (such as fibre-cement slates), the neatest renovation is achieved by re-forming the valley in close-mitred slates interleaved with lead soakers.

Verges. The junction of a slated roof with a gable is most simply achieved by carrying the slates across the full width of the wall and terminating them on top of a wooden bargeboard, the top surface of which is level with the tops of the fixing battens. As in the equivalent treatment of the verge of a tiled roof, the bargeboard supports the edge of the slates, protects the end grain of the battens from rot and grants the opportunity for decorative treatment of the top of the gable. A humbler treatment of the verge exhibited a mortar fillet, which was applied to the underside of the slates where they oversailed the outside face of the gable wall. As this plain appearance is common in traditional rural buildings, it is sometimes found in

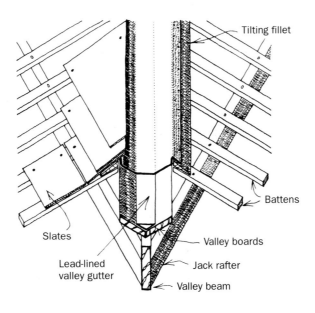

FIG. 100. Open-valley gutter with sheet-lead lining.

Slates

Lead-lined valley gutter

Tilting fillet

Battens

Valley boards

Jack rafter

Valley beam

95

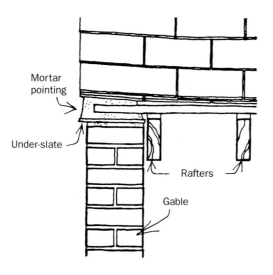

FIG. 101. Close-clipped verge in slating.

cut slates of the slate-hanging which overhang the secret gutter.

A cheaper and less satisfactory detail for parapet verges relies upon sheet-metal soakers, interleaved between slating courses, being turned up against the flanking masonry and capped with a continuous mortar fillet. Sometimes, tile slips are bedded in this mortar to give a more 'crafted' appearance (Fig. 102). The main shortcoming of this arrangement is the risk of a fracture between the mortar and the masonry, inviting water into the roof at the rear of the upstand of the soakers. In incompetent repairs, even the soakers are sometimes omitted, reliance being placed entirely on a dense mortar mix to exclude rainwater from this joint, and in this circumstance, the inevitable small splits in an inflexible cement mortar fillet provide a clear route for rainwater to enter the roof. Hence it is prudent to replace such features with

Edwardian and inter-war houses of the Vernacular Revival. The most satisfactory way of constructing this detail was to bed an underslating course of slates in mortar on top of the gable masonry and below the battens. The gap between these slates and the roof covering would then be pointed up with mortar as the slated verge was completed (Fig. 101).

Where the gable (or party wall parapet of terraced houses in Greater London) is carried above the roofslope as a sloping parapet, the best waterproofing detail is the inclusion of a stepped metal flashing built into the bed joints of the stones or brickwork of the parapet, cladding sheet-metal soakers which exclude rainwater from the otherwise open joint between roof surface and flanking masonry. Smaller masonry features that penetrate the roof surface, such as chimney stacks, are treated in exactly the same way. The junction of slating with the cheeks of dormer windows was most often achieved with a sheet-metal *secret gutter*, partly obscured by the lap of the slates and constructed in the same way as an open valley gutter, the metal lining of the channel being continuous with the metal cladding of the dormer cheek where, as often applies, the dormer construction is metal-clad. If the cheek of the dormer is slate-hung or tile-hung, the metal gutter lining is continuous with the vertical hanging flashing concealed by the

FIG. 102. Outworn tile-and-mortar fillet at the junction of roofslopes and party wall parapet. It should be replaced with a stepped lead flashing. (Redland Roof Tiles.)

ABOVE: *Terraced houses complying with the 1877 Model By-laws continued to be built throughout the years leading up to World War I. (Robin Bishop.)*

RIGHT: *To attract respectable tenants, developers of late Victorian and Edwardian houses often embellished front elevations with ornament. Here, moulded stonework and coloured ceramic tiles enrich the porch of a terraced house in north London. (Robin Bishop.)*

Simple original features contribute to the character of a period house. Here a part-glazed timber partition dividing ground-floor kitchen from scullery evokes tranquil domesticity. (Robin Bishop.)

The Arts and Crafts Movement reappraised and revived forms of building traditional in the English regions: a house clad in the tarred weatherboarding of the south in Hampshire (c.1902).

Appreciation of the qualities of the vernacular architecture of pre-industrial England was at the heart of the endeavours of Arts and Crafts Movement architects: The Deanery Garden, Sonning-on-Thames, Berkshire (Edwin Lutyens, 1901 & 1912). (Robin Bishop.)

Vernacular and Tudor prototypes were stretched to the limit of their applicability in creating a living-hall bay suited to the owner of Country Life magazine (The Deanery Garden). (Robin Bishop.)

LEFT: *Letchworth Garden City, Hertfordshire (founded 1903) is home to many bespoke houses by Arts and Crafts Movement architects: a detached house by M. H. Baillie Scott (1865–1945).*

BELOW: *A pair of semi-detached houses 'Laneside' and 'Crabby Corner' (1904–05) by the architect Barry Parker (1867–1947) at Letchworth Garden City.*

ABOVE: *Edwardian semi-detached houses in Teddington, Middlesex, liberally adorned with fretwork-framed balconies and porches.*

RIGHT: *'Littleholme' Kendal, Cumbria: a bespoke villa of 1909 for the furniture maker A. W. Simpson by C. F. A. Voysey (1857–1941).*

LEFT: *A detached villa of the 1930s in a west Kent town. Its rustic weatherboarding and high tiled roof testify to the continuing influence of the cottage prototype, even in the age of the motor car.*

BELOW: *Designs for inter-war council houses in many English towns and villages were often inspired by the features of traditional local rural houses.*

RIGHT: Tile-hanging, usually adopted to clad only the upper storeys of houses, was sometimes applied over the entire exterior.

BELOW: Bricks made locally, tarred weatherboarding, painted roughcast render and plain tiles produce a convincing image of cottages suited to twentieth-century use in a Kentish town.

The standard form of inter-war semi-detached house proved to be a versatile vehicle for expressing a range of architectural styles; here flat-fronted examples combine painted render with modern steel windows.

Flat-roofed modern movement houses of the inter-war years failed to appeal to more than a small minority of buyers but many builders believed that the 'alien' associations of the continental prototypes could be mitigated by constructing external walls in exposed brickwork.

a stepped-metal-flashing cladding soakers when renewal of part or whole of the roof covering is implemented.

Eaves. As the slates at the verge conventionally end on a bargeboard, so the eaves slates normally terminate over a continuous wooden fascia. As with tiles, the edge of the slates should project not less than 50mm (2in) in front of the fascia and into the zone occupied by the gutter. Also, the underslating felt should always be run into the gutter below the projection of the slates, and excess felt should be trimmed off to prevent the flow of rainwater in the gutter from becoming obstructed. Some slated roofs exhibit the sprocket-eaves treatment often found in older tiled roofs and the dangers of using narrow slates in this zone have already been described. However, it cannot be stressed too strongly that great care should be taken to ensure that the slates used in any re-roofing are sufficiently wide to prevent rainwater creeping in between the courses. Similarly, amateur restorers of slated roofs must remember that, as in tiled roofs, the lowest course always shows an edge of two thicknesses of material at the eaves. Accidental or careless omission of the eaves underslate (a little more than half the length of the first full course) invites rainwater or melted snow into the roofspace at its junction with the wall top.

Stone Slates

Stone slates or tiles are obtained from beds of stone, which have the property of laminating in thin slabs along the planes of bedding. *Yorkshire slates* are of sandstone and are the largest roofing slabs that can be obtained in England. Almost equally large sizes could be found in the *Horsham slabs* of West Sussex. The slates were formed by splitting conventionally quarried blocks of stone with hammers and chisels or metal wedges. Northamptonshire also had celebrated quarries supplying stone slates, the best known being *Collyweston*. These slates are thinner and lighter than the Yorkshire slabs; they are also more regular than the *Cotswold stone slates* formerly won from the Eyford, Guiting and Stonesfield quarries, but the modern material is unlikely to be as durable as the products of these Oxfordshire and Gloucestershire pits. The preference of architects of

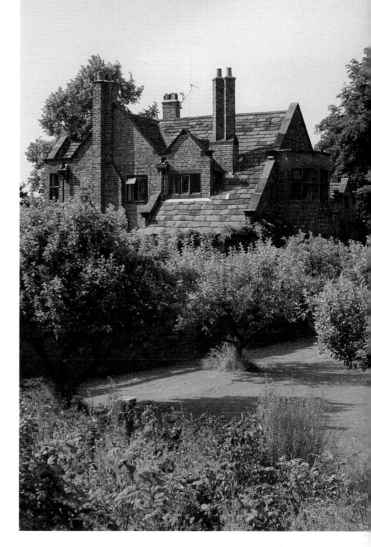

FIG. 103. Pennine stone-slate roof. Brae Cottage, Knutsford, Cheshire: a neo-vernacular house built for Henry Royce, co-founder of the Rolls Royce Motor Company.

the Arts and Crafts Movement that local building materials should be used wherever possible meant that expensive rural or suburban houses pre- and post-First World War were sometimes roofed with stone slates in the manner of ancient local buildings (Fig. 103). The material gives a picturesque appearance and is reasonably enduring. However, because of the very heavy load imposed by stone slates, a stronger roof structure than that used for any other type of pitched-roof covering is necessary.

Stone slating is executed under the same principles

of lap and bond applicable to other forms of random-sized slating. Traditionally, the slates were hung on cleft oak or deal pegs, which are driven by the slaters tightly into holes near the head of each slate. The slates usually outlast these pegs and in more modern work brass screws were sometimes used instead. Today, wedge-shaped aluminium alloy pegs or stainless steel nails are more often used (Fig. 104). A stone-slate covering which was installed before 1939 is also likely to demonstrate that individual slates were bedded and pointed up in mortar in addition to their mechanical fixing. This technique is not employed today; friction between the units, maximised by skilful sorting and laying, their considerable weight and a sound mechanical fixing are deemed to be adequate to secure stone slates on the steepest roofslope.

FIG. 104. Head-nailed Cotswold stone slates being reinstated on a village house in Oxfordshire.

Suitable pitches for stone-slate roofs vary according to the size of slate available in the district. In Pennine Yorkshire and Lancashire, and in old Sussex roofs, the larger slates make roofs watertight at as low an angle as 24 degrees. As they are immensely heavy, a pitch steeper than 45 degrees is unusual. The small Cotswold slates were customarily laid to a pitch of 55 degrees, whilst Northamptonshire stone-slate roofs of middle-sized slates are pitched at a compromise angle of 45–50 degrees.

Stone-slate roofs are commonly finished at the apex with sawn stone ridge tiles. Hips are almost unknown in stone-slate roofs because of the difficulty of obtaining a neat appearance in such coarse-grained material, although the slates can be mitred in the same way as Lakeland slates. The typical valley in Cotswold slating was 'swept' by using tapered slates in twos and threes in alternate courses (Fig. 105). In preference to 'new-fangled' sheet-metal fittings, an inverted length of ridge tile was sometimes used to form a cross-gutter above a meeting of valleys to keep rain out of the junction. The eaves were commonly projected 150–200mm (6–8in), the doubling course resting on a course of large (or *cussome*) slates bedded on the wall, projecting outwards and slightly upwards to form an eaves soffit. An open verge can be formed in the same way, but a better treatment often found in ancient buildings (and thus reproduced by the Arts and Crafts architects) was to end the roof against a gable projecting slightly above the roof surface and finished with a coping, as this allowed the slates to tuck in against the gable and below the coping, the resultant gap being closed with a mortar fillet.

Shingles

Wooden shingles have been used to some extent for roofing in the British Isles, particularly for the cladding of turrets, outhouses and the roofs of garden buildings. They continue to be widely used as a roof covering in Canada and the USA. Shingles are made by sawing and splitting wood, cleft shingles being more serviceable than sawn shingles because splitting guarantees continuous fibres throughout the length of a unit, resulting in maximum durability. British shingles were traditionally of oak, which gives a fairly watertight covering. In America, red cedar, white cedar, cypress and white pine are woods that convert

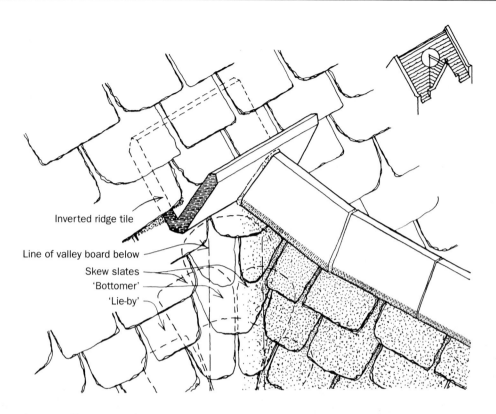

Inverted ridge tile

Line of valley board below
Skew slates
'Bottomer'
'Lie-by'

FIG. 105. 'Swept' valley in stone slates.

well into shingles, and red cedar shingles are now the standard type in Britain.

Softwood shingles are 400–450mm (16–18in) or 600–675mm (24–27in) long and range in width between 75–250mm (3–10in). Thin shingles measure 10mm (⅜in) thick at the bottom and reduce to 2mm (¹⁄₁₆in) thick at the upper end. By contrast, English oak shingles are 300–400mm (12–16in) long and 100–200mm (4–8in) wide. It is not uncommon to find a consistent triple thickness on roofs in exposed locations, the lap being the distance the shingle extends over the third one below it. Where a thickness of two shingles only is adopted, as applies generally in Britain, the gauge is obtained in the same way as in plain tiling, being half the difference between the lap and the length of a shingle.

Shingles may be laid on the two types of pitched-roof construction most suitable for slates; the open batten roof and the boarded, counterbattened and battened roof. It is not advisable to omit the counter-battens in the second system of construction, as some circulation of air below the roof covering is essential if premature rotting of the shingles is to be avoided. Where shingles are laid on an open-batten roof, one to three roof boards are laid along the eaves and valleys to receive a few of the first courses of shingles. The purpose of these boards is to protect the shingles if it is necessary to walk along the eaves to make repairs. The eaves course of the shingles is doubled in the same way as tiles or slates and they should overlap the fascia by about 40mm (1½in). Each shingle is fastened with two non-ferrous nails at a point about 50mm (2in) above the upper line of exposure. In this way, the heads of the nails are protected by the laps and the shingles are further secured by the nails of each succeeding course passing through the heads of the previous course (Fig. 106). Steel nails, even if galvanized, should never be used for fixing oak

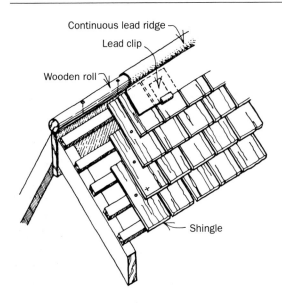

Continuous lead ridge

Lead clip

Wooden roll

Shingle

FIG. 106. Ridge junction of a roof clad with timber shingles.

shingles as the wood contains tannic acid, which will readily attack the iron and its zinc coating.

The durability of shingles is greatly increased by setting them from 5–12mm (¼–½in) apart. This permits the water to drain off quickly, secures quick drying of the roof, allows for swelling of the shingles and thus prevents them from buckling. Wide shingles demand the use of a wide joint, though the joints may be made as narrow as 3mm (⅛in) if small units are employed. Conventional double-pitched roofs covered in shingles usually include two further features that require special treatment.

Ridge. A durable ridge detail is obtained by using a wooden roll covered in sheet metal in the same manner as the lead-clad ridge roll which crowns the apex of some slated roofs. To achieve this, the ridge board is carried up slightly above the shingles and a wooden roll is spiked to its top surface. After the shingles are laid, the roll is covered with lead extending about 150mm (6in) down from the shingles on each side. To prevent the metal being lifted by the wind, clips are formed from slips of lead about 150mm (6in) long and 65mm (2½in) wide which are nailed at 600mm (2ft) intervals along the roof under

the flashing, and then turned up and dressed not less than 25mm (1in) over the 'free' edge.

Hips and valleys. In the construction of hips, a metal-covered roll similar to a ridge roll may be used and a sheet-metal valley gutter suitable for other tile-type roof coverings can be used in valleys. The use of sheet-metal soakers below carefully mitred shingles on hips and valleys can also provide a weathertight detail. In the USA, sheet tin was the metal favoured for this purpose and for the finish of ridges and hip rolls. Where oak shingles are employed, zinc should on no account be used for soakers because it will react adversely with the timber.

Thatch

Although regarded as an obsolete roofing material by the late nineteenth century, thatch enjoyed something of a revival through the influence of the Arts and Crafts Movement architects (Fig. 107) and it was employed to roof a meaningful number of outer-suburban houses of the inter-war period, particularly when the enthusiasm for 'Old English' was at its height in the late 1920s and a conspicuously antique appearance in 'stockbroker villas' was fashionable, even to the extent of parts of old buildings being re-used in new dwellings.

Though the principle is not at first obvious, the countless straws or reeds of a thatched roof exclude the weather by exactly the same arrangement of overlapping units as do roofs of tiles, slates or shingles. Thatch acts as excellent thermal insulation, ensuring warmth in winter and coolness in summer, but it is readily damaged by birds, sometimes invites infestation by vermin and represents a considerable fire risk, as is evidenced by the high insurance premiums paid by thatched-house dwellers.

A roof is prepared to receive thatching by nailing to the rafters wooden battens at 200mm (8in) centres. As the thatched covering is quite light, common rafters of conventional cross-section (for example, 50 × 100mm (2 × 4in)) may be spaced more widely than applies in a tiled roof – 600mm (2ft) centres are common. The thatching commences at the eaves and is laid in courses or 'lanes' from eaves to ridge, each lane being about 750mm (2½ft) wide. Bundles of straw or reed about 80–100mm (3½–4in) thick are laid on the battens and, where traditional techniques are followed religiously, are secured to them with tarred rope yarn drawn by a thatcher's needle. An alternative fixing for the bundles is to hang them on the battens with thatching hooks tied to the head of each bundle. Starting at eaves level at the right-hand gable, the bundles are laid to the full thickness of 300–375mm (12–15in) until the lanes reach the ridge. After two or three lanes have been put on, they are interlaced with *withies* or reeds forced diagonally through the bundles of thatch in a criss-cross pattern. The ends of the withies are bound together and either nailed to the rafters or tied to the battens with yarn. When a 3m (10ft) width of thatch has been laid, hazel rods are run through the thatch at 600mm (2ft) centres on lines parallel to the eaves. These rods or *runners* are secured by looping the withes over them and nailing their ends to the rafters with iron pegs.

Where old thatch is to be renewed, all the loose and rotten straw and moss is combed out and, if the decay is restricted to small areas of the roof, these can be repaired by patching the surface with new straw. A generally poor surface has to be completely covered with fresh material secured with hazel runners and pegs. To limit the damage that can be caused by birds, a complete covering of galvanised chicken-wire netting is sometimes pinned to the finished surface.

Thatch is unsuitable as a covering for roofs of less than 45 degrees pitch. Dormers cannot be satisfactorily formed in thatch except at the eaves, where the characteristic 'eyebrow' profile of the thatch sweeping over the dormer window is the natural visual result. The verge cannot project far and, to project at all yet still drain efficiently, the straw must be raked to project diagonally outwards from the roofslope. After trimming, the straw at the verge must be well secured with rods or twine, as of all types of roofs formed from overlapping units, thatched roofs are most at risk from stripping in high winds and the verges are the most exposed features.

If well laid and carefully maintained, rainwater rarely penetrates thatch, though collection of the run-off which drains from the top layers of straw can be difficult to achieve because the great thickness of straw at the eaves and the pronounced eaves overhang

FIG. 107. Thatched roof of an architect's studio, constructed for the planning of Letchworth Garden City, Hertfordshire (1903).

(elevations should be shielded by a projection of not less than 450mm [18in]) rules out the fitting of a conventional metal or PVCu eaves gutter. Hence it is conventional to omit the gutter, and where it is necessary to secure good drainage of the ground on the line where the rainwater drops, this is assisted by installing a land drain of 75 or 100mm (3 or 4in) diameter clayware pipes with open joints, embedded in a trench filled with broken brick hardcore or pea shingle, and surfaced with garden earth.

RESTORING PITCHED ROOFS WITH NEW MATERIALS

Although use of the original roofing material in any re-roofing is to be recommended in all cases, in some instances, perhaps for reasons of excessive cost or unavailability of an obsolete product, it may prove impractical to adopt this policy. In addition to the traditional materials, there are some modern products that can provide durable roof surfaces of reasonably period appearance.

Fibre Cement Slates

A form of synthetic slate or tile has been in use in Britain since Edwardian times. Asbestos cement slates were used from around the turn-of-the-century to roof sports pavilions and similar 'temporary' buildings of lightweight construction. Their use produced pink, diagonally gridded roof planes which were susceptible to early disfiguration from algae growth. In more recent times, they were used as a low-cost substitute for slate on roofs where the natural material had deteriorated to a point where piecemeal repairs were inadequate. Worries over the health hazard posed by the inclusion of asbestos-based products in buildings have prompted manufacturers to cease production of asbestos-cement slates and to substitute mineral fibres for the asbestos formerly used as the binding agent for the Ordinary Portland Cement which is the main ingredient of this material. The arrangement of bond, lap and fixing for fibre-cement slates is exactly the same as that for natural slates, but because the fibre-cement sheets are much lighter than the quarried material, the tail of each slate has to be restrained against stripping by the wind. This is usually achieved by locating a disc-headed copper rivet in the narrow joint between the slates of the course below and hooking the lug of this rivet through the top slate via a hole provided for this purpose. All the ridge and hip details suited to natural slate may be used for the synthetic substitute and the half-round or tapering semi-cone-shaped ridge and hip tiles, which are also available as fibre-cement products, are appropriate to these locations. However, mitred cutting of the slates is difficult unless a powered disc cutter is used with great care, and precautions should be taken against inhalation of the resultant dust, which, though likely to be less harmful than asbestos-cement dust, could provide problems for respiration. Even when it proves possible to form mitred slates for use at the hip, it may be difficult to obtain secure fixings for these irregularly-shaped slates.

As the natural colour of Ordinary Portland Cement is a rather lifeless pale grey, a blue-black coating is applied to the proprietary slates so that a reasonable approximation to the colour of Welsh slate is achieved. There is no doubt that in new roof coverings, this 'semi-gloss' coating distinguishes the material from the matt surface of natural slate. Following a few years' exposure to polluted city atmospheres, the surface begins to resemble that of natural slate as the sheen of the applied finish recedes. Abrasion of this surface from particles contained in rainwater also causes the self-colour of the fibre-cement to start to 'grin through' giving a streaked or blotchy appearance which has some affinity with the look of weathered natural slate roof coverings.

Fibre-cement slates are readily available in the two sizes most common in natural slate used on houses; the *Countess* of 250 × 500mm (20 × 10in) and the *Duchess* of 300 × 600mm (24 × 12in). They are normally guaranteed by the manufacturers to last for thirty years.

Concrete Tiles

The familiar profiles of clay plain tiles, pantiles and even large natural slates are reproduced in a modern roofing material that is in widespread use today – plain and interlocking concrete tiles.

With the exception of stone slates, interlocking concrete tiles are the heaviest generally available pitched-roof covering. The slate-like tile was the first type to be introduced, and it can be laid to a roof pitch as low as seventeen-and-a-half degrees. The flat top surface of these 'interlocking slates' displays a matt finish similar to that of natural slate, but the machine-made appearance of each unit and its considerable thickness (necessary to maintain the integrity of this cast-concrete product) which is most apparent at any open verge, reduces the resemblance to natural slate. Being a concrete or 'reconstructed stone' product, the tile will remain in place by its own weight on a roof of low pitch and nailing may not be needed. The bolder, corrugated or 'pantile' profiles that are also available are only suitable for more steeply pitched roofs, and a proportion of these tiles must be nailed rather than simply located on the battens. It is clear that the pantile-profile tiles more closely resemble the clay products on which their design is based than does the flat variety that aims to reproduce a slated surface. The ribbed or corrugated types of interlocking concrete tiles have to be accepted as a frankly modern system of roofing although they bear only a slight resemblance to clay plain tiling through the coloured finish applied by the manufacturers, despite the makers' many ingenious efforts to create an 'antique' look in a new roof covering by subtle shading of the finish applied to a proportion of each sorted pallet of tiles. A reasonably convincing copy of Cotswold stone slate or North Country roofing is also achievable through the medium of reconstructed-stone concrete tiles which have been moulded to give a markedly 'rustic' shape and surface texture.

Because of the enormous weight of the concrete covering, a careful assessment must be made of the capability of an existing roof structure to accept the increased load. In the mid 1970s one inner London borough was experiencing annually some twenty roof collapses in houses where the original slates had been replaced with interlocking concrete tiles without any attempt having been made first to reinforce the roof structures. Many of these houses were terraced dwellings erected in the Edwardian period. If such a change of roof covering is planned for any older house, it is advisable firstly to obtain the opinion of an architect, structural engineer or building surveyor on the suitability of the existing structure to accept the increased load.

Most manufacturers of concrete tiles offer the standard tile as part of a roofing system, so that special verge and valley tiles as well as ridge and hip tiles compatible with the standard product are available.

Bituminous Felt

The underslating felt, which should always be installed below the battens or counterbattens of any pitched roof clad in tiles, is a less durable version of the bituminous felt that is sometimes used to finish small areas of flat roof and the pitched roofs of ancillary buildings such as summerhouses and garden sheds. This stouter type of felt usually has a granular surface, which may be green or red if it is not the natural blue-black colour. To offer acceptable durability it should be at least three layers thick with flashings into any adjoining masonry, and saddle-section ridge cappings formed in additional thicknesses of roofing felt. It suffers the shortcoming of all continuous sheet materials that it is likely to be badly affected by climatic extremes; contraction or expansion of the felt or the boarding on which it is laid

eventually causes blisters or fractures in the felt which will open up and admit rainwater or melted snow to the boarding below. For this reason, felt should only be regarded as a means of covering house roofs temporarily, pending the application of more permanent materials. The increasingly untidy appearance of ageing felt roofs supports this recommendation.

Bituminous Wash

Slated roof surfaces that appear to have been coated with grey or matt black paint are a common sight in areas of older housing. They are the result of an expedient that attempts to defer the 'evil day' of re-roofing – the application of a bitumen-based paint to the surface of the slates with the intention of rendering weathertight a decaying roof surface.

It should be clear that a main advantage of a roof covering of small, overlapping units is its capacity to tolerate thermal movement in the structure – the slates or tiles are able to slide backwards and forwards over each other without endangering weathertightness. Once covered with a continuous skin of paint which does not match this flexibility, this property of the slating becomes disadvantageous because the extremes of surface temperature experienced in Britain over a year will produce hair cracks in the paint film, drawing water by capillary action on to the increasingly porous surface of the slates. The rainwater will accumulate at places from which it was formerly able to drain away and if these spots coincide with decaying, delaminating slates, it will enter the roof. Therefore the application of bituminous paint to slating may actually accelerate the decay of the roof covering and its use cannot be recommended if an enduring repair of defective construction is sought.

SHEET METAL ROOF COVERINGS

As well as the tile-type roof coverings and thatch, the third main roof-covering method used in the early twentieth century and still practised today is the cladding of structures with malleable metal sheeting. At the turn of the century, lead and copper were the materials most commonly employed, but zinc became quite popular in the early decades of the twentieth century, not least because it was cheaper than the other metals. However, it weathers to a rusty colour that is not nearly so attractive as the whitish patina that forms on lead or the brilliant blue-green of oxidising copper.

Sheet metal is most noticeable as the roof covering of those cupolas and turrets of Edwardian houses that are either too small or too awkwardly shaped to be finished in tiles, slates or shingles. In terms of durability, copper is to be preferred to lead for the purpose of covering steeply pitched roofs and domes because it remains static whilst lead tends to 'creep' under its own weight and the expansion and contraction induced by exposure to the wide range of temperatures experienced over the year (sheet copper is about one-sixth of the weight of sheet lead of equivalent durability).

Where copper is laid on pitched roofs of any shape, allowance is made for expansion and contraction of the metal by joining the sheets with flattened welts (joints formed by folding together the edges of neighbouring sheets). A secure fixing of the metal to its substrate is achieved by folding into each welt at 600mm (2ft) intervals copper clips about 120mm (5in) long and 50mm (2in) wide which are nailed to the roof boarding.

Other details familiar in the sheet-metal cladding of cupolas, domes and spirelets are also used in flat roof coverings and are described in the following section.

FLAT ROOFS

Sheet Metal Coverings

It is an advantage of sheet metal roof coverings that they can be laid to the very low pitches (12 degrees and below) conventionally classified as 'flat' roofs.

Where copper is used on flat roofs, roll joints are generally employed. Copper clips about 190mm (7½in) long and 40mm (1½in) wide are nailed to the roof boarding at 900mm (3ft) centres below the line of a timber roll of tapering section, the roll being about 32mm (1¼in) wide at the top, 40mm high and 40mm (1½in) wide at its base. The edges of the copper sheets are then turned up against the roll on each side and the clips are bent down and turned over these edges. The roll joint is completed by the addi-

tion of a continuous copper cap that has stopped ends where the roll is not terminated against a vertical surface. Alternatively, the sheets flanking the tapering sides of this 'batten roll' can be flanged over at the top, parallel to the roof surface (Fig. 108). A prepared capping strip is then folded and slipped over these two flanges, and the whole assembly is dressed down the sides of the roll. The joints of sheets that lie in the path of draining rainwater are formed with a *double-lock cross-welt*. Where the sheets meet brickwork at the top of the slope, they are turned up the wall surface under a copper flashing continuously fixed into a horizontal joint of the masonry. The junctions of rolls with the wall are capped by purpose-made copper saddle pieces.

Copper coverings of flat roofs may also be found with the joints of sheets formed as *standing seams* or *flattened welts*. It is difficult to guarantee the water-tightness of flattened welts where they run across the slope of the roof and standing seams (effectively, welts which are left projecting up from the roof surface) cannot be used on flat roofs where much maintenance traffic is expected because they are easily damaged. When renewing copper roofs it is important to obtain a perfectly level surface of the substrate as any projecting nail heads in the boarding may eventually punch through the copper sheet. Above the boarding a continuous layer of brown flax felt or building paper should be laid to lessen the possibility of 'wearing' of the underside of the sheet metal on top as it expands and contracts.

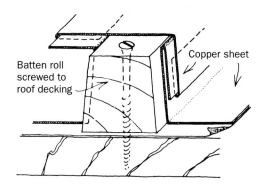

FIG. 108. Batten roll joint of sheet copper roof covering.

The same care in the preparation of the sub-surface is essential in the renewal of *lead* flat roofs. This material is the metal most widely used for covering small roofs over bays and dormer windows as well as for flashing pitched-roof surfaces to adjacent parapets, dormers and chimney stacks.

Lead sheet is available in two forms, *cast lead* and *milled lead*. Though cast lead is the more difficult to obtain today, it was a familiar roofing material until the First World War and it is more durable than the milled product. Cast in sheets from the molten metal, it is not of a consistent thickness. Sheets containing flaws and sand holes should be re-cast because it is hazardous to apply such material to any roof surface, particularly steep roofslopes where creep of the lead under its self-weight will act to enlarge any small fissures or voids.

In common parlance, lead continues to be specified by its weight in pounds per square foot, though '5lb' lead is also currently termed 'Code 5' and so on. The weight of lead sheet commonly used for flashings, soakers and roof coverings varies between 4lb and 8lb (1.81 and 3.6kg) per square foot, the heavier – and thicker – material obviously being more durable. Because lead sheet expands and contracts considerably with changes of temperature, the length of any one piece used for a gutter lining or flat roof covering should not exceed 2.7m (9ft) and the fall of a gutter or roof surface should be not less than 25mm (1in) in 2.7m (9ft). If the pitch of a 'flat' roof exceeds 75mm (3in) in 3m (10ft), the lead sheet is induced to creep down the slope and, with a rise in temperature, the sheet metal covering will expand but not contract back to its former length when the temperature falls; this permanent stretching will eventually produce cracks in the surface.

Milled lead being normally only available in rolls up to 600mm (2ft) wide, and the maximum recommended length of sheets being 2.7m (9ft), there are very few lead roofs that can be renewed without forming joints between adjacent sheets. The joints fall into two categories; those sited across the flow of rainwater (*lap* and *drip* joints) and those parallel with the flow of water (*rolls, hollow rolls, seams* and *welts*). Like copper, lead sheets may be joined with flat welts or seams. These are made by fixing lead, copper or stainless steel clips at about 600mm (2ft) centres at

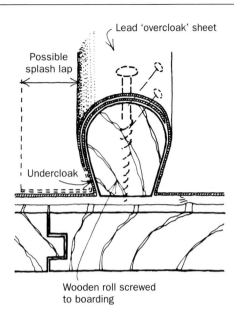

FIG. 109. *Solid roll joint of sheet lead roof covering.*

the junctions of the sheets. One sheet is bent up against the clip which is hooked over it and the adjoining sheet is bent over both as an *overcloak*. This profile is then folded flat on to the lead roof surface. On flat roofs, such welts are not as reliable as rolls in excluding rainwater.

Wooden rolls for lead coverings are made round or 'loaf shaped' in section in contrast to the tapering profile of copper rolls. Usually they are about 50mm (2in) in diameter and are best installed at the joint of sheets by screw fixings into the roof decking (invariably butt-jointed or tongue-and-grooved boarding in Edwardian or inter-war construction). The sheet lead is then dressed around the roll and tucked well into internal corners at the interface with the boarding to obtain a firm grip. This lower sheet or undercloak is dressed to half the height of the roll and tapered off with a rasp to a fine edge. The sheet is then nailed to the roll along this edge and the overcloak is dressed completely over the roll and its partial lead covering to finish on a line on the flat not less than 38mm (1½in) beyond the further face of the roll (Fig. 109). Sometimes this *splashlap* or narrow extension of the lead on to the roof surface is omitted, for if snow is likely to lie for long on the roof, it is possible that

FIG. 110. *Lead-clad finial and concave curves of the corner-turret roof of an Edwardian villa.*

water produced by the melting snow will be drawn up over the roll between undercloak and overcloak by capillary action. To obviate this possibility, the overcloak may be dressed over only about three-quarters of the roll. In either case, the free edge of lead should be on that side of the roll which is *not* exposed to the prevailing wind (generally south-west in Britain).

Rolls without a wooden core – hollow rolls – have been extensively used for centuries on the steeply pitched roofs of churches and in Edwardian houses they may be found on porches, roofs of bays, cupolas and convex, concave and ogee roofs of turrets (Fig. 110). They are made by fixing to the boarding with two brass screws, at the joint of lead sheets, a lead or copper clip every 600mm (2ft). The edges of each sheet are turned up the clip in exactly the same way that a seam or welt is formed, but the greater width of material allows the combined thicknesses of lead to be formed into a hollow cylinder. Although this detail is watertight, obtaining a consistent thickness in the completed rolls demands great skill from the plumber. Because they are fragile, hollow rolls are unsuitable for use on flat roofs where even infrequent

foot traffic is anticipated. Rolls of both types are usually sited at about 500mm (20in) centres, a spacing determined by the standard width of mass-produced milled lead sheet. Lap joints should not be found on flat roofs because good practice restricts them to horizontal joints on the inclined surfaces of lead-covered pitched roofs. Where a steep pitch is lead covered and a short lap of sheets (say 100mm (4in)) is sufficient to keep the surface watertight, lead clips fixed to the boarding and sited at 600mm (2ft) centres are used to restrain the edge of the lap, because high winds endanger the adherence of sheet roof coverings. Shallower roof pitches call for correspondingly deeper laps to resist water penetration by capillarity and an uneconomical use of lead naturally results.

The problem of joining adjacent lengths of lead sheet in gutters and on anything more than the smallest flat roof is overcome by treating the area as a number of planes, slightly inclined and raised a little one above the other by low steps called *drips* which should not be more than 2.2m (7ft) apart (Fig. 111). Drips in existing construction are commonly about 50mm (2in) high, though 75mm (3in) is to be preferred if it can be achieved in any reprofiling because of its better resistance to water penetration by capillarity. Thus a drip joint is simply a lap joint with a step built into it (Fig. 112). Where it is impracticable to improve an existing step to a height of at least 50mm (2in), a groove should be formed in the vertical surface before the lead is dressed over. If this anti-capillarity groove is omitted from a shallow drip, water will be drawn up through the lap, leading to rotting of the substrate.

Where flat roofs terminate above vertical surfaces, the lead covering may be formed in a nosing that allows the metal to shrink or expand freely. This is achieved by nailing a half-round timber moulding on to the vertical surface. The horizontal leadwork is then dressed around the moulding and the flange forming its underside is secured against wind action with lead clips (Fig. 113). Alternatively, a welt may be formed as the nosing at the top of the vertical surface. In this case, lead, copper or stainless steel clips must be folded into the welt and fixed to the edge of the roof decking to anchor the joint of the sheets. Where a lead flat roof abuts a wall surface, the roofing sheets are turned up against the masonry and cloaked by a

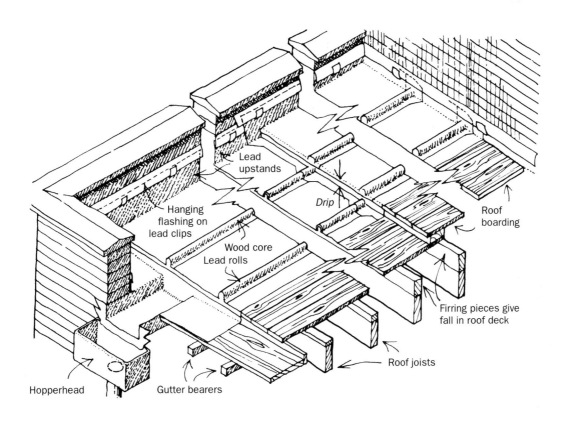

FIG. 111. Sheet-lead flat roof construction.

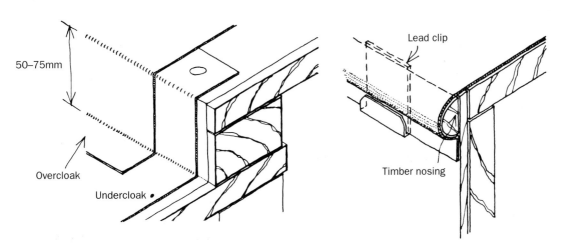

FIG. 112. Stepped (or 'drip') joint of sheet-lead roof covering.

FIG. 113. Edge nosing of a sheet-lead flat roof covering.

flashing secured in a horizontal bed joint with lead wedges. In exposed locations it is also necessary to restrain the lower edge of this cover flashing with lead clips, spaced at regular intervals. Most DIY stores now stock rolls of thin lead sheet, pre-bonded to bitumen adhesive, a material that has done much in recent years to simplify repairs to gutters and flashings. However, it will not endure for the sixty to eighty years normal for the pure metal where it is correctly installed.

As a highly malleable material, it should be no surprise to learn that lead sheets can be welded together satisfactorily and, by the same technique, defects in the material may be patched to restore watertightness. Welding also plays a part in repairs to lead-lined parapet or valley gutters where sheets of excessive length were used in the original construction and it is not acceptable or practicable to revise timber substrates to the profiles demanded by current practice. One or two companies manufacture a product that unites two sheets of milled lead (not exceeding 600mm [2ft] deep) with a flexible

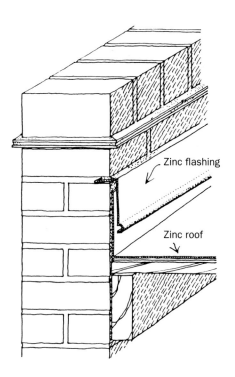

FIG. 114. Junction of sheet-zinc flat roof with parapet.

'Neoprene' gasket. These sheets may be welded (*lead burned* in trade parlance) to the retained or new lead sheets to either side, replacing an overlong sheet susceptible to early corrugation and cracking with one which offers an integral flexible joint that will take up thermal expansion and contraction before the lead is affected, thus lengthening the lifespan of the construction.

The third type of period sheet metal roofing is *zinc*. It is lighter and cheaper than either copper or lead but will not last as long. In polluted industrial areas it may be good for only twenty years, though forty years is its usual lifespan under average conditions. It is worth noting that zinc is quickly corroded by cat's urine, suggesting that zinc-covered flat roofs should be inaccessible to these pets. Zinc sheet is less liable to expand than lead, but it moves more than copper and this property is acknowledged in its detailing. No. 14 gauge zinc is the minimum grade used for roofing and joints between sheets are formed in the roll-cap system (similar to the batten-roll method of laying copper roofs) or with standing seams. The latter method is much more popular in mainland Europe than the UK and it is also more appropriate to pitched roofs than to flats because of risk of damage to seams from maintenance traffic. In the treatment of roll ends and corners, the most important difference between zinc and lead is that zinc can be bent but not 'bossed' (formed to a domed shape) or dressed into corners. When the work is done by the plumber, angle junctions are formed by cutting and soldering. *Soldered shields* are used to clad the roll ends, and saddle pieces similar to those employed with copper sheet are used where walls abut vertical surfaces. Elsewhere, soldering should be avoided because it may restrict the capacity of the zinc to move without fracturing. As sheet zinc can be obtained in widths of up to 900mm (3ft), the rolls on which it is joined may be set further apart than the spacing dictated by milled lead. Drips can be spaced as much as 2.8m (9ft) apart, and hanging flashings of the roof covering against perimeter walls – also carried out in zinc – differ only from the lead detail in that the bottom edge of the metal is turned into a 'bead' to stiffen the edge (Fig. 114).

Because lead sheet is quite thin and does not lose any shape to which it is formed, it is often used for

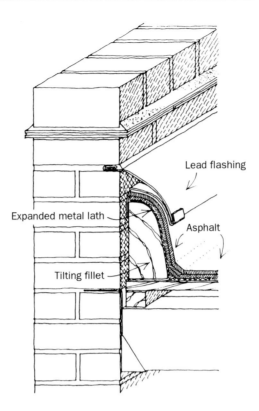

Lead flashing

Expanded metal lath

Asphalt

Tilting fillet

FIG. 115. Junction of asphalt
flat roof with parapet.

soakers below hips of slated roofs and under mortar fillets masking the joint of tile-type roof coverings with parapets and chimney stacks. Its susceptibility to early deterioration in city atmospheres suggests that any outworn zinc soakers should be replaced with sheet lead fittings.

Asphalt

Even in the mid-nineteenth century it was appreciated that sheet-metal coverings were unsuitable for flat roofs over which there was likely to be much foot traffic. For this reason, asphalt was adopted as a finish for the flat roofs of many city and large industrial buildings and it is also the roof surface of many bays, porches and other small, flat-roofed projections on older houses.

Rock asphalt consists of rock impregnated with a natural pitch called bitumen. The asphalt used for roofing is mastic asphalt which, at best today, consists of a mixture of rock asphalt imported from mainland Europe and bitumen-rich Trinidad lake asphalt from the Caribbean. Asphalt is laid hot in at least two layers to a total thickness of 20 or 25mm (¾ or 1in). If it is carefully installed, it forms a sound and substantial covering for flat roofs. It can also be used on vertical and sloping surfaces and it is conventional to form skirtings to an asphalt flat in the material itself. Where it is turned up against an abutting wall surface, its thickness must be increased to three coats in order to guard against splitting as the different substrates expand and contract at different rates. The particular risk posed by a right-angled junction with a flank wall is tackled nowadays by installing a triangular bitumen fillet against a timber kerb clad in expanded metal lath, over which the asphalt is carried to give a watertight upstand which can 'slide' below a continuous lead flashing built into the wall (Fig. 115). The problem posed by applying asphalt to deep vertical surfaces or sloping planes is the tendency of the material to creep under its self-weight – a characteristic that is heightened by its exposure to sunlight. Such movement eventually opens up splits in the surface, which will admit water. On flat surfaces this shortcoming is mitigated by laying light-reflective white limestone chippings across the asphalted area, but this solution cannot be adopted on sloping sections or on roofs which regularly carry foot traffic. A special solar-reflective paint is sometimes applied to these panels and it undoubtedly increases the lifespan of the material.

One great advantage of asphalt over other forms of sheet roof covering is its tolerance to being 'patched' in situ. Small repairs may be made to a damaged surface by flooding the affected area with molten asphalt after the defective section has been cut out. The eventual physical breakdown (or 'embrittling') of the material is delayed by careful preparation of the substrate and it has always been safer to lay asphalt on thermally stable roofs of solid construction (such as concrete or stone slabs) than on boarding. Where an asphalt roof on boarding is to be renewed, the plane-boarded surface *must* be covered with a bituminous felt separating membrane before the asphalt is laid. The felt then acts to isolate movement in the boards from the asphalt, the natural elasticity of which may not be sufficient to absorb such movement. Where the asphalt meets vent pipes or other features which project above the roof surface, it is dressed around the projection in the manner of an asphalt skirting but the top of the asphalt must be shielded and this is done by fixing a metal collar to the projection which cloaks the joint of the different materials.

Bituminous Felt

Bituminous felt is often used as the finish of new flat roofs or the new surface of old roofs. The limitations of the material were indicated in the earlier section of this chapter: Restoring Pitched Roofs with New Materials, but it is necessary to add that the tendency of felt to stretch, deform and puncture under long-term exposure to the weather is much less marked in its use on flat roofs than where it is pressed into service as a pitched-roof covering, because the essential precaution of covering felt on a flat with light-reflective stone chippings reduces thermal movement. To further stabilise the condition of the finish, it is also advisable to ventilate the substrate on which it is laid so that a fairly consistent temperature and moisture content is maintained within the decking. This policy accounts for the colony of small mushroom-shaped ventilators that are sometimes seen 'sprouting' from felted flat roofs. A good specification and careful workmanship are the best guarantees of durability in a three-layer felt flat roof, though the performance of this finish is invariably inferior to that of rock asphalt.

Flat roofs finished in sheet metal or asphalt – materials tolerant of thermal movement – are also prone to the internal deterioration that sometimes befalls felted flat roofs. The incorrect positioning of the impervious vapour barrier, or worse still, its omission, may cause an increase in the moisture content of the timber decking, creating conditions conducive to dry rot and with disastrous consequences for the entire building construction. Opinions differ on the best position for the vapour barrier, but it would seem safest to locate it on the warm side of the roof insulation. Where an existing flat roof construction is being relined internally, a useful vapour check is automatically incorporated by installing aluminium foil-backed plasterboard as the new ceiling surface.

CHAPTER 6

Upper Floors, Internal Walls and Staircases

UPPER FLOORS

Floors constructed from timber joists supporting wooden boards constitute the vast majority of upper floors in Edwardian and inter-war houses, despite the enthusiasm of 'advanced' architects of the 1930s for forming all elements of structure of even small houses in reinforced concrete. In addition to the floor load, wooden floors usually carry the weight of ceilings of plaster and wood, fixed to their undersides. In the building construction integral to modest houses, which is the main subject of this book, *single-joisted floors* were the most widely used form of wooden upper floor. In the single-joisted floor, the members span the entire distance between the bearing walls, and their ends either rest on wallplates incorporated in the masonry, or are built directly into the supporting walls. In the rarer *double-joisted floor*, the joists rest on wooden beams (also termed *binders* or *bressummers*) which are supported at their ends by the bearing walls.

The joists of a single-joisted floor are commonly spaced between 300–450mm (12–18in) centre-to-centre and vary in size, related to the distance they are required to span, from 75 × 50mm (3 × 2in) to 280 × 75mm (11 × 3in), though the vast majority of timber floor joists used in house construction are of dimensions not exceeding 200 × 63mm (8 × 2½in).

Where the joist ends are built into thick external walls, best-quality work provided padstones (or stone 'templates') to support these members because they are less liable to be crushed or displaced by the loaded joists than is common brickwork. However, the danger of damp entering the joist ends through the thin residual section of wall is not obviated by this detail. Chapter 4 notes that outside walls were often reduced in thickness at the top of each storey, providing ledges to accommodate the continuous timber wallplates to which the joist-ends were fixed by skew-nailing. Alternatively, wallplates could be bracketed off a wall surface on a continuous brick corbel or iron angles built into the masonry. Both of these methods more securely insulate the joist ends from damp penetration than building-in and the projecting construction could be concealed behind the curve of the cornice of the room below the floor.

Logic dictates that floor joists also terminate on internal walls. In this case, a wallplate permitting simple timber-to-timber fixings was sited on top of the internal wall. Any 'packing-up' of joists sited on an uneven surface to achieve a common level was usually effected by installing thin slivers of slate beneath joist-ends; wood packings were less satisfactory as they are easily crushed. Even where joist-ends were built into the walls, the timbers will tend to topple over or curl out of position unless some side-restraint is provided and the measure adopted in traditional construction was the installation of *herringbone strutting* – short struts of timber, in section 38 × 63mm (1½ × 2½in), fixed diagonally between the joists, to which they were nailed (Fig. 116). Scrap wood was often used for this purpose. A quicker method which, however, required greater accuracy from the carpenter in the fabrication of components, was to fix short lengths of joist tightly between the main spans. In either case, the strutting

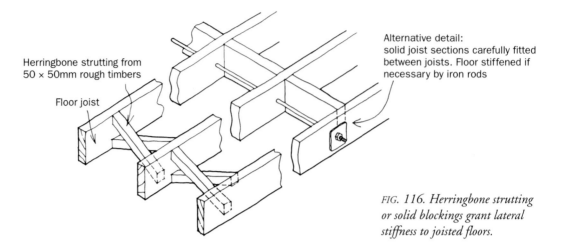

Herringbone strutting from
50 × 50mm rough timbers

Floor joist

Alternative detail:
solid joist sections carefully fitted
between joists. Floor stiffened if
necessary by iron rods

*FIG. 116. Herringbone strutting
or solid blockings grant lateral
stiffness to joisted floors.*

would be fixed at not less than 1200mm intervals along the joists, so that a room in which the joists spanned only 3.6m (12ft), and where the builder considered that lateral restraint was necessary, would contain only one central range of strutting. In small houses where the spans are short (say 3m (10ft)), there may be no strutting to stiffen the joists, but its omission from small areas of floors will not cause problems. Although unusual in domestic construction, where floors were required to carry large loads, iron tension rods were sometimes drilled through the joists alongside the solid struts. Tightening the nuts at the end of these rods compressed the struts and the floor was thereby stiffened.

A complication in timber floor construction that arises in almost every upper-storey room is the integration of the fireplace hearth and its flammable contents into a fire-resisting structure. Reconciliation of these apparently incompatible demands was achieved by forming a zone of floor, clear of all timbers, in front and to the side of the fireplace. This was done by terminating three or four joists on a line about 600mm (2ft) in front of the chimney breast, with their ends housed in trimmer or cross-joist, transferring the load from that area of floor to flanking trimming joists built into brickwork to either side of the chimney breast. These three timbers, framing the void in which the hearth was constructed, were conventionally up to 25mm (1in) thicker than the standard floor joists (Fig. 117).

Brickwork was then the main means of filling the hole to provide a fireproof hearth, in the form of a trimmer arch ('semi-vault') which spanned between the body of the brickwork of the chimney breast below, through a section of segmental arch, on to wedge-section timber plate nailed to the side of the trimmer (Fig. 118). On top of this semi-vault some other incombustible material such as tiles or strong cement provided a finish level with the floorboards, extending out at least 450mm (18in) in front of the grate and 150mm (6in) to either side of the fireplace opening. In good-quality construction, a hardwood border was fixed around the hearth to give a neat finish between it and the boards.

The original floorboards are likely to be one or other of two distinct types and qualities. A floor of plain-edge or square-jointed boards comprises 'second-quality' boards nailed directly to the joists, each board having a plain, butt joint edge-to-edge with its neighbour and being between 150–250mm wide (narrower boards, nominally 100mm (4in) wide may be found in some of the youngest inter-war houses). A tongued-and-grooved or *matched* floor consists of selected material, the joining edges of which have been machine-moulded with a tongue-and-groove profile so that the boards interlock. Such 'T & G' flooring is often 22–29mm (⅞–1⅛in) thick and was always secret-nailed in the original installation. The nails were driven into the upper angle of the tongue (Fig. 119), and in hardwood boards they

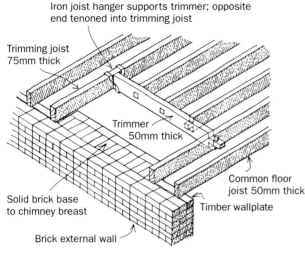

FIG. 117. *Aperture in joisted floor to accommodate hearth.*

would be punched in so that their heads lie well below the surface of the wood. The grooved edge of the next board then covered the tongue, hiding the fixings. Thus only one line of fixings was necessary and fixings through a board's top surface were confined to the first and last boards abutting the walls.

Though matched flooring appealed to the original occupants as a means of excluding draughts, its advantages are much less obvious in the modern home. The boards being fixed through their tongues, it is effectively impossible to remove them without damaging these mouldings, and even if the boards can be removed intact, their successful reinstatement may be difficult because the tongues tend to deform

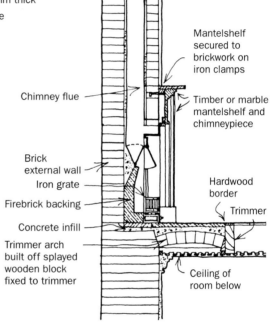

FIG. 118. *Cross-section through chimney flue, fireplace and hearth.*

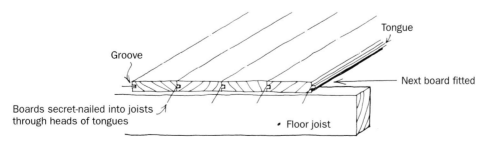

FIG. 119. *Secret fixing of tongue-and-groove floorboards.*

or splinter as the boards are taken up. Operations such as rewiring, or the installation of central heating, which usually necessitate the temporary removal of individual boards, may make a T & G-boarded floor seem like more of a liability than an asset. On reinstating a previously raised board over a pipe run or cable route, it is advisable firstly to remove the tongue so that the board can function as an easily removed access trap for future maintenance or replacement of services.

An even more frustrating form of floor decking which may be encountered in the largest Edwardian houses is the *double floor* in which a surface of tongue-and-groove boards is laid on top of a plain boarded substratum. The advantage of such extravagant construction for the builder lay in the opportunity of completing the coarse work such as plastering and the first coats of painting over the plain-boarded sub-floor, which granted easy access to all areas, yet was able to tolerate damage from this heavy work. The better-quality T & G boards would then be laid on top of this sub-floor when the joinery work was in progress. To prevent shrinkage in the boards of the sub-floor from causing open joints in the finished floor, the lower layer of boards was often laid diagonally across the joists so that the top layer, laid at right angles to the joists and nailed into them through the lower-level plain boarding, was also aligned diagonally to the sub-floor. In this way, shrinkage of the lower boards tended to pull the upper boards together more tightly. In reinstating the upper layer of such floor-deck construction, it is essential to fix the boards through to the joists, not just to the sub-floor boarding, as otherwise future shrinkage of the sub-floor will cause the top layer of boards to buckle and split.

Brick Jack Arches

Although it is a form of construction more common in commercial buildings than in houses, ground floors spanning basements in large Edwardian villas were sometimes formed from a series of shallow brickwork vaults or *jack arches*. These segmental brickwork vaults were usually of quite small span (not exceeding 2m [6ft 6in]) and were built side-by-side in series in order to obtain a soffit as close to a flat plane as possible. This was achieved by arching the brickwork between inverted wrought-iron 'T' sections, which spanned between the side walls (Fig. 120). The top, ground-floor, surface of this construction was then made level by infilling the spaces over the springing of the arches with fine rubble or mass concrete and forming a level floor finish in concrete or a sand/cement screed.

Concrete Floors

Reinforced concrete upper floors are unusual as a form of upper-floor construction in any period house, except for the arrangements adopted in many Modern Movement dwellings of the inter-war

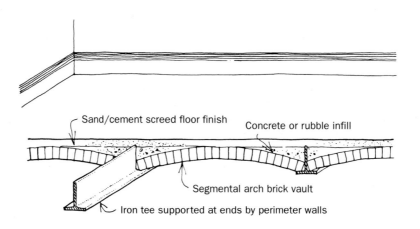

Sand/cement screed floor finish

Concrete or rubble infill

Segmental arch brick vault

Iron tee supported at ends by perimeter walls

FIG. 120. *Solid suspended floor formed from brickwork jack arches.*

period. The principle of reinforced-concrete construction is that steel bars are cast into the concrete at the time it is formed in the temporary moulds (*formwork* or *shuttering*) in order to provide stiffness in vertical elements such as walls or columns and, more importantly, tensile capacity in horizontal members such as beams or floor slabs.

Although this combination of materials offers many advantages, including lighter and less space-consuming structure/construction and the possibility of ready adaptation of floor plans to suit changing circumstances (particularly where a reinforced-concrete structural frame has been employed), it is not without its disadvantages, a condition dealt with in the later chapter on problems of Modern Movement dwellings. However, it is plain that one advantage of a concrete floor construction is that it is sufficiently stiff and solid to accept a wide range of floor finishes, from the most fragile and light-weight cork tiles, through to the heaviest types of stone slabs.

Floor Finishes

Although in modern construction, solid concrete floors are generally covered with a level sand/cement screed 50 or 75mm (2 or 3in) thick, and it is left to the occupier to provide his own floor finish in the form of carpet, this was not the practice followed in Edwardian houses. A considerable range of floor finishes was available even before the First World War. Sometimes the finish was also the floor construction that was intended to exclude rising damp; this applied particularly to stone and slate-slab basement or ground floors. Slabs of stone or slate in thicknesses between 32 and 63mm (1¼–2½in) thick were simply laid on a roughly level surface with no damp-proof membrane between the floor finish and the earth. By the start of the twentieth century, this treatment was extremely rare as ground-floor construction in houses lacking basements, because it was more or less obligatory to provide a mass concrete oversite slab in these circumstances, but it continued to be the means of providing a floor finish in many cellars. According to the normal condition of the ground, such surfaces may not be affected by dampness, although slate slabs will prove more impervious to rising damp than other types of natural

stone. A superior arrangement where slate formed the floor finish over a concrete slab, was adopted in the halls and kitchens of the many of the more expensive Edwardian and inter-war houses and placed thick slate slabs on mortar bedding on continuous minimally 100mm (4in) thick concrete.

Tiles

More popular than natural stone as a floor covering were the many varieties of tiles. The proliferation of small tile factories still operating in the Edwardian years produced a bewildering variety of tile patterns which it may be difficult, if not impossible, to match with modern products. However, Edwardian tiled-floor finishes can be categorised into four main types.

Quarry Tiles. In spite of their title, quarry tiles are *not* quarried from the ground. Like bricks and roof tiles, they are a fired clay product and the name is probably a corruption of the French word *carré*, meaning 'square'. Like many clay products, they were mainly manufactured in Staffordshire, though a famous brand of 'Heather Brown' quarries originated at Ruabon in North Wales, where they are still made today. Staffordshire quarries have traditionally been available in red, blue and buff, and they were a favourite floor covering for kitchens, larders and downstairs lavatories.

Quarry tiles are normally unglazed, the vitrification caused by the firing process granting them the silky top surface they normally display. Staffordshire quarries could be up to 300mm (12in) square and 38mm (1½in) thick, 225mm (9in) square being also a standard size, although the 150mm (6in) square tile is nowadays the most familiar size and in Edwardian times these were 25mm thick. Contemporary tiles of this face size are 19mm (¾in) thick. Plain *geometric* floor tiles of quarry-tile type came in smaller sizes too; 115mm (4½in) square, 75mm (3in) square, and so on, in diagonal halves of these sizes (triangles) and in octagons, hexagons and diamond shapes. Rectangular tiles were also made for use in border strips. These geometrics were normally 13mm (½in) thick.

From this great variety of types it was possible to form tessellated paving in an almost unlimited range of designs, and patterns unique to individual rooms will be found in expensive Edwardian houses. The quality and complexity of tiled-floor designs in Edwardian houses was closely related to the status of the rooms so treated. The areas seen by visitors; the garden path to the front door, the entrance hall and conservatory, received most attention and displayed the showiest tiles and tiling patterns. Kitchens and sculleries not visited by guests would have cheaper floors of six-inch square quarries, red tiles being the most favoured material. In such floors of one colour, it was unusual to find the gridded layout generally adopted in new work today; the tiles were often laid with staggered joints, in the same manner as stretcher bond in brickwork, or they might be laid diagonally.

Modern quarry tiles are laid on a minimum 10mm (⅜in) thick bed of sand and cement mortar on a recently laid 20mm (¾in)-thick floor screed of the same mix, on concrete. Alternatively, they can be laid directly on to a firm surface (preferably concrete) with a stiff mortar mix at least 16mm (⅝in) thick. A thicker mortar bed reduces the likelihood of obtaining a level surface in the finished work. Where new tiles are used to replace broken units or to extend an area of antique tiles, it is necessary to match the new material to a thoroughly-cleaned sample tile taken from the existing floor. Most modern tiles are thinner than the Edwardian products, making it necessary to build up the mortar bed below the patched-in unit or area. Where cracked tiles have been lifted, the imprint of the tile backs is left on the mortar bed, and if the thickness of the new tile is identical to, or greater than that of the original unit, it will be necessary to carefully chip away at this profile to provide depth for the new mortar bed.

The width of joint in the old work must be followed, and it is clear that using very fine joints, with the tiles butted closely together, was the normal policy in Edwardian construction. However, in entirely new quarry-tiled floors, it is advisable to adopt an 8–10mm (⁵⁄₁₆–⅜in) wide joint to conceal small irregularities in the tile shapes, which may be more characteristic of the modern product than the period tiles. If it is difficult to incorporate a damp-proof membrane below a newly quarry-tiled ground-floor finish, this is unlikely to invite problems from rising damp because the tiles are as impervious to ground water as they are to cleaning water. In a modern, centrally heated environment, quarry-tile floors will expand and contract appreciably, so that an expansion joint, filled with cork strip, and pointed with polysulphide or silicone mastic, at the junction of the tiling with the enclosing walls, reduces the risk of fractures which are unsightly, trap dirt and draw in moisture.

Quarry tiles are simply cleaned by mop, using one of the proprietary floor cleaners, dissolved in warm water. To give a lustrous finish to any tiled floor, the traditional treatment after cleaning was the application of a thin slick of warmed linseed oil, which was allowed to penetrate the tile surface before a wax polish was applied. Rapid wearing of the wax seal encourages yellowing of the linseed oil, which also attracts dirt, and this treatment cannot be recommended as a practical policy today when modern cold-wax polishes will prove to be both easier to apply and more durable.

It has been noted that quarry tiles were sometimes used for paving garden paths and external terraces. Fractured tiles in such locations are as likely to result from severe winter weather as from impact damage from, say, a garden roller, because quarries are not immune from frost attack. Therefore it is wise to restrict the thinner modern tiles to sheltered locations if they are to be used externally.

Because they are extremely hard and dense, quarries are notoriously difficult to cut. Rather than adopting the laborious technique of 'nibbling' away the excess area of a tile with a hammer and chisel, where many tiles must be cut neatly (as at an exposed joint between floor finishes) it is well worth hiring a powered rotary tile cutter from a local tool hire service for the purpose.

Encaustic and Transfer-printed Tiles. These types of tiles allowed more intricate designs in tiled floors than quarry tiles, because they not only contributed to the overall tiling pattern, but each tile also incorporated its own motif. Encaustic tiles were produced by stamping a design into the body of a plain clay tile when still in its plastic state. The depressions so formed were then filled with liquid clay of a contrasting colour before the tile was fired, producing a tile with a design created from at least two colours of clay. The surface of the tile was level and the pattern was generally contained within each individual tile, although it could extend over a series; in this way it was possible to achieve a large number of varied designs for differing floor surfaces. *Incised tiling* is a version of the encaustic tile. This variation on the principle retained sunken lines or patterns so that, like the joints between individual tiles, they might be filled with cement of contrasting colour after the tiles were laid. Encaustic tiles were always expensive because a good deal of handwork was involved in their manufacture and they cannot be obtained as standard 'catalogue items' today. They continue to be available to order from one or two Midlands tile companies.

Most decorated tiles produced both in the late nineteenth century and the Edwardian years aped the appearance of the encaustic tile by printing the desired pattern on the tile surface, a treatment which naturally produces a less durable product because the pattern is prone to wear off where tiles are exposed to foot traffic and regular cleaning. These *transfer-printed* tiles were originally produced by transferring a dark outline, drawn on tissue paper, to the dried tile. This design would then be coloured in by hand before the tiles were glazed and fired. Later, the development of lithography made it possible to print flat areas of colour directly on to the tile surface, dispensing with the need for hand painting. Tiles of this type (carrying only superficial decoration) are much more likely to be found in middle-size Edwardian houses than are encaustic tiles.

Ceramic Mosaic. Mosaic paving in which the small elements, or tesserae, providing the design, are made of clay, is distinguished from marble mosaic and vitreous mosaic (in which the paving material is glass) by the title *ceramic mosaic.*

'Roman' ceramic mosaic comprised 13mm (½in) tile cubes, which were laid in succession, or in a series of concentric arcs. Tending to be adopted in only the most opulent Edwardian houses, this treatment was accomplished either by placing the tesserae one-by-one in position on a prepared bed of cement and afterwards levelling the pavement before the cement set, or by a clever technique of the manufacturer in which the pieces were fixed with glue, face downwards on a full-size drawing of the design. The complete pattern was then divided into manageable sections and these fragments were taken to their intended positions in the house where the mosaic pieces with their paper upwards were placed on a prepared bed of cement and carefully levelled. The paper pattern was afterwards removed by soaking it in water. It should be clear that repair or restoration of such a delicate construction is best left to an expert paviour.

Marble Tiles. Where it can be afforded, marble in small slabs has for long been used for paving entrance halls and passages because it is admired as a stylish and very durable floor finish. Almost endemic to the material was the familiar pattern of white tiles 300 or 450mm (12 or 18in) square, laid parallel, or diagonal to, the enclosing walls. Also popular, and yet more elegant, was the combination of white octagonal tiles with smaller square black tiles set diagonally to them. Old tiles may be 19–25mm (¾–1in) thick, but their modern replacements may be as thin as 10mm (⅜in) for 150mm (6in) square slabs. Normally they are laid on a thin bed of cement and sand mortar on a level concrete sub-floor, but some varieties of marble are stained by Portland cement and so should be bedded on, and pointed with, one of the special cements called *Keene's* or *Parian.*

Varnished Boards and Wood Blocks

Boarded surfaces of joisted upper floors were often covered with sheet floor finishes; carpet, rugs, oilcloth or linoleum. Alternatively, boards might be left exposed to be varnished or polished, a treatment usually applied in the case of expensive beech, oak and maple-boarded floors because these timbers exhibit distinctive colours and patterns of grain for which they are admired. Often such boards were quite wide, giving an opulent effect in contrast to the standard plain-edge deal boards found in meaner Edwardian houses. The 'fitted carpets' conventional today were hardly known throughout the Edwardian and inter-war years; where carpets were laid on wooden floors, the boards were usually exposed between the edges of the carpet and the enclosing walls. To grant an acceptable appearance, these sections of boards received a dark oak stain followed by a glossy varnish and, in bedrooms, it was the

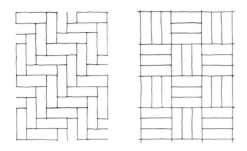

FIG. 121. Herringbone (LEFT) and basket weave (RIGHT) patterns in wood-block floor surfaces.

convention never to carpet under beds; raw boards sufficed as the floor finish in these locations.

Where they could be afforded, wood-block floors were popular as they are durable and quiet in use. Because of their small size, wood blocks (sometimes known as *parquet*) cannot do the structural job of boards which, in spanning between the joists, stiffen a suspended timber floor. Therefore, parquet is generally laid on a solid sub-floor of concrete or brick vaults levelled with a sand/cement screed. Individual blocks are commonly 75mm (3in) wide, from 225–375mm (9–15in) long and 25mm (1in) thick. Connections between the blocks were made with dowelled or tongue-and-groove joints, with complete interlocking of the units generally being achieved by adopting herringbone or basket-weave patterns in the blocks (Fig. 121). The blocks were often secured to the sub-floor and protected against rising damp in ground floors by setting them in a thin bed of hot bitumen. Unfortunately, this pitch bedding becomes brittle with age and the consequent loss of adhesion will lead to loose or hollow-sounding areas which it may be possible to replace or secure only by taking up and relaying a large area of floor. A durable repair can be effected by using an appropriate modern epoxy adhesive that will provide a more secure fixing than the adhesion achieved with the original bedding material. A wide variety of timbers was employed for such wood-block floors, including mahogany (light red-brown), teak and oak (light yellow-brown where unstained). Mahogany is liable to indent slightly with use. Among softwoods, pine and fir were also used in wood-block floors.

Sheet Coverings

It has been noted that carpets in Edwardian and inter-war houses rarely extended to the enclosing walls of rooms; they appeared as large rugs, bordered by a rim of exposed, stained and varnished boards, tiles or wood blocks. In the same way, stair carpets never extended to the full width of the stair flight, but were bordered by the exposed timber treads (usually 'grained' rather than painted) to either side, the carpet being secured at the junctions of treads and risers with stair rods of wood or brass.

The most common 'overall' surface for cheap, boarded floors was *linoleum*. This is made from powdered cork mixed with mineral fillers and oxidised linseed oil and resins on a jute canvas backing. Pigments were added to this compound to achieve the desired colours, which in the 'lino' that dominated sheet-flooring materials until the 1960s, were many and varied. It was also possible to inlay a pattern through the whole thickness of the material or to print it on the surface. *Oilcloth* is an inferior form of linoleum, being simply canvas coated with an oil that sets hard, though the two terms often seem to be interchangeable in common parlance.

It may be possible to find stocks of old material in small, traditional carpet shops, but because linoleum has been largely superseded by sheet-vinyl floor coverings, the small range of products which still exists is unlikely to contain many of the elaborate patterns of former times (often imitating wood-block or marble flooring), these products having been discontinued by the manufacturers in favour of simpler designs and plain colours.

Granolithic and Terrazzo Paving

Most of the floor finishes already described were used in the main living rooms of middle-class houses, but cellars and service rooms (termed 'domestic offices' in the grandest houses) often did not merit even a slate-slab floor, and various types of 'composition' flooring were employed instead. The means did not exist to 'power-float' the top of a concrete slab, a method which is used today to achieve a smooth floor surface, and although a thin sand/cement screed could be laid on concrete to achieve a smooth walking surface, this material is prone to dusting with wear, a drawback not entirely overcome by attempts to seal and paint the surface. A small improvement over the short-comings of a sand/cement screed was effected by the adoption of *granolithic* as a jointless floor covering. Although today it is always laid on a concrete sub-floor, a firm and roughly level surface sufficed for many Edwardian speculative builders. The material consists of Portland cement and fine hard stone chippings in definite grades and proportions, and produces a hard, grey surface that is almost as prone as a regular sand/cement screed to dust where it is not sealed. Because it is jointless, the surface can be turned up the surrounding wall surfaces to give a matching skirting.

The laying of granolithic is a skilled job. The top surface is levelled and steel-trowelled, and is then allowed to cure for seven days under a covering of wet sand or sawdust. Small repairs to cracked granolithic can be made with sand/cement mortar. In view of the 'patched' effect this produces and the material's tendency to dust, coating the surface with a propri-etary floor paint is recommended.

Terrazzo is a more exotic form of granolithic, and may be found as a finish for floors and stairs in Modern Movement houses of the 1930s. Instead of chippings of indigenous hard stone and ordinary grey cement, terrazzo includes chippings of imported marble together with coloured cement. According to the size and colour of the marble chippings and the colour of the cement binder, a wide range of effects can be achieved, ranging from a fine-grained black finish, through pronounced patterns incorporating large chips of vivid green marble to an almost homo-geneous white terrazzo, again containing very small chippings of white marble carried in a matrix of white cement.

Nowadays, new terrazzo floors tend to be of pre-cast material (small slabs to the required finish are cast, cured and ground-off at the factory, before being taken to the site where they are laid on a thin sand/cement mortar bed to provide the finished floor). Older installations were always of *in situ* terrazzo, laid as a continuous surface in the same way as granolithic, the main distinction with terrazzo being that the surface was laboriously ground off level when the material had set in order to expose the 'sliced' marble chippings, giving visual 'texture' in a somewhat abstract pattern. This surface was then polished to give a shiny, marble-like surface and durability may be improved by coating the floor with an appropriate clear sealant.

Because it was recognised that continuous surfaces of *in situ* terrazzo may be prone to crack with expan-sion of the material itself or the concrete floors and stairs to which it is applied, brass *parting strips* were often incorporated to break the floor finish into smaller bays. These features will not entirely prevent cracking unless the resulting bay sizes are quite small (not exceeding 2m (6ft 6in) square). Consequently, it is common to find a considerable number of hair cracks in even quite recently laid *in situ* terrazzo surfaces, and as these can only be removed by cutting-out the affected area and patching-in new material, with detrimental results for the appearance, it is often better to tolerate these small defects, making sure that the clear sealant finish is maintained so that floor-cleaning liquids are prevented from entering these fine cracks, to cause worse distress to the floor finish.

INTERNAL WALLS

Other than the comparatively few Modern Movement dwellings incorporating structural frames that were erected in the inter-war years, British houses built before 1940 are universally of *mass* construction; that is, they rely on load-bearing brick-work or masonry to support the intermediate floors and roof. Except in the smallest houses, the unbraced 'box' of the external walls alone was insufficiently strong to guarantee the stability, in all conditions, of two or three-storey construction. Accordingly, certain internal walls were also carried out in brickwork or blockwork. These solid partitions supported the timber floor joists and the trimmers of staircase open-ings too, where these members could not be sited to span between the external walls.

Timber-framed Partitions

Internal walls that have no load-bearing function and simply subdivide the internal space can afford to be of lighter construction. They are normally assembled in the same way as balloon-frame external walls, with timber stud uprights 100 × 50mm (4 × 2in) in section sited at 300–400mm (12–16in) intervals, housed in continuous wooden soleplates at floor level and continuous head members which were fixed to the underside of the ceiling joists, with intermediate horizontal rails and cross-bracing to give rigidity.

It is important to recognise that the presence of timber-framed partitions does not guarantee that they play no part in supporting the structure. In many Edwardian houses, timber-framed walls were used to support the ends of floor joists, and where the plan allowed it, in large houses, such partitions might be carried up through two or three storeys, the top members of each wall panel supporting the joists of the intermediate floors. Where it was necessary to include wide openings in the internal walls of lower storeys (for example, double doors between inter-

FIG. 122. Diagonal structural bracing in the framing of a denuded upper-storey partition. (Robin Bishop.)

communicating ground-floor rooms), some degree of trussing, in the form of diagonal braces, would be included in the partition occupying the identical location in the upper storey, so that higher-level loads could be transferred down to the panels of partition flanking the opening of the lower storey (Fig. 122). It is clear that it is essential that the construction at the head of any existing timber partition is fully investigated before any attempt is made to adapt or remove it. It may be holding up a floor, part of the roof, or both, either in itself or through similar construction on an upper floor.

The fact that the floor joists run parallel to a timber-framed partition does not mean that the wall is not helping to support the floor. The ceiling plate of the partition may be supporting short blocking pieces that span between the joists (Fig. 123). It is possible, too that owners of Edwardian houses may find that seemingly solid internal walls are in fact, timber-framed partitions, the gaps between the studs and transoms being filled with solid *brick nogging*. This form of construction seems to have been an attempt to build rigidity into the structure whilst avoiding the laborious task of bonding partition brickwork into the external wall construction. It has already been noted that many Edwardian and inter-war speculative houses share the shortcoming that brickwork or blockwork internal walls were rarely bonded into the external brickwork; they simply butt up against an adjoining surface, allowing the two walls to move independently, with resultant cracking of the plaster internal wall finish. Timber-framing of internal walls or *bonding timbers* – horizontal wooden members, equal to the wall thickness, which are often found at around 450mm (18in) intervals vertically in internal walls – introduced a type of continuous construction which was probably intended to provide some 'tying-in' of the parts. These wooden members were also useful as *grounds* for fixing joinery (for example, doorframes at openings in the wall).

The brick-nogging of a fully framed partition may be a simple infill which it may be possible to be remove without adverse effect on the wall's structural stability (although the plan should be endorsed by a structural engineer and its removal will reduce the partition's sound-insulating properties) but continuous brickwork layered between bonding timbers

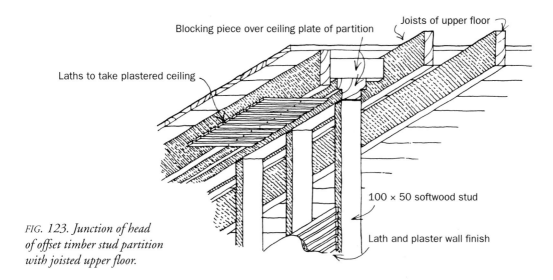

Blocking piece over ceiling plate of partition

Joists of upper floor

Laths to take plastered ceiling

100 × 50 softwood stud

Lath and plaster wall finish

FIG. 123. Junction of head of offset timber stud partition with joisted upper floor.

obviously supports these members and few bricks can be extracted before the stability of the wall is threatened.

Door Openings

A door opening in any internal wall naturally introduces a structural weakness. In a conventional half-brick-thick partition, door openings are almost invariably spanned by timber lintels, the brick panel above the door opening being built off the top surface of the timber. In later inter-war construction, concrete or steel lintels began to replace the wooden type and today, lintels of either type have entirely superseded wooden members, which are too readily overstressed and are susceptible to fungal and insect attack. In a timber partition, it was a simple matter to span a horizontal brace between the studs flanking a door opening to form a lintel. Where the partition is load bearing, it was good practice to incorporate double studs at each jamb so that the internal pair could support the lintel and gain stiffness from the outside posts to which they were nailed, and which extended up to the full height of the partition. The oversize gap opened up between the studs by the door opening might necessitate trussed construction above the lintel in order to transfer load down to the double studs framing the opening. Clearly, such an opening cannot be enlarged without the expert advice of a structural engineer first being obtained. Where

double studs exist, the lathing was sometimes terminated against the outer faces of the internal pair which, being deeper than the outer studs, could also provide a ground for fixing the architraves (the wooden 'trim' to a door opening) but in a timber-framed partition, it was more normal to fit a 'false jamb' into an opening formed slightly larger than the finished door opening. This deeper section of joinery granted the opportunity to correct small dimensional inaccuracies in the carpentry, as well as providing a surface against which to terminate the lath and plaster.

Wall Claddings

Lath and Plaster. Where airspace rather than brickwork formed the 'infill' between the members of a timber partition, no background was available for the conventional plaster wall finish and so some backing for the plaster had to be added to the face of the timbers. Before the advent of *plasterboard*, which slowly came into use in Britain from the 1930s, this was achieved by nailing horizontal wooden laths at very close intervals across the surface of the timber framing. The laths were most often thin riven or sawn strips of pine (the riven or split material was preferred for durability), nominally 25mm (1in) wide, up to 6mm (¼in) thick and about 1200mm (4ft) long, a gap of 6–10mm (¼–⅜in) being left between adjacent laths. The plaster was then applied

121

to this horizontally slatted surface, and it adhered to the lathing because some of the material squeezed through the gaps, causing the plaster to 'grip' the lathing on setting.

At a right-angle junction of two framed partitions there is a potential lack of fixing surfaces for the lathing. This problem was avoided by inserting a wider stud than the standard posts into the thickness of the main partition and against the end stud of the abutting partition (Fig. 124), thus providing a narrow timber surface for fixing the ends of the laths. This detail is equally helpful in modern construction as a means of providing an end fixing for the sheets of plasterboard that have replaced lath and plaster.

The plaster used in all Edwardian and most inter-war houses was composed of lime and sand, horsehair or ox hair being added to the mix to ensure cohesion of the material. To those familiar only with modern, lightweight gypsum plasters (for example, 'Carlite'), the traditional material is surprisingly heavy, even at its conventional thickness of 25mm (1in). This is readily apparent when the need arises to demolish the lath and plaster finish of a wall or ceiling, and this operation should only be undertaken with great care.

A hollow-sounding surface at all points on the plastered internal face of an external wall may betray lathing behind the plaster (localised 'hollowness' may merely indicate loss of adhesion of areas of plaster from its brickwork backing). Sometimes, plaster was applied to lathing on vertical battens fixed to the structure, rather than directly to the masonry, though this treatment tended to be reserved for irregular internal wall surfaces (encountered most frequently in solid rubble stonework construction) which would have required an impractically thick coating of plaster to give a smooth finish.

Where the laths remain behind a small hole in lime plaster, they will provide sufficient support for a 'patch' of new gypsum plaster. If they are damaged, an additional 'key' must be provided. If the hole is not more than 75mm (3in) wide, key is obtained by inserting into the hole a piece of jute sacking (or *scrim*) soaked in plaster of Paris before the new surface is formed with gypsum plaster. The repair of larger holes calls for the use of panels of plasterboard or sheets of expanded metal lathing, the former being

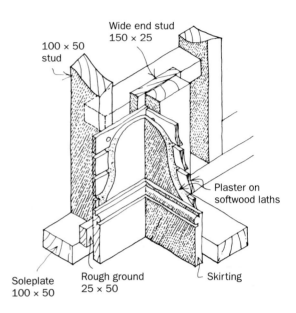

FIG. 124. Internal corner construction at junction of stud partitions.

fixed to the studs with short, galvanized clout-head nails at close intervals to provide a flat substratum for the new *in situ* plaster skim-coat finish.

Plasterboard and plastering. Expanded metal lath came into use during the nineteenth century and is the modern substitute for split or sawn pine laths. Much more convenient than metal lathing and in situ plaster if the complete re-cladding of an old partition is necessary is plasterboard, which is a prefabricated paper-faced sheet of gypsum plaster either 1.2 × 2.4m (approximately 4 × 8ft) or 0.9 × 1.8m (approximately 3 × 6ft) in area, being approximately 9 or 12mm (⅜ or ½in) thick. Variants of the standard product include sheets that are laminated with expanded polystyrene. This form of plasterboard may be used as a new internal finish for old external walls and offers the advantage of upgrading their thermal insulation.

Where small areas of defective plaster need to be replaced, modern gypsum plasters ('Carlite', 'Sirapite' and so on) will adhere well to the old lathing and are chemically compatible with the retained lime plaster, though it is unwise to re-coat internal surfaces of solid external walls from which corroded lime plaster has been removed with lightweight gypsum plasters. The reason is that gypsum plasters perform badly in damp conditions and breakdown of the new finish will occur quite quickly where these modern materials have been applied to the internal surfaces of damp external walls. A satisfactory specification for such work demands the application of a sand/cement render base coat, restricting use of gypsum plaster to a Sirapite finishing coat.

Curved or complex shapes or small surfaces in new work, like the underside of an arch, are best formed from timber framing clad in expanded metal, which is itself coated to the required profile with new *in situ* gypsum plaster. Installation of plasterboard sheets to create large flat areas is a fairly simple operation, but the skills required of a plasterer to achieve plain or decorative finishes are not easily learned and there is much to be said for employing suitably skilled tradesmen to carry out this work.

Although many elaborate mouldings in *fibrous plaster* (plaster profiles cast in moulds at the factory to produce prefabricated features later erected at the building site) became available from the mid-eighteenth century, cornices in rooms were often 'run' in *in situ* plaster in precisely the same way as external rendered ornament (that is, the required profile was formed in thin zinc sheet and this 'horse' was either run along short sections of the plaster mix on the bench to form the moulding which was then installed on the wall or ceiling, or run across 'green' plaster on the wall to create the desired feature).

For householders undertaking an ambitious restoration of an opulent Edwardian interior, a wide variety of fibrous plaster ceiling roses and medallions is produced by several manufacturers, though it is often difficult to find patterns of appropriately simple design and adequate size in the catalogues, most manufacturers wishing to replicate elaborate eighteenth-century designs in diminutive sizes suited to the small rooms of modern houses. Where no suitable design can be found from stock items, it is worth considering replicating any original mouldings that have survived in the house, as this is an exercise easily effected by fibrous plaster manufacturers, though the resulting bespoke moulding will be far more expensive than a catalogue item.

Skirtings. At the foot of a conventional plastered wall, whether it was of timber-framed or solid construction, a wooden skirting was installed. In Edwardian and inter-war houses many different patterns of skirting may be found, and Edwardian houses in particular display a bewildering range of mouldings, the products of myriad small joinery works, some of which may be extremely elaborate – especially those of the main and most prestigious living rooms of the house. Therefore it may be difficult to match exactly a complex existing profile with period-pattern mouldings generally available today, although several joinery manufacturers have recently expanded their ranges to include patterns from each of the more common types. Profiles similar to the simpler mouldings used in Edwardian and inter-war houses are readily available, one such being the 'Torus' pattern which is supplied in a range of heights (Fig. 125). In the final few years before the First World War there

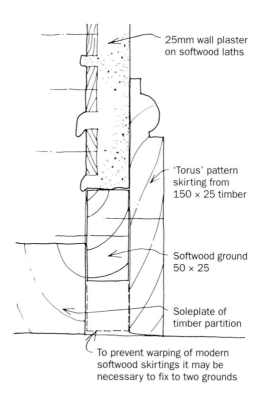

25mm wall plaster on softwood laths

'Torus' pattern skirting from 150 × 25 timber

Softwood ground 50 × 25

Soleplate of timber partition

To prevent warping of modern softwood skirtings it may be necessary to fix to two grounds

FIG. 125. Cross-section through Torus pattern skirting board trimming foot of plastered stud partition.

seems to have grown up an increasing preference for simpler joinery mouldings, particularly the 'ovolo' pattern which, together with the 'lamb's tongue' moulding, remained a popular form throughout the inter-war years (Fig. 126). The ovolo moulding had long been familiar in frames and glazing bars of timber windows, but from around 1910, this profile was also applied to skirtings and door and window architraves, often in preference to the 'ogee' type which was the first choice of late-Victorian speculative builders, and which can be found in Edwardian houses of conservative design.

Perfectionists may wish to consider commissioning exact copies of existing mouldings to obtain complete authenticity; most joinery works are able to reproduce surviving profiles in new material, though a small order will generate a disproportionately high cost for this service. Economical use of material tends to be untypical of Edwardian detailing; skirtings of drawing rooms of large villas might be of two or three

parts and as much as 350mm (14in) in height. Like other joinery items, including broad architraves around door and window openings and picture rails, skirtings were fixed to the walls through wooden grounds. In a timber-framed partition, these grounds were thicker than the laths by the thickness of the plaster finish, so that they would act not only as a fixing for the timber trim but also as an edge against which to finish the plaster (see Fig. 125). On brick walls, the grounds were fixed to wooden plugs or *pallets* built into the vertical joints between bricks. Fixing a continuous horizontal ground to the studs of a timber partition was a simpler operation. In a timber-framed partition constructed from modern materials, wooden grounds are equally useful because it is hard to obtain secure fixings into plasterboard for a skirting, even if modern 'toggle' fixings are used.

Wainscoting. The clear hierarchy of wall finishes defined by the Victorians continued to be applied in the first four decades of the twentieth century. Painted plaster was superior to painted brickwork and was favoured for service rooms such as kitchens and sculleries. Wallpapered plaster was better regarded and was certainly the most common wall covering, though superior to this were the forms of wooden wall cladding. Painted softwood panelling was second-best to a surface of polished hardwood, which was regarded as the most sumptuous and durable wall finish.

The shallow moulded skirting at the foot of a wall is the most minimal form of panelling, but wainscoting was a 'half-way house' sometimes adopted in the more costly Edwardian houses (rarely in inter-war dwellings) to provide a partially panelled wall finish in halls, on staircases and in passages which were subjected to heavy use. A *chair rail* was installed in front of a wooden ground not less than 900mm (3ft) above the floor to prevent chairbacks damaging the plastered surface. Between this rail and the skirting, continuous wooden panelling was inserted by the joiner. The resulting wainscot or *dado* might be painted or *grained* in imitation of a more expensive timber, if of softwood, or waxed and polished, if of hardwood.

Cheaper than a fully panelled dado was a surface of tongue-and-groove matchboarding of a type

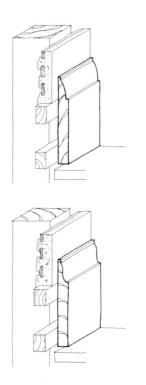

FIG. 126. (TOP) Ovolo-moulded and (BOTTOM) lamb's tongue-moulded skirting boards.

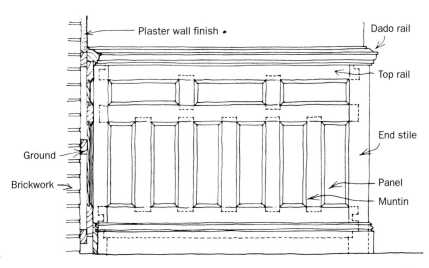

FIG. 127. Wainscoting.

similar to that used in flooring, but incorporating a bead moulding in the joints in this application ('bead-and-butt' boarding). This form of panelling was often used to flank minor staircases leading to roof-space servants' rooms. Although the construction of panelled wainscotings may differ according to their complexity, the basic principle of their assembly was the prefabrication of a framework of posts and transoms carefully jointed into each other which was infilled with panels of thin sheet timber, housed in grooves in the framing members and able to shrink and swell independently of the framework (Fig. 127). This arrangement is essentially that of panelled door construction, but on a larger scale. The frame and its infilling panels were assembled on the joiner's bench where the tenoned joints were clamped and glued together. The ground that finished the plaster on a horizontal line at the rear of the chair rail (applied as a separate moulding on top of the dado) was used as the top fixing for the wainscot, and the ground at the foot that secured the skirting board, also secured the underside of the panelling. An intermediate ground was usually provided for additional fixings along the horizontal centre-line of the wainscot, and in a long run of panelling, vertical grounds were also installed to provide further fixings at 2.4–3m (8–10ft) intervals.

Providing replacement timber comparable in quality to the original material can be obtained (to minimise the risk of non-uniform movement in the hybrid construction of the restored wainscot) the repair of panelled dados with modern wood glues and the ingenious fixing devices now available can be successfully executed by the skilful handyman.

Ceramic dados. Where resistance to rough treatment was the prime quality demanded of a wall surface in a porch, entrance hall, staircase or passageway, or for hygienic conditions that were essential in a bathroom, WC, or kitchen, a tiled or glazed brick dado, which required no maintenance other than an occasional wipe with a damp cloth, was sometimes installed. From the 1870s it became fashionable to incorporate dados of brightly coloured decorative tiles in the entrance porches of many speculative houses and in some cases this treatment was extended into entrance halls. The policy received a boost in the first years of the new century as *art nouveau* patterns of tile obtained great popularity (Fig. 128). *Faience* was also used in this application, a green glaze being the most popular finish for faience tiling, although ochre, maroon and peacock blue can be found among other distinctive colours. It was common for the tiles to carry some relief patterning; either built up from the general face or incised into the material. The latter effect was achieved by applying patterned metal dies to the clay when it was in its plastic state.

FIG. 128. Porch flanked by a dado and overpanel of art nouveau *tiles. Note also the heavily moulded entrance door (c.1905).*

Even today, faience tiling has institutional associations for many people – it is remembered as a wall finish in municipal slipper baths and similarly 'sanitary' buildings. For this reason, in many houses the original shiny surface of a tiled dado has disappeared behind cladding or sprayed and textured paintwork. With mild paint stripper and much careful effort, the latter finish may be removed to reveal the original surface, which will probably be found to be undamaged. Less easily concealed than the flat surface of the plain tiles is the moulded waist rail of matching material which invariably trimmed the top of such a glazed panel and which is equally susceptible to restoration by application of paint stripper and 'elbow grease'.

Panelling. A really sumptuous effect could be obtained in grand rooms by extending the panelled treatment of a dado to the whole wall surface, thus creating a completely panelled interior. To achieve this result, the techniques adopted for the assembly of wainscoting were simply extended to the entire wall area. Following the fashion set by avant-garde designers from the 1870s, by the start of the twentieth century it was widely recognised that full-height panelling was apt to make a room rather gloomy and it had become conventional to terminate panelling at an intermediate level, the remainder of the wall extending up to the ceiling being treated as a plastered and painted frieze. This frieze might be painted the pale plain colour of the ceiling or it could carry elaborate stencilled decoration in multi-coloured paintwork on a pale-painted background. Ending painted softwood or exposed hardwood panelling at an intermediate level on the walls was the favoured treatment for the low-ceilinged drawing and dining rooms which proliferated in Arts and Crafts Movement houses of the Edwardian era, because adequate natural lighting of these rooms, with their small windows, depended on some reflection of light from the pale ceiling and frieze surfaces. A deep wooden cornice moulding surmounting the top of the panelling was sometimes used as a shelf on which to display a frieze of decorated dinner plates or other items of 'blue and white' china. Painted, grained or varnished panelling is quite a rarity in all but the most expensive bespoke or speculative Edwardian or inter-war houses and deserves careful conservation where it has survived.

Doors

The plain surface 'flush' door familiar in modern buildings first appeared in the UK in pioneering Modern Movement houses of the 1930s but was not widely adopted in speculative house building until after World War II. Two main types of door are found in older houses: *ledged* doors and *panelled* doors.

Ledged doors. Although they were sometimes used as room doors in Arts and Crafts style houses, ledged doors were most often used as rear or side entrance doors. The simplest ledged door is formed from tongue-and-groove boarding nailed to three horizontal *ledges* (back bars) extending across the width of the door. This is a weak form of construction, and with use, such simple doors will 'drop' away from the hinged edge because they do not incorporate cross-bracing. The *ledged and braced* door avoids this difficulty. In this type of door, diagonal braces are introduced between the ledges to stiffen the construction, and if the door is hung from the side from which the braces rise to reach the 'leading' edge, it is prevented from dropping (Fig. 129). Making a new ledged and braced door from v-jointed tongue-and-groove boards and standard-size planed softwood planks is a straightforward job for a competent handyman.

A more sophisticated form of ledged door which was often installed at the external entrance to kitchens and sculleries was the *framed and ledged* door in which the boarded surface was framed with solid timber members which were tenoned into each other. The *stiles* (vertical framing members) and *rails* (horizontal members) of this type of door are as thick as the combined thickness of the boarding and a conventional ledge, but a regular back-bar is retained as the intermediate lock-rail or mid-rail which passes behind the boards so that an uninterrupted boarded surface appears externally (Fig. 130). Even more robust than this substantial form of door was the *framed ledged and braced* door, which added diagonal braces to the framing.

Panelled doors were almost invariably the original doors of Edwardian and inter-war houses, and those fitted to the cheapest houses represent the simplest kind of panelled joinery to be found in these dwellings. The frame of the door is formed from solid stiles and rails tenoned into each other. These members are grooved on their inside faces to accept the infilling panels which, before 1914, were slabs of solid timber as little as 8mm (⅜in) thick. In the inter-war years, *plywood* was introduced, allowing the infill panels to be thinner. Locks or latches were sometimes mortised into the leading edge of the outer stile of the door, but as the insertion of the lock-case could destroy the tenon which joined the mid-rail to the stile, in the best internal doors of expensive Edwardian houses, a single mid-rail was sometimes replaced by a pair of intermediate rails framing an additional shallow, central panel. In this way, the outer stile was left solid so that a mortise lock could be inserted without weakening the construction. In

cheap houses, this difficulty was avoided by the use of *rim locks*, which are applied to the face of the stile/mid-rail, thus obviating surgery on the outer stile. By the inter-war years, in contrast to the four-panel internal door universally adopted in late-Victorian and Edwardian houses, the danger of weakening door construction by the fitting of mortise locks and latches was reduced by introducing a

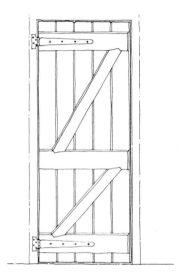

FIG. 129. A boarded, ledged and braced door.

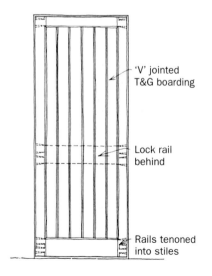

'V' jointed T&G boarding

Lock rail behind

Rails tenoned into stiles

FIG. 130. A framed and ledged door.

pattern of panelling which placed a deep mid-rail at quite a high level, below a broad top panel (Fig. 131). Alternatively, the mortise latch could be housed in the stile below the joint of stile and mid-rail, where it did not threaten the integrity of the door construction.

Some enrichment of the junctions between the panels and framing members was almost always included in panelled doors (only internal faces of panelled doors serving coal stores, under-stairs cupboards, and so on, being entirely devoid of decorative mouldings). The simplest treatment was a moulding formed on the inner edges of the stiles and rails to 'soften' the joint between framing and panels. More elaborate – and more expensive – was the adoption of 'planted' mouldings, enriching and sometimes masking these junctions (Fig. 132). This enrichment could be carried further by incorporating mouldings in the infilling panels themselves. Projecting panels of large internal doors (e.g. those serving the drawing and dining rooms of large Edwardian villas) are known as *raised and mitred* or *fielded* panels. These treatments are much more commonly found in front entrance doors where some show of status was thought to be necessary, and despite a general simplification of design (and therefore manufacture) encouraged by the larger building companies of the inter-war years, complex geometry and heavy

mouldings continued to grace front entrance doors down to the outbreak of the Second World War (see Fig. 28 in Chapter 2).

Internal doors of all types – single, double, folding or sliding – met wooden frames which were either inserted in the rough framing of a timber partition or a masonry opening spanned by a lintel. The wide joint of this 'finished' frame with the wall finish of the brick or timber background was concealed by a continuous moulded wooden architrave, which also terminates the skirting at floor level (Fig. 133). Like skirtings, architraves could be machined from one section of timber, or if a more complex appearance was wanted they would be assembled from two or more separate mouldings. A bewildering range of moulded profiles was produced by the many local joinery works operating before the First World War, which may make it difficult to match surviving trim with stock mouldings. The picture is different for inter-war houses because standardisation of components among a smaller number of larger building companies engendered a greater uniformity of style in the joinery trim of modest speculative houses and the ovolo moulding referred to earlier as an option for the treatment of skirting boards was even more generally adopted as the pattern for door and window architraves. Where stock mouldings cannot

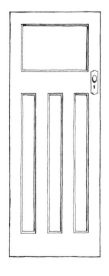

FIG. 131. A panelled door with high mid-rail.

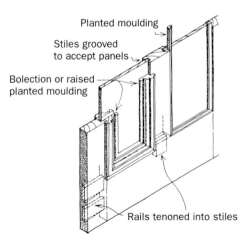

FIG. 132. Alternative treatments in panel-retaining mouldings of panelled doors: bolection or planted mouldings.

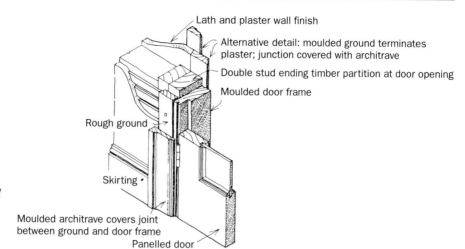

Lath and plaster wall finish

Alternative detail: moulded ground terminates
plaster; junction covered with architrave

Double stud ending timber partition at door opening

Moulded door frame

Rough ground

*FIG. 133. Jamb
construction at the
junction of panelled
door/doorframe/
plastered stud
partition.*

Skirting

Moulded architrave covers joint
between ground and door frame

Panelled door

be found to match the original material, most manu-facturers of architectural joinery will be prepared to copy surviving mouldings, machining an identical profile from solid timber sections of a stock size slightly larger than the desired form.

Glazed panels were almost as common an infill between the stiles and rails of panelled doors as the timber panels already described. In Edwardian houses in particular, internal doors, as well as panelled front entrance doors, sometimes incorporated colourful panels of stained and painted glass above the mid-rail. Clear glazing or translucent glazing in 'obscure glass' was also incorporated in fanlights over internal doors or other sections of internal wall construction such as partitions screening 'service stairs' (flights and landings of servants' staircases) from family accommodation, where it was necessary to borrow daylight from the better-illuminated main rooms.

Wall Finishes

Wallpapers. The use of wallpaper as a decorative wall finish was established in Britain in the sixteenth century, but the mechanised printing of wallpapers introduced in the nineteenth century brought about an enormous expansion of the range of papers and the number of firms producing them. Important innovations of the late nineteenth century were 'Anaglypta' and 'Lincrusta', dense papers into which a raised pattern was embossed during manufacture by

the use of metal dies. Anaglypta, formed from a hard-ened paper pulp, pressed into moulds to give the desired relief pattern, was durable and the cheapest of the relief wallpapers. Lincrusta was a more expensive material, its cheapest form being produced by spreading solidified oils on to paper, which was then pressed into moulds to produce patterns imitating low-relief decorative plasterwork. Both products were popular as low-cost substitutes for wood-panelled dados in areas of the house subject to heavy use such as the entrance hall or staircase. When painted or varnished after they were applied to a wall, the raised pattern remained prominent, giving a richer effect than that of simple, flat, printed papers.

The handful of national wallpaper manufacturers operating today are the direct descendants of the many firms that produced a vast range of papers in Edwardian times. However, changing fashions have dictated that very few of the patterns popular before 1940 are available now, although circumstances have improved somewhat with the recent revival of some traditionally patterned relief papers. Fortunately, smaller specialist firms also exist and it may be possible to find examples of patterned papers from their ranges which emulate the spirit and detail of Edwardian and inter-war papers.

Paint. The range of proprietary paints available in Edwardian times was much narrower than that available today. Although a few manufacturers offered pre-mixed distempers or enamels in a range of colours, it was conventional for painters to mix pigments at the building site in order to produce the hues required for interior or exterior decoration. The cheapest form of overall paint finish, often reserved for utilitarian rooms such as cellars, coal stores and washhouses, was *limewash*, a solution of powdered lime and water. It was also applied to the faces of external walls of yards and areas to increase daylight by reflection in these otherwise gloomy enclosures. A slightly superior material was *whitening* which was a solution of finely powdered chalk, size and water. This was more widely used than limewash as the paint finish for ceilings. It suffered the limitation of all distempers that the pigment or colour (in the case of whitening, white chalk) was not dissolved but merely suspended in the solution, and relied upon the size to fix it to the surface after the water had evaporated. Dilution of the mixture simply reduced the effectiveness of the size, rendering the colour unstable and liable to drop off the surface as a powder. This property accounts for the patchiness and dusty texture of the unmaintained distempered ceilings and friezes surmounting the picture rails of Edwardian houses that have not been modernised. White was the pigment most generally used in distemper, but pastel colours were also employed. Modern *emulsion paints* containing polycarbonates have enormously improved the performance of water-based paints, causing them to supersede the old distempers.

Oil-based paints have for long been viewed as superior to water-based paints. Modern gloss paint may owe its viscosity to a petroleum by-product, but Edwardian oil paint was based on linseed oil, which is produced by the compression of flax seed. It was the oil most used for house painting and could only be used where white lead gave pigment to the paint. *Boiled linseed oil* was used in combination with all powdered or dry colours.

An important limitation of the old oil-based paint and which contrasts with the performance of today's gloss paints, was its slowness in drying. It was also prone to discoloration after drying, light tones becoming progressively more yellow. Despite these shortcomings, it was preferred to water-based paints for the painting of wall surfaces that did not require

wallpaper (such as plain or patterned plaster friezes above the picture rail). Treatment of such freshly plastered areas ideally called for four separate applications of oil paint, the first two coats – which would be largely absorbed by the plaster – being mixed thinner than the finishing coats. On wide surfaces, the final coat was often applied in such a way that a matt appearance resulted. The special composition of the paint used in such 'flatting' caused it to dry very rapidly so that two, four or even six workmen might need to be employed at the same time in decorating a large wall surface in this way. Doors too were sometimes finished in 'flatted' paintwork, but as it was appreciated that better durability was obtained with a glossy surface, the general preference was to lay on the oil paint so that a gloss finish resulted. The high gloss of today's mass-produced alkyd paints could only be achieved by applying a clear varnish over the surface of the dried oil paint. At least one specialist paint manufacturer has recently recommended production of oil-based distempers and oil paints (both 'eggshell' and gloss) in a range of period colours.

As common a treatment of internal joinery in Edwardian and inter-war houses as oil paint in plain colours was *graining*. Through this process, essentially cheap timber was made to look like more expensive wood by applying patterns to its surface in imitation of the rarer timber's grain. Water-based paints were used for graining in imitation of softwoods (such as pine and fir). The grainer began his work only after the painter had given the new wood three or four coats of plain paint. His first job was to lay-on the graining ground, which differed in composition according to the wood to be imitated. On top of this ground, a further coat of paint matched to the tone of the desired timber was applied, and the grain of the wood was reproduced by drawing steel combs of different sizes across the still-wet surface. When the desired effect had been achieved, and the grained surface had dried, the finish was sponged down with a mixture of beer and whitening before over-graining with a thin coat of complementary colour, after which the final varnish coats were applied. Plainly, the apparent ease with which a convincing copy of the natural wood was obtained was owed entirely to the skill of the grainer, and among interior decorators competence in graining was rated much more highly than skill in plain painting. Happily, there has been something of a revival of interest in the decorative techniques of graining and *marbling* (paint treatments simulating the characteristic 'veining' of these metamorphic stones) in more recent times and an increasing number of specialist interior decorators, as well as enthusiastic amateurs, are practising these skills.

It is important to appreciate that period paints almost invariably relied upon lead compounds to provide the colour or to accelerate the drying of the paint. Although the adhesion of these old, lead-based paints on external woodwork compares favourably with the performance of modern paints (as house-holders who have laboured to strip these ancient coatings from original window-frames will testify) lead compounds can be injurious to health, and for this reason they have been excluded from modern paints. Indeed, it is only in relation to any essential use of traditional lead paints on listed buildings or works of art that an exception to the legal ban on these materials can be made. In these cases, it is necessary for the owners to certify to the manu-facturers that lead paint is required, before it may be made.

Despite the poorer adhesion of today's paints resulting from the omission of lead compounds, it must be said in their defence that they are much easier to apply than period products. In decades when labour was cheap (even in the 1930s, the outside of the average 'semi' could be redecorated for about £5) time could be lavished on the careful preparation and laborious application of purpose-mixed paints. The use of factory prepared, mass-produced paints spares the handyman an irksome sequence of tedious and very time-consuming procedures.

STAIRCASES

External Steps

A hard stone step was generally used as the threshold of a main entrance door, and in London and the south of England, Portland stone was favoured for this application. It was normal to slope the top surface of the step from front to back by about 3mm

(⅛in) to throw water off, and the front edge was often moulded as a *nosing*. In pursuit of the cottage ideal, Edwardian or inter-war houses erected on flat ground rarely incorporated ground floors raised substantially above external ground level, although steeply sloping sites might make this arrangement necessary, in which case a flight of stairs connected the garden path to the front entrance door. If carried out in solid stone steps, each step was made to overlap the one below by at least 38mm (1½in). Alternatively, the *treads* and *risers* might be made out of separate slabs, bearing on thin brickwork flank walls. A favourite material for the construction of external stairs in this way was York stone, the treads being made 63 or 75mm (2½–3in) thick, with risers 50mm (2in) thick. Where a stair flight was narrow (as in the case of external access stairs to a cellar) stone slab treads might be installed without risers.

Many risers below front entrance steps, although they appear to be stone, are actually formed from a type of 'artificial stone' – cast concrete with a stone-dust surface. Where this form of construction was adopted, the risers are often very thin (perhaps 19–25mm (¾–1in)) inviting serious damage to the material through heavy use and continuous exposure to the weather. Generally, this defect does not threaten the structural stability of the steps and cosmetic repairs can be carried out with sand/cement mortar.

Timber Stairs

Wood is the material most commonly used for stair building in dwellings. In the characteristic Edwardian London terrace house, which places the rooms of the back extension on mezzanine levels, the *dog-leg* stair was the type almost invariably used. In this type, the central well-hole is omitted, causing the handrail of the lower flight to meet the soffit of the upper flight because the outer *string* of the upper flight is vertically over that of the lower one.

A more generous arrangement, which allowed a continuous handrail guarding a central well-hole was the *open-newel* stair. More sophisticated still was the *geometrical* stair, in which the string (that is, the fascia forming the exposed edge of the stair flight) was continued, unobstructed by *newel posts*, in a curve around the well-hole. The existence of a string

131

inclined in elevation and curved in plan usually results from the incorporation of *winders* (radiating steps) in the staircase. By the Edwardian period, it was unusual to find examples of geometrical stairs in any but the grandest houses, although a fashion for the revival of eighteenth-century French urban architecture reintroduced this stair type in some central London houses of the years immediately preceding the First World War.

Straight-flight stairs

There are two distinct types of construction for straight-flight timber stairs, the first of which was normally reserved for rough work such as cellar stairs. In this version, rough timbers or *carriages* cut to the saw-tooth profile of the undersides of the treads and backs of the risers, were installed between levels, the wearing surfaces being simply fixed on top (Fig. 134). To obtain the wall string (or 'sloping skirting') abutting the stair, boards at least as thick as the standard skirting to which it was connected were cut to fit closely over the treads and risers. Clearly, it is very difficult to fit the wall strings satisfactorily, and even when a good fit is achieved, shrinkage of the timber and jarring of the wooden surfaces with continuous use of the stair are likely to reveal imperfections. A more satisfactory form of wooden stair construction is obtained where the individual treads and risers are *housed* (grooved) 10–16mm (½–⅝in) into the strings. In this arrangement, any carriages sited below the steps between the strings are not cut to the profile of the undersides of treads and risers but are simply standard joist-section timbers of sufficient strength to help support the stair and its likely load. Where a finish to the sloping underside of the stair was required, they served the additional purpose of providing a central fixing for the laths of the plastered soffit. These carriages were often *birdsmouthed* on to the trimmer that supports the landing at the head of the flight. Rough brackets nailed to the sides of the carriage and fitted tightly under the treads, to which they were secured with angle blocks glued in position, guaranteed a firm intermediate support for a wide stair flight (Fig. 135).

However, 'standard' staircases within speculative houses were generally constructed without such centre carriages. The strings in which the treads and

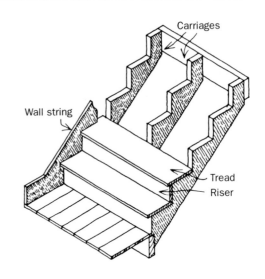

FIG. 134. Straight-flight timber cellar stairs.

risers were housed on both sides were deemed to provide adequate support. Although formed from only three basic elements – treads, risers and strings – the manufacture of such a staircase was quite a complicated operation, as is clear to anyone who inspects the debris resulting from a demolished staircase of even the cheapest speculative house. The string adjacent to the flanking wall – the *close string* – was first of all marked out with the profile of each step by drawing around a triangular template (*pitch board*) placed on the broad surface of the string on a line parallel to its top edge. Templates representing the thickness of the treads and risers but with sloping, rather than flat undersides, were then sited on these lines to give the outline of the housings. To form the housings, holes were bored 10–16mm (½–⅝in) into the string adjacent to the position of the nosing of each tread and a small amount of adjacent timber was cut away to give a guide for the straightforward removal of the rest of the wood with a saw and gouge. The grooves of the housings having been formed, the treads and risers were then located in the housings, jointed and glued together, and also glued to the strings. A close fit of treads and risers with the strings was ensured by driving hardwood wedges into the tapered parts of the housings remaining below and behind the treads and risers, thus forcing these

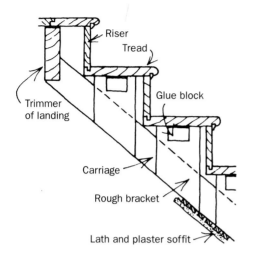

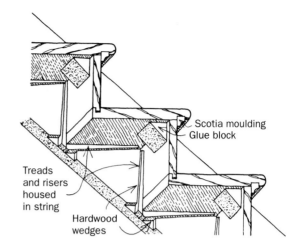

FIG. 135. Straight-flight timber stairs carried on rough brackets.

FIG. 136. Housed stair-flight construction.

components tightly against the slots in the strings (Fig. 136). The depth of string adjoining the stair (the top surface of which was always finished with a moulding except in the humblest stair flights serving cellars and attics) was reconciled with the standard skirting moulding on landings by ramping its top surface at the foot of the stair and incorporating a knee at its head (Fig. 137).

Various methods of joining tread to riser were practised. The full thickness of the riser was commonly housed into the underside of the tread behind the housing, the joint being reinforced with angle blocks. More sophisticated than this was a rebated joint of tread and riser. A simple butt joint of tread and riser was also widely adopted, woodscrews joining the tread to the riser at 300mm (12in) intervals to ensure that the two components did not pull apart (Fig. 138). An improvement in the appearance of the junction between the underside of the tread which was commonly adopted, particularly in Edwardian houses, was the housing of a small *scotia* moulding into the tread's underside to mask the adjacent joint (See Fig. 136 above).

Where stairs terminate over a cut string rather than against a close string (where the edge of the stair is exposed to view) the ends of the treads and risers were prepared to fit the return nosings and the shape

of the string. The risers were mitred at their ends to fit corresponding bevels on the string, whilst the treads were mitred behind the nosings to intersect with the return nosings. These latter pieces were machined from the same timber as the tread, and moulded to the same section as the combined nosing and scotia. When planted at the ends of the treads, they give the impression that the nosings are

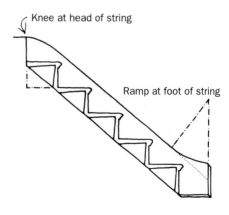

FIG. 137. 'Knee' and 'ramp' features at head and foot of close string of a housed-stair flight.

133

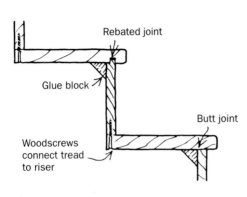

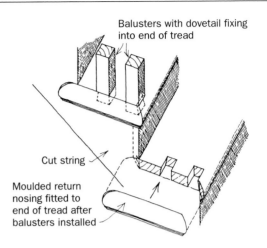

FIG. 138. Screw-fixing of timber stair treads and risers.

FIG. 139. Junction of balusters and treads over 'cut string' of timber stair concealed by moulded 'return nosings'.

continued across the ends of the steps. These *return nosings* also serve to conceal the dovetail sockets formed in the ends of the treads to accept the balusters that support the handrail and guard the open side of the stair (Fig. 139).

Balustrades to timber stairs

Where thin wooden balusters flank a stair flight showing a cut string (two per tread being the most common provision, though opulent Edwardian houses may display three balusters per tread) they give insufficient support to the handrail. Even where a proportion of these slender posts are of metal rather than wood, it is normal for the handrail to have an end-fixing into the underside of the stair's upper flight (in the case of a dog-leg stair), and/or into heavier and otherwise freestanding posts sited at changes of direction, called *newels*. Those placed at the bottom of a staircase are called *starting newels*, and at this location the centre of the newel post is normally in line with the face of the first riser. *Angle newels* at landings are usually less elaborate than starting newels, and are invariably smaller. Again, the face of the adjoining riser should be on the centre-line of the newel. There should also be a common centre-line to handrail, newel post and cut string and the centre-line of the balustrade should also be that of the cut string and handrail.

Balusters of almost numberless different designs may be found, particularly in houses erected before the First World War. In the last decades of the nineteenth century, ornate wooden balusters turned to a 'spindle' profile became fashionable, and this treatment continued to be applied in speculative houses until at least 1914. A square base gave a better fixing than a round end and the spindle treatment therefore tended to be restricted to the middle section of each baluster. Holes were drilled up to 25mm (1in) into the underside of the handrail to receive the tops of the balusters, whilst a dovetailed fixing into the treads prevented the balusters from pulling out if there was any settlement of the stair flight that did not equally affect the handrail (See Fig. 139 above).

Handrails surmounting such balustrades were usually of hardwood. If continuous over 2.4–3m (8–10ft) they were often stiffened with an iron flat-bar core 6–10mm (¼–⅜in) thick and 25–50mm (1–2in) wide, fitted in a groove in the underside of the handrail. The balusters were fixed to this core with screws, and the core was screwed to the handrail. The cheapest form of handrail was the plain deal *mopstick*, almost circular in section. A flat plane was formed on its underside to facilitate its connection to the balusters. In Edwardian houses, more complex mouldings were favoured, including the *toad's back* pattern (Fig. 140) in polished hardwood.

Some timber merchants stock a version of this section called the 'frog's back' handrail, but it is usually available only in softwood and is of much slighter section than the Edwardian prototype.

Lengths of handrail were butt-jointed together and, in the best work, secured with handrail bolts, which have a square nut at one end and a circular nut at the other. A hole for the bolt was drilled in the ends of adjoining lengths of rail as closer to the centre of the section as possible and the nuts were lodged in small mortises in the underside of the rail, the bolt then being screwed into the captive square nut. After this, the circular nut was tightened on to the handrail bolt by rotating it with a screwdriver engaging in slots in its surface. In this way, abutting lengths of handrail were drawn tightly together, and an inconspicuous joint was made more likely if two or more hardwood dowels and a glued connection were also incorporated at this point (Fig. 141). In the rare cases where wall-mounted handrails were required, they were normally supported on curving painted iron brackets screw-fixed to timber plugs set in the flank wall of the stair. Alternatively, if great strength was sought, the brackets could be built into the masonry as the wall was being erected.

Replacement and repair of timber staircases

As one of the largest timber constructions in an average suburban house, the staircase is particularly susceptible to attack from dry rot or wood-boring beetles. It is in danger from the dry-rot fungus because most under-stairs spaces are poorly ventilated, causing them to be both damp and warm, particularly if they provide access to a cellar. If dry rot is present, it may not become apparent until finishes (normally plaster over timber laths) are stripped away, revealing the skeins of fungus on the laths, and undersides of treads and risers. If this condition exists, the whole of the affected stair flight must be replaced. Where woodworm infestation is found (and damage from the common furniture beetle is very common in under-stairs spaces) a small area of timber peppered with the flight holes of the insects does not threaten the structural integrity of the stair, but a timber surface in which shallow channels unite these holes suggests that the internal substance of the wood has been largely eaten away. In the first case,

treatment of the timber with a wood preservative incorporating an insecticide will arrest the damage; in the latter condition, replacement of the ravaged wood is essential.

Timber staircases for use in houses continue to be made in the time-honoured way described above, and prefabricated stair flights, virtually identical in detail to the typical Edwardian or inter-war pattern continue to be made. However, the contrast with the bespoke installations original to Edwardian and inter-war houses lies in the dimensional format of these products. Modern mass-produced timber staircases are manufactured to comply with the requirements of current building regulations, particularly in respect of the prescribed maximum pitch of the stair, the depth, in plan, of the treads, and the height of the risers. The resulting pitch of the proprietary prefabricated stair and sizes of these critical components are unlikely to match the dimensions of an original wooden staircase, installed at a time when regulations were more liberal. The new, ready-made stair is almost certain to be of lesser pitch and will have been manufactured to suit a modern-house room height

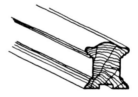

FIG. 140. A 'toad's back' profile moulded hardwood handrail.

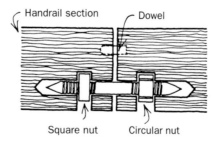

FIG. 141. Concealed bolt for joining lengths of hardwood handrail.

somewhat lower than that found in either a typical Edwardian or inter-war house.

This provides the first difficulty in any plan to use a standard prefabricated timber stair – the possibility that there is no single-flight proprietary item long enough to do the job. Of course, where an original stair was split into two or more flights, it is more likely that adaptation of standard items will produce an acceptable arrangement, but it will be appreciated that use of elements of lesser pitch than the original staircase also absorbs more space in plan. Thus, the price of adoption of ready-made elements that comply with current building codes may be the inclusion of a small additional area of floor – which might otherwise be put to other uses – for the purpose of accommodating the stair. The ready-made items sold by today's builders' merchants and DIY stores are made to standard formats, the most common widths of flight being 865mm (34in) and 915mm (36in). Stair enclosures marginally wider than these standard dimensions can be reconciled with narrower stairs by adding appropriate timber mouldings to the top surfaces of the unmoulded strings. Where replacement of an original staircase is unavoidable and there is general incompatibility between a proprietary item and the staircase zone/local construction, replication of the original arrangement is likely to be necessary, although the cost of manufacture of such a bespoke assembly will far exceed the price of 'off-the peg' timber stairs.

Metal Staircases

With the introduction of 'international style' modern-movement architecture to Britain in the inter-war period, the 'open plan' arrangement of many of these houses made it legitimate once more to incorporate metal spiral staircases as a prominent feature of interiors.

The metal spiral staircase had enjoyed its first period of popularity in the middle years of the nineteenth century when cast iron was still a recent addition to the range of materials used in building construction and there was a desire to demonstrate both the slenderness that could be achieved in spiral staircases of cast-iron construction and the decorative potential of the new material. Metal spiral staircases might also be incorporated in large houses and public buildings to grant access to basements, attics and library or conservatory walkways, in place of the more space-consuming, straight-flight or dog-leg stairs. Dislike of the products of modern industry and its concomitant, the enthusiasm for 'unselfconscious' traditional rural buildings which took hold in the final decades of the nineteenth century, caused the frank use of metals in domestic architecture to be disliked and metal staircases will not be found in Arts-and-Craft-style houses, though metal external escape stairs may have been added to some of these buildings in alterations to allow multiple occupancy.

By the time a further change of fashion towards modern or modernistic styling re-established the appeal of displaying the qualities of industrial products, ideas on what was acceptable as decoration had also changed and the elaborate naturalistic castings used for the stair treads, risers and balusters of metal staircases by the Victorians were unacceptable. So it is that modern versions of the metal spiral stair, from the examples incorporated in the earliest British modern movement houses of the 1930s, down to the catalogue items available today, tend to be of pressed steel (often with solid timber treads and open risers). Paradoxically, the fairly recent revival of interest in Victorian design has meant that many cast-metal staircase components first produced in the mid-nineteenth century are once again being manufactured and may be more readily available than the plainer patterns adopted in modern movement houses. Although there has also been a considerable revival of manufacture of components in cast iron, many small foundries continue to prefer to replicate period castings in aluminium, which appeals to them because of its lower melting point, ability to reproduce fine detail precisely and light weight in comparison with iron. When painted to match the appearance of surviving painted iron or steel construction, aluminium parts are effectively indistinguishable from the original components.

CHAPTER 7

Windows and Glazing

Chapter 4 External Walls, deals thoroughly with the treatment of window openings in outside walls, but it will be appreciated that the windows sited in these openings make a very important contribution to architectural design and many variations upon the types of windows described below are to be found in Edwardian houses, with only a little less variety apparent in houses of the inter-war years.

BAY WINDOWS

The most common type of complex window incorporated in Edwardian and inter-war houses is the bay window. By the late nineteenth century, most house builders had recognised that the sitting rooms of suburban terraced houses would seem more spacious and distinctive if their windows, located in the front elevation, could offer more than one aspect. Thus the square bay and the splayed bay window came to be a prominent feature of the street elevations of countless speculative dwellings, and in the inter-war period there was equal enthusiasm amongst builders for the curving, segmental bay, applied to many semi-detached houses as an alternative to the splayed bay, which remained in widespread use. A view up and down the road from such a window was as possible as a view across the street to the identical house opposite. Early morning or evening sunlight could slant into a room which, without a bay window, would merely face a sunlit street.

As an external architectural feature, the bay 'broke up' an otherwise sheer front elevation, creating shadows and gradations of tone which a flat surface would lack; it also suggested complex (and therefore expensive) construction and detailing and so provided a good 'selling point', although the embellishment accorded to the bay and any adjoining porch were usually superficial, such elaboration being restricted to the front elevation. Hence the additional expense of incorporating a bay, even in cheap houses, was thought worthwhile.

Construction of Bays

Bay windows may be multi-storey or single-storey. Single-storey construction is straightforward; the structure is conventionally of timber posts and lintels, or stone or brickwork corner piers bearing timber lintels and masonry arches, raised off a stone or brick dwarf-wall erected to the desired plan shape. Sliding-sash or casement windows were then inserted within this structure to form the facets of the bay. A timber roof structure was erected on top of the structural frame and covered with a finish either consistent with that of the main roof covering, or in contrast (for example, in deference to the enthusiasm for 'cottage' styling, and acknowledging the practical problems of covering the small surface areas presented by bay-window roofs, the bay of an Edwardian terraced house might be covered with clay plain tiles whilst the larger main roofslopes continued to be finished in Welsh slate).

Multi-storey bays might also be framed up in timber, and a rendered finish of the *spandrels* located between the windows of succeeding storeys usually indicates that there is a lightweight framing behind this weather-excluding coating. Panels of brickwork below the windows of upper-storey rooms dictated corners piers of brickwork or stone to support this heavy construction, so that the window area was restricted to only part of each facet of the bay and much of the transparency gained by the addition of a bay was therefore sacrificed.

Roofs of bay windows may be flat or pitched, and in Edwardian and inter-war houses they often comprise a structure of 75 × 50mm (3 × 2in) or 100 × 50mm (4 × 2in) timber rafters and 75 × 50mm (3 × 2in) ceiling joists, providing a flat soffit internally even where a pitched roof was employed. Flat roofs were finished in asphalt or sheet metal where surrounded by a parapet and were clad in metal where finished with a projecting eaves. Pitched roofs display most of the tile and sheet materials used on main roofs such as slates, clay and concrete tiles, pantiles, shingles, zinc, copper and lead.

The presence of a bay window can act to conceal distress in the main structure of a house of traditional mass-masonry, load-bearing construction. This applies because the wide aperture in the main wall which had to be formed to allow the floor plan to 'flow' into the bay was usually spanned by deep timber beams, some of the load on which might be lessened by a higher relieving arch (Fig. 142). Where the flashings capping the open joint of bay-window roof and front elevation are defective and allow rainwater to pass into the building fabric, rotting of the

beams at their bearings is a distinct danger and it is not unusual to see some evidence of distress in the form of open joints of sagging brickwork above the bay-roof apex as the rot-affected ends of the timber beams are crushed by the weight of superincumbent masonry. It will be appreciated that, owed to the obscuring effect of the 'added' bay, even subtle visual evidence of distress may signify very serious problems demanding dismantling of the bay, replacement of the rotted beams, rebuilding of a section of the front-elevation brickwork and reconstruction of the bay.

Oriel Windows

A variant upon the bay which was quite frequently used, particularly in Edwardian houses, as a device for maximising natural light available through a window lighting a small bedroom, landing or staircase, was the *oriel* window. This type differs from the bay only in being independent of the ground because it is cantilevered off the main building structure. Except in the case of small two-light triangular-plan oriels, sometimes employed to light box rooms and staircases, it was necessary to reinforce the wooden structure of oriels with timber or metal brackets supporting the underside of the projecting construction (Figs. 143 and 144). In the case of upper-storey oriels, a 'full-height' window can utilise the floor construction of the upper storey for its support, the

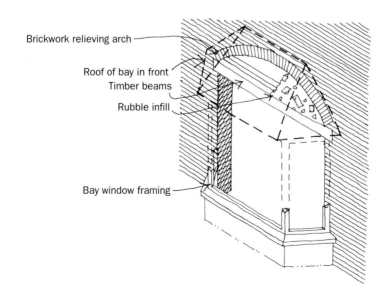

Brickwork relieving arch

Roof of bay in front
Timber beams

Rubble infill

Bay window framing

FIG. 142. Typical structure concealed behind the lean-to roof of a bay window.

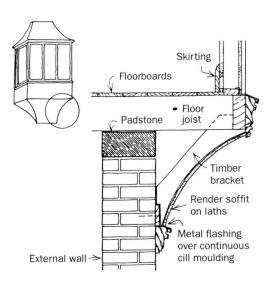

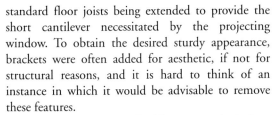

ABOVE: FIG. 143. Oriel window and the structure concealed behind its rendered soffit.

RIGHT: FIG. 144. Oriel window of a 1908 semi-detached house.

standard floor joists being extended to provide the short cantilever necessitated by the projecting window. To obtain the desired sturdy appearance, brackets were often added for aesthetic, if not for structural reasons, and it is hard to think of an instance in which it would be advisable to remove these features.

When renovating or rebuilding an oriel window, where the opportunity offers, it is wise to introduce thermal insulation not only into its roof construction, but also into its soffit, because an uninsulated underside will lose heat to the fresh air as efficiently as the glazing itself.

AESTHETIC PREFERENCES IN WINDOW DESIGN

Throughout the Edwardian and inter-war years, the desire to install windows in new houses reminiscent of those of traditional rural houses was satisfied in one of two ways – either by using side or top-hinged casement windows in preference to the ubiquitous sliding sash window, or by retaining the double-hung type and using sashes displaying a pattern of glazing bars which attempted to reproduce the forms of glazing adopted in traditional country dwellings. The latter treatment was most simply achieved by subdividing one or both of the sashes of the conventional double-hung window with glazing bars, to produce an appearance approximating to that of the windows of houses of seventeenth and eighteenth-century country towns before the invention of plate glass allowed window sashes to be glazed with single sheets. In speculative development in particular, no doubt to minimise expense, it was thought to be an acceptable compromise to subdivide only the upper sashes with glazing bars, the lower sashes retaining their single sheets of clear plate glass and the possibility of an unobstructed view for the occupants (Fig. 145). This treatment had been devised by a London architect in the 1870s but was not widely taken up by builders of modest houses until the turn of the century. It is illustrated alongside the detail of a sash window box jamb in (see Fig. 150 below). Of course,

139

FIG. 145. Subdivided upper sashes and sheet-glass lower sashes in a turn-of-the-century London terraced house.

in speculative houses, even this token gesture towards vernacular architecture tended only to be applied to windows of front elevations. Side and rear elevations not exposed to the general public received sash windows of more utilitarian design, comprising two, or at best, four panes of plate glass.

CASEMENT WINDOWS

The casement is the simplest form of opening window. It hangs on hinges fixed either at its side, top or bottom, or it can be fixed so that it swivels vertically or horizontally. The *French window* or *French casement* is the grandest type of casement window.

The Victorian and Edwardian architects who led the 'domestic revival' by synthesizing the elements of traditional rural houses recognised that in these buildings the breadth of the wooden frame surrounding the glass in an outward-opening casement is often surprisingly wide. In small windows, the area of wood can easily equal the area of glass, and many house owners renovating older dwellings make the mistake of replacing the stout frames of the Edwardian or inter-war work with mass-produced modern windows comprising slender posts and transoms which, accordingly, look feeble alongside the old woodwork. It was not unusual for the fixed frame of a casement to be machined out of 125 × 100mm softwood, and for the frame of the opening light to be from 75 × 63mm (3 × 2½in) timber, the wider dimension being the width of the outside face. If painted white, as was usual with softwood frames, the surface would appear even wider by contrast with the adjacent, darker, glazed area.

Casements are sometimes paired, closing against one another at rebated *meeting stiles*, and a conventional arrangement in Edwardian and inter-war houses was to group them together in a range – as many as six or seven identical lights in a segmental bay and hardly fewer in a timber-framed square or splayed bay (Fig. 146). Individual lights might be separated by timber, brick or stone mullions.

The conflict between the functional and cost benefits of using clear, plain sheets of glass and the desire to achieve 'cottage-style' glazing presented almost as many problems for the design of casements as it did for sliding sashes. Of course, the overall size and shape of a casement might be contrived so as to resemble the rural prototype, but the use of wide or deep panes of sheet glass still hit the wrong note. Thus many casements were subjected to the same compromise applied to sashes – the top section of each casement (or possibly a top-hung fanlight riding over it) would be subdivided into several smaller panes, as a memory of the 'quarries' which made up the windows of ancient cottages (Fig. 147). This treatment of wooden casements of bay windows, in its simplest form (squarish fanlights surmounting deep rectangular casements, the two elements being separated by a heavy wooden transom) continued to be a standard arrangement in all but the smallest windows of detached and semi-detached speculative houses of the inter-war years (See fig. 19 in Chapter 2).

Wrought-iron casements were still being produced

FIG. 146. Splayed bay window of an inter-war house comprising fixed lights and side-hung casement windows.

in the years preceding the First World War. They were favoured by some architects (their most famous advocate being C. F. A. Voysey) for their freedom from rattling in high winds – a flaw to which wooden windows, shrinking and swelling with changing climate, are susceptible. After World War I they were superseded by steel windows, problems with the durability of which being dealt with under the Steel Windows section of this chapter.

CASEMENT WINDOW FITTINGS

Wooden casements were almost universally hung on cast-iron butt hinges similar to those used to hang internal panelled doors, but other, more specialised ironmongery is required to retain and secure a casement.

A *pin-stay* or *peg-stay* secures the casement to the fixed frame and allows graduated opening of the window; the horizontal bar of the stay, which is pivoted off the bottom rail of the window, contains a series of holes that engage on the pin fitted to the window sill. Peg-stays were made in a wide range of designs and 'black iron' (wrought iron) fittings ending in the traditional metal spiral are still available today (Fig. 148). They are much more suitable in a restoration than the brass or aluminium-alloy fittings

FIG. 147. Subdivided fanlights surmount plainer casements in the fenestration of an Edwardian semi-detached house.

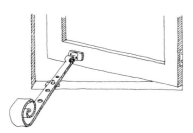

FIG. 148. Wrought-iron peg stay restraining a side-hung casement window.

which tend to dominate the window ironmongery sections of DIY stores.

Sliding stays and *telescopic stays* were more elaborate (and less reliable) types of casement stay that gave a graduated opening. On small and unimportant windows, a simple hook-and-eye stay was used.

The most common form of fastening of casement to frame was the *cockspur fastener*. This device is fixed on the casement and there is a corresponding striking plate on the fixed frame. A slot in the face of the striking plate accepts the tongue of the fastener. Like the peg stay, the handle of the cockspur fastener was often finished with a spiral of metal (Fig. 149); alternatively, the handle might be made so that it curved away from the glass, assisting manipulation of the fitting.

On French windows, further fastenings of the

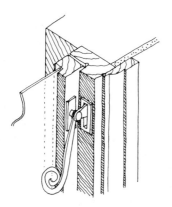

FIG. 149. Wrought-iron cockspur fastener securing side-hung casement to fixed frame.

casements to the fixed frame are necessary. A modern answer to this need is the fitting of bolts at the head and sill of the window, often by recessing special *flush bolts* into the joinery, but such slender items in light-weight alloys were unknown to the Victorians and a much clumsier arrangement, which was often adopted, involved the fixing of full-height *French* or *espagnolette* bolts to the inside face of one of the window's meeting stiles. Both devices incorporate a central lever or handle that causes the bolt to engage in keeps fitted to the fixed frame at the head and sill of the door opening. In spite of the ornamental appearance intended in the design of these fittings, the multitude of bracket fixings to the wood which are required to retain the bolt in the correct align-ment and ensure its efficient operation make it an ugly addition to the door surface, and in any renova-tion of French windows where absolute fidelity to the original is not essential, a much less obtrusive detail results from the use of brass flush bolts.

Where they are arranged to open, *fanlights* are a type of casement window. They invariably open inwards and are hinged at the bottom (this type of window is also called a *hopper vent*). The most common type of stay for a fanlight is a *quadrant stay* which consists of a curved metal flat bar on which slides a small catch attached to the fanlight. Plain cast-metal quadrant stays (without a retaining catch) may also be fixed alongside both sides of a hopper vent, in which case a spring catch must be fixed to the inside face of the fanlight's top rail to engage in a keep plate on the head of the fixed frame. *Shad-bolt stays* are thin metal flat bars springing from the fixed frame of the window in which screws or pins attached to the sides of the fanlight move. It should be clear that the latter two devices allow the fanlight to take only two positions; fully open or closed. Simple butt hinges are a suitable means of hinging the fanlight from the sill.

SASH WINDOWS

More sophisticated in construction than casements, and still very common in Edwardian speculative houses despite the contemporary preference for 'cottage' fenestration, were double-hung *sash* windows. In this type of window, the sashes slide

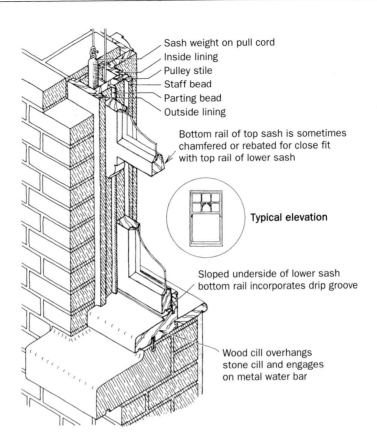

Sash weight on pull cord
Inside lining
Pulley stile
Staff bead
Parting bead
Outside lining

Bottom rail of top sash is sometimes chamfered or rebated for close fit with top rail of lower sash

Typical elevation

Sloped underside of lower sash bottom rail incorporates drip groove

Wood cill overhangs stone cill and engages on metal water bar

FIG. 150. Box-sash window construction.

vertically and are counterbalanced by weights hung on flax cords or chains, or by spring sash balances. Where weights were used, a complicated construction had to be adopted for the window jambs because they were required to house the weights as well as to provide a frame to retain the sashes (Fig. 150). In individual windows located in masonry, the full thickness of the weights box is not apparent from outside, part of its thickness being concealed behind a nib of the brickwork or stonework. Against this nib is sited the outside lining of the weights box which is generally of timber up to 25mm (1in) thick. This is grooved to accept the pulley stile at right-angles to it, which may be 25–32mm thick. The internal tongue of this part in turn engages in a groove in the inside lining of the weights box, which again may be 25mm thick. With a back lining added, these parts form the box in which the two sash weights hang. Where the weights were large or the space containing them was

small, they were separated by a thin wooden tongue to prevent them from clashing when a sash was raised or lowered. The pulley stile was grooved on its face to receive a *parting bead* projecting either 13 or 16mm (½ or ⅝in), providing a vertical channel in which the sash slides and retaining it in the correct alignment. The parting bead was sometimes made of hardwood 13 × 25mm in section (½ × 1in) or 16 × 32mm (⅝ × 1¼in), merely nailed in place so that it could be removed if it was necessary to take out the top sash from inside. The lower sash slides inside the parting bead and is retained by a similarly removable *staff bead* that projects about 16mm (⅝in) in front of the pulley stile.

At the head of the window, the three-sided arrangement of the wooden jambs is reproduced but here there is no requirement to house the sash weights and so an upper lining is omitted, the head lining being grooved into the inside and outside linings, which match the equivalent parts of the jambs. In the same way that the outside linings of the jambs may be partly hidden by nibs of single-skin brickwork, so much of the outside lining of the window head is commonly concealed by the soffit of the brickwork flat or segmental arch that spans the window opening.

At the meeting of the horizontal top and bottom rails of the lower and upper sashes respectively, it was normal to rebate or chamfer the adjoining wooden surfaces so that draughts filtering through the resultant gap were minimised. It was also good practice to slope the underside of the bottom rail of the lower sash and incorporate a drip groove (or *throating*) so that wind-blown rain penetrating this joint would naturally trickle out over the complementary sloping surface of the timber sill.

When the fixed frame of a double-hung window had been fixed in position, it was necessary for the joiner to hang the sashes by attaching the weights housed in the jambs. Installation of the weights was achieved by means of a void formed in the face of the pulley stile, which was sealed when this task was complete with a bevel-edged board or trap kept in place by its tight fit in the void, or by the use of woodscrews.

Where two or more double-hung sashes formed part or all of a range of windows, neighbouring sashes were separated by mullions, which usually accommodated the sash weights for both flanking frames. As each mullion might have to contain four weights, its inside and outside linings had to be wider than those used for the jambs of a single window. The pulley stiles, staff beads and parting beads were detailed in exactly the same way as those in a single frame. In high-quality work, a parting strip was placed between the two sets of weights to prevent them knocking against one another and jamming in the box, and this refinement necessitated access traps in the pulley stiles on both sides of the mullion (Fig. 151), otherwise access to all four weights via a single flap in one side of the mullion could be obtained only with difficulty.

The sizes of the various wooden components forming a sash were fairly standardised. Frames of sashes in modest houses were 40–63mm (1⅝–2½in) in thickness, the bottom rail being 87–102mm (3½–4in) deep, the stiles around 50mm (2in) wide and the top rail 50mm (2in) deep. The meeting rails at the centre of the window were 35–45mm (1⅜–1¾in) deep. Meeting rails of very large sashes glazed with heavy plate glass are likely to be at least 50mm (2in) thick, the bottom rail of the lower sash being 100–125mm (4–5in) deep.

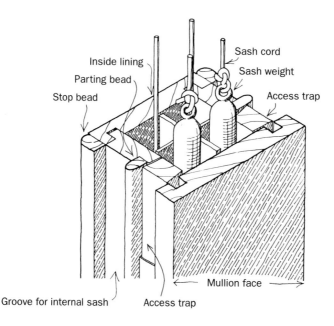

Inside lining

Parting bead

Stop bead

Sash cord

Sash weight

Access trap

Groove for internal sash

Access trap

Mullion face

FIG. 151. Central mullion of a pair of box-sash windows.

The bottom edge of the lower sash of a double-hung window is vulnerable to water penetration by capillary action, and for this reason a groove was sometimes incorporated in its underside; similarly, the fixed wooden sill sometimes included a groove in its vertical face in the plane of the outside face of the lower sash with the identical intention of inducing any wind-blown rain entering the joint to drain outwards (See Fig. 150 above). Plainly, it is wise to insist on replication of these features in any new joinery required to replace badly decayed windows.

Sash Ironmongery

The sash pulleys used in old double-hung windows are of two types; *frame pulleys* and *axle pulleys*. A frame pulley is a cast-iron fitting containing a cast-metal wheel (sometimes of brass) which revolves on iron pins projecting from the inside face of each cheek of the case. The pulley fixing plate, which is fitted flush with the inner lining of the weights box, also commonly displays a brass finish though this is often only a thin brass face riveted on to the cast-iron case.

Axle pulleys were a superior product in which the pulley wheel revolved on an axle that passed through the wheel and cheeks.

Continual use of the window sash was less likely to dislocate the wheel of such a pulley from its case than equivalent treatment of a window fitted with frame pulleys. The integral construction of frame pulleys made them more susceptible to damage from over-vigorous handling of jamming sashes and they tended, therefore, to be employed in low-quality work and in association with light sashes. Heavier windows and careful building construction demanded the use of axle pulleys, which normally combined brass faceplates, pulley wheels and axles, with cast-iron cases. By Edwardian times, the smooth operation of heavy sashes was assisted by adopting ball-bearing pulleys, a grease-packed race of ball bearings allowing the concave-section pulley wheel to revolve freely around a hollow circular moulding formed in the pulley case. All patterns of well-made sash pulley were produced with faceplates made semi-circular, rather than square, at the ends, so that the plate could be easily fitted flush with the weights box

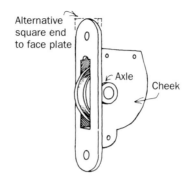

FIG. 152. *Sash pulley.*

inner lining by occupying a recess formed with a brace-and-bit (Fig. 152).

Standard sash pulleys were made in sizes from 44–75mm (1¾–3in) in diameter, increasing in 6mm (¼in) increments. Sash cord was available in a range of thicknesses between 5 and 10mm (¼ and ⅜in), the thickest cord being suitable to support a load eleven times heavier than the 5mm (¼in) diameter product. Very heavy sashes necessitated chain connections to the sash weights. Chains were available in steel, brass and copper in about five sizes. Unlike sash cord, which is still obtainable from many DIY stores, sash chain may prove impossible to replace with identical modern material, though various patterns of light-gauge brass chain may be bought by length at many DIY shops.

In low-cost houses, cast-iron sash weights were standard equipment. Where only a narrow space was available for the weights boxes sited to either side of a double-hung window, or where the use of plate glass resulted in very heavy sashes, lead sash weights were employed because this material is about 80 per cent heavier than an equivalent mass of cast iron. Lead weights were usually made to special order, in contrast to the mass-produced, cylindrical cast-iron components. The bespoke nature of a lead weight was reflected in its price, which before the First World War was approximately five times that of an equivalent iron weight. The latter were invariably cast from low-quality waste iron, and each incorporated an eye at its upper end through which the sash cord was knotted. They can be found in weights varying from approximately 2kg (4lb) up to around 23kg

145

FIG. 153. *Sash fastener.*   FIG. 154. *'Fitch' sash fastener.*   FIG. 155. *Sash lift.*

(50lb) and in length from about 300–800mm (12–32in). No volume producer of cast-iron sash weights operates today, so it is wise to retain any apparently redundant sash weights found in your house for possible future use. In the absence of a local supply of new or salvaged cast-iron components, weights replacing those missing from windows scheduled for restoration may have to be purpose-made in lead.

Sash fasteners of many different makes were available until recent years but it is possible to distinguish a few main types, all of which continue to be available. One of the most familiar is a latch which operates horizontally, instead of vertically like a door latch. A metal bar swings through a quarter-circle to engage in a keep fitted to the top of the lower sash (Fig. 153). The *Fitch* fastener comprises a helical metal cam, which is fastened to the top of the meeting rail of the lower sash and engages in a hook fixed on the top surface of the bottom rail of the upper sash. Its chief advantage is that its operation draws the two sashes together horizontally and forces them in opposite directions vertically; in this way it holds the upper sash tightly and prevents rattling and draughts (Fig. 154). The screw sash fastener performs similarly, drawing the sashes together by the tightening of a thumbnut on a fine-pitched screw. This circular nut operates against a shaped lug fitted to the lower sash, thus developing great pressure in the desired direction. Though it takes much longer to operate than the other types of fastener, it may be preferred for the greater security it offers against attempts to force the sashes apart from the outside.

Small double-hung windows can be raised and lowered by pushing against the meeting rails or hori-

zontal glazing bars, but the tendency of the wood to pull away from the glazing, which is encouraged by this procedure, makes sash lifts essential fittings for large windows. The simplest type is the hook sash lift that was often produced in an alloy, 'BMA' (bronze metal antique) being favoured, particularly in the inter-war period (Fig. 155). A pair of such fittings might be fixed to the inside face of the bottom rail of the lower sash to facilitate easy opening of the window. Modern versions of the fitting are usually of polished brass, which may be too 'showy' a finish to give an authentic look to this humble detail. A stronger type of fitting, which preserved a plain appearance in the internal frame surface, was the flush sash lift, which had to be housed in the wood of the window's bottom rail. This type of sash lift also remains available, albeit most readily in brass, from the few builders' ironmongery manufacturers still operating today.

REPAIR AND REPAINTING OF WOODEN WINDOWS

Careful repair of windows may be the most time-consuming part of a renovation project, but it may offer the most satisfaction for the outlay of time. As will be clear to all those who have witnessed the replacement of the original wooden-framed double-hung sashes with aluminium or plastic-framed (PVCu) double-glazed casement windows, from both inside and outside, the windows do much to set the tone and establish the personality of the house. Out of practical considerations they must operate efficiently to provide daylight and some insulation from cold and noise as well as offer security and the option of fresh-air ventilation. Repairs to the opening lights of casement windows are often easily effected on the workbench, either by scarfing-in new timber of matching type and profile, or, in the case of more minor problems (for example, local damage from wet rot), plastic repair with epoxy-resin compounds to replace rotted timber or to rigidify corner joints loosened by shrinkage or loss of timber. Repair of the built-in fixed frames may be more problematical, particularly if wet-rot damage is well advanced, causing entire sills to soften, and extensive decay may necessitate manufacture of replica window joinery in durable timber for wholesale replacement of the original installation. Despite their comparative complexity, layman repairs to wooden double-hung sash windows are equally feasible.

Overhauling Sash Windows

If the sash windows of an old house 'stick' or are painted shut, it is incorrect to assume that there is nothing that can be done to improve this condition. It is often not very difficult to make them operable again and for the general health of the building it is advisable to do this. Painted-shut windows result from the lack of maintenance stemming from neglect and freeing them may not require much work.

It may be necessary to attack the problem from both inside and outside. The paint seal between the window frame and the sash may be slit with a sharp knife. Then the blade of a wide putty knife can be tapped into the joint and this should act to free the window (if the sash remains stubbornly immobile, insertion of a wide-blade wood chisel or a small crowbar may be required). Where the sash is found to be bowed or swollen, it may be necessary to remove it from the fixed frame, in which case the staff beads must be carefully prised off and removed from the frame. The lower sash can then be swung into the room on its cord ends and these cords – which are sometimes nailed into grooves in the edges of the stiles or simply 'knotted' into cavities therein – can be detached from the window, freeing the sash to facilitate careful repairs carried out on the workbench. As the suspension cords are detached from the stiles of the sash, their ends should be knotted before they are released so that they do not disappear over the pulleys into the weights boxes. To remove the upper sash it is also necessary to take out the parting bead. The

exposed faces of the pulley stiles and the parting beads should be cleaned and, if necessary, the outer edges of the sash stiles should be planed for a more comfortable fit before the sash is re-hung.

Replacement of broken sash cords is the most common reason for repairs to double-hung windows, but if the sash weight is missing or needs to be replaced it is essential that the combined weight of the replacement weights for an upper sash are at least 0.23kg (½lb) heavier than the window, whilst for the lower sash the weights must be at least 0.23kg (½lb) lighter than its weight. This displacement of weights tends to keep the sashes close together and tight against the window head and sill when closed.

To reunite a top sash with weights that have become detached from the window, the pockets have to be opened by removing the traps to gain access to the weights. Then the new sash cords are carried over the pulleys by threading fine but strong string, attached to the cord, through the small void between the pulley wheel and its fixing plate. The string is led over the pulley and down the void of the box jamb by a small lead weight called a 'mouse' (though a bent nail is equally good for guiding the thin cord of a small sash). When the sash cord is visible through the open trap at the foot of the lining, the string and mouse are detached from it, and the cord is tied to the top of the sash weight. With the top sash resting vertically on the window sill, the sash weights are pulled up to the pulleys and the cords are cut off just long enough to permit knots to be tied at the required level. Then the sash is removed from the frame far enough to permit the cords to be pushed down through the grooves in the edges of the stiles and secured by means of the knots, which sit in purpose-designed circular voids at the ends of the grooves. The sash is then replaced in the frame and pushed up and down a few times to test its efficiency. After refixing the parting bead, the lower sash is re-hung in a similar manner and re-assembly of the window is completed by refitting the internal staff bead. It is important to re-fix the access traps tightly in their pockets to prevent them from fouling the lower sash.

Sashes sometimes work inefficiently because the pulley wheels are rusty. Removal, de-rusting and cleaning of the pulleys are called for in this circumstance. Care is needed to avoid damage to any brass faceplate of a pulley if it is necessary to prise the cast-metal case from the lining.

Painting Windows

A definite sequence of operations can be recommended for painting windows. In general, it is advisable to start from the centre of an assembly and work outwards; from the top and work down. Paint any glazing bars first, then the top and bottom rails, the stiles and finally the fixed frame.

The painting of double-hung sash windows follows the same plan but requires a little more thought. Painting (or repainting) should begin by raising the lower sash and lowering the upper sash until the top rail of the lower sash is exposed to the outside above the top rail of the upper sash. Paint this top rail first, then slide the sash back to a near-normal position and continue painting this lower sash from the centre and outwards, working down so that any glazing bars are painted next, then the bottom rail and lastly the stiles (do not paint the underside of the bottom rail). Move both sashes back to 25mm (1in) from their closed position and paint the upper sash. Any external architrave or sill may be painted next. The sashes should be raised and lowered before the paint is completely dry to prevent sticking. When the paint is dry, move both sashes down as far as they will go towards the sill and paint the upper jambs (outside lining, pulley stiles and parting beads). When these sections are dry, raise both sashes to their fullest extent and paint the lower sections of the jambs. Finally, remove any masking tape that has been used to give a neat edge to fresh paintwork and inspect the work thoroughly for any touching-in that may be required.

STEEL WINDOWS

Advances in technology and the comparative scarcity of craft skills available in the inter-war period, together with the increasing size of house-building companies and the developments undertaken, led to a preference to standardise and mass-produce building components for residential development. Windows were a prime candidate for this treatment

and the economics of setting up a factory for large-scale production suggested that steel was a more suitable material for this process than timber. Crittall Ltd of Braintree, Essex, were early in the field and quickly recognised the merits of associating the new architecture that was sweeping mainland Europe with their new product, first of all in an estate of flat-roofed, art deco style workers' housing at Silver End, Essex, in the mid 1920s. Another prominent brand was Hope's Metal Casements.

All these windows were fabricated from mild steel of angle-iron section, giving thin fixed and opening frames and glazing bars of virtually uniform size. Despite the scope to glaze large areas in plate glass, subdivision of even quite small lights by several horizontal glazing bars seemed to be the preferred treatment, vertical subdivisions being fewer (this treatment no doubt being thought to be more in sympathy with the horizontality favoured in many Modern Movement buildings and also with the treatment of fenestration then fashionable in Europe – particularly Holland). Of course, this horizontal gridding ran counter to the vertical stress that is conventional in traditional glazing patterns.

Despite this inversion of convention, the arrangements for opening and restraining steel casements were identical to those employed in wooden windows; casements were hinged from fixed frames and restrained on peg stays, a type of cockspur fastener being used to secure the frames in the closed position.

The chief problem associated with steel windows is corrosion. Only recently has hot-dip galvanizing been offered as part of the protective treatment of these windows and even where this coating exists, corrosion is likely to occur at any points where the protection can be breached. Such a point exists at a corner where the frame sections have to be mitred – cutting through a galvanized section exposes the untreated steel to the air and, in time, rusting will cause swelling and lamination of the metal. It is plain that in the case of a mild steel unit lacking any protective galvanizing, breakdown of the paint film will invite corrosion at any point on the window frame and most steel windows installed in inter-war buildings have suffered badly as a result of this shortcoming. The consequences of rusting of these features include stiff or jammed casements, rainwater penetration as the metal of the fixed frames corrodes and exfoliates, and cracking of glass induced by swelling of the frames as the metal rusts. It is possible to repair such rusted steel windows where sufficient sound metal remains for new sections to be welded in place, but as this task involves temporary removal of the frames to a workshop where properly controlled repairs can be carried out, many will conclude that manufacture of replica windows of superior specification is a wiser option.

Fortunately, the angle-iron frame profiles employed in steel windows in the 1930s continue to be used today, so that fidelity to the original section sizes is easily achieved. Also, the companies which supply windows of slim steel frame section offer the option of post-fabrication hot-dip galvanizing of the frames, which acts to protect vulnerable corner joints, amongst others. Paint finishes too, have improved markedly since the inter-war years and excellent durability is offered by the 'baked-on' enamel finishes which have been in use in the UK for more than three decades. A very wide range of colours is now available in these baked enamel powder-paint treatments, and it should not prove difficult to obtain a match for existing paintwork on new steel windows that will prove to be far more durable than that applied to the original frames.

GLASS AND GLAZING

There was a common principle for glazing all types of wooden-framed windows glazed with low-cost sheet glass throughout the Edwardian years and the inter-war period; the glass was bedded in the rebate of the window frame in linseed-oil putty and was secured with small metal pins or *sprigs* (copper preferred) before the sprigs were concealed by a continuous wedge-section fillet of putty. Ideally, this putty fillet was terminated 1.5mm (1⁄16in) below the top surface of the internal frame so that slight over-painting of the putty on to the glass was not noticed from inside. This method is still perfectly suitable for fixing single glazing today. A very similar technique was used for glazing wrought-iron casements, the difference being that short metal pegs fixed into pre-drilled holes performed the function of the sprigs.

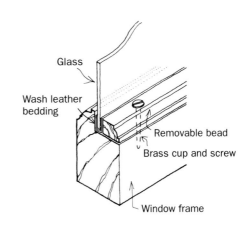

FIG. 156. Beaded glazing.

Beaded Glazing

Glazing of top-quality hardwood window joinery demanded a better means of securing the glass than simple putty fillets. Separate glazing beads of matching material were fixed to the wooden frames with fine metal pins or brass screws located in brass cups (Fig. 156). In this arrangement, the edges of the glass were first bedded in wash leather to remove the risk of fractures posed by direct contact with the rigid timber window frame and to prevent rattling. When replacing such glazing, it is satisfactory to replace the obsolete wash leather with a proprietary glazing tape.

Period Glass

Modern sheet glass is widely available in 4mm, 5mm (approx. 3⁄16in) and 6mm (1⁄4in) thicknesses, and it is almost all produced by the float glass process in which the molten material is 'floated' over a tank of molten tin, producing very large clear sheets of consistent thickness. Very large sheets of polished plate glass are at least 6mm (1⁄4in) thick, but individual lights in even the grandest Edwardian houses are unlikely to be of glass of this thickness. However, the 'picture' windows incorporated in some Modern Movement houses of the 1930s may have necessitated the use of polished plate glass in sizes and thicknesses appropriate to shop windows.

Until quite recent times, glass was sold according to its weight per square foot: 15oz, 21oz, 26oz, 32oz, 36oz and 42oz glass being the readily available weights. A great deal of domestic glazing was carried out in 26oz glass which is less than 3mm (⅛in) thick and the small panes of lights subdivided by glazing bars were of yet thinner glass. The 3mm (⅛in) glass which is the modern equivalent of 26oz glass is suitable for glazing small windows where the glass size is not more than 600 × 400mm (24 × 16in), but larger sizes require 4mm or even 5mm glass. If it was unacceptably thin by current standards, glass made in the first half of the twentieth century also sometimes contained blemishes that are not found in the modern material. These defects are particularly apparent in the optical distortions caused by the low-quality sheet-glass used in bomb-damage repairs during the Second World War, though they are representative of the inconsistencies found in all sheet glass made in the old-fashioned way – by blowing the molten material into the shape of a large-diameter hollow cylinder which was then converted into a single flat sheet in an oven. Indeed these inconsistencies are often valued as contributing character to old buildings glazed with this material, but the value of this additional 'texture' to ordinary Edwardian and inter-war houses where this may not have been a quality sought by the designer or builder, is questionable.

After manufacture, sheet glass was sorted into classes according to quality, known as 'bests', 'seconds', 'thirds' and 'fourths'. Cost considerations dictated that much low-quality sheet glass was installed in speculative housing and a wavy or broken appearance in objects seen through the windows lighting the humble rooms of a back extension or roof-space servants' quarters may point either to wartime repairs or survival of the original fourth-quality sheet glazing.

Leaded Lights

Clear glass was only one of the types of glazing installed by the Edwardian and inter-war builders. In a period in which the elaborate decorative treatment of most materials was still a legitimate aim, patterned glazing remained as popular as it had been in the late nineteenth century. This was most often achieved by installing leaded lights, in which small pieces of glass (*quarries*) are carried in channel-section lead strips called *cames*. The cames were made in a range of sizes

of the H-section channel bar, the width of the lead on the window face being as little as 5mm (³⁄₁₆in) or as much as 19mm (¾in). Each small pane of glass was inserted into the grooves in the encircling cames, bedded in a special cement containing plaster of Paris, linseed oil and lampblack among other ingredients, and the thin lead wings were folded back on to the surface of the glass to secure it.

To prevent rattling and to rigidify large panels of leaded lights against possible damage from high winds, horizontal iron square- or circular-section *saddle bars* were fixed into the jambs of the window frame across the rear of the glazing. Twin copper wires soldered to the junctions of the lead cames were twisted around these saddle bars, strengthening the lead 'grid' which frames the quarries in a typical leaded light. Joints between cames were soldered and a finished light would be secured in a front entrance door with removable beads fixed on the inside, though the fixing of small stained glass panels in opening fanlights might be as modest as the conventional putty fillet.

Used as the glazing of a fixed window, a leaded light could be fixed directly into a timber frame or stone mullions without the intervention of a

FIG. 157. Pattern in leaded lights. LEFT: art nouveau tracery. RIGHT: gridded.

casement. This was done by forming a groove in the wood or stone surrounding the opening. The leaded light was worked into this groove by bending back the leaves of the perimeter cames, and, once inserted, straightening them out again. If in stonework, the groove was then filled and pointed with cement, and putty was used for securing a fixing into wood. The light was never bent or 'sprung' into position in case the cement in the glazing should be cracked, inviting rainwater penetration.

Plainly a limitless range of patterns can be formed in leaded lights. Patterns based on a simple rectangular grid containing obscure-glass quarries (sometimes of 'Cathedral glass', either clear or pastel-coloured) are common in houses of the 1920s and 1930s, not least in front entrance screens and as windows lighting staircases, bathrooms and WCs. In Edwardian houses, erected at the time that enthusiasm for *art nouveau* was at its height (1900–1910), the geometrical composition and colour combinations of stained-glass lights were often much more complex, advertising the impressive skills of the glazier (Fig. 157).

Coloured Glass

Coloured or stained glass produced before 1940 was of two types; *pot metal* and *flashed glass*. The colours were obtained by adding metallic oxides to the glass constituents before firing. Pot metal is a glass uniformly coloured all the way through. Flashed glass is ordinary clear glass with a thin film of coloured glass on one side. It could be patterned by removing the coloured film to form the desired geometrical shapes, and this treatment was often adopted to provide part-transparent panels of coloured glass in front entrance doors. Alternatively, clear glass could be painted. This treatment was often reserved for the central panel of any leaded light and might only be adopted as the centrepiece of the design for the most prestigious application in the house, the upper panel (or panels) of the front entrance door. Images of flowers or animals were popular (Fig. 158). A durable finish to the painted glass was ensured by firing the glass after its surface had been painted with pigments formed from the mixing of iron oxide and other mineral oxides. Truly luminous colours were obtained only if the glass was fired three times.

FIG. 158. Roundels of painted glass central to the two main leaded lights of a front entrance door.

Coloured glass is not nearly so readily available today as coloured plastics. Various brands of acrylic sheets are available in a wide range of colours, surface finishes and thicknesses. Although it may prove satisfactory to replace very small pieces of broken coloured glass with panels cut from acrylic sheet of identical colour, the latter material is not as reflective as glass, is warmer to the touch, scratches and marks more easily on contact with fingers and tools, and melts at quite low temperatures, giving off toxic fumes. In the light of this final property, on no account should it be used for replacing large panes of broken glass in attached conservatories and so on. Any official approval required for such building work (for example, Building Regulations Permission) is likely to specify at least 'self-extinguishing' properties in the re-glazing material.

Replacement Leaded Lights

The repair of leaded lights is specialised work best performed by a suitably skilled tradesman. Many local glaziers continue to offer services of repair and

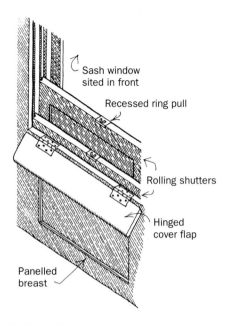

FIG. 159. Vertically sliding internal window shutters.

fabrication of leaded lights and ranges of standard-size lead cames continue to be available from the traditional suppliers of these products. To increase the appeal of their products, many double-glazing companies offer tailor-made double-glazed units, patterned with lead cames, simulating the surface treatment of traditional leaded-light single glazing, for use in houses so treated where the installation of double glazing is planned. In these products, the size and shape of the individual quarries is measured and the complete pattern is carefully reproduced on the outer and inner surfaces of the external sheet of glass of the double-glazed unit by applying thin lead strips bedded on adhesive. It is a decorative treatment in contrast to the decorative *and* structural purpose of the old lead cames. Because a single sheet of glass has a grid of lead strips applied to it, the rattling – in high winds – of quarries that have worked loose from their encircling cames, is eliminated. However, some of the texture of the traditional leaded light is sacrificed and it is essential to insist upon the pattern of leads being reproduced on the inside face of the outer leaf of glass (often omitted in cheap work) as otherwise the view through the undecorated inner sheet of each double-glazed unit will be of the adhesive-fixing of each lead strip to the outside face of the outer sheet.

SHUTTERS

In the Edwardian and inter-war years the fear of civil unrest, which had haunted householders throughout the larger part of the nineteenth century, had receded and the fitting of internal shutters as a security measure was less necessary. The trend towards simplification of the design of the domestic interior also tended to reject the sometimes fussy panelled assemblies which were necessary to house folding shutters flanking main windows, and where internal shutters were fitted in Edwardian houses, they tended to be of the *rolling shutter* type (Fig. 159). These features operate on precisely the same principles as the double-hung sash window. A pair of framed panels counterbalanced by lead or cast-iron weights on sash cords is sited internally, behind and below the window sashes. When lowered, the shutters are concealed behind the panelled back of the box in which they are housed when not in use. The top of this box is both the internal window sill and a hinged flap which lifts to allow access to the shutters so that they may be raised in the same way as the conventional window sash, in this case to *exclude* daylight. Clearly, the upper shutter has to travel twice as far as either window sash and so the sash cords and weights boxes are proportionally longer than those of the windows. The lower section of each weights box is concealed behind the panelled back, which also conceals the retracted shutters. To raise the 'parked' shutters, a recessed staple or ring pull is provided in the top surface of the top rail of each shutter. This fitting allows the hinged flap to close tight to the top of the retracted panels and it is easily pulled out, enabling the operator to roll the shutter upwards.

In many Edwardian houses, these fittings have fallen out of use, but if the finish of the over-painted hinged-flap sill is penetrated and the accumulated dust and dirt sucked out of the cavities between the panels and their carcass with the nozzle of a vacuum cleaner, it is usually found that the high quality of the original timber and workmanship makes reconditioning of the surviving shutters a fairly simple job.

External Shutters

The internal window-shutter had entirely disappeared from speculative houses of the inter-war years, but from the 1920s the appeal of a 'continental ' image in new houses brought about a revival of interest in external shutters. Many purely decorative external shutters can be seen on the elevations of modern and 'modernised' houses, but the value of genuine external shutters in excluding rough weather has always been acknowledged by the inhabitants of exposed rural and coastal settlements. When open, these shutters lie flat on the sections of external wall which flank the windows, an arrangement made possible by the use of projecting butt or *parliament* hinges which pivot the shutter leaves out of the window opening. Such shutters are normally hinged from a hanging stile separate from the outside lining of the weights box, in the case of a sash window, or the jamb frame of a casement. Sometimes a demountable iron frame from which the shutters were hinged was fitted into the external recess of the window opening, the whole assembly being removed during the mild summer months.

External shutters were commonly made from durable softwood such as pine. To admit some light and air even when the shutter was folded across the window, the external frame enclosed panels of pivoting horizontal louvres. Modern 'decorative' shutters reproduce this treatment, but the louvres are fixed and for best protection of these essentially flimsy features from the weather, the panels are invariably (and unauthentically) fixed back-to-front on the external wall surface alongside elevations. In authentic, functioning installations, to allow room for the pivoted, overlapping louvres and the integral vertical control rod that is located behind them, the framing of the panelled construction was never less than 28mm (1⅛in) thick. Therefore, external shutters of large windows can be very heavy, and substantial non-ferrous (non-rusting) hinges will be needed if it is intended to reinstate fittings that have been demounted and stored for some time.

In shutters shielding high windows, it was unwise to incorporate only a single panel of louvres because this assembly would quickly suffer damage from high

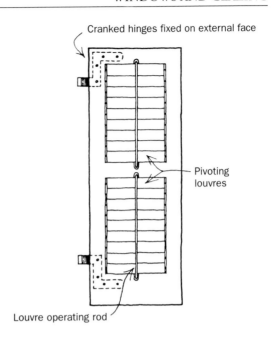

FIG. 160. External timber shutter.

winds. Each shutter was therefore split into two or more panels of louvres, each actuated by its own operating rod and separated from the other panels by horizontal mid-rails which strengthened the wooden framing (Fig. 160).

Reconditioning louvred external shutters is made more difficult by their elaborate construction, as paint-stripping of the complicated profiles can be very time-consuming. It is much easier to remove the shutters temporarily from the building's elevation and to have old, peeling paintwork removed by a specialised process in which the complete unit is immersed in a bath of sodium hydroxide. Repainting of the bare timber surfaces and refitting of the overhauled ironmongery is then a much less formidable operation. Neither is paint-stripping with a blowtorch a sensible way to prepare dowdy shutters for restoration. The heat of the blowtorch will almost certainly char the thin wooden louvres during attempts to extricate old paintwork from the multitude of corners and crevices contained by the shutter framing.

CHAPTER 8

Services and Fittings

It was only with the early years of the twentieth century that piped mains services became a standard provision for most urban dwellings. When there was no legal compulsion to install sewerage connected to an organised system or to provide piped fresh water from a public supply, new rural houses (including those we would now consider to be in outer suburban locations) would often lack these facilities. However, the increasing confidence of the new local authorities following the founding of urban and rural district councils in 1894 caused standards set by contemporary public health legislation (initially the Model By-laws of 1877) to be extended to such 'peripheral' developments, a process which was assisted by the publication of model by-laws for rural authorities in 1901. Section 157 of the Public Health Act of 1875 gave urban authorities powers to make by-laws relating to drainage and the practical consequence of these powers was official insistence on a rational system of foul and storm-water drainage for every new dwelling, and its connection to a public sewerage system. Hence, from the start of the Edwardian period, virtually all new houses in England and Wales were required to have an adequate means of foul-water disposal, which for most meant connection to the public sewerage system, and in advance of commencing work on site, developers were required to submit plans illustrating their proposals to the local authority.

Water was supplied either by private companies or local authorities. Although it was possible (even into the inter-war period) to erect a new house in a rural area without a mains water service, the Public Health (Water) Act of 1878 stipulated that no new house should be built in a rural area unless it was within reasonable distance of a mains water supply.

Changes in the artificial lighting of houses through the Edwardian and inter-war years were caused more by technological advances than by new legal requirements. Town gas had established itself as a suitable fuel for artificial lighting from the early years of the nineteenth century and reliable fittings were made more possible with the invention of the incandescent mantle that was introduced in the UK in 1897. It was an open-ended cylinder of woven fabric saturated with a chemical solution which, when fitted over the gas burner, produced a much brighter light than that of the naked burner flame. The incandescent mantle allowed gas burners to be inverted (to hang downwards in contrast to the 'vertical' arrangement of earlier naked flame burners), obviating shadows at floor level and making it possible to shield the light source with attractive glass shades or diffusers. Although there were municipal gas undertakings, much provision of town gas for lighting was made by private companies and to avoid undue expense for the manufacturer and consumer, the supply network was local to the source of fuel – the gas works – excluding rural and outer suburban houses from this option. To remedy the anarchic circumstances that had developed in London because of unregulated competition between private suppliers, the Metropolis Gas Act of 1860 required agreements to be made between formerly competing companies to confine their operations to designated areas. By the inter-war period, because of the high cost of laying mains to provide a supply to individual dwellings of the new suburban estates, the gas companies generally insisted on guarantees from developers that a certain minimum number of rooms in each house would be 'carcassed' with pipework before street mains were laid.

Electrical lighting was not subject to the same limitations. Certain public buildings and large houses had been lit by experimental installations using locally generated electricity from the early 1880s, but the significant capital costs associated with the provision of this service in a new and untried technology probably acted to deter private enterprise and most electricity supply concerns were run by local authorities from an early date until nationalisation of the industry in 1948. A further disincentive to private investment in this industry was the provision of the Electric Lighting Act of 1882 (the basis for all later legislation) that allowed local authorities to purchase private companies after 21 years of operation.

In the Edwardian years, speculative houses in suburban locations where mains electricity was readily to hand might be provided with electric lighting from the outset (though any provision of power points was less likely until the ready availability of electrical household appliances in the inter-war years) but many houses of the inner suburbs continued to receive gas lighting as a standard service until the First World War. After World War I, new houses almost invariably incorporated electric lighting and this form of lighting also began to replace gas lighting in any refurbishment. Not surprisingly, early patterns of electric light fittings (both pendant and bracket types) tended to be based on forms familiar in gas mantles; an example of a bracket-type fitting being shown in Fig. 161 below. Fortunately, the braided flex used to supply power to these fittings, yet meeting current safety standards, is again available, allowing an authentic look in any restoration of period fittings (that is, free of PVC cables).

HEATING AND VENTILATION

Britain lagged behind the USA and many European countries in research to improve conditions of the internal environment of buildings. Lacking a context in which extremes of climate play a significant part, there was little incentive to invent and refine systems of mechanical ventilation, air conditioning or even central heating except in cases where very large buildings or buildings housing specialised processes presented particular requirements. Certainly it was not thought necessary to devote such research to improving environmental conditions within individual family houses (which were, in any case, generally rented from landlords who were reluctant to make an inessential additional capital investment). Consequently, the provision of central heating within new UK houses has been viewed as desirable only since the 1960s. For many decades, house builders continued to rely on the efficacy of the open coal fire as the sole source of heating, and its physical properties were also often employed to promote better fresh-air ventilation, the prime source of which was windows that opened.

The hearth opening in a chimneybreast was usually finished with splayed sides to maximise the flow of combustion air from the room into the grate. The opening above the fireplace into the chimney flue was constructed as an inverted funnel in order to guide the ascending current of heated air and smoke towards the bottom of the flue. This throat to the chimney was formed by drawing over the brickwork which flanked the fireplace opening, each course of bricks adjacent to the opening being corbelled – that is, made to advance slightly in front of the course immediately below it. The projecting lower corners of the bricks were then cut off with the edge of the bricklayer's trowel and the corbelling produced a

FIG. 161. *Electric light suspended from wall-mounted metal bracket.*

curved profile leading to the neck, or inlet, of the flue proper (Fig. 162). The effectiveness of the flue depended upon the temperature of the gases flowing through it and therefore the height of the opening over the fire was often limited to about 750mm (2ft 6in) so that cold air from the room would not readily pass up the flue without first coming into contact with the fire. It was preferable to build flues curving rather than straight because this policy prevented rain and sleet from falling vertically on to the fire and also tended to check the downward passage of currents of cold air (downdraughts). To be effective, the divergence of a flue should be such that daylight cannot be seen by a person looking up the flue from the fireplace recess. The normal size of a flue for an ordinary fireplace was 225 × 225mm (9 × 9in) whilst for larger fireplaces and kitchen ranges a void 337 × 225mm (13½ × 9in) in plan was used. Fireplaces serving the same storey were often placed back-to-back so that their separate flues could be carried up together into a common chimney stack. Where hearths were located immediately above each

other (as in upper storey rooms) it was necessary to divert the upper parts of the lower flues to one side of the upper-storey hearth to avoid the niche of this fireplace (Fig. 162). To ensure the efficiency of such flues in carrying away smoke and fumes, this divergence had to be gradual because friction in the flue caused by sharp angular offsets drives smoke back down the chimney. A gently curving route for a flue was usually achieved by building-in large-radius curves formed in corbelled brick construction.

The grouping together of several fireplaces serving the same storey, and the consequent grouping of the flues, offered a significant advantage to the builder – it minimised penetration of the roof covering by chimney stacks and thus simplified roof construction and weatherproofing. Grouping the flues also increased their efficiency because an up draught of combustion air in one flue induced a similar movement of air in adjoining flues. This phenomenon was sometimes exploited as a means of ventilating rooms. To achieve this result, it was necessary to construct a vertical air duct about 150mm (6in) square alongside the chimney flue, terminating at its upper end in the roof space of the house, with its lower end issuing at high level into the room served by the adjoining chimney flue and fireplace. When the fire was lit, combustion gases in the chimney flue heated the surrounding brickwork and the air in the neighbouring ventilation duct and induced it to rise, thus drawing stale air out of the room. To minimise the draughts induced by the burning fuel from badly fitting windows and doors, fresh air was sometimes fed to the fireplace through a 50mm (2in) diameter iron pipe which connected the hearth opening directly to outside air. Cold downdraughts in the ventilation duct were obviated by fitting a fabric flap over the grille that vents the head of the duct into the roof space. The existence of this system in a period house is declared by the presence of pierced metal vent grilles just below ceiling level on chimney-breasts.

Even chimney flues that have not served a solid fuel fire for many years are likely to contain large deposits of soot and they must be swept clean if a chimney fire is to be avoided when a new fire is lit in the grate. This accumulation of soot occurs in spite of the fact that most flues incorporate smooth internal

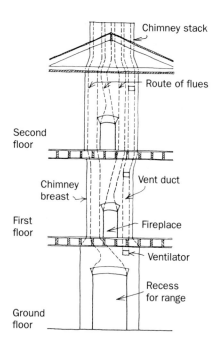

FIG. 162. Typical layout of chimney flues in a three-storey terraced house.

surfaces. This finish was achieved by applying *parging* to the flue walls. This process involved the application of a continuous cement-mortar lining to the flue (ox hair was often included as a binding agent). If the parging was omitted, soot could settle in any open mortar joints of the flue walls, introducing the risk of chimney fires.

The positioning of chimney stacks in relation to roof surfaces is crucial to the efficient operation of fireplaces. When the wind blows horizontally, air compressed against the surface of a chimney pot flows up over its top edge in such a way that a zone of still air is created directly over the chimney opening, allowing the chimney gases to pass over the pot's leeward edge into an area of low pressure. As wind speed increases, the pressure of this area is reduced and the chimney draught is correspondingly augmented. When the wind blows upwards, the area of low pressure is formed closer to the top of the chimney and the escape of flue gases is greatly assisted. When the wind blows downwards, the escape of chimney gases is cut off, and unless there is sufficient pressure behind the combustion gases to deflect or lift the wind at the mouth of the chimney, a downdraught results.

A chimney sited at or near the ridge of the main house roof which is not in the lee of higher roofs will invariably function well, because the wind deflected upwards by the inclination of the windward roofslope assists the escape of chimney gases as it passes over the chimney pots. Chimneys sited below the ridge of the main roof on the leeside will be adversely affected by wind driven down the roofslope on which they are located, as will chimneys crowning the apex of any lower roof on the leeside of the main roof. A traditional remedy for the downdraughts created in such chimneys was to extend the chimney pot with a metal pipe, fitted at the top with a conical cowl (Fig. 163). In this way, the top of the chimney was removed from the zone of downward air currents. However, the fitting of a protective cowl was almost as likely to prove counter-productive. By partly blocking the chimney opening it excludes downdraughts but it may also inhibit the escape of flue gases.

An alternative modification to chimneys, which was believed to be an effective cure for the smoking

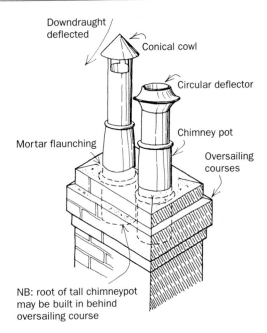

FIG. 163. *Brickwork chimney stack and fireclay pots modified to improve smoke venting.*

fireplace that resulted from downdraughts, was the fitting of a circular deflector to the top of the chimney pot. The curved top surface of this deflector caused that part of the wind that it blocked, to be lifted well above the top of the chimney. Thus the chimney gases were given an opportunity to escape over the leeward edge of the modified chimney-pot terminal (See Fig. 163 above).

To prevent chimney pots from being dislodged by strong winds, each pot was usually secured to the supporting stack by building-in its bottom rim behind an oversailing course of corbelled brickwork at least one course below the top of the stack and surrounding the lower part of the pot with a sloping profile of cement-mortar flaunching, bedded on the top surface of the chimney-stack brickwork (Fig. 164).

Grates

The 'register grate' which was introduced in the UK in the early nineteenth century was the first step towards production of a standard fireplace design that included all the improvements to the domestic

157

FIG. 164. Chimney stacks used to sublime effect: The Deanery Garden, Sonning-on-Thames, Berkshire (Edwin Lutyens, 1901). (Robin Bishop.)

of the nineteenth century. However, from the 1870s a new style of cast-iron fire surround began to replace the arched-top pattern of register grate; the grate aperture was rectangular and the splayed cheeks were clad in glazed tiles. This type of grate remained the standard pattern throughout the Edwardian period. The bars retaining the fire were cast in one piece and dropped into a slot at the front of the grate, or held in place by integral hooks fitting into slots formed in each vertical edge of the grate aperture. A floor-level ash pan, its fascia usually embossed with decoration, controlled the draught from below. As successive models moved the grate further forward, it became necessary to introduce a projecting metal smoke hood above the fire to guide the smoke into the flue.

The style of the chimneypiece (fireplace surround) could vary from the simplest pattern of flat jambs and a lintel supporting a mantelshelf (of wood, iron, slate or marble) to elaborate assemblies reflecting contemporary patterns of interior decoration. The 'Adam Revival' style simulating the chimneypieces of late-eighteenth-century stately home interiors exercised an influence on the fire surrounds installed in many speculative Edwardian houses – in this case, white paint over moulded timber or cast-iron products was the formula adopted. Interest in English vernacular architecture prompted by the Arts & Crafts Movement led to a revival of traditional English forms of fireplace, notably the 'inglenook', diminutive forms of which began appear in Edwardian houses following its inclusion in country houses designed by leading late Victorian architects such as Norman Shaw. Where oak lintels would have been too expensive, brick arches provide the necessary 'Old English' look and were much used in the smaller houses designed by notable architects of a later generation such as Edwin Lutyens. Beaten copper smoke hoods were incorporated in the design of many such chimneypieces and lustre-glazed tiles designed by William de Morgan graced the cheeks of the grandest designs. For those who could not afford such bespoke splendour, proprietary ceramic tiles, tube-lined with Art Nouveau patterns or plain glazed tiles and finished in bold colours – peacock blue, sage green, maroon or ruby red were popular – flanked the grates of simple chimneypieces of small suburban houses. Recognising this enthusiasm for the natura-

hearth recommended by the American inventor Count Rumford in the 1790s. Ordinary register grates consisted of a metal frame (usually cast iron) which closed in the fireplace opening and which was fitted with a receptacle for the fuel, comprising front and bottom furnace bars and a fireclay or metal back and sides, over which was fitted an adjustable flap valve, damper or hinged canopy. A firebrick lining about 75mm (3in) thick surrounded the fire on three sides. After 1840, the Carron Ironworks, the most famous manufacturer of cast-iron fittings, produced a register grate incorporating a semi-circular arch, which remained a popular pattern until the last years listic forms and 'whiplash' patterning of the style, at least one enterprising manufacturer of cast-iron fittings introduced a range of art nouveau style fire surrounds which were widely employed in the bedrooms and lesser living rooms of speculative houses erected in south London from around 1905 until the beginning of the First World War (Fig. 165).

Gas fires for domestic use appeared as early as the 1860s. Formidably ugly cast-iron gas grates incorporating a mat of asbestos fibres as the heating surface were superseded only after 1918 by equally ugly fires fitted with the more familiar ceramic honeycomb burners. Gas heating was not very popular before the First World War because gas fires were said to dry the air. Also, gas was about four times more expensive than coal. Therefore the preference was to install gas fires in bedrooms where a cleaner and more instant form of heating than the open fire was desired, the comparatively high cost of the service being tolerated because the fires were used only sporadically.

The first modern British electric fire appeared in 1912 when nickel heating elements were introduced. In earlier fires the elements had been sealed in narrow glass tubes to protect the wires from oxidation in air; an arrangement which severely limited the effectiveness of this heating medium. By 1921, fires sold by the same manufacturer included an imitation coal-effect model, setting a precedent to be followed in many electric and gas-grate designs down to the present day.

Kitchen Ranges

Before the advent of gas and electric cookers, cooking was generally carried out on a solid-fuel stove integral to a kitchen range. Even the most humble terraced houses incorporated such a cast-iron fitting containing an oven, hot plate and register-grate open fire. A more sophisticated type of range comprised a fire with a high-pressure 'boot' pattern boiler at the rear, roasting and baking ovens to either side of the fire, hot plates over these ovens and a plate rack spanning the full width of the fitting at high level. The heat of the fire was concentrated on each oven and the boiler by an arrangement of horizontal and vertical flues controlled by dampers.

As the overall height of the kitchen range might

easily be 1500–1800mm (5–6ft) and its width could be as much as 1800mm (6ft), a very large fireplace recess had to be provided for it in the chimney breast. The great heat generated by the cast-iron construction necessitated the building-in of a solid brick lining grouted with fireclay or fire cement on the floor of the fireplace recess below the ovens. A similar lining was built vertically at the back of the recess, the flues also being formed in this material. Baffle plates were inserted below the ovens to break the flow of hot air under these chambers and to prevent it from going directly up the flue before it had properly circulated around, and thus warmed the ovens. The seating for the boiler was solid brickwork built up from the floor. Soot doors were always provided in the brick lining of the range to give access to the flues, which required frequent sweeping.

Few cast-iron kitchen ranges, original to Edwardian houses, survive. Most were the victims of modernisation of kitchen facilities in the two decades after the Second World War and mass-produced gas

FIG. 165. A moulded cast-iron art nouveau chimneypiece.

cookers had been developed sufficiently by the early 1920s to ensure that the cast-iron range was not an original appointment of the standard speculative inter-war house. The promise of cleaner cooking with modern equipment and the association of the old fittings with grim times caused many householders to dismantle and demolish these characterful fittings in spite of their massive and heavy construction. Enlargement of a tiny room by removal of a range was also a cause for disappearance of this feature, but where a range survives and room enlargement is not desired, retention of the fitting, if only for its decorative value, is recommended.

Central Heating

Modern domestic central heating commonly comprises a gas, oil or solid-fuel fired boiler supplying hot water at low pressure to metal panel radiators via metal pipes. Edwardian hot-water central heating systems operated on the same principles, though circulation of hot water was through large-diameter steel pipes to cast-metal column radiators and the cast-iron boiler was coke-fired. Early twentieth-century central heating systems lacked the control devices familiar today such as electronic programmers, electric pumps and motorised valves. The circulation of hot water was achieved by the water attaining the pressure necessary to raise it to the highest radiators, and gravity was relied on to return it to the boiler. This was the main reason that the small-diameter pipes familiar today were unknown, and radiators were served by 38 or 50mm (1½ or 2in) diameter steel pipes of the type seen in older hospitals and schools.

A conventional Edwardian central-heating system for a six-bedroomed villa would include fourteen radiators fed from a 50mm (2in) diameter main, although flow and return branches to each individual radiator would be 19mm (¾in) in diameter with a 25mm (1in) return main to the solid-fuel-fired boiler located in the cellar or basement furnace room. Where it was impractical to install the heavy column radiators of grouped oval loops of cast iron in upper-floor rooms, the main heating pipe could be arranged simply to perform a horizontal circuit around an upper storey to take the chill out of the enclosed air.

ARTIFICIAL LIGHTING

Gas Lighting

Artificial lighting by gas has fallen almost entirely out of use today except in some older houses in remote rural districts where mantles are kept burning with liquid petroleum gas. Yet in many Edwardian houses the greater part of the pipework installed by the gas fitter was to supply gas lighting.

A good proportion of the Victorian and Edwardian iron gas-supply pipes located below city streets and pavements continue to supply North Sea gas which, although now dwindling, is a main source of heating fuel in Britain today. A gas supply to an individual Edwardian or inter-war house was made with a cast- or wrought-iron pipe of smaller diameter than the street main, but the connection to the main is nowadays carried out in a flexible plastic pipe colour-coded yellow to identify it visually as a gas pipe. This service pipe always terminates at a meter – a practice unchanged since the days of the Victorian town gas companies. Connections from the meter to all fittings were made in plain wrought-iron tube with screwed joints. These joints were sealed with red lead compound and the pipes were fixed to external walls with hooks or patent pipe clips. The service pipe was never less than 19mm (¾in) in diameter and a large gas stove might require a supply pipe 25–38mm (1–1½in) in diameter. The distributing pipes or branches of a modern gas supply system are usually of copper, precisely like those used to circulate hot water through a conventional central heating system, but in an original gas-lighting installation, branches of the wrought-iron pipework used to feed individual mantle locations might be as small as 6mm (¼in) in diameter so it is not unusual to find sections of defunct gas supply pipework embedded in the 25–32mm (1–1¼in) of plaster that was used to clad internal wall surfaces of Edwardian houses. The surface of a chimneybreast over the mantelshelf often obscures small-bore, dropping vertical branches of the gas supply, because an eye-level location over the fireplace was a favoured fixing point for gas lighting brackets.

An example of the care that was necessary in installing gas lighting to ensure an even moderately efficient system was the slight inclination of the pipes and brackets so that the small amount of water vapour that condensed in the pipes and flowed back to the lowest points could be drained off, instead of impeding the gas supply. Sometimes a whole system of house pipes was arranged to drain back into a siphon at the meter position. Surviving and functioning gas brackets in Edwardian houses are certain to be of the mantle-mounted type because the incandescent mantle, an innovation of the final years of the nineteenth century, quickly superseded the less efficient 'bat's wing' and 'fishtail' naked flame burners.

Electric Lighting

Before 1918, electricity supplied to houses was used only for the purpose of artificial lighting. Although from about 1880 electric lighting seemed to promise improved illumination, the earliest light bulbs produced only a dim glow and were very unreliable. Similarly, there were districts where the mains electrical supply was far from dependable. It was only after World War I that technical developments radically improved the quality of electric light, and it is clear from contemporary comments that the Edwardians greatly desired improvements in domestic illumination. The demand for circuits supplying electricity through power points was engendered by the ready availability of affordable mass-produced powered domestic appliances, including electric irons and vacuum cleaners, which were the products of new industries of the inter-war period.

Edwardian designs for electric light fittings tended to reproduce the style of fittings adopted in domestic gas lighting (Fig 166). For this reason, bracket fittings tended to proliferate. The central ceiling-mounted pendant fittings familiar in modern speculative houses were generally outnumbered in an electrically lit Edwardian house by bracket fittings incorporating a single lamp. These were cantilevered off the walls on curved or 'swan-neck' metal brackets. Sometimes the lamps were simply hung on the flexible, braided electric supply cable, which was itself suspended from an ornate projecting bracket (See Fig. 161 above).

A plain Edwardian pendant would consist of a ceiling rose, a supply cable suspending a brass lamp

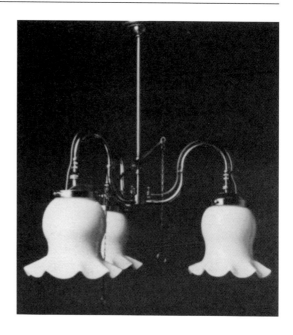

FIG. 166. Three-arm pendant light fitting with inverted incandescent mantles operating on natural gas or LPG. (Sugg Lighting.)

holder, a clear glass light bulb and a conical opal glass shade which gave a 'finished' appearance as well as diffusing light upwards and reflecting it downwards. More 'Heath Robinson' in appearance and characteristically Edwardian were *counterweight pendants* which allowed the height of the lamp to be adjusted. This type of fitting comprised a plain pendant with a counterweight added and pulley wheels fixed both to the ceiling and to the counterweight. The cable serving the lamp passed through an eye attached to the counterweight in order that lowering of the lamp and reflector, causing raising of the counterweight, did not induce the weight to rotate around the supply cable (Fig. 167).

Much less common except in grand houses were *electroliers* (electric chandeliers). A simple form of electrolier consisted of a rigid tubular metal stem, containing the supply cable, which ended in a circular cast-metal body to which the tubular arms of the electrolier were connected, and a spun metal shell and pendant knob respectively enshrouding the body and 'finishing off' the underside of the fitting. The

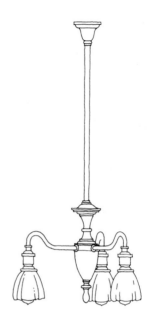

FIG. 167. *Counterweight pendant ceiling-mounted electric light fitting.*

FIG. 168. *Three-arm electrolier.*

arms of such an electrolier could be curved upwards or downwards, or they might be at right-angles to the stem (Fig. 168).

Library and dining-room pendant fittings often boasted a gilded chain stem through which the supply cable was threaded and an 'art glass' shade finished with a silken fringe. This impressive form of fitting, like the ornate oil lamp it superseded, was sometimes installed as a low centre-feature over a dining table. The art-glass shade was formed from slivers of glass held in position by a gilded or nickel-plated metal frame and the silken fringe was sewn on to a thin-gauge metal band that was connected to the shade with setscrews. Similar pendant fittings, adjustable in height by means of a complicated system of pulleys, ornamental counterweights and suspension cords, and clad in highly patterned or scintillating fabrics, were also installed in expensive bespoke houses.

The continued existence of previously undiscovered Edwardian light fittings is questionable because period wiring which has survived to the present day is likely to represent a safety hazard. The rubber-coated cables which were used to wire new houses even as late as the 1950s are liable to perish over three or four decades, introducing the risk of short circuits and fires resulting from the contact of exposed wires. Thus an Edwardian house that was fitted with electric lighting at outset may have been rewired on at least two occasions, the period fittings having been 'retired' at each rewiring. The position is hardly better for inter-war houses because they too will have been subjected to at least one re-wiring and fringed celluloid lampshades of cubist design (Fig. 169) or art deco wall-mounted fittings of chromium-plated brass and etched glass are likely to have been the victims of a 1960s' re-wiring exercise.

The reconditioning of any surviving period electric light fittings to the high safety standards of modern fittings is better undertaken by appropriately skilled tradesmen than by enthusiastic amateurs but the increasing availability of reproduction items makes it a fairly simple matter for the diligent restorer to obtain new fittings which will harmonize with surviving features of an Edwardian or inter-war interior.

FIG. 169. A cubist-style fringed celluloid lampshade of the 1930s.

WATER SUPPLY

By the beginning of the twentieth century, municipal and private enterprise was meeting the requirements of new urban and suburban buildings for reliable supplies of fresh drinking water. In England, the corporations of Liverpool and Birmingham were supplying drinking water from specially constructed reservoirs established in valleys in North Wales, whilst Manchester met its needs from the natural lakes of the Lake District of north-west England. In London, the New River, an initiative of the seventeenth century, brought fresh water to large reservoirs at Finsbury from its source at Amwell in Hertfordshire and the River Thames was increasingly used as another main source of drinking water. Distribution of the purified water from local surface or subterranean reservoirs was accomplished via cast- or wrought-iron water-main pipes located beneath the streets. A supply to an individual house was arranged by forming a hole in the street main – the supply having first been isolated from this section – and a screw thread was then formed in this hole. Into

this opening a hollow brass or iron ferrule was screwed. The plain end of this ferrule was then soldered to the lead pipe serving the dwelling with a *wiped joint* in which the solder uniting the two materials was made to encase the joint completely. If a wrought-iron service pipe was used, a threaded socket finished the 'house' end of the ferrule so that the iron pipe could be screwed into it. A valve or *stopcock* was then attached to the pipe near the ferrule or where the service pipe entered the building. Such stopcocks are generally found in cast-iron boxes with hinged covers fitted flush with the earth in a garden area close to the front boundary with the street or in the front pavement surface. They enable individual houses to be isolated from the street main without disrupting the general water supply in that important pipe.

In addition to the stopcock located close to the connection with the street main, a similar valve was usually fitted to the service pipe in a convenient place close to its point of entry into the house, so that repairs to pipes within the house could be made without the water company's stopcock at the front boundary needing to be closed. A still more practical arrangement placed a draw-off tap on the rising main (the domestic cold water supply pipe rising to the storage tank) on the house side of this stopcock so that the house pipes could be emptied to prevent them freezing (and consequently bursting) in a severe frost. Water expands as it freezes and soft lead piping is notorious for its susceptibility to split under the increased internal pressures resulting from freezing water. All these arrangements continue to be the means by which mains water is supplied to new houses or faulty service pipes are renewed, although blue PVC pipework has replaced the iron street main and in internal work, copper tube has replaced the old lead pipework.

Where a water service pipe passed under a foundation wall, allowance was usually made for possible settlement of the wall by leaving a space of 50mm (2in) or more on all sides of the pipe. Good practice called for a lead pipe to be enclosed in a *thimble* of iron pipe, two or three sizes larger than the service pipe, built into the foundation wall. Such underground pipes were as likely to be adversely affected by frost as the integrity of the internal pipes was to be threatened by freezing conditions. For this reason they were often located about 750mm (2ft 6in) below ground level which was safely below the frost line. To guard pipework from corrosion by the soil, iron pipes were normally painted with a bituminous protective compound, or lagged with a special pipe covering applied when the pipe was heated on installation. Lead pipes were sometimes protected by encasing them in rough deal tarred boxes filled with bitumen. It is unlikely that this original protection will have endured to the present day. In any case, lead pipes are much less likely to corrode in most soils than is iron pipework.

Water Storage

Even today in some areas, the mains supply system cannot be relied upon to provide water at a pressure that will guarantee a consistent supply to the highest sanitary fitting in the house. Partly for this reason the route of the rising main has for many years been arranged so that a high-level water storage tank is almost the first device to be fed from the supply pipe. The one exception to this rule is the direct connection to the kitchen sink, which is tapped off the main before it rises to the storage tank in order to ensure at least one source of uncontaminated mains water. An equally important reason for the adoption of a system in which most of the fittings received their cold water supply by gravity from a high-level tank or *cistern* was the need to prevent negative pressure in the street main from sucking back potentially contaminated

water contained in the domestic fittings. The supply of mains water to the cistern is regulated by a floating ball valve attached to the incoming pipe. When the tank is filled and the ball valve floats almost level with the supply pipe, it cuts off a further supply of water until some stored water is drawn off. To guard against malfunction of the ball valve and consequent overfilling of the tank, an overflow pipe sited a little below the tank's top rim, discharging into the outside air through an external wall, is incorporated. Operation of this pipe gives clear notice of a defective ball valve. The pipe is fixed a little below the inlet level of the supply pipe so that stored water cannot rise to the level of the inlet, sending possible contaminants back down the rising main (Fig. 170).

Today's domestic water-storage tanks are commonly of moulded polypropylene construction and tend to be available in metric capacities equivalent to the old 50 gallon, 100 gallon and 200 gallon sizes. Water storage tanks employed throughout the Edwardian and inter-war years were generally made of metal – galvanized steel cisterns being available in a range of standard sizes. They were made from thin plate (not exceeding 3mm (⅛in) thick) riveted to steel corner-reinforcing angles. Such cisterns are quite light and durable but the water in some districts tends to attack the zinc coating, causing the steel to corrode, inviting fractures and inducing leaks. Modern moulded plastic cisterns entirely avoid this problem. It was common to fit a removable wooden

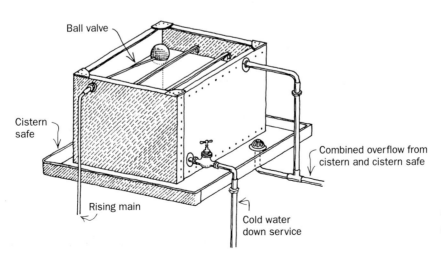

Ball valve

Cistern safe

Combined overflow from cistern and cistern safe

Rising main

Cold water down service

FIG. 170. Cold-water supply cistern and 'cistern safe'.

cover to the top of a steel cistern to prevent 'foreign bodies' from falling into the stored water. Tanks of this type were most suitably sited in the roof space directly above the bathroom, thus economising on pipe runs, but in some circumstances shortage of space caused the cistern to be mounted on heavy wooden bearers sited at high level in the bathroom itself. Small domestic cisterns were also available in stoneware or glazed fireclay.

It would be unusual to discover in a large Edwardian suburban house an original cistern with a capacity of more than 150 gallons (a common overall size for a tank of this capacity being approximately 1200mm long, 900mm wide and 750mm high [4ft × 3ft × 2½ft]) although sometimes, sufficient water was stored to cater for the needs of the household over two days on the basis that each person would use 25 gallons per day. The water storage capacity of modern domestic tanks tends to be smaller than this, not only because space taken up by large tanks can be put to better use, but also because today's supply of mains water tends to be more reliable than it was in the early years of the twentieth century. The minimum capacity acceptable today for a tank providing a cold-water service only is 50 gallons, but a tank supplying the hot water service too should store at least 80 gallons.

The standard galvanized steel cistern favoured by builders before the Second World War not only suffered the shortcoming that its seams were likely to rust and eventually, to cause leaks, but also that in humid weather the metal construction invited condensation on to its outer surfaces, which would then drip on to the supporting building construction. To protect absorbent materials from saturation by the dripping water, a *cistern safe* – a shallow tray of thin galvanized steel – was sometimes installed below the tank. The provision of this drip tray necessitated inclusion of an overflow pipe in a wall of the safe itself which could be combined with the tank over-flow before it passed through an external wall to discharge into the outside air. A small cistern required a 32mm (1¼in) diameter safe waste pipe and a larger installation would be fitted with a 38mm (1½in) pipe. To prevent rust or sediment clogging the pipe, in the best work the end connected to the safe was protected by a convex brass grating soldered over

its open mouth and fitted with a removable rim so that the grating could be extracted in order to clean out the pipe (see Fig. 170 above).

Modern polypropylene cisterns are almost equally likely to create condensation in humid weather, but this tendency can be checked by insulating the tank with a glass wool or mineral fibre quilt or expanded polystyrene or polyurethane slabs. In any case it is wise to insulate water storage tanks located in a roof space which is otherwise not insulated from the outside air in order to prevent the stored water from freezing in severe winter weather. All connecting pipework that is similarly exposed must also be insulated. Preformed sections of tubular foam polyurethane, which fit over the small-diameter copper pipes used nowadays to carry a cold-water down service, are readily available for this purpose. Less efficient early twentieth-century attempts to prevent exposed lead or iron pipes from freezing included covering the pipes with hair felt and a continuous canvas jacket that was stitched tightly over the felt or secured with copper wire. Where pipes ran horizontally between ceiling joists, a measure of insulation was achieved by filling up the void with sawdust or slag wool and a modern version of this detail might be achieved by covering the pipes with a deep layer of polystyrene beads.

Cold Water Down Service

The delivery of cold water to fittings is effected by a pipe, which connects with the storage cistern about 50mm (2in) above its underside, so that any sediment that collects in the tank will not be sucked down the pipe as the water is drawn off. Apart from the tap over the kitchen sink, which draws drinking water direct from the rising main, all the fittings, including WCs, bathtubs, wash-hand basins and bidets (rarely fitted before the Second World War but nevertheless available) are conventionally supplied from the cistern. Today, a copper delivery pipe usually fulfils this function but iron or lead pipes were the norm until 1939.

Where a lead water supply pipe ran horizontally, hooks or lead tacks were used to support it at intervals not exceeding 900mm (3ft). Though the policy was not often adopted, it was good practice to set pipes in sleeves where they passed through walls or partitions in order to prevent their expansion and contraction from cracking plasterwork. To conceal the resultant open space between the pipes and the wall surface, small circular shields or *escutcheons* sleeved on to the pipes were used. Such horizontal runs were commonly distribution branches fed from the dropping delivery pipe of the cold water down service at each floor level in order to serve a local group of fittings. Each fitting in the group was supplied through a branch taken off the distributing branch. In a well-installed system, valves were provided off the down-service supply pipe at the head of each distributing branch so that the supply of water could be shut off from each group of fittings. The best (and most expensive) installation included valves on each branch so that individual fittings could be isolated from the supply.

A common size for the main supply pipe dropping from the tank in the roof space was 38mm (1½in) diameter; distribution branches springing from this pipe might then be 25mm (1in) diameter with individual fittings being served by 19mm (¾in) or 13mm (½in) pipes. Copper pipework conventionally used for this purpose today is 15mm, or exceptionally, 22mm (⅝ or ⅞in) in diameter.

SANITARY FITTINGS

Three varieties of pottery were used in the manufacture of period sanitary fittings; earthenware, stoneware and porcelain. Earthenware is made from various clays mixed with powdered flints and other ingredients to give a quality of finished product varying from a porous terracotta-like texture to a strong, dense, semi-vitrified material. Stoneware is made from refractory clays burnt at higher temperatures and is close-grained, hard and impervious. It was usually glazed by a process in which the main ingredient was common salt, and thus went under the name; 'salt-glazed ware'. Porcelain is made from china clay mixed with powdered flints, powdered bones, sand and so on. So-called porcelain sanitary fittings were usually manufactured from very carefully prepared earthenware composed of fireclay covered with an enamel of porcelain. The finish of this highest standard of pottery sanitaryware in many ways resembles the fine china of a dinner service.

The moulded polycarbonate baths, basins and shower trays which proliferate today were unknown before the Second World War and are likely to look out-of-place if used in conjunction with surviving original sanitaryware or where it is desired to restore a period arrangement.

Sinks

Before the introduction of pressed stainless steel sinks after the middle years of the twentieth century, the kitchens, sculleries, pantries and housemaids' cupboards of Edwardian and inter-war houses were fitted with sinks in porcelain-glazed moulded cast iron, glazed stoneware or porcelain-enamelled fireclay. They were supported on pedestals, standards, brackets or corbels and it was not customary to mount the sink on a range of cupboards as applies with modern lightweight stainless-steel units or vitreous-enamelled steel sinks. By the start of the twentieth century, a pattern of moulded fireclay sink incorporating an adjacent sloping grooved draining surface was familiar, but separate draining boards of hardwood, edged in non-corroding metals and fixed alongside the sink on cantilever brackets projecting from the rear wall were equally prevalent in Edwardian houses.

After many years' use, glazed fireclay sinks become unhygienic because the glaze wears thin and the porous earthenware begins to absorb waste water. Therefore, although fireclay 'Belfast' sinks are still obtainable, the retention of elderly clayware sinks in kitchens in preference to replacement by more impervious modern products cannot be recommended.

Wash-hand Basins

Wash-hand basins or lavatory basins continue today to be of the two basic types that were familiar to our Edwardian ancestors. They were either formed in one unit, the basin, slab, skirtings and apron being made from one moulding of cast metal or pottery, or they were built up from two or more pieces and often two or more materials. This second type consisted of a basin of moulded sheet metal, cast iron or pottery, with the lavatory top or slab and skirting being made of slate or marble perforated with an opening which was sited centrally over the basin. Today, this latter

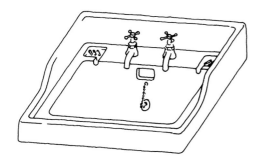

FIG. 171, ABOVE. Bracket-mounted porcelain lavatory basin.

FIG. 172, RIGHT. 'Onyx' freestanding lavatory basin.

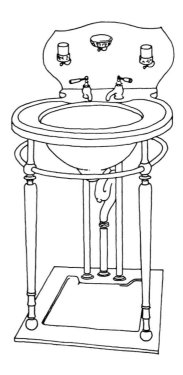

type of fitting is often called a *vanitory unit* and an impervious top slab of polycarbonate or decorative laminate (often patterned in imitation of marble) commonly replaces the real marble slab used in the Edwardian version.

The cheapest form of lavatory basin, which was installed in many pre-1940 speculative houses, was the plain wall lavatory on brackets. It was made of white enamelled earthenware, the basin, top and skirtings being in one piece. It was supported on two plain enamelled iron brackets and fitted with 13mm (½in) diameter gunmetal taps, strainer waste and overflow (Fig. 171). Although this fitting seems primitive by the standards of modern sanitaryware, it is worth remembering that in rural households, even in the inter-war period, washing was accomplished in a large ceramic dish filled with cold water from a large clayware jug or ewer which had been filled with water the previous evening.

Edwardian built-up basins might incorporate a carved marble top encircling a round or elliptical opening over the basin, and a low carved marble splashback or skirting fitted against the wall surface at the rear of the basin. This skirting would be extended along the sides of the basin where it was built into a full-depth recess. Where basins were built into corners, a basically triangular shape of slab with a curving front rim was a common treatment. However, this space-saving arrangement tended to look cramped, and even if a corner location for the

basin was inescapable, a rectangular slab might be employed, not only to give a more generous appearance but also to give more space to the user. The slab was supported at the back by a cleat or shallow bracket built into the wall and at the front by metal legs or brackets. Sizes for such marble slabs ranged between 600 × 475mm (24 × 19in) and 900 × 550mm (36 × 22in), their thickness ranging from 32–76mm (1¼–3in) with the matching skirtings being 19–25mm (¾–1in) thick.

The most elegant type of Edwardian lavatory basin was an 'open' lavatory consisting of an elliptical basin fixed below an onyx marble slab supported on its front edge by two slender metal legs. A matching marble splashback of very decorative shape complemented the slab and the waste and water supply pipes, legs, soap tray, towel rail and taps would be nickel-plated (Fig. 172).

Baths and Showers

Until the final years of the inter-war period, the most common type of bath was the cast-iron tub, coated inside with white porcelain enamel and outside with metallic or vitreous enamel (where not boxed-in to give a simpler shape and more easily cleaned surfaces; a treatment which gained popularity through the 1930s). The rim of the tub was made in the form of a roll moulding, cast in one piece with the bath. The rounded head, square foot, parallel or tapering sides and deep bulbous form carried on cast-iron feet are hallmarks of the traditional bathtub, characteristic of original installations in Edwardian houses, which endured fifty years of unpopularity before regaining appeal during the early 1980s. If the original bathtub in your house remains in good condition, it may be possible to recondition a discoloured interior either by employing specialists to 're-enamel' these surfaces or by repainting them with proprietary bath enamel. The taps and waste grating may also be replaced in any upgrading because good copies of ornate plated Edwardian-pattern taps are obtainable from several manufacturers (Fig. 173). When the fashion for 'boxing-in' the bathtub to simplify its form took hold in the 1930s, the favourite material for the panelled side of the bath and a sheer, wipe-clean dado on the enclosing walls was 'Vitrolite', an opaque glass, fixed, in quite large sheets, with chrome-plated dome-head screws, angles and cover strips. Favoured colours for this material included yellow, green and eau-de-nil, often contrasting with large areas of black glass.

Perhaps it is surprising to learn that much of the technology intrinsic to modern bathroom fittings existed at the beginning of the twentieth century. The predecessor of the modern 'mixer' tap was the combination bath tap, through which water was supplied to the bath via a single discharge nozzle containing the shut-off valves for the hot and cold water. A combined shower and plunge bath equivalent in operation to many modern installations was also available to the more affluent turn-of-the-century households. A standard cast-iron tub was modified to this arrangement by adding a U-plan, metallic-enamelled zinc or steel shield to the foot of the bath, accommodating vertical supply pipes serving the side spray and the overhead shower nozzle, the supply of water through these pipes being controlled by a tier of valves on the edge of this canopy (Fig. 174). An example of this type of fitting may be seen in the bathroom of Julius Drewe, client for Edwin Lutyens' great mansion of Castle Drogo, Devon, the building

FIG. 173, ABOVE. *Edwardian-style brass basin tap. (Sanitary Appliances.)*

FIG. 174. *Combined roll-rim, cast-iron bathtub and moulded zinc shower screen.*

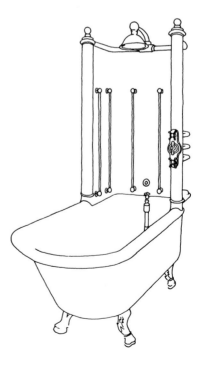

of which was an initiative of the years immediately before and after the First World War. A cheaper type of combined plunge and shower bath substituted for the zinc shield a flexible rubber curtain hung on rings sliding on a circular tube around the shower nozzle. Inclusion of a side spray from vertical supply pipes was impractical in this 'budget' arrangement.

Purpose-made, independent shower baths were rarely installed in pre-World War houses, and the typical speculative builder did not consider their inclusion in the bathrooms of small houses of the inter-war period to be necessary. Today, many ingenious shower fittings and complementary compact shower trays in porcelain-enamelled fireclay, moulded polycarbonate, resin-bonded reconstituted marble and so on, are available to make the inclusion of a shower bath in a refurbished house more of a standard feature than a luxury. A new shower bath is best built into a fully tiled recess so that the impervious surface of the tiles protects the other elements of the local building construction from the detrimental effects of steam and water.

Water Closets

As with lavatory basins, so with water closets: the basic types still installed today were familiar to the Edwardians. The pedestal wash-down closet is the 'classic' WC. The essential features of this fitting are: 1) an impervious basin of suitable shape and area to be completely drenched by the flushing water, 2) the retention of sufficient water in the trap at the base of the fitting to ensure the immediate immersion and dilution of excreta and to prevent the pan from venting the soil pipe, 3) the provision of a flushing rim which thoroughly distributes the flushing water, and 4) a trap which immediately refills with fresh water when the foul water has been evacuated. A standard installation incorporated a cast-iron flushing cistern fixed about 1800mm (6ft) above the closet, the ball valve that released the water being operated by a pull chain. The manufacturer's name was often embossed on the front face of a metal cistern or sealed into the glaze coating of the fireclay in the case of a ceramic cistern. Before the advent of plastics ('Bakelite' was the first, introduced in the late 1930s) WC seats were always of wood – varnished hardwood such as west African mahogany in expen-

sive houses, enamelled or painted softwood in cheaper dwellings.

The syphonic type of flushing WC was sometimes installed in expensive houses. It tends to be quieter in operation than the simple washdown closet as it operates on the principle that the syphonic action of its deep-seal trap draws the contents of the pan down to the soilpipe as fresh water flushes the basin. The fireclay moulding of this type of WC is much more complicated than that of a washdown closet and a larger-capacity cistern giving a minimum 3-gallon flush was necessary in early models. Again, the flushing cistern was almost always sited at high level, an arrangement ensuring efficient flushing which is rarely employed in modern houses. Yet the low-level cisterns, which proliferate in new and 'modernised' dwellings, were known to the Edwardians, and even a type of low-level cistern with push-button flushing apparatus similar in its operation to the modern space-saving 'flush panel' cisterns was available. In the inter-war years, builders of speculative houses, ever keen to economise in the interests of producing a saleable product at a competitive price, had recognised that the low-level cistern offered an advantage over the traditional high-level installation because it could be sited under a window, an arrangement which was potentially space and cost-saving. Thereafter, the close-coupled, low-level suite quickly became the standard arrangement. In order to compensate for the less efficient flush of a low-level cistern, many early installations included a large-diameter flush pipe between cistern and pan (minimum diameter 63mm [2½in] but modern suites rarely incorporate a flushing pipe greater than 38mm (1½in) in diameter.

Hot Water Supply

In a modern centrally heated house where low-pressure hot water is the heating medium, a supply of hot water is normally provided by employing a branch of the heating system to warm cold water stored in an insulated cylinder or *calorifier*. Water in this tank is heated by a coil of copper pipe integral to the central heating system, which passes through the vessel. Cold water from the high-level storage tank refills the cylinder as the hot water is drawn off. This system is easily assembled from the small-diameter copper pipes, which are standard to modern low-pressure, hot-water, panel-radiator central heating, but these components were not available before the Second World War and domestic water heating was usually achieved by a more direct method.

The standard domestic arrangement of an Edwardian house comprised the *back boiler* of a cooking range or living-room grate, which received heat from an open fire when a damper was disengaged. The heated water, becoming less dense, ascended a flow pipe into a large storage cylinder, thus displacing cold water already stored in this tank, which was induced to enter the boiler, there to be heated, until hot water filled the entire system. Hot water for washing could then be drawn off at the bathroom and kitchen taps. These storage cylinders were generally built into the internal brickwork of the house – normally at high level within the chimneybreast, which also housed the range or grate, thus economising on the connecting pipework. This arrangement ensured good insulation of the cylinder and conserved the heat of the stored hot water. Siting the system at the centre of the house also ensured that radiant heat from the stored water and adjacent building fabric helped to keep the rooms warm. Where the parts of such a system remain in good condition despite disuse, it may be possible to return the storage cylinder and supply pipes to working order, even if the original heat source of an open fire is defunct, by installing an electric immersion heater in the tank. This device, which is cheaply purchased but can be costly in operation, heats the stored water when energised by throwing a switch.

The condition of the pipework connecting the back boiler to the cylinder is clearly a main consideration in any scheme to bring an antique hot water system back into use. Four main types of tube were used for this purpose and to supply hot water to the taps: lead, galvanized iron, brass or copper tube. Although copper pipe was highly valued because the metal is not corroded by pure water and it is sufficiently elastic not to be adversely affected by the expansion caused by passage of hot water, it was rarely used before the Second World War because of its high price. Similarly, brass pipework was unusual, not only because of its high cost, but also because it was more likely than copper to split in service.

Galvanized iron pipe was most commonly used for cold and hot water distribution, but it is prone to corrode at joints and bends where the protective galvanizing can be eaten away by friction or maintenance. Equally liable to fail, but by reason of their poor elasticity rather than any special susceptibility to corrode, were lead hot water pipes which were the favoured means of conveying hot and cold water in most houses of the north of England.

Range boilers were made in various shapes and sizes from cast iron, wrought iron and copper. Cast iron, being the cheapest material, was very widely used in speculative houses and if a cast-iron boiler was imperfectly made or in any way misused, the brittle nature of the material might result in an explosion and the possibility of serious injury to people. Used with soft water, cast-iron boilers very soon rusted and discoloured the water. Wrought-iron boilers were usually made from 6–10mm (¼–⅜in) thick plates welded together. Standard shapes for these back boilers included the boot, arched and saddled forms, all of which were arranged to arch over a horizontal duct of the flue leading from the open fire.

By the later inter-war years, technical developments allowed the newer heating fuels – gas and electricity – to be applied to the task of water heating. Electricity could be used to heat water in the storage cistern through operation of an immersion heater and hot water for the bath and wash-hand basin was readily obtained in this way. The same fuel could provide hot water to the kitchen sink from a local storage cistern – often sited over or adjacent to the sink. The 'Sadia' electric water heater was one of the favourite brands for this application. Of course, the competing gas companies were not keen to let the electricity suppliers have the field of local water heating all to themselves, and even more common than the electric water heater was the 'Ascot'; a small gas-fired water storage cylinder which occupied the same position alongside the sink, hot water to the sink being supplied via a swan-neck-profile chrome steel pipe which could be swung away to give clear access to the sink after the hot water had been provided. Many present-day flats, either purpose-built or resulting from conversion of houses, continue to be served by this form of localised hot-water heating, though the 'instant' water heaters that are used tend to be fuelled by electricity in preference to gas which continues to be viewed as the optimum fuel for combination and balanced-flue boilers serving conventional central heating/hot water installations.

In larger houses and blocks of flats, neither the simple domestic range boiler nor localised water heaters were adequate to meet the water-heating needs and an independent boiler had to be installed for this purpose. Normally constructed from 8–10mm (⁵⁄₁₆–³⁄₈in) thick wrought-iron plate in the same way as good-quality back boilers, they were much more powerful than the built-in type. A chamber for burning the solid fuel fed in through an iron fire door was surrounded by water contained in a wrought-iron jacket. When heated, the water ascended into the pipework of the hot water system through a flow pipe on top of the boiler and was displaced by colder water returning from the system through a pipe entering the boiler casing at low level. An independent boiler required two basic features unnecessary to a back boiler; namely, its own flue or pipe connection to a conventional chimney flue, and a high-level steam pipe fitted with a safety valve.

DRAINAGE

Drainage Below Ground

The method of disposing of soil and waste water from a house depends upon the availability of a public sewer. By the beginning of the twentieth century many urban and suburban areas were provided with the public sewerage systems that remain largely unmodified today.

Rural houses

In the Edwardian period, new labourers' cottages in rural locations still relied on the primitive sanitation deemed acceptable by the Victorians before the introduction of public health legislation. Even artistically advanced architects such as M. H. Baillie Scott (a contemporary of Edwin Lutyens and a leading designer of Arts and Crafts style houses) did not feel it was necessary to include baths in artisans' cottages before the First World War and this indifference to what we would consider basic sanitary provision

extended to inclusion of water closets. Particularly in the absence of a public sewer, there was little stimulus to install a WC and purpose-built cottages from this period were often not served by any sanitation more sophisticated than an *earth closet*.

The principle of this fitting was that dry, loamy earth, freshly applied, would deodorize excreta, which could then be dug into the top surface of the garden earth. The fitting consisted of a perforated hinged seat on brackets, which extended over and held in place a portable pail. At the rear of the seat was a wooden box containing the dry earth, which was released into the pail by pulling up a stirrup-shaped handle located alongside the seat. When the pail was almost full, its contents were disposed of into the garden earth and the empty disinfected pail was re-fixed below the hinged seat.

More expensive rural houses were provided with water closets, which demanded the installation either of a watertight underground cesspool to collect the sewage or a septic tank for its purification, the latter device being effectively a small sewage treatment works. Even into the inter-war years, because it was an expensive facility to construct and maintain, the septic tank system of sewage treatment tended to be reserved for use with the largest rural houses.

Cesspools intended only to drain waste water from washing and food preparation were also called *soakaways* because they were built 'dry' in stone or brickwork with open joints, allowing the accumulated waste water to soak into the surrounding earth. Such underground chambers were usually cylindrical with a domed roof that might incorporate a circular opening in the crown fitted with a cast-iron airtight cover lying flush with the garden surface. Soakaways of this type function well only in certain types of earth. They were never located in clay soil, which is virtually impervious. Present-day local authority building control officers will not approve use of soakaways to drain waste water into any type of earth, but, subject to official approval, in some areas it may be possible to install new soakaways to serve new or modified rainwater drainage installations.

Watertight cesspools used in clayey soil where the liquids would not filter away, or in loose soil where pollution of the earth from sewage was unacceptable (variations in the requirements of local by-laws, particularly before the 1936 Public Health Act, meant that use of soakaways for sewage disposal was not proscribed in all areas), were built of bricks laid in cement mortar and a ventilating pipe was provided. The inside of the cylindrical chamber was finished with a coat of Portland cement in an attempt to make it watertight. Although good-quality construction demanded a 215mm (9in) thickness for the enclosing wall and vaulted roof of a 'tight' cesspool, if the supporting soil was dense and stable, the cement-rendered floor of the chamber was often applied over a single thickness of bricks rather than a more solid concrete-slab base. Sometimes a cesspool was split into two separate compartments, the first, smaller chamber being a settling tank for the solid waste and the second, larger vessel being the liquids chamber. In this arrangement, the accumulation of potentially explosive gases in both compartments would be avoided by the provision of piped outlets to a common air vent above ground.

The neatest type of cesspool currently available is a prefabricated GRP (glass-reinforced polyester) chamber that is simply buried in a large hole in a garden area adjoining the house. Local authorities covering rural areas generally provide a cesspool-emptying service, which involves pumping the accumulated waste into a mobile tank.

Apart from the foul-drainage system discharging into a cesspool or septic tank, and the gutters and downpipes draining rainwater from roofs into water butts or an external tank so that it might be used for washing and garden watering, land attached to rural houses was often safeguarded from flooding by installing a separate system of field drains. These consisted of short sections of earthenware pipe about 75mm (3in) in diameter, laid with open butt joints to allow percolation of the subsoil water through the joints. The pipes were placed about 1m below the surface in parallel lines about 1.8–2.4m (6–8ft) apart, the trenches in which they were housed being partly filled with loose stones to encourage drainage of the subsoil water into the pipes. In sparsely populated areas, such field drains were run to a convenient ditch, but in suburban locations where field drains were used to dry out otherwise marshy garden paths and so on, the drain was usually terminated at a soakaway sited in porous ground.

Urban houses

Two types of public underground drainage system exist in urban areas, namely combined and separate systems. The latter arrangement provides drains for foul water emanating from sinks and WCs, completely separate from those carrying surface water from roofs, yards and gardens. As its name suggests, the combined system discharges both types of drainage into a single sewer, introducing the risk of flooding at the sewage treatment works following a downpour. Where separate systems apply, the local authority will insist upon the installation of entirely separate foul and surface-water drains in any modification of the existing drainage necessitated by a proposed enlargement or alteration of a house or flat. In an area where separate systems do not exist but are proposed, the local authority may require new domestic drains to be kept separate to the line of the site boundary, beyond which they may discharge through a common pipe into the existing combined sewer.

Current building regulations require that drains sited below ground shall run straight between manholes (more properly termed *inspection chambers*) giving access to the pipes. This arrangement was reckoned to be good practice even before 1900, many years before the introduction of national building regulations prescribing a common standard, but the proliferation of local by-laws laying down differing requirements caused the details of underground drainage to vary from area to area. Therefore, it is not unusual to find wholly inaccessible curves built into drains below ground, particularly in the shallower drains clearing surface water. In the rectilinear arrangement of late-Victorian and Edwardian suburban estate development, it was generally an easy matter to ensure that drains ran straight between inspection chambers, but when the fashion for more picturesque, sinuous road layouts began to be followed by speculative builders in the inter-war years, a non-rectilinear, yet rational, hierarchical system of drainage was sometimes difficult to achieve and curves are often built into underground drainage in these layouts, reducing the reliability of the local system.

However, principles which were generally observed in house-drainage installations included discharging

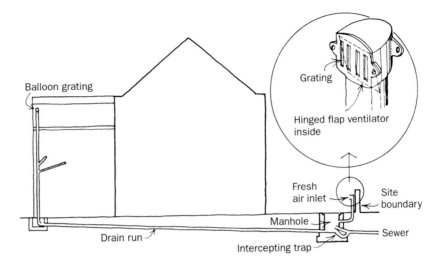

FIG. 175. Venting of external foul drain through the soil-and-vent pipe terminating above the house eaves and at the site boundary.

kitchen sinks into a waste pipe separate from that serving the bath, wash-hand basin and WC, providing trapped gullies for the waste water discharged from kitchen sinks, and avoiding locating drains beneath dwellings. In many provincial towns, rainwater pipes and sink, basin and bath wastes were required to discharge into the open air over a gully, and some districts permitted the discharge of bath and basin wastes into rainwater hopperheads, although this practice is prohibited today. In London the arrangement of rainwater or bath and basin wastes discharging into a gully above the level of water in the trap and below the grating was allowed, and this prevented dead leaves etc., which are carried down the rainwater pipes, from fouling the gully grating.

British sanitary regulations traditionally required underground drains to be disconnected from the house at one end and from the sewer at the other, causing the house drainage to be doubly disconnected from the public sewer. Disconnection at the house end was effected by the water-retaining traps fitted below the sink, wash-hand basin and bath and incorporated in the WC as well as by the gullies over which the wastes discharged. Disconnection at the other end of the drain was achieved by means of an intercepting trap or *interceptor*. In many areas, ventilation of the drain by at least two untrapped openings sited at its opposite ends was a supplementary

requirement. This connection was usually satisfied by providing a fresh-air inlet at the foot of the drain which vented the manhole nearest the sewer with a single short length of vertical pipe sited against the back of the front boundary garden wall or fence. This boundary manhole provided access to the interceptor. At the top of the fresh-air inlet a mica flap valve was fitted for the purpose of admitting fresh air and preventing foul air from escaping. At the head of the drain a foul-air outlet was provided by extending the soil pipe serving the WC above eaves level and covering the open end of this *soil and vent pipe* with a balloon-shaped wire cage, preventing birds and leaves from getting in (Fig. 175).

Although every attempt was made to avoid laying drains below a house for fear of the damage to pipes that could be caused by differential settlement between the house foundations (through which the pipes passed) and surrounding earth, in terraced houses drained to the front, the location of drains below the structure could not be avoided. In best-quality work the portion of the drain that passed below the house was carried out in cast-iron pipes, giving a very rigid construction, which was not susceptible to distortion or collapse. However, the high cost of this arrangement caused many builders of suburban houses to rely instead on encasing conventional salt-glazed stoneware pipes in a concrete 'jacket' about 150mm (6in) thick where they passed below the building. To further protect the drain against damage caused by settlement, a space was left between the top of the pipe and the brickwork or stonework of any foundation wall through which it passed. An arch, turned over the drain, leaving a 50–75mm (2–3in) deep airspace over the encased pipe, gave a satisfactory detail. Pipes of 102mm (4 in) internal diameter (the conventional size), laid to a fall of 1 in 40, were sufficiently large to serve the combined foul and surface-water drainage discharged from even a large detached house.

Medium-size terraced and semi-detached houses draining to the front or rear may utilise only two manholes – one in the rear yard that accepts connections from the soil stack, waste and rainwater gullies, and one by the front boundary, which gives access to the interceptor. In contrast, large detached houses may boast six or seven separate manholes, receiving connections from a multiplicity of waste and rainwater gullies scattered around the external walls and accommodating the sharp changes in direction of the main drain that are necessary to carry it around the perimeter of the house.

Drain Construction

Only two types of pipe suitable for underground house-drainage were available before the Second World War: cast-iron pipes and salt-glazed stoneware pipes.

Cast-iron pipes were made in stock lengths of 915mm, 1830mm and 2745mm (3ft, 6ft and 9ft), exclusive of the *socket* or swelled end, into which the plain or *spigot* end of the next pipe was fitted. Pipes

were available from 51–254mm (2–10in) internal diameter, increasing in approximately 25mm (1in) increments. Cast-iron pipes used below ground were bedded on concrete and the joints between sections were always caulked with molten lead. They are still used today for high-quality underground drainage but the old technique of sealing joints with lead has been superseded by quicker and more reliable patented jointing systems.

Much more widely used in early twentieth-century underground drainage were salt-glazed stoneware pipes. These were made with internal diameters of 51mm, 76mm, 102mm, 153mm and 229mm (2, 3, 4, 6 and 9in) for use in residential development. Pipes of 51 and 76mm diameter were used only for surface water drainage. Stoneware pipes were 686mm (27in) long, 76mm (3in) being taken up by the socket so that a standard distance of 610 mm (2ft) between sockets resulted. Joints between pipes were made with Portland cement mortar composed either of neat cement or cement and sand in equal proportions. To help the drain layer to centre the spigot of an upper pipe in the socket of a lower section in a slightly inclined drain, a gasket of tarred yarn was sometimes inserted in the socket. However, this technique was frowned on by some local authorities who insisted on the joint being formed purely with cement. A circular cement joint of consistent thickness was the correct result of this method of joining pipes, the cement being finished with a ramped profile on the pipe's outer surface, to form a collar around the upper pipe (Fig. 176). The drain layer

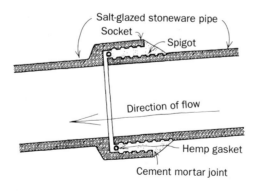

FIG. 176. Joint of socketed, salt-glazed earthenware underground drainage pipes.

accounted for excess cement being squeezed into the pipe as it was laid by drawing a semi-circular wooden scraper (a *badger*) through the sections of pipe in which joints had been freshly made, in order to clean out any cement droppings. In most districts it was common practice simply to bed a run of pipes directly on earth but this was known to be a defective arrangement and in good-quality work pipes were laid on a continuous bed of concrete.

This method of drain-laying prevailed until the 1960s, but since that time, technical developments have revolutionized underground drainage installations. A type of fireclay pipe is still commonly used for buried drain runs, but instead of the rigid construction resulting from the use of cement-jointed socket connections (which are susceptible to fracture with settlement of the supporting ground), a flexible system is adopted, the connections between pipes being formed with a moulded polypropylene collar containing gaskets which prevent the joints from leaking. Because a flexible drain run will tolerate small movements without fracturing, the rigid base essential to a traditional installation may also be dispensed with, and the pipes are often run in a trench partly filled with carefully graded gravel or pea shingle which spreads rather than concentrates any loads imposed over the drain-run, thus minimising deflection and distortion of the pipes. These flexible systems include the pipe sizes and standard accessories, such as clayware trapped gullies that are conventional in traditional stoneware drainage, so it is quite possible to modify or extend an existing rigid installation with pipes joined by flexible connections if the necessary adaptors are obtained. Robust PVCu (unplasticised polyvinylchloride) pipes are also increasingly used for underground drainage in new work.

Manholes

Nowadays it is recommended that manholes should be built from 215mm (9in) thick brickwork on a base of 150mm (6in) thick concrete, but in older domestic drainage it is common to find manholes enclosed only by 102mm (4½in) thick, single-skin brickwork. The internal dimensions of even shallow manholes are rarely less than 750 × 600mm (2ft 6in × 2ft), dimensions often matched in the

cast-iron access cover which seals the top of the chamber. Current standards require the walls to be built of hard, impervious brick of semi-engineering quality, but this requirement is fairly new, and common bricks were often used in old construction. Where such soft bricks were used, it was customary to render the internal surface of the brickwork with cement. This treatment did nothing to protect cheap bricks from the frost damage to which they are susceptible.

The internal arrangements of manholes differed according to the pipework adopted for the drainage. In cast-iron drainage, the channels and bends used in manholes are of full circular section. They differ from those used in less accessible locations only by incorporating openings in their top surfaces for inspection purposes. These openings are fitted with screw-down iron covers and thus the openings to the manhole from the drain are completely closed. In stoneware drains the drain is wholly open to the manhole, the channels being of half-round section and the connecting bends from branches being of three-quarter-round section. For a 'standard' manhole of a domestic system, built in the time-honoured way, the following construction sequence applies; the circular-section main drain and branches from the sanitary fittings are built into the chamber walls at precise levels above the concrete base slab to ensure the correct fall of the drain, and these outlets are then connected up with the semi-circular and three-quarter-round sections of channel and branch bends which are cut to lengths and profiles which will guarantee an unimpeded flow of solids and waste water. The spaces left between the sides of the channels and the manhole walls are then filled with dense, fine concrete finished to a sloping profile with an absolutely smooth surface. This *benching* ensures that in a drain which overflows because it has to cope with a sudden torrent of rainwater, the excess water will always return to the main channel and not lodge in a low area where it can become stagnant and infectious (Fig. 177). For this reason, fractured or damaged benching should always be restored to a smooth, impervious finish without delay. Sub-standard benching is usually the most easily noticed defect when a manhole cover is lifted for inspection of a drain. Where a deep manhole was necessary, as on a

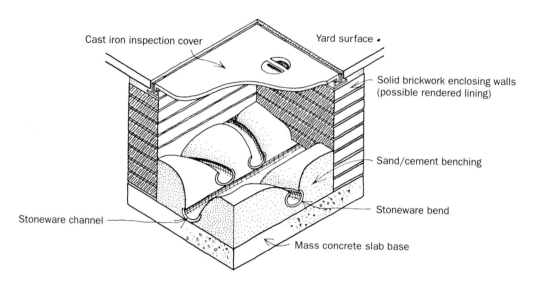

FIG. 177. Brickwork inspection chamber ('manhole') construction.

steeply sloping site, it was usual to arch the enclosing brickwork over the outlet from the manhole to the drain to protect the drain connection from any settlement of the brick chamber.

Defects in Underground Drainage

Defective joints are probably the most common cause of blockages in stoneware drains. Where the drain layer failed to centre the spigot of the upper pipe truly in the socket of the lower section, the internal moulding of the socket may project above the general *invert* (flow) level of the pipe, thus causing an obstruction that will trap sediment and eventually block the pipe. This defect was made worse if excess cement from the badly formed joint was allowed to fall on to the offending projection. Clearly, the risk of blockage was thereby increased, and the danger of sewage seeping into the surrounding earth through an incomplete cement joint was introduced. In a case where sewage percolates out of a pipe, not only is public health endangered by contaminated soil, but also blockage of lower reaches of the pipe is threatened because liquid sewage flowing out of an incomplete joint forms a current under the pipe which will work sand and mud into lower open joints, ultimately blocking the

pipe at a point where its slope is not great enough for the sediment to be washed forward.

A further problem invited by cracked or incomplete cement joints is the tendency of the leaky construction to attract tree roots. All tree roots, and particularly those of the willow, grow towards water. The fine roots furthest from the tree then enter the pipe through very small holes, ultimately choking the drain through the growth of small fibrous roots inside the pipe.

Where a leaking drain is not in danger of blockage from tree roots but occupies a narrow gangway alongside the house, greater problems are posed by the adverse effect on the adjoining foundation of the constantly saturated soil. A previous owner may have ignored a leaking drain carrying only waste water or rainwater because it did not seem to represent a health hazard, but as the ground below the adjacent footing becomes more marshy, it is less able to support the foundation, and if this condition arises at a corner where there is no scope for the footing to span over this soft spot, collapse of the foundation and the wall it supports will follow.

Almost all defects in old underground drainage are due to the inflexibility of the pipework. Settlement of the surrounding earth imposes stresses on the pipes, which cause the hard cement joints to fracture. This shortcoming has been largely corrected in modern drainage systems through the adoption of flexibly-jointed pipework.

The wide range of possible defects in underground drainage confirms the particular importance of conducting a thorough inspection of this element of the building before completing the purchase of any older house.

Drainage Above Ground

Lead and cast iron were the two materials from which pipes carrying external drainage above ground were made. Lead was preferred to cast iron, not only by architects but also by local authorities, as late as 1914, though in imitation of American practice, cast iron was increasingly adopted for cheaper buildings and by the inter-war period it had almost entirely superseded lead as the material for the downpipes of urban and suburban buildings.

Cast-iron soil and waste pipes were lighter than underground drain pipes of the same material, and those used to convey rainwater were of lighter section still. Soil and waste pipes were invariably of circular cross-section, as indeed were 'standard' rainwater pipes, but pipes of square, rectangular or even octagonal section were often used in prestigious buildings. Circular, square and rectangular-section pipes continue to be available today, but local authority building control officers may disallow the use of square and rectangular-section cast-iron rainwater pipes if they also vent a drain because the generous tolerances necessary to the casting process remove the possibility of a consistent fit at spigot/socket connections, making it impossible to guarantee impervious joints. The connection of vertical cast-iron pipes was achieved by the method described earlier for joining underground drainage.

The accessories of an exposed cast-iron rainwater drainage system are its most attractive features. Sections of pipe with ears already cast on for fixing the vertical assembly to the wall were manufactured, but often separate ornate pipe clips or *holderbats* were used for this purpose, each clip being secured to a horizontal brick joint with two 100mm (4in) long, wrought-iron, rainwater pipe nails. Where the roofs drained to a lead-lined internal parapet gutter,

openings lined in lead had to be formed at suitable intervals in the parapet to carry the accumulated rainwater out into hopperheads, which were sometimes of quite elaborate design, even in some cases incorporating the date of the building's construction and the initials of its owner (Fig. 178). These details were borrowed from the traditional forms of lead downpipes and hopperheads, the skills necessary to the creation of these features being greatly valued by the British Arts and Crafts Movement architects, who endeavoured to preserve or revive this dying expertise in their detailing of several large, late-Victorian and Edwardian houses. Lead, because it is easily moulded, is much more able than cast iron to be formed into highly ornate and even fanciful shapes. The clips or tacks securing old lead pipes are invariably more elaborate than mass-produced, cast-iron holderbats.

Whether of cast iron or lead, the sizes of the soil and waste pipes that were carried externally to the vent stack connecting with the drain were fairly consistent. The vertical soil and vent pipe itself was usually at least 88mm (3½in) in internal diameter, a pipe 102mm (4in) in diameter being widely employed in cast-iron drainage. Soil pipes feeding into this stack from WCs were of equal diameter. Bath and sink wastes were of smaller diameter –

FIG. 178. A cast-iron rainwater hopperhead embossed with the house construction date.

usually in the range 38–63mm (1½–2½in), lead being the favoured material for these thinner pipes. The problem of connecting lead to iron pipes was overcome by sleeving the end of the lead in a brass ferrule, to which it was bonded with a wiped solder joint, and securely caulking the ferrule into the socket of the iron pipe with molten lead. Where a lead stack pipe had to connect to a stoneware socket (as applied at the head of the underground drainage), Portland cement rather than caulked lead filled the joint around the brass ferrule.

Dwellings fitted with overground drainage entirely of cast iron which also had overhanging eaves, also used cast-iron gutters. Although these were often of half-round section to suit the simpler forms favoured by the later years of the inter-war period, the ogee profile continued to be a popular and decorative pattern. This gutter pattern is once again readily available, thanks largely to the introduction of a portable machine that forms colour-coated aluminium strip to ogee profile. Modern aluminium ogee guttering avoids the chief defect of the cast-iron product; namely, rusting of the flat vertical backplate of the gutter around its fixing nails, causing leaks and the eventual collapse of the worst-afflicted sections. As the aluminium product is thin-walled (unlike cast-iron guttering), a less attractive feature of the modern version is its insubstantial appearance, which is particularly noticeable at the end of a run because the gutter profile is usually blanked off with a shaped piece of sheet aluminium. This form of gutter is also readily distorted when ladders are leaned against the eaves. A range of more robust components that also replicates the traditional cast-iron ogee gutter is available in the form of cast-aluminium guttering, which will accept the pressure imposed by an access ladder

and, when painted, appears indistinguishable from the cast-iron prototype.

The continued availability of cast iron for soil and rainwater pipes has led to its use in many restoration projects, but the high cost of the material and its susceptibility to fracture when roughly handled rules it out for low-budget repairs and renovations. Moulded PVCu piping is almost universally used in new work and in the rehabilitation of old houses, standard colours being white, beige, light grey and black. Black is perhaps the most suitable colour for replacement gutters because a line of black guttering seen against the background of a pale-coloured painted fascia tends to look slighter than it is. Also the carbon black, which is a constituent of the material, safeguards black plastic rainwater goods against early degradation by the ultra-violet wavelength of sunlight. Various patented systems of half-round, deep half-elliptical, trapezoidal trough-section and ogee-profile PVCu guttering are available for fixing by the moderately skilled handyman. Light grey seems to be the finish favoured for new PVCu external waste, soil and vent pipes. This neutral colour is fairly inconspicuous in the context of most traditional building materials but it can be over painted with conventional gloss paints, with some hope of a reasonably durable finish, if a different colour scheme is required or it is necessary for new work or adaptation to harmonise with retained features. Joints between sections of pipe are achieved either with 'push-fit' couplings incorporating flexible gaskets, or by use of a plastics solvent cement. A full range of fittings for the various proprietary systems, including the moulded plastic versions of all the accessories germane to cast-iron drainage, is available through the larger DIY stores.

CHAPTER 9

Outside the House

The walls, fence, railings or hedge enclosing the site on which your house stands may have as much aesthetic impact as the building materials exposed on the outside of the house itself.

Garden walls were commonly of the same materials as the main house walls, and even low brickwork walls (*dwarf walls*) in Edwardian work tended to be at least 225mm (9in) thick with impervious copings of terracotta or durable stone where a creasing tile course below a brick-on-edge coping was not adopted. The modern method of building single-skin (102mm (4½in) thick) brickwork garden walls reinforced with frequent piers was unknown, though small panels of single-skin brickwork were sometimes incorporated in dwarf walls which were otherwise 225mm (9in) thick.

Although they may appear robust, garden walls of Edwardian and inter-war houses were generally erected in continuous ranges without expansion joints and with poor or inadequate foundations, so that many examples have suffered badly from settlement with compression of the topsoil of the supporting ground that is attempting to bear their weight. The piling of garden earth behind the inside face of a garden wall at the site boundary (for example, at the rear edge of the pavement) is also a common cause of problems, the wall being induced to overturn, threatening injury to passers-by with potential legal consequences! Short of complete demolition and rebuilding, there is little that can be done to salvage such poor-quality construction, although it may be possible to renew only the most defective sections of such a wall by rebuilding them above improved foundations, the rest of the retained

construction having been underpinned. Where a considerable length of wall is to be rebuilt, it is wise to incorporate expansion joints at not more than 6m (20ft) intervals, because use of the Portland cement mortars that are conventional today will produce a mass brickwork construction which is far less tolerant of thermal movement (and hence resistance to unsightly and stability-threatening cracking) than the lime mortar which dominated domestic construction for at least the first three decades of the twentieth century. Various compressible joint fillers of foam polyurethane or bitumen-impregnated fibreboard, varying in thickness between 3–30mm (⅛–1¼in) are available for insertion in expansion joints.

In a brick wall it is usually most convenient to break a continuous surface with a 10mm (⅜in) wide vertical gap. Once filled to within 10mm of each face with a proprietary joint filler, this joint is then sealed in the plane of both wall surfaces with a water-excluding polysulphide or silicone mastic. These mastics are available in a range of colours which make it possible to achieve a close match to mortar-joint colour or a colour complementary to most facing bricks.

It is hardly worthwhile to offer advice about existing timber fences, because by the inter-war period the appeal of erecting cheap fences instead of brick walls had become clear to the speculative builders, and most put up rather ephemeral barriers to screen gardens from those of neighbours to either side and the rear. In many cases these were very nominal post-and-wire constructions and it will be appreciated that even more substantial timber-boarded fences erected as late as 1939 are unlikely to have survived to the present day. A front boundary treatment once seen fairly widely in association with inter-war suburban villas, and favoured by at least one leading contemporary architect and critic of suburban development (Clough Williams-Ellis) was a series of white-painted timber posts linked by hanging black-painted spiked chains. This was a fashion imported from the USA which is rarely seen today, no doubt because the posts are very ready to rot at their interface with the pavement or garden earth and the chains both invite vandalism and present more of a decorative than practical barrier to intruders unless reinforced by a hedge.

Hedges were a very popular treatment for defining boundaries, particularly the once-ubiquitous privet hedge which was adopted as the front boundary treatment of countless suburban villas. Unfortunately, expanding car ownership has endangered the very existence of the suburban front garden, all too many of which have been converted into hard-standing for the family motor car, necessitating the removal of the front garden wall and hedge, to produce a street scene more ragged than the neatness and uniformity which typified suburbia in the inter-war and immediate post-war periods.

RAILINGS AND GATES

The decorative potential of cast-and wrought-iron in architecture was very fully exploited in the nineteenth century, though highly ornate treatments lost some of their appeal in the context of general enthusiasm for simpler cottage-style dwellings from the 1880s. Thus, metal railings are rarely found in association with Edwardian and inter-war suburban and rural houses, though some sophisticated examples of *art nouveau* style railings were installed to enclose the sites of turn-of-the-century urban houses. By the beginning of the twentieth century, cast iron was rarely used in railings. It tends to be brittle and consequently cast-iron balusters needed to be thicker than the sizes dictated by the aesthetic preferences of the time. The revival of traditional building crafts, which was a main ambition of the Arts and Crafts Movement, meant that forged-iron or wrought-iron work, which displayed the skill of the blacksmith in exploiting the malleability and ductility of the mate-

rial, was preferred to that of mould-formed, cast-iron components.

Wrought iron is obtained by the elimination of carbon and other impurities from the basic *pig iron* that is the initial product of the iron-smelting process. It reached the blacksmith's shop in the form of bars, ready for working. Ornamental features were produced by hammering red-hot iron into the form required, or by bending and twisting it, when cold, into the desired shapes. The former technique is known as forged work and is the superior method. Only in this way can the metal be controlled so that delicate ornament, such as flowers, can be formed. Today, a request for 'wrought-iron' gates or railings will invariably result in features fabricated from mild steel, which is easily formed when cold and is more readily welded than the traditional material. As the mild steel used for this purpose is often obtained in strip form, these products tend to lack the solidity seen in true wrought-iron features and unprotected mild steel rusts much more readily than wrought iron.

Wrought-iron Railings and Gates

A railing is formed from many separate components, jointed together in one of two ways; by welding or by mechanical connections – usually collars and bolts. The simplest form of railing is an assembly of vertical bars, 22–25mm (⅞–1in) in diameter, spaced at 150–175mm (6–7in) centres, passing through the top and riveted to the bottom rail, and forged in the form of spikes at the top. The horizontal rails are likely to be about 50mm (2in) wide and around 13mm (½in) thick. Another familiar and less basic type of railing incorporated a third horizontal rail, sited not less than 225mm (9in) above the bottom rail. In the space between these two rails, metal scrolls or additional vertical dog bars were inserted to prevent the intrusion of dogs and also increase the strength of the railing.

Where railings were unusually high, or masonry piers giving firm fixings were not provided, or the spacing of the piers was too wide to secure the railings properly, it was necessary to provide *back stays*. These are merely 'props' extending from the back of the railing to give lateral strength. The back stay is always attached to a bar thicker than the regular standards located at either end of a bay of such bars, and, other than in the most utilitarian railings, it was common to turn the need for backstays into a feature of the design. A favourite means of incorporating such back stays and achieving a decorative effect was to site two principal vertical bars, strengthened by back stays, about 375mm (15in) apart, the space between them being filled with bold scrollwork or other complex geometry hammered from heavy bar iron. To make the railings a consistent deterrent to trespassers and to complement the integral decorative scrollwork, this panel might be surmounted by a scrollwork finial incorporating a spearpoint (Fig. 179).

The vertical standards of iron railings were placed in holes of dovetail section in a continuous sill formed from stone blocks, a stone coping or a hard brick coping to a brick dwarf wall, and were secured

by 'running' the holes with lead or neat Portland cement after the standards had been located. Lead, carefully caulked after having been poured, is the best fixing material, except in a very damp location, where corrosion of the iron at the point where it meets the lead is likely to occur. In such a case Ordinary Portland Cement (OPC) should be used for re-fixing dislodged railings.

Although bar steel is available in a range of sections and sizes, some of which are almost identical to the bar sizes found in wrought ironwork, it may be impossible to obtain an exact match for missing components of an incomplete iron railing from the 'stock' steel sizes. Where facsimile fittings in cast- or wrought-iron cannot be obtained, to achieve a completely inconspicuous repair it may be necessary to replace a complete range of standards with steel bars of the section most closely resembling the original components.

The simplest form of metal gate comprises a rectangular frame, infilled with vertical bars. Modern garden gates in 'wrought iron' are invariably fabricated from sections of mild steel strip and bar, bent to shape and welded together, often in forms alien to the blacksmith's craft as it was traditionally practised in Britain. The bar from which the body of the gate is hung is called the *back standard* or *hanging bar*, and the opposite post is called the *front bar*. In the case of double gates without any fixed post between them, the front bars are called *meeting bars*; a *slam plate* riveted to one of these enables the gates to engage on each other and eases the exercise of fastening them together. As the back standard bears the whole weight of the gate, in authentic wrought ironwork the bar used in this position can vary from 32mm (1¼in) to 100mm (4in) square according to the size of the gate. The bottom rail is then of the same width but much less thick. The top rail can be thinner than the bottom rail but is often of equal width because it must be sufficiently wide to allow the standards forming the 'infill' of the gate to pass through without seriously weakening it. In the case of a gate with 25mm (1in) square-section standards, the top and bottom rails must be 50mm (2in) wide.

Iron gates may be hung on *pintles* projecting from the flanking masonry, which engage on tubular lugs welded to the back standard. This arrangement

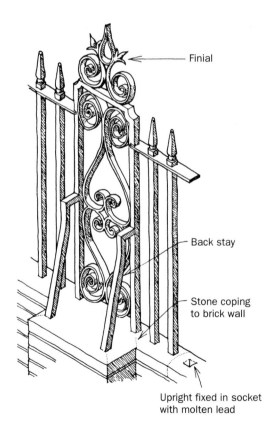

Finial

Back stay

Stone coping
to brick wall

Upright fixed in socket
with molten lead

FIG. 179. Decorative panel in wrought-iron railings rooted in a low brickwork plinth.

suffers the disadvantage that the gate is readily lifted off the pintles, limiting its usefulness as a security barrier. Light gates can be hung on butt hinges like internal doors, though this method was rarely adopted. A looped hinge or hanger at the top of the back standard and a pivot at its foot, on which the whole weight of the gate is imposed, was the most suitable way of hanging heavy iron gates. In this arrangement, the back standard of the gate is rounded where the hinge clasps it and the hinge is formed from a loop of thick strip-metal bolted around a short piece of bar iron, one end of which is formed in a semi-circle, the other end being *ragged* (formed with jagged edges) for the purpose of fixing the hinge into the flanking surface of brickwork or masonry (Fig. 180). In careful construction, the inside of the hinge was lined with a gunmetal collar. This detail prevented the hinge and back standard from coming into contact and thus reduced the risk of rust forming at this point.

The cheapest means of providing a pivot at the foot of the back standard was to locate this member in a dished metal socket set firmly in the ground. Many householders will confirm that this method suffers the disadvantage that accumulated dirt eventually clogs the socket and the gate becomes difficult to move. A neater and more reliable detail places the dished profile in the underside of the back standard, the projecting pivot on which it engages being set into the ground. The joint between the two components is thereby raised above ground level and the risk of jamming is consequently reduced. If a small oil hole is drilled through the flared end of the back standard, seated on the pivot, it is a simple matter to lubricate the joint periodically, so preventing squeaks (see Fig. 180).

Wooden Gates

Few original wooden gates of even inter-war houses are likely to have survived until the present day. Continuous use and continuous exposure to the weather quite quickly take their toll on wooden gates, particularly if they are not repainted fairly regularly. When renewing a decayed wooden gate, it is advisable to arrange for its replacement to be made in hardwood, even where a painted finish is desired or appropriate, because the hardwoods used in building are more rot-resistant than any of the easily available softwoods. Many large DIY stores stock a range of 'standard' garden gates fabricated from hardwood, but the look of a traditional garden gate, largely resembling a ledge-braced and battened external door but with voids alternating with the vertical wooden slats to partially screen the garden beyond, is likely to be achievable only if it is made by the householder or commissioned as a 'special' from a joinery workshop. This formula is even more essential where more individual, yet authentic designs are desired (one thinks of the timber gates bearing a 'sunburst' motif, which were a very popular way of sealing entrance paths and vehicle drives at the front boundary of semi-detached houses of the 1920s and 30s).

New gates should be hung on metal strap hinges fixed to a stout hardwood post set tightly in a galvanized steel socket secured in a concrete foundation sited considerably below ground level. In this way, even with eventual rotting of the timber at its point

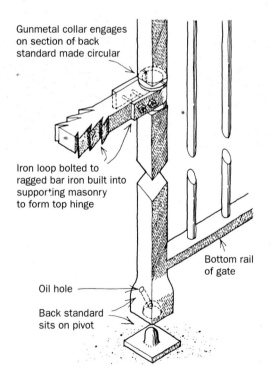

Gunmetal collar engages on section of back standard made circular

Iron loop bolted to ragged bar iron built into supporting masonry to form top hinge

Bottom rail of gate

Oil hole

Back standard sits on pivot

FIG. 180. Fixing and hinge details of a wrought-iron gate.

of contact with the ground, removal of the decayed post from its subterranean steel sleeve and its replacement with new timber, is simplified.

BALCONIES, PORCHES AND VERANDAHS

In suburban houses, elaborate carpentry is often seen in association with balconies, porches and verandahs and the decorative treatment of the timber complexities of these features is readily recognised as an essential quality of Edwardian villas.

A verandah, which is roofed by an upper storey of a house or a projection of the main roof, or a lean-to roof, is sometimes termed a *loggia* (Fig. 181) even if it is open (or openable) only on its main elevation and not at the sides, as the description strictly requires. However, the principles of the construction of the timber floors and balustrades integral to these features are the same.

The wooden floor of a verandah or timber balcony was made to slope at about 1 in 50 from the main house elevation to its front edge. For this reason, the floorboards were usually laid from the front to the back of the projecting verandah or balcony and not across its width, discouraging rainwater from lodging in the joints. Joists running parallel to the main elevation rather than perpendicular to it resulted from this arrangement and support for these joists was obtained by notching them into stout timber girders built into the house elevation and the brick or timber structure supporting the verandah's outer edge (Fig. 182). In a long verandah these girders would be sited at intervals not exceeding 3m (10ft), but a small balcony might require only two girders, one supporting each end. To give the required outward slope to the verandah floor, these girders could be laid at the necessary inclination or their top surfaces could be sloped to the desired pitch. In either case, the joists were installed so that their top surfaces were flush with those of the girders, the flooring being laid directly on this common surface.

To be enduring, verandah flooring was at least 32mm (1¼in) thick, of tongue-and-groove profile, and laid in white lead; that is, the joint between any two boards was thoroughly filled with a paste composed of white lead and linseed oil. This was

FIG. 181. *Loggia projecting from a sun-washed face of an inter-war detached house.*

regarded as a means of sealing the joint, although long-term breakdown of this compound introduces fine cracks that act to admit, rather than repel rainwater. Where the timber was carefully selected from suitable types of wood such as close-grained pine or teak (a very durable hardwood), this assembly may have a fairly long lifespan, but flimsier constructions, original to Edwardian houses, are unlikely to have survived to the present day without frequent repair or modification to improve their durability.

Although verandahs that cover nothing more than

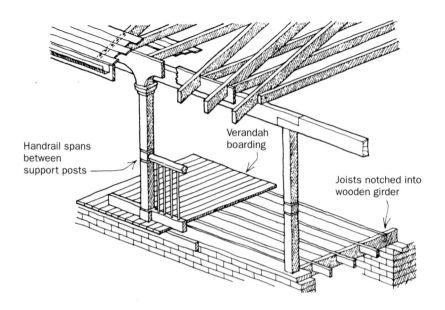

Handrail spans
between
support posts

Verandah
boarding

Joists notched into
wooden girder

*FIG. 182. Structure
of a timber-framed
verandah under a
lean-to roof.*

a shallow basement or ventilated crawl space were satisfactorily finished with a boarded surface, wooden boards alone are eventually penetrated by rainwater, and any balcony surface required an impervious finish. As a balcony is meant to be walked on, the sheet-metal covering conventional for roofs of bay and dormer windows was not a suitable finish and asphalt was normally laid over the boards to give a level, watertight surface. If the original installation did not incorporate a membrane of bituminous felt separating the poured asphalt from the boards, differential movement of the timber and the wearing surface may have introduced cracks into the asphalt that invite water into the inner building construction. In any renewal of an asphalt surface laid on boarding (including plywood or chipboard, modern substitutes for tongue-and-groove) it is essential to insist on the molten asphalt being laid on a continuous separating membrane of bituminous felt.

Wooden balustrades screening verandahs, balconies, loggias and porches were framed up as panels of vertical slats located in continuous timber top and bottom rails, themselves fixed to the main supporting posts of the verandah structure. In this way, a multiplicity of joints between individual balusters and a generally damp floor finish was avoided and the risk of wet rot penetrating the ends of the

spindly wooden balusters was much reduced. For the same reason, the undersides of the main supporting posts of a verandah or porch structure were sometimes set above the floor by means of metal shoes or cast-iron buttons 25mm (1in) thick and 50mm (2in) in diameter. Four such buttons were placed under a square post, the metal pins that projected from the top and bottom surfaces of these components being let into the floor and the underside of the post and bedded in white lead. Another method was to rivet the buttons to an iron plate which was itself secured to the underside of the post. A simple but effective decorative treatment of the main verandah or covered-balcony posts was to chamfer their corners, the octagonal cross-section resulting from this chamfering being returned to a square profile at the ends by terminating the splay faces with oblique-cut chamfer stops (Fig. 183).

A verandah projecting from the house must have a separate roof, and where this roof was added to obscure as little as possible of the main elevation, a low pitch was employed, which necessitated a sheet-metal roof covering on a substratum of tongue-and-groove boards. In good-quality construction, the ceiling of the verandah was formed from narrow strips of pine or hardwood, laid on and secret-nailed to the ceiling joists. A better appearance resulted if the ceiling boards were installed at right-angles to the building, in which case firring strips had to be run at right angles to the ceiling joists to carry the boards. In cheaper work, the verandah roof was left open on the underside, exposing the assembly of timber rafters and roof boarding, the narrow, planed, tongue-and-groove boards being laid with their finished side downwards.

CONSERVATORIES

Changing aesthetic preferences caused the Victorian enthusiasm for conservatories of cast-iron construction to wane, and elaborate painted timber construction took on appeal (Fig. 184), though elements like the tension members of trusses of glazed roofs tended to continue to be of wrought iron. Conservatories attached to modest houses were most commonly of the 'lean-to' type (Fig. 185) their walls being framed in timber posts and transoms enclosing the glazing, with the roof formed in patent glazing which was either of lead-capped, moulded wooden bars or proprietary metal sections where very slender glazing bars were required. The wood framing is on the lines of balcony balustrade construction, with panes of clear glass replacing the balustrade panels, the whole framework often being erected on a dwarf wall of single-skin brickwork. This choice of a largely wooden construction for Edwardian conservatories

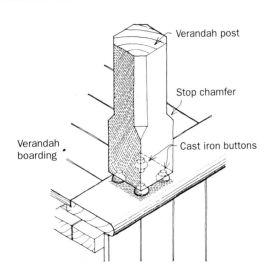

FIG. 183. Foot of a timber verandah roof-support post.

explains the ramshackle appearance of many surviving examples. Timber is prone to shrink or swell with changes in temperature and humidity, and posts or soleplates in contact with the ground will have rotted over the years, causing sections of the structure to subside, bulge and sag. Where such decay is well-advanced, nothing less than the complete replacement of the shaky structure with modern rot-resisting materials will suffice, but, where

FIG. 184. The free-standing conservatory of a detached Edwardian Thames-side villa.

FIG. 185. Lean-to conservatory with roof of patent glazing.

replication of the original wooden construction is not considered essential. a sagging roofslope is quite easily rectified by replacing bowing wooden glazing bars with aluminium patent-glazing sections

The interiors of conservatories might be elaborately decorated, quarry tiles of contrasting colours in chequerboard pattern, or patterned encaustic tiles often constituting the floor finish. Coloured or patterned glass in leaded lights or secondary panes that contrast with the clear glazing of the main lights were also used, providing privacy and adding interest to the views from inside and out.

YARD AND PATH SURFACES

The use of quarry tiles for external pavements such as garden paths or terraces has been touched on already. It may be difficult to find replacement tiles that match exactly the size and colour of period items, although the revival of interest in the components of vintage building construction means that there is now a wider range of period-pattern floor tiles than those available even ten years ago. This judgement also applies to glazed fireclay garden-edgings and certain types of Staffordshire blue clay pavers that were also used for yard surfaces. These hard tiles or brick-shaped pavers commonly displayed a top surface patterned with rectangles or diamond shapes thrown into relief by a grid of incisions made in the clay. This incised surface reduced the risk of pedestrians slipping in wet or frosty weather. Where a particular pattern of blue-brick paver or channel is no longer made, it may prove possible to find matching

items in the stock of an architectural salvage company. As they are extremely hard-wearing and not easily damaged, salvaged items are more likely to achieve an exact match with the original work, not least in terms of texture and colour, than the new product.

Where maximum durability against damage from horseshoes and the iron tyres of cartwheels was desired (plainly, these concerns only informed the site treatment of the grandest Edwardian houses), granite setts (sometimes erroneously called 'cobbles') were used to pave driveways and stable yards. Cornish granite was favoured for this application and was also widely used for the paving of city streets in the period up to the First World War. In most British cities, highly patterned road surfaces of setts criss-crossed by tramlines disappeared below tarmac only in the 1950s.

Pavements formed from a continuous surface of slabs are more common than surfaces laid with setts. Before the advent of the pressed concrete paving slabs which provide the wearing surface of many modern urban pavements (the interest offered by even these synthetic products is increasingly threatened by the ever more widespread use of tarmac for pavement surfaces), York stone was the most popular pavement and it may survive as the surface of garden paths serving Edwardian houses. As it is still quarried today, it is easily replaced, if expensive. Although it may be a better match for surviving slabs, salvaged York stone paving slabs are in such demand for restoration projects that, when bought in bulk, they are likely to be as costly as the new material.

CHAPTER 10

Restoration of Modern Movement Dwellings: the Particular Problems

The flat-roofed Modern Movement houses of the late 1920s and 1930s present problems for building construction additional to the concerns that need to be satisfied in houses of traditional construction. Perhaps the advantages to constructional and environmental performance of traditional building forms – thick walls of porous masonry and free-draining pitched roofs – were insufficiently appreciated by many of the pioneer modern movement architects. Certainly, in their zeal to create revolutionary architectural forms, to some extent 'the baby was thrown out with the bathwater'.

By the inter-war period, many buildings demonstrating the advantages of new construction technology were to be found in contemporary textile mills, factories and dockside grain silos, all of which seemed to declare the suitability of making roofs from flat slabs of reinforced concrete, allowing pedestrian access and admitting the possibility of sunlit terraces and rooftop gardens. The adoption of reinforced concrete for the general building structure – most excitingly, the potential it offered to reduce building structure to an array of highly-stressed point supports (freestanding columns) in substitution for the thick walls required in load-bearing, mass-masonry structures – granted greater freedom to the designer of elevations and interiors. With the perimeter structural elements confined to point supports along or adjacent to the elevations, the external wall surface was 'freed' and, at one extreme, could be composed entirely of glazing if that was the designer's preference.

Similarly, any aspirations to create 'open-plan' interiors were more easily satisfied as the reduction of the necessary structure to a grid of columns allowed planning to break away from the cellular plans, composed of an aggregation of small rooms, demanded by load-bearing masonry construction. In adopting reinforced concrete (rather than the steel frame, an earlier technical development which had first liberated designers in this way) structure and construction could be largely of one material rather than the complex 'kit' of interdependent parts demanded by mass-masonry construction. The constructional format of the building was simplified in a way that sympathised with the contemporary architectural aim of simplifying the formal composition, and it was thought as suitable to apply this formula to house design as it was to factories and warehouses.

However, there are sound foundations for the claim that the use of reinforced concrete in domestic architecture tests this form of construction more severely than its application in commercial and industrial structures that are not required to accommodate either continuous occupation or such a wide range of human activities. The extra stress placed upon reinforced-concrete construction by its use in dwellings will become clear with the later part of this account of its properties and failings, but it is important, first, to note the shortcomings of the material as they may be found in any of the building types in which it is employed (Fig. 186).

187

FIG. 186. A daring cantilevered corner balcony of this flat-roofed house illustrates the sometimes experimental nature of reinforced-concrete construction in inter-war Modern Movement buildings.

DECAY AND REPAIR OF REINFORCED CONCRETE

It would be comforting to think that the hard and dense product we know as reinforced concrete is a permanent material – a sort of 'cast rock'. Unfortunately, as applies even with rock, it is in a continuous chemical reaction with its environment and it can decay. The prime shortcoming of reinforced concrete is the possibility of its disintegration in the long term. When reinforced concrete was a new technology the need to 'bury' the steel reinforcing bars well into the concrete to protect them from premature corrosion was not fully appreciated – the material was still in its experimental phase. Consequently, over the decades, water has penetrated the fine pores of the concrete to reach and rust reinforcing bars. This causes swelling of the steel and bursting (*spalling*) of the concrete cover, exposing the reinforcing bars and accelerating their corrosion. Tell-tale streaks of rust-staining, emerging through the concrete even before lumps of concrete fall off, are a conspicuous warning of this change.

This deterioration is accelerated by the process of *carbonation*, which is the chief contributor to concrete failure. As the name suggests, carbonation is a long-term chemical reaction of the concrete with the atmosphere. The alkaline-rich character of fresh concrete alters considerably over time as atmospheric carbon dioxide and rainwater react with the calcium hydroxide in the concrete to create calcium carbonate, producing an acidic quality in the material that causes corrosion of the steel reinforcement. Rusting of the reinforcement reduces its tensile strength and leads to spalling and fracturing of the concrete. The scope for this deterioration is conditioned solely by the cover to the reinforcing steel. If the cover to reinforcement adjoining an external face is considerably less than the 75mm (3in) dimension required by current Codes of Practice (and this always applies in inter-war buildings), the bars may be in contact with continuously damp and acidic concrete, which will engender corrosion.

Pessimists could speculate that such serious damage to a material that works structurally only when both of its constituents (the dense concrete and the reinforcing steel) fully bond and act together, might only be remedied by demolition and rebuilding of the construction. However, in most cases – even where decay is well-advanced – such drastic action is not necessary. The increasing incidence of long-term deterioration of reinforced-concrete structures has created a market for concrete repair products – a range of treatments for the protection of reinforcing steel and the replacement of spalled concrete.

Clearly, the first action where deteriorating concrete is suspected, is finding of the cause of the problem. As the culprit is almost invariably rusting reinforcement, householders will be relieved to learn that determining the depth of the concrete cover to the suspect bars does not demand physical investigation – opening-up of the construction to reveal the reinforcement. An electromagnetic 'cover meter' survey can be made to determine the exact location of reinforcement. Some physical investigation of suspected zones of carbonation is necessary, however, and their extent can be gauged by applying a solution of phenolphthalein to the freshly exposed concrete and noting changes in colour which signal either continuing alkalinity or the change to an acidic, and thus deleterious condition.

In modern movement houses constructed largely from reinforced concrete, deterioration of the concrete is sometimes accelerated by the use of unsuitable surface finishes. Raw, reinforced concrete is generally considered to be an unattractive material and from the outset, all early modern houses showed painted concrete external surfaces. Where porous cement-based paints (which are quite quickly stained by sooty atmospheres) continued to be used for this purpose, a surface treatment sympathetic with the need of the concrete to 'breathe' existed, but adoption of an impervious finish such as gloss oil paint exacerbates the problem of carbonation because it traps moisture within the walls, preventing its evaporation into the outside air.

Rectification of the damage caused by carbonation must begin by drilling out all the areas found to be defective, then grit-blasting the newly exposed surfaces of sound concrete and the rusted reinforcing bars to clean them thoroughly. It is then necessary to prime the retained steelwork with a cement-based protective and anti-corrosive coating before proceeding with repair of the concrete. A compatible, proprietary 'bonding-bridge' slurry is then applied over the newly protected steel before a special concrete-repair mortar with good waterproof qualities is added to restore the original profile of the concrete. As the repair mortar is likely to be rather coarse-grained, it may be necessary to apply final 'fairing coats' of a special levelling mortar – a brush-applied slurry giving a close-grained surfaces that

enhances protection against future carbonation. Repainting with a vapour-permeable masonry paint concludes the restoration.

This description of concrete repair is most relevant to treatment of vertical surfaces – walls and columns – though concrete floors and beams may be treated similarly in the unlikely event that they have suffered the deterioration from carbonation to which walls and columns, exposed externally, are prone. Concrete flat roof slabs provide a different set of problems for serviceability.

Special Problems of Reinforced-concrete Flat Roofs

The apparent indifference of most designers of inter-war Modern Movement houses to the need to incorporate good thermal insulation in roofs has certainly contributed to problems with the durability of this construction. It does not seem to have been appreciated that some measures would be needed to enhance the thermal performance of the plain concrete slab at least to the level of that of the air incidentally entrapped within a conventional pitched roof. In the absence of this useful thermal insulation, condensation presents a threat to the comfort of the occupants and the integrity of building materials because warm internal air will readily condense on the underside of a cold, uninsulated roof deck. Consequently, many flat-roofed Modern Movement houses have had to be adapted by the inclusion of additional fresh-air vents at high level in the external walls for the purpose of venting away humid air before it has the opportunity to condense on cold internal surfaces (Fig. 187).

Fortunately, designers of the first flat-roofed houses did recognise that simple exposed concrete would not grant a weather-tight roof construction. The practice established in earlier industrial buildings was followed; it was realised that it was necessary to apply a waterproof coating and this was achieved by laying asphalt over the slab. The addition of this material does very little to improve the insulating properties of the construction; the underside of the roof slab continues to expose a cold surface to the interior, inviting condensation. Even in the 1930s the threat of damage to an unprotected asphalt surface was appreciated (under hot summer skies the material can revert to a semi-molten condition, posing the threat of serious damage to the membrane from simultaneous foot traffic). Accordingly, it was common to add a more durable wearing surface above the asphalt, asbestos-cement based *promenade tiles* being a favoured treatment (Fig. 188).

This treatment hints at a sympathetic modification of sub-standard arrangements, which will act to improve the thermal performance of an uninsulated concrete flat roof. Accepting the 'chequerboard' appearance of a flat roof finished in promenade tiles, it is easy to see how an identical configuration of heavier pressed-concrete slabs might be used to secure new, continuous thermal insulation added on top of the asphalt membrane. This 'inverted' roof construction involves the addition of rigid, thick polystyrene slabs in a continuous layer above the asphalt (protecting this waterproof coating and granting it a more stable thermal context which improves its durability). Held down by heavy concrete slabs laid on top as a walking surface (themselves mounted on special corner pedestal supports) (Fig. 189), the main consideration in upgrading a concrete-slab flat roof in this way is to ensure efficient sub-slab rainwater drainage. Accordingly, the paving slabs are laid with open joints so that the rain-

water drains through and there is no danger of saturation of the insulating layer because the sealed cells of the polystyrene will not absorb and hold rainwater. Clearance of storm water is achieved via special rain-water outlets that collect the run-off from the asphalt substratum. One limitation of this method of upgrading a flat roof which should be emphasized is that although the modification is readily achieved where the roof is surrounded by a parapet, offering scope to contain and screen the thickness of the added materials, these extra layers are not easily accommodated on flat roofs that project beyond external walls, or on cantilevered canopies, without producing an effect that may be aesthetically unacceptable.

METAL WINDOW REPAIR AND REPLACEMENT

If optimistic judgements were often made by the first architects of the Modern Movement about the benefits of employing a 'simple' reinforced-concrete construction, this approach was no less marked in contemporary enthusiasm for the adoption of steel-framed windows in lieu of the timber-framed products conventional in house building.

FIG. 187. A pair of flat-roofed Modern Movement houses with air vents high in the external walls.

FIG. 188. An English detached house of Modern Movement design.

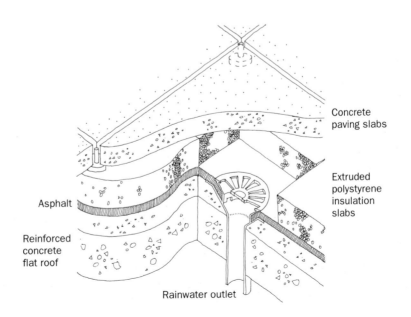

FIG. 189. 'Inverted' flat-roof construction: paving slabs secure polystyrene foam insulation above an asphalted reinforced-concrete flat roof.

Concrete paving slabs

Extruded polystyrene insulation slabs

Asphalt

Reinforced concrete flat roof

Rainwater outlet

FIG. 190. Steel-framed windows pattern the front elevation of an inter-war detached house.

Steel-framed windows promised the standardised quality of material and construction achievable in modern factory-based mass production and the reputation of steel suggested durability far superior to that of wood-framed windows that are prone to rot in the absence of continuous careful maintenance of the protective paint film. Unfortunately, the pioneering steel-framed windows, while manifesting the visual crispness, guarantee of a standard quality of product and adherence to fine tolerances offered by mass-production techniques, failed to incorporate protective coatings to ensure long-term durability. Today's steel-framed windows are galvanized at the factory to give good protection to the steel before highly durable paint finishes are applied. These treatments ensure the long-term serviceability of the product, but the painted mild-steel frames of the 1920s and 1930s (and, indeed, the 1940s and 1950s) are likely to have shown their shortcomings after not more than 30 years (Fig. 190).

The problems likely to be encountered with steel windows have already been touched on in Chapter 7, but it is worth emphasising that deterioration of painted mild-steel-framed windows begins with the breakdown of the paint film at points of stress – notably mitred and welded corner joints – allowing rainwater to penetrate into these fine joints by capillary action, causing corrosion, swelling, and lamination of the steel, which often causes cracking of the glazing as it is put under pressure by the rusting metal. Although it may be practicable to temporarily remove rusting steel-framed windows and to pass them to a workshop for shot blasting to remove rust – any badly corroded sections being cut out and new metal of matching section being welded in before a new protective paint system is applied – this is an expensive and disruptive procedure.

It has been noted that almost from the outset of UK steel-window production for house building in the 1920s, a product now known as the original Crittall window range, was developed, and a virtually identical product continues to be available today. In the light of this, it is usually preferable to commission replacement replica windows fabricated from the new material with its superior protection of galvanizing and an enamel paint finish. This applies even where upgrading glazing to the higher thermal performance of double-glazing is necessary. Although of quite slender section, the profiles of the slim steel hinged-casement or fixed-frame sections are sufficiently deep to accommodate standard 14mm (%6in) thick sealed double-glazed units in substitution for single glazing. As well as boasting a galvanized and tough baked-on polyester-powder paint finish, the new frames also incorporate flexible vinyl weather seals to better exclude wind-blown rain at joints between fixed and opening frames – a feature not built into the pre-war product. Yet, except under the most detailed inspection, the new frames will be indistinguishable from the original fenestration.

CHAPTER 11

Care of Edwardian and Inter-War Houses, Alterations and Improvements

STRUCTURAL ALTERATIONS

'Knocking Through'

It should be clear that mid-twentieth century ideas on house planning – the promotion of the 'open plan' in particular – tended to be inimical to the planning policies adopted for houses erected before the First World War whose plans were usually a cellular aggregation of small rooms. Although the last few years have brought an increasing appreciation of the merits of traditional house-plans, modern lifestyles, central heating and residual respect for the open-plan policy all place pressure on householders to consider complete or partial demolition of internal walls to enlarge 'poky' rooms of modest Edwardian or inter-war dwellings.

'Knocking through' is usually achieved by installing a rolled steel joist (RSJ) on the line of the partition wall that formerly supported the upper-floor joists, and then removing the partition. The steel beam spans a wide opening between brick piers which replace the extreme ends of the original wall. In this way, some householders have converted adjoining small rooms into continuous 'through lounges' up to 10m (33ft) in length. There is some truth in the claim that there is a period precedent for this treatment. Ground-floor parlours or sitting rooms of Edwardian houses of all but the smallest types were sometimes arranged to open into rear living rooms through double or folding doors (Fig. 191). It will be appreciated that this is a very different arrangement from an almost full-width opening from

which the doors and their framing are omitted – the latter treatment tends to emphasize that the result of the alteration is a large, amorphous, irregularly shaped room which is completely out of sympathy with the cellular spaces of the rest of the house. Each case must be looked at on its own merits because larger houses may absorb 'knocking through' without the character of the accommodation being destroyed. Where it is decided to compromise and to fit high timber double doors, it must be made clear that wooden doors replacing a heavy, plastered brickwork

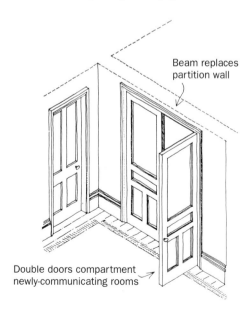

Beam replaces partition wall

Double doors compartment newly-communicating rooms

FIG. 191. Living rooms joined by double doors.

or timber-framed partition will not provide equally good sound insulation. The joinery is light in weight and gaps at the joint of doors and frame cannot be completely sealed against airborne noise.

Loft Conversions

Another rearrangement of the layout of older houses that is often carried out is the conversion of vacant roof space into additional rooms. That this is a popular policy is proved by the rash of bulky dormer windows, which continues to spread through suburban streets, usually disfiguring the 'settled' silhouette of the affected houses. The insistence upon making such dormers very large in relation to the roof planes from which they spring is the main cause of this disfiguring effect. The policy is understandable as an attempt to maximise the usable volume of the house, but its potentially disastrous aesthetic consequences should not be ignored. Although there are many precedents for flat-topped dormers in Edwardian and inter-war houses, the dormer structures were kept quite small – generally up to 2m (6ft 6in) wide and 1.5m (5ft) high at most. The use of standard mass-produced softwood windows that do not correspond in overall size, configuration of lights or frame thicknesses with the original purpose-made windows underlines the alien character of an over-bulky dormer. Modern 'off-the-peg' windows invariably display a far greater proportion of glass to framing than the original provision in pre-1940 houses, with the result that their mullions and transoms look worryingly insubstantial. This unattractive flimsiness is emphasized in a flat-roofed dormer because the mullions of a multiple-light window appear to 'support' the roof structure.

Even worse than an oversized dormer leaning out of a small roofslope is a flat-topped dormer, the upper part of which visually breaks the roof ridge or 'severs' the hip of a pyramidal roof. Most local planning authorities are in any case opposed to this type of domestic extension, but they tend to be less concerned about overlarge dormers located on roofslopes surmounting rear elevations. Those concerned about conserving the character of a period house will wish to avoid the incorporation of large dormers altogether, and one radical but rather more sympathetic means of creating additional roof space for conversion to living accommodation is to transform the hipped gable of the pyramidal roof conventional in inter-war detached and semi-detached houses into the similarly commonplace pitched-roof profile surmounting a triangular masonry or tile-hung gable (Fig. 192). Where new dormer windows cannot be avoided, householders will receive a more

FIG. 192. Less disruptive of the simple geometry of the 'standard semi' than a flat-roofed dormer may be replacement of the hip by a gable.

FIG. 193. The ground-hugging compactness of a pair of chalet 'semis' is badly compromised by flat-roofed side extensions (compare with FIG. *19 in Chapter 2).*

sympathetic hearing from local authority planning officers in proposing a form which is in scale with traditional treatments, relates to existing windows in the wall surface below and adopts claddings and fenestration patterns characteristic of the treatment of surviving original windows. The inter-war house type worst affected by the creation of new roof-space accommodation is the semi-detached chalet, which in its unaltered state displays a vast area of catslide roofslope. The natural temptation is to fill this triangle of air with additional first-floor accommodation, adding a dormer which is effectively the larger part of an additional storey and which reduces the roofslope to a shallow strip of tiling below the roof ridge, the remainder of the 'lid' being an asphalt or felted flat roof covering the new upstairs rooms. The baleful effect of this type of alteration on the pleasant ground-hugging profile of the chalet-type, semi-detached house is all too apparent (Fig. 193).

Where a roof surface is sufficiently steep for the low space behind the eaves to be converted to living accommodation, it may not be necessary to enlarge the roof volume with a dormer. A modern product that has replaced the old-fashioned skylight is the roof window, already referred to in Chapter 5. This device is fixed in the plane of the roof with its protec-tive weather-tight flashing projecting slightly above the surface of the surrounding tiles or slates. These factory-glazed, prefabricated units are invariably double-glazed so that condensation on the underside of the glass is obviated. The window pivots at its centre to admit fresh air and to allow cleaning of the external glazing from the inside. An independent ventilator is also often incorporated so that it is not essential to pivot the window (and thus admit wind-blown rain in bad weather) in order to draw in fresh air. As it lies in the plane of the roof, a roof window is much less conspicuous than a dormer window, though a rash of these windows is almost as disrup-tive of the otherwise calm appearance of a broad roof-slope as an ill-sited dormer.

Rear Extensions

Where a roof void or other unused internal space is not available to provide space for expansion, the option of extending the plan outwards is usually considered. This normally means adding space to the house either at the side or at the rear. Clearly, extensions to mid-terrace houses are restricted to the rear elevations.

Perhaps fortunately, in the light of some of the enormities perpetrated in the past, planning officers are increasingly concerned about the design of rear extensions (in the case of detached and semi-detached houses, the treatment of side extensions is at least as important an issue) and for houses located in Conservation Areas it may prove difficult to establish the acceptability of any substantial modification unless it can be shown to 'preserve or enhance' the character of the Conservation Area. In the case of these houses, additional to the standard requirement to obtain Planning Permission for a proposed extension, Conservation Area Consent must be obtained and this is the official control which will determine the possibility of erecting an extension. Designation of areas as Conservation Areas is now quite widespread and leafy suburban neighbourhoods of typical Edwardian houses are increasingly candidates for this designation, though, to date, this distinction has been accorded to very few areas of inter-war housing.

Rail travellers will confirm that the most basic design of rear extension comprises a flat roof surmounting a one or two storey 'box' of brickwork or rendered blockwork, the walls of the box being perforated by 'off-the-peg' softwood-framed windows and sliding, aluminium-framed patio doors. As additions to houses of very utilitarian design, such extensions may be aesthetically acceptable, but they usually stand in stark contrast to the careful and complex detailing of Edwardian houses and are almost equally unsympathetic to cottage-style dwellings of the inter-war years. With a little thought, it is easy to see where modifications may be made to this formula to achieve a more harmonious blend of old and new. If the flat roof is replaced by a pitched roof that reproduces the slope and covering of the main roof, some affinity between the two structures is achieved automatically. The use of a constructional form and materials matching those of the adjoining main block for the outside faces of the extension's external walls is also a prerequisite if a strong visual unity of the old and new is sought.

The very first difficulty likely to be encountered in the construction of a rear extension is the necessary depth of the new foundations. The footings of pre-1940 houses are usually quite shallow and new foundations of identical depth are unlikely to comply with the requirements of current building regulations. Therefore the foundations of a new extension

may need to go down deeper than the original footings and this condition introduces the risk that the old work will be undermined. In some cases it may be necessary to underpin a section of the old footing to reconcile its founding level with that of the new work. The existence of a shrinkable-clay subsoil or nearby mature trees are two causes for the local authority's building control officer to require deep excavations (to perhaps 1.5–2m (5–6.5ft) below external ground level even for a single-storey extension). As this requirement frequently emerges only when the original footings have been exposed, where this circumstance was not established by a preliminary investigation and accounted for in the design, is quite likely to cause a doubling of the foundation work and a proportional increase in its cost.

Where the external walls of the house are of 225mm thick solid brickwork with a brickwork external face, and a matching appearance in the walls of the extension is desired, the new walls cannot be of identical thickness and appearance because this arrangement will not fulfil the requirements of modern building regulations either in terms of weather-resistance or thermal insulation. Accordingly, most modern brick-faced external walls are cavity walls in which the external leaf is of facing brick and the internal leaf is of aerated concrete blockwork. If the blockwork inner leaf is of dense concrete (for maximum crushing strength) or merely as thick as the brickwork outer leaf, despite the good insulating properties of an air cavity at least 50mm (2in) wide, this construction will still not satisfy the thermal insulation standards of current building regulations. Its insulating properties can be improved either by adopting thicker blocks for the inner leaf, adding insulation between the internal wall finish and the inner leaf, or building some insulation into the cavity. (Fig. 194).

Where Edwardian or inter-war houses have their external walls coated in roughcast or pebbledash render, an inexpensive form of solid construction can be adopted for extensions. High thermal performance, lightweight concrete blocks rendered externally, satisfactorily exclude wind-driven rain and provide a reasonable level of thermal insulation. According to the product used, in order to achieve the level of insulation required by building regulations, it may be necessary to supplement the blockwork with additional thermal insulation, over which the internal wall finish is applied (Fig. 195). A type of plasterboard laminated with extruded polystyrene sheet is also a satisfactory insulator but on no account should the aluminium-foil backing (or similar impervious membrane) to the plasterboard inner lining be omitted, because this vapour check reduces the risk of troublesome condensation forming within the wall construction. Alternatively, the external render may be applied over special expanded-metal lath cloaking an external layer of insulation.

Few details are as unsympathetic with the format of all Edwardian and most inter-war houses as a bituminous-felt flat roof finished at the eaves with a boarded fascia, yet the low construction cost of this arrangement has caused it to be widely used in small domestic extensions. Roofs of this type are prone to leak unless the roof finish is well maintained and periodically renewed. Current requirements for good thermal performance and effective roof-space ventilation demand quite complex constructional arrangements to achieve this form and this consideration alone may highlight the benefits of adopting a pitched roof instead. Where use of a flat roof is inescapable, in aesthetic and constructional terms it may be preferable to install a roof-deck of solid construction (such as a reinforced-concrete slab or deck of precast-concrete trough sections, complemented by adequate thermal insulation and ventilation measures) behind a parapet. The top surface of the deck may then be securely waterproofed with a poured-asphalt roof covering.

It is obvious that the pitched roof is far superior in its capability of throwing off rainwater and providing an easily ventilated roof void (itself an insulating medium) in which it is a simple matter to install additional insulation. The lean-to roof is a common form of capping for the original back extensions of many Edwardian and inter-war houses, so that the integration of small rear extensions into the form of such houses which lack any rear extension is assisted by its adoption (Fig. 196). Where a 'back extension to a back extension' is planned, the necessarily narrow plan of the second extension and its distance from the rear wall of the main block may militate against the use of a simple lean-to roof and a 'mono-

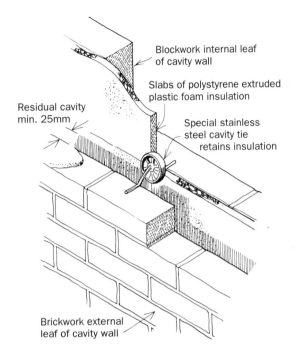

FIG. 194. Cavity wall construction for new extension external walls.

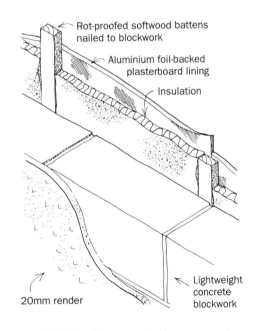

FIG. 195. Solid wall construction for new extension external walls.

197

pitch' or regular pitched-roof form may have to be adopted. Monopitch roofs were used over small back extensions to Edwardian houses, though if the span of the ceiling joists of the added block exceeds 3m (10ft), the roof takes on a scale which conflicts with the forms of the original house. Broader extensions, which cannot be roofed satisfactorily with a lean-to, should be capped with a conventional pitched roof. Short-span pitched roofs may be simply constructed on the 'couple-close' principle (see Fig. 79 in Chapter 5). The span of a pitched roof capping a new rear extension – or even a pair of extensions sited back-to-back – is unlikely to approach the more than 6m (20ft) width most economically spanned by standard prefabricated timber trusses.

Replacement Windows

The general design, detailing and siting of new and replacement windows in extensions to the accommodation or in the original structure is crucial to the successful renovation of Edwardian or inter-war houses. Most of these houses were fitted with French windows giving direct access from a living-room to a

FIG. 196. New back extensions can harmonise if the simple forms of unadorned rear roofslopes and elevations are replicated.

garden (Fig. 197). A modern equivalent of this feature is the sliding aluminium-framed 'patio door' which tends to be installed in new or enlarged openings in the walls of old houses, with no consideration of its visual effect on the adjacent architecture. Yet there are few modern building products that are more alien to the original window detailing of cottage-style houses. Modern, mass-produced, soft-wood-framed French windows hardly represent an improvement over the metal fitting because the thickness of the timber used for the doors and the fixed frame is so slight that it causes a disproportionately large area of glazing to contrast with a small and mean-looking area of wooden frame. Therefore, where surviving joinery is too badly decayed or damaged to be repaired, restorers seeking complete authenticity are obliged to commission purpose-made joinery replicating the original feature. For durability, bespoke replacement frames are best made entirely in hardwood, but if this material cannot be afforded for all the parts, it is essential that the sill at least is of hardwood to resist premature rotting caused by rising damp and saturation by driving rain.

If the most familiar modern versions of French windows display too much glass and too little frame to 'fit in', this quality is no less marked in the smaller sizes of mass-produced wood windows. The width of the fixed frames of these windows is always unconvincingly narrow, and for this reason, as well as the distinction between the pattern of subdivision of a modern frame from that seen in pre-1940, cottage-style houses, it is always easy to identify modern, wooden-framed windows in older façades. Paradoxically, purpose-made aluminium windows of the type installed by most double-glazing contractors generally display more frame area in relation to glass than do mass-produced wood-framed windows. Notwithstanding this accidental affinity between modern aluminium and antique wood frames (particularly apparent where the aluminium frames are finished in white enamel paintwork), replacement of painted timber frames with aluminium is not recommended because even in the long view, the detailed treatment of the metal frames at sills, corner joints and junctions between lights is readily distinguished from the way in which these features are handled in wood-framed windows. It is far better to employ every feasible measure to retain the original windows, undertaking careful repairs through scarfing-in of new timber, where necessary. In the few cases where wholesale replacement of rotted timber windows is unavoidable, the new frames should replicate the details seen in the original joinery except where an original detail has invited problems from the outset (for example, bedding a softwood sill on to a stone sill which falls towards the interior of the house).

In relation to materials most suitable for fabrication of new wood-framed windows, the most enduring materials are the indigenous and tropical hardwoods. Although some ranges of mass-produced, hardwood-framed windows are available, these products are unlikely to harmonise with the general format or details of traditional fenestration and hardwood must be the first choice for manufacture of purpose-made frames. To obtain total fidelity to the 'look' of the period windows, it will be necessary to apply a matching paint finish to the new frames. Care is needed in the selection and application of a paint system for hardwood surfaces because the resinous nature of many of these woods tends to act against good adhesion of the paint film to the timber.

It is general knowledge that softwoods are far less durable than hardwoods as materials for the manufacture of purpose-made window frames, and in view of the renowned longevity of much period softwood joinery, the question arises of why this is so. The cause of the disparity between the performance of most modern softwoods and pre-1940 material lies in the difference between the way freshly cut timber is treated today and the way it was treated before the Second World War. Traditionally, the roughly squared logs were often carefully stacked and allowed to season in the open air for several years before being machined into joinery sections. In contrast, modern softwood is invariably kiln-dried quite soon after it is felled. The accelerated drying-out quickly makes it suitable for shaping but thereafter the wood is more prone to distort and decay than the well-seasoned timber of yesteryear. Some varieties of softwood are less susceptible to these shortcomings than others and where dense, close-grained timbers such as Baltic Pine or Douglas Fir are used, dimensional stability

FIG. 197. Timber-framed French windows opening on to the back garden are an attractive feature of many early twentieth-century houses. (Robin Bishop.)

across the temperature range and resistance to warping are likely to be almost as good as the performance offered by tropical hardwoods such as Lauan or Iroko.

Porches

A common minor alteration to modest houses made by many new owner-occupiers is the addition of an external 'storm porch' to reduce draughts admitted through the front entrance door. In houses with an integral porch, this modification is often made by fitting an outward-opening door in the plane of the front elevation, thus creating a 'draught lobby' in front of the original entrance door. In many cases this alteration has the unfortunate result of reducing the area of shadow contained by the front elevation and consequently reducing the architectural interest of this main feature of the house. The radical change in the appearance of the elevation caused by this modification can be reduced if the new external door is almost entirely of glass contained in a minimal metal frame. Various types of double-glazed, metal-framed, outward-opening doors incorporating efficient draught seals largely meet this requirement but such a door is even less conspicuous if it is obtained colour-coated in a dark paint or bronze-anodized finish so that it will more successfully hide in the shadows.

In the smallest houses where the main entrance door sits in the plane of the front wall, sheltered only by a modest canopy, infilling of a porch enclosure to form a 'storm porch' is not a possibility and, for many, there is a natural temptation to improve draughtproofing by adding an external porch. Often, such additions are viewed as a manageable DIY project and receive the sort of attention better accorded to fully independent structures by being formed from random rubble walling, or in a timber frame clad in varnished boards. Where it is considered essential to add an entrance porch, it is advisable to aim for the simplest possible shapes and to choose materials for the roof and wall construction uniform with those of the main house roof and external walls.

Upgrading Bathrooms and WCs

Rear extensions are sometimes added to the original accommodation to house a new bathroom. Although almost all new houses of the Edwardian years incorporated an internal WC, baths were not built-in in every case and original bathrooms of the smaller houses of this period tend to be cramped, spartan and out-of-tune with current ideas of comfort and convenience. For economy, the most basic sanitary installation in a small Edwardian house placed the WC at ground-floor level so that the drainage pipework would be minimised. Even in larger houses of this period that incorporate an internal WC on an upper floor, it is normal to find an additional WC at ground level, usually accessible only from the outside via a rear garden or yard. Naturally, in the conventional domestic arrangement in which the bedrooms are located upstairs, a main disadvantage of siting a new bathroom on the ground floor is the extended distance from the bedrooms to this amenity. However, adopting this arrangement minimises new pipework and this aspect of the work may find more

favour with the local authority's building control officer than an upper-storey installation in which the new fittings are remote from a retained soil-and-vent pipe.

The plans of many small terraced Edwardian houses are identical to those of late-Victorian dwellings in which a two-storey back extension flanked a rear yard. Where the upper storey of the back extension contains a third bedroom or 'box room' accessible only from the central upstairs room, it may be logical to convert this space into a combined bathroom and WC, or a bathroom and separate WC. As the route to this rear room very often takes a diagonal line across the central bedroom from a central, lateral staircase, reversal of the stair may be necessary to make sense of this rearrangement (Fig. 198).

Because bathrooms have become the vehicle for flights of fancy in interior design and decoration, something should be said about the finishes that are suitable for bathrooms newly installed in Edwardian and inter-war houses, and the remodelling of existing bathrooms. Full or half-height wall tiling is an appropriate treatment, but the impressionistic pastel shades and floral patterns of many imported ceramic tiles are alien to the forms of tiles found in surviving bathrooms from the period 1900–1940. Naturalistic or floral patterning in Edwardian wall tiles was much more 'sharp' or conventionalized geometrically than the images which appear on most modern products, though it is possible to find modern products which approximate to the somewhat mechanical look of early twentieth-century tiles. Where patterning was employed, it also tended to be regular; it was not the custom to insert patterned tiles in apparently arbitrary places in areas of plain tiling. In the later inter-war years, as the influence of *art deco* was being felt, installation of bands of patterned tiles in contrast to areas of plain tiling gave way to patterning wall surfaces with tiles of different colours; the combination of pale yellow or eau-de-nil with gloss black was a popular treatment, and patent coloured glass, or 'Vitrolite' in a matching colour might be used where a large plain surface was required alongside the bathtub or flanking the mirror over a wash-hand basin. Although 'Vitrolite' cannot now be obtained as a new product, plain ceramic tiles in suitable

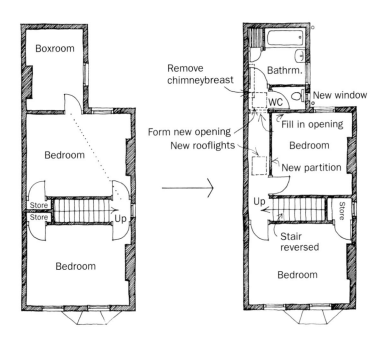

FIG. 198. Achieving modern standards in simple houses may necessitate the reconfiguration of bedrooms and the reversal of a 'spinal' staircase.

colours can be found and the revival of interest in antique patterns of sanitary fittings means that various patterns of 'thirties'-style WCs, baths and wash-hand basins are again available.

In relation to floor finishes for bathrooms and WCs, the carpets often installed today were not thought suitable in the pre-war period and the ubiquitous linoleum was the most common floor finish, though it is interesting to find that cork tiles ('compressed cork') which remain readily available today, were well-regarded because of their warmth and resilience. Modern, highly patterned vinyl tiles are less appropriate but the more subdued patterns of vinyl sheet may give an appearance quite close to the old-fashioned 'lino'.

Boarded walls, ceilings and bulkheads may also have found a place, particularly in Edwardian bathrooms, but if new or restored construction of this type is contemplated, it is important to recognise that such woodwork should be painted, not stripped or varnished so producing an overly textured and 'busy' appearance.

TREATMENT OF ENDEMIC DEFECTS

Renewal of Damp-proof Courses

Often the most conspicuous defect in poorly maintained older houses is the failure of the original damp-proof course to resist rising damp and the consequent deterioration of the building construction. It is virtually impossible that any of these houses could have been built without a damp proof course because national legislation required this feature after 1875, but the asphalt used in most as the damp-proof course is likely to have worn out. A range of measures are available for controlling rising damp.

A modest method of limiting the effects of rising damp – it is essentially a 'damp alleviation' technique – consists of atmospheric siphons which are installed at low level and at quite close centres in the outside face of the external wall. Moisture contained in the base of the wall is reduced by drawing it through this series of porous tubes which, once inserted, are left permanently in the brickwork. The distance between the tubes and their angle of inclination has to be carefully calculated according to the type of wall and the local ground conditions. The tubes terminate in small circular gratings fitted flush with the outside face of the wall. The system is useful for reducing the amount of water contained in a wall rather than entirely eliminating it and it may become less effective as the pores of the ceramic siphon tubes become clogged with salts crystallising from the water they attract.

A second type of 'tentative' installation that aims to combat rising damp without causing major disruption to the structure or finishes is the electro-osmotic system. The principle of its operation is that if an electrical potential can be set up between a building and the adjoining earth, moisture can be encouraged to flow from the former to the latter. Only a small amount of current is used but results 'from the field' suggest that the method is not always successful. At the opposite extreme from these modest attempts to discourage rising damp is the classical procedure for renewing a damp-proof course: the affected wall is shored up and alternate sections of the lowest brickwork course are removed and rebuilt, a damp-proof course of slate or other impervious material being incorporated in the new structure. When these renewed sections are complete, the retained sections are demolished and these, in turn, are rebuilt, thus completing the continuous stratum of the new damp-proof course. This operation is both disruptive and expensive and the last thirty years have witnessed the development of alternative methods designed to achieve almost equally effective results.

Insertion

Insertion of a new physical damp-proof course may be achieved by using a special chain-saw to cut out a continuous slot in a low-level horizontal mortar joint of the affected wall. A new damp-proof course of polyethylene or lead sheet bonded to bitumen-impregnated hessian is then inserted into this slot, a section at a time. The damp-proof course is inserted in approximately 1m (3ft 3in) lengths. It is wedged in place with pieces of slate and the part of the slot not occupied by the damp-proof course is packed with mortar. It is not normally practicable to make the cut

below the internal floor level, but the type of saw now in general use allows the cut to be made in the horizontal mortar joint closest to the internal floor level. The shallow strip of internal wall face left below the damp-proof course and above the floor surface should be denuded of any remaining plaster and be finished with two coats of bituminous paint to seal out any dampness. To further reduce risk of rot returning to afflict new materials, skirtings re-fixed over this vulnerable area should ideally be of an inert and impervious material such as glass-reinforced polyester (GRP).

The many contractors who specialise in the installation of new, physical damp-proof courses usually insist that any adjacent internal wall plaster that has been affected by dampness is removed – the hacking off of a continuous 1m (3ft 3in) depth of plaster from the affected wall is standard procedure. Following the insertion of the damp-proof course, the denuded brickwork is given some days to dry out before a sand/cement render containing a water-repellent ingredient (the basecoat of the new plaster finish) is applied.

Injection

Plainly, the sawing of a wall for the insertion of a damp-proof course may be a practical treatment for rising damp in detached houses and some semi-detached houses, but terraced houses in which the party walls, rather than the easily accessible front or rear elevations, act as the main route for rising damp, present a different condition. Unless adjoining owners jointly resolve to install a new physical damp-poof course for their mutual benefit, sawing of the party wall is out of the question. Impregnation of the lowest brick courses of the affected wall with a water-repellent fluid containing silicone may provide a solution. To be effective, this *injected chemical damp-proof course*, like any new physical barrier, requires the removal of a 1m (3ft 3in) high band of plaster from the internal surface of the affected wall. Small holes at 150mm (6in) intervals in a horizontal row are then drilled down into the heart of the wall and the proprietary liquid is poured into these openings or injected under pressure until the foot of the wall is saturated with the water repellent. Just as the plaster that is applied after the installation of a physical damp-proof course should include a water repellent, so the plaster coating a wall that has been impregnated with a chemical damp-proof course must be equally damp-resisting if the installer's guarantee is to hold good.

Chemical damp-proof courses have been in general use only for the past four decades, which provides little evidence of their reliability in the long term. Yet most firms offering this treatment guarantee their work for a thirty-year period. Only if this is offered by the long-established companies is this warranty to be taken seriously. Clearly, it is wise to be sceptical about the likelihood of the business lifetime of some of the smaller and newer firms extending to thirty years.

Easily Cured Causes of Rising Damp

Conditions quite distinct from the breakdown of the original damp-proof course can help to propagate rising damp. Where the damp-proof course of a solid external wall remains effective, the manifestation of rising damp inside is often due to the piling of garden earth against the wall and above the damp-proof course. This defect is very simply corrected by lowering the external ground surface below damp-proof-course level.

A familiar feature of the external treatment of many brick-built Edwardian and inter-war houses was the application of a continuous cement-render plinth to the foot of the external wall, a purpose of which seems to have been the concealment of the 'ugly' damp-proof course, as well as to improve the weather-tight quality of the foot of the wall, the brickwork being shielded against saturation from rainwater deflected off the local ground surface by the rendered plinth. It follows that such a plinth was sometimes added some years after the house was completed, as a measure intended to improve damp-proofing. Unfortunately, it was often not appreciated that, in this arrangement, the plinth 'bridged' the damp-proof course, thus providing a route for groundwater to permeate the brickwork above its level. To be effective, a damp-proof course must extend through the entire thickness of the wall and not stop short of the external face, be pointed up with mortar, or be concealed by a rendered plinth. The removal of an offending rendered plinth above

the line of the damp-proof course will markedly improve the efficiency of a damp-proof layer which is otherwise intact and effective.

Concealment of Rising Damp

Perhaps it is natural for discovery of the effects of rising damp to prompt measures not so much for its cure as its concealment. It is probably safe to guess that measures to conceal rising damp in the short term are as widely practised today as they have ever been, and there is nothing to recommend such action. However, there are durable damp concealment techniques, which may prove helpful in circumstances where correction of the cause of dampness would demand a very expensive remedy (for example, demolition and rebuilding, which might be necessary for an external wall also acting as an earth-retaining wall).

A traditional form of repair along these lines involved stripping the internal wall surface of plaster and fixing to the masonry a patent, corrugated, bitumen-impregnated sheet lathing which was then concealed by the new plasterwork. This lathing has been superseded in recent years by a studded polyethylene-sheet membrane which is fixed into the masonry with steel screws located in polypropylene plugs, sealing the membrane against water penetration through its fixing holes. The material is faced with a fine-mesh grid of polyethylene internally, which provides a good 'key' for application of the new plaster surface.

To obviate future problems that may be generated by these low-cost, damp-concealment techniques, it is essential that the narrow cavity left behind the corrugated or studded lath is well ventilated, giving the dampness still passing through the newly clad, mass-masonry construction an opportunity to evaporate away. For this reason it is advisable to provide continuous shallow voids at both the head and foot of panels of damp-resisting lathing, venting the void at the rear of the lathing through grilles incorporated in the skirting board just above floor level, and into the ceiling void at high level. It should be stressed that this damp-alleviation technique is not to be recommended where there is the opportunity to install a new damp-proof course, which will dry out the entire building construction.

Decay and Treatment of Timber

It is mainly rot or insect attack that affects the serviceability of timber used in house construction. When an attack is found, it is advisable to obtain the opinion of a specialist who will be able to identify the type of decay and advise on the treatment of the timber, including designating any parts that should be removed. Where fungal decay is found, this expert should specify the cause and suggest measures for its elimination. Plainly, the existence of timber decay is likely to be related to other shortcomings in the condition of the house and these faults may have to be rectified in addition to treatment of the timber. Problems may have emerged because of an original design or sub-standard alterations that failed to provide protection of timber from ground moisture or adequate ventilation (creating conditions conducive to fungal and insect attack). Problems may also arise where roofslopes are not sufficiently steep to drain away all rainwater. A more likely cause of problems is lack of maintenance that has led to blocked or broken rainwater drains, displaced roof tiles or peeling paint finishes, all of which invite timber decay.

Rot in Timber

Timber decay that is not owed to insect action is normally the result of fungal attack. If it is appreciated that the function of all timber pests is to break down and convert dead trees into soil, allowing new trees unimpeded growth, it should be clear that these pests cannot discriminate between dead wood lying on the forest floor and that used in the construction of dwellings.

The fungi are parasitical and can only live by feeding on organic matter, including wood and leaves. In contrast to most plants, they breathe in oxygen and give out carbon dioxide. All fungi require about 20 per cent moisture content in the host wood to germinate, and in a heated, ventilated, sound, dry building of modern construction (where constructional timber does not occupy locations where it is likely to be penetrated by rainwater or groundwater) there is no need to fear fungal attack, as the moisture content of the timber will stabilise at around 12–14 per cent.

The most serious and devastating wood fungus and the species most frequently found in older houses is *dry rot* (*serpula lachrymans*). Having established itself in damp timber, this infection can spread to dry wood or brickwork. Its life-cycle starts with a spore, of which there are countless millions in the atmosphere. These spores are highly resistant to extremes of heat and humidity and are very long-lived. A spore which lands on wood with a moisture content of 20–25 per cent in a still and stuffy atmosphere where the temperature is between 7 and 27°C (44–80°F) can germinate and then throw out hollow strands known as *hyphae*. These initially hair-like fibres seek out and feed off the cellulose in the wood which is digested by the fungus to leave a dry, dessicated and fragile shell of wood fibre (*lignin*) which, in the absence of the binding cellulose, cannot continue to perform any structural role required of the timber. Having drawn the cellulose from one section of the wood, the hyphae reach on to adjacent sections to continue the process whilst the strands of the initial attack unite to into an equally fast-spreading cotton-wool-like growth called *mycelium*. In the later stages of an attack, different strands develop from the mycelium to convey moisture from the decomposing wood to sound timber, sometimes many feet away, weeping 'tears' on to it until it too is subjugated and ripe for attack. When this action is well established, the fungus will produce a fruiting body (*sporophore*), which produces millions of fresh spores. This growth bursts at intervals to release into the atmosphere an enormous number of rust-coloured spores that are carried in the air to germinate in distant damp timber, starting the process afresh.

Dry rot seems to possess an almost uncanny knowledge of the presence of timber and is able to thrust through brickwork mortar joints and to travel large distances across brickwork behind plastered surfaces in its search for fresh food. It is quite capable of travelling into an adjoining house through the masonry joints of a thick party wall. Evidence of the existence of dry rot may be found in a musty smell pervading a suspect space; the presence of a whitish cotton-wool-like fungal growth on timber; cracking and bulging of joinery mouldings such as skirtings and door linings, owing to the shrinkage of hidden fixing timber which has been attacked by the fungus; and readily apparent ravaged timber showing deep cracks across the grain, giving a 'cubed' appearance. Once dry rot has been discovered, the only remedy is extermination of the fungus together with correction of the unhealthy conditions that invited the attack. Unless it is completely destroyed to its limits, the fungus will develop fresh strength and start again to devour the timberwork.

For the householder, there are two broad options for treatment of a dry rot attack. One may either employ an experienced jobbing builder to undertake the work of opening up and eradication, or call in one of the numerous specialist 'building preservation' companies. If a builder is entrusted with the work, it must be ensured through a full briefing and careful supervision that only conscientious, knowledgeable and skilled tradesmen are employed who are able to give rational advice on the proper nature and extent of remedial treatment if (as is often the case) the initial assessment of the degree of damage proves to be inaccurate. An advantage of employing a specialist firm is that its tradesmen are more likely to be thoroughly acquainted with this area of building preservation. However, it is also true that many of the specialised companies sub-contract the rebuilding aspects of their service to general builders and that any well-established firm that offers a guarantee will inevitably err on the side of over-zealousness, doubtless dictating removal of an excessive amount of original construction and thereby adding to expense.

The first step in eradicating dry rot is both to find the heart of the outbreak and to trace its full extent with great thoroughness. Each branch of the fungus must be traced from its source to the growing tip, and finishes should be opened up to reveal timber at least half a metre (20in) beyond evidence of infection. Floorboards, plaster, timber trim – including architraves and skirting boards – and other finishes (including apparently impenetrable wall tiling) must be removed from timber and masonry if there is the slightest suspicion that the fungus has reached beneath or behind them. Only when the full extent of the attack is known, can treatment begin.

If fruiting bodies have been found, these should be treated with fungicide to prevent the spread of airborne spores. Then all infected timber is cut out so that all affected wood – including apparently sound

wood at least half a metre (20in) away from the visible extremities of attack – is removed. Where important structural timbers are infected but have not been weakened by the fungus, it may be practical to treat them with fungicide and to retain them. All fungus-infected timber that has been removed should be burned immediately, together with any shavings or sawdust from the infected area. Brickwork into which the mycelium has spread and any apparently unaffected masonry that adjoins an outbreak must be similarly poisoned. If a structural wall is too thick to absorb surface-applied fungicide to its core, it must be drilled with a series of holes into which the liquid is injected in order to permeate the entire thickness. Wherever possible, walls should be treated from both sides. Leaking gutters and roofs, defective rainwater downpipes, mounding of garden soil which bridges the damp-proof course and all other sources of penetrating dampness must be removed. Poorly ventilated and stagnant spaces must be opened up to a constant current of air by the introduction of new ventilation ports as even a vigorous attack of dry rot can be arrested (but not reduced) by exposure to fresh air.

New timbers installed as replacements should be thoroughly treated against infection. Pressure-impregnation of the new wood with rot-resisting chemicals is the favoured approach and the treatment of any untreated wood intended for repairs can only be obtained to order as these are industrial processes. It is more normal to purchase pre-treated timber. Even though these treatments drive the chemicals into the timber to a much greater depth than surface application by spray or brush, the wood may not be completely impregnated, particularly in the heartwood, so that any ends or notches in the wood cut on site should be dipped in preservative or touched up with a brush.

Other forms of fungal decay of built-in timbers are relatively unimportant because they are unable to spread to sound wood. However, they do signal the existence of unhealthy conditions, which may invite more serious trouble. As this observation suggests, combined or separate attacks from dry rot and less voracious fungi are common in neglected and decaying structures. The minor fungi are generally termed *wet rot* and cannot prosper in wood with a moisture content of less than 25 per cent (that is, too damp for dry rot). The long-term result of a wet-rot attack is the survival of a paper-thin shell of sound wood on the surface of the infected timber, showing deep cracks along the grain, but rarely across it as would result from dry rot. Eradication of the less damaging fungi entails cutting out and burning only the infected timber, replacing these sections with treated timber, although it is wise to coat the affected area with fungicide before adding new material as a precaution against any subsequent outbreak of dry rot which could emerge as the construction dries out. This circumstance is most unlikely in the comparatively well-ventilated location that is a common site for wet-rot damage – namely, poorly maintained external timber window sills.

Insect Action on Timber

The destructive action of beetles on timber is rarely as serious as fungal attack because an infected member is only weakened by the combined cross-sectional area of the tunnels, made by the insects, that it contains – the strength of the surrounding wood remains unimpaired. Beetle action that has ceased requires little attention except for any necessary repairs to the damaged timbers. In contrast, an active attack should not be left unattended and can be identified by the clean appearance of the *flight holes* and the little patches and piles of fresh bore dust that fall from them.

The main insect enemy of timber in twentieth-century houses is the *common furniture beetle* ('woodworm'). This insect can be found in both hardwood and softwood, chiefly in the sapwood that lies close to the bark in the tree. Therefore it is a serious pest in the lighter structural timbers found in houses of the last one-hundred-and-fifty years, where the proportion of sapwood is high. Although, as is apparent in 'woodworm' damage to furniture, flightholes are frequently seen in polished surfaces, the insect lays its eggs in cracks, joints and unvarnished recesses. They hatch out in 3–4 weeks and the larvae bore into the wood. After a period of 12–36 months, the grub becomes a fully grown beetle. It immediately finds its way to the surface and emerges to fly and mate in the months of June, July and August. The flight holes of the furniture beetle are about 1.5mm (⅟₁₆in) in diameter (Fig. 199). Wet or damaged timber is the most

FIG. 199. Flight holes of 'woodworm' pepper a ravaged section of floorboard removed from an Edwardian villa.

appetising food for the insect but apparently sound wood may be equally badly afflicted.

Other timber pests that are encountered much more rarely than the furniture beetle include the *death-watch beetle* and the *house longhorn beetle*. The death-watch beetle tends to prefer hardwoods, a preference which has made it the greatest enemy of the oak roof timbers of English mediaeval churches and which suggests that it cannot be viewed as a major threat to the timber structural elements of Edwardian and inter-war speculative houses. The house longhorn beetle, on the other hand, though confined to parts of south-east England centred on Hampshire and south-west Surrey, should evoke some anxiety from householders living in this region because it is mainly found in softwood timber less than fifty years old and prefers to attack fresh, sound wood. Dry, warm timbers in roof spaces adjoining chimney flues are favoured and the larvae of the beetle (which is much larger than the furniture beetle) bore voraciously to and fro along the grain of the wood, emerging, in June or August, through few and scattered flightholes up to 12mm (½in) long.

As applies in the treatment of fungal attack, in the

eradication of insect pests it is necessary to identify the unhealthy conditions that have invited the attack, and to cure them at source. Dampness and lack of ventilation are as welcoming to insects as they are to wood fungi and once these conditions are corrected the beetles will feel less inclined to stay. All local dust, dirt and rubbish should be cleared away, partly to remove conditions congenial to the beetles but also to facilitate treatment with insecticide. Formulation of a rational plan of action demands an assessment of the severity of the attack, which can only be made when its full extent has been revealed. It is important to establish if timbers have been so badly eaten away that their strength has been reduced, thus necessitating replacement, or if the damage is more superficial, leaving enough sound wood for the members to continue to do their original jobs. Timber which is so badly honeycombed that it is virtually useless – termed 'frass' – is likely to coincide with the sapwood content of structural timber. Thus, stout beams and bressummers that are riddled with holes and, on this evidence, may be thought to be useless, may be found, on investigation, to contain solid heartwood adequate to perform the structural role.

Wholly infested wood must be removed and any beetle-riddled frass eliminated by scraping or wire-brushing. All infested wood must be cleared away and burnt and any local construction cavities must be cleaned out carefully. When the retained sound timber is clean and readily accessible it can be treated with insecticide either by brushing, spraying or injection. The technique in brush application should be to spread the liquid generously over the surface and into all cracks. Spraying is an operation best left to a specialist company and is carried out with a coarse spray at low pressure. Where bearings of affected timbers are inaccessible, it may be necessary to drill deep holes for saturation of the buried beam- or joist-ends by injection. Sound timbers such as wallplates and lintels which are built into masonry, showing only one or two faces to the building interior, may be protected by coating their exposed faces with a thick 'mayonnaise' preservative paste.

The success of the insecticidal treatment depends very much on the skill and intelligence of the operatives and careful supervision to ensure that attention is given to the full extent of affected areas. Clearly, the right result is more likely if the working areas are easily accessible, well-lit and well-ventilated.

Any new timber introduced into the treated areas in repair or replacement work should also be treated with preservative containing an insecticide. In practice, the proprietary liquids that are used in the vacuum-impregnation of timber against fungal attack also contain insecticides and effectively identical products are available through builders' merchants and DIY outlets for brush application on site.

ENERGY CONSERVATION

Thermal Insulation

At points in some of the previous chapters, something has been said about adding insulation to uninsulated wall and floor surfaces, yet the part of the house most frequently associated with installing insulation is the space contained within a conventional pitched roof. It is true that most of the energy used in heating a house quickly leaks away through an uninsulated roofspace and for several years the local authorities, as the agents of central government, acknowledged this shortcoming by making available grants to householders whose houses lacked any form of 'loft insulation'. Government generosity in this connection is now at an end but insulation of uninsulated roofspaces still offers advantages to the householder, not least in the form of reduced energy bills. Satisfactory types of insulation include glass-fibre or mineral-wool quilts or mats at least 80mm (3in) thick (100mm or more is to be preferred if space allows), exfoliated vermiculite at least 130mm (5in) thick, as well as polystyrene beads, another form of 'loose fill' material.

The installation of glass-fibre or mineral-wool quilts is extremely simple. Unrolled between the ceiling joists to form a continuous insulating layer, the conventional roll-width ensures that they are held in place by the sides of joists. It is often more difficult to obtain a consistent thickness of loose-fill material. This applies particularly at the point where the ceiling joists terminate against the rafters that are descending to meet the back of the eaves fascia. To prevent the loose fill from spilling over this edge and filling a void which should be kept open to ensure good ventilation of the roof space, it is necessary to

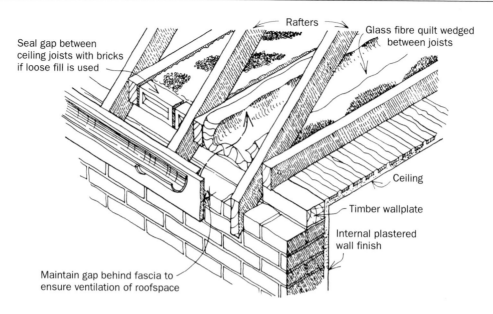

FIG. 200. Alternative materials for roof-space thermal insulation.

'dam' the channels between ceiling joists with bricks or wooden blocks cut to size (Fig. 200).

The necessity of maintaining permanent ventilation of the roof space prompts a question of how roofs enclosing rooms may be satisfactorily insulated because there is often very little space between the external roof surface and the internal plaster finish. Clearly, it is unwise to fill the cavity with insulation, preventing through-ventilation and introducing conditions conducive to dry rot. Ideally, a shallow void should be retained below the roofing felt, which lies underneath the tiles and to discourage *interstitial condensation* (condensation of moisture within the insulating material) it is necessary to introduce a vapour barrier on the warm side of the insulation. Fulfilment of the first requirement may be met by introducing corrugated-profile polyethylene sheets, specially developed in recent years to guarantee good eaves-level ventilation, below the roofing-felt layer, and the latter demand can be satisfied by inclusion of a mineral-fibre quilt laminated with sheet polythene, installed in the sloping plane of the roof by stapling this composite material to the sides of the rafters, the polythene face showing to the interior. An alternative method for incorporating a vapour check where

relining the underside of the roof timbers is in order, is installation of vapour-check plasterboard carrying an aluminium-foil vapour-check on its rear face, which supports the thermal insulation.

Harnessing Solar Energy

Installing additional insulation is only one aspect of energy conservation in the home. In the design of new houses, the need to satisfy stricter official performance standards has caused greater attention to be paid to the contribution to energy conservation that might be made by practising 'passive' solar design. This approach recognises that a new dwelling can be sited and constructed in a way that its energy needs will be reduced. Most older houses were erected with little consideration for the optimum orientation of living rooms in relation to energy-saving and with no concern at all for a good standard of thermal insulation, so the techniques of 'active' solar design, which aims to exploit the contribution of solar energy to house or hot-water heating, are of greater relevance to owners of Edwardian and inter-war houses.

Naturally, householders will wish to balance the environmental and running-cost benefits of alterations with their impact on appearance, but a new conservatory which offers environmental benefits is not necessarily inimical to the period image of an Edwardian or thirties house if its architectural potential is handled carefully. An attached conservatory on the south side of the house acts as an effective sun-trap in winter as well as in summer, and some of the heat generated can be vented into the house through an opening fitted with doors that also prevent heated air in the main accommodation from leaking into a glazed room made cold by a cloudy sky. Less easy to accommodate architecturally are solar panels which, when fitted on a south-facing roofslope, harness some of the sun's energy in assisting domestic water-heating. These black-painted panels are connected, by pipework passing into the house, to a tank through which passes a section of the pipework of the hot-water system. The panels, their connecting pipes and the tank, are filled with an oil which responds quickly to a change in temperature. An increase in the temperature of the oil caused by sunlight striking the panels is rapidly transferred to the section of hot-water pipework that passes through the tank and thus the water-storage cylinder is charged with warm water independent of the action of any connected central heating boiler or electric immersion heater. Even intermittent sunshine may be adequate to ensure a constant supply of warm water from a very well-insulated cylinder; watery winter sunlight striking the solar panels will generate a small amount of heat, reducing the amount of fuel required to raise the temperature of stored water to a warmth suitable for washing, whilst in summer, hot water requirements may largely be met from exploitation of the sun's energy. Against these savings has to be set the significant capital cost of installing the system which is likely to run into thousands of pounds as constructional alterations to the house as well as the system's purchase price are accounted for. Neat visual integration of the large panels into the architecture also presents a considerable challenge, and it is hard to avoid the conclusion that the new 'plumbing' can only be accommodated as a frank overlay of modern technology on the period shell, which will not be to everyone's taste. Solar heating panels are hardly less liable to offend than a blatantly exposed satellite TV dish (Fig. 201).

CENTRAL HEATING

Even among the older houses of Britain's housing stock, there must now be fairly few examples where no attempt has ever been made to install central heating, either at the outset or in a refurbishment, but for those contemplating upgrading a house which lacks this amenity and who are uncertain about the relative merits of the various options, some outline guidance may be helpful.

For most householders, central heating means a system of panel radiators fed through copper pipes with hot water under low pressure. The boiler that heats the water may be oil, gas or solid-fuel-fired. This arrangement is the direct descendant of the steel-pipe installations original to many inter-war houses, already described in Chapter 8. Simplification of the techniques required to achieve the modern installation places less demand on the

FIG. 201. Satellite TV dishes do not enhance house elevations!

talents of the heating engineer, and in consequence DIY installation of central heating systems has become commonplace. Accordingly, it is possible to visit countless houses where this job has been clumsily or insensitively carried out. Pipes hurtle out of stair risers and career across walls and through cornices; no regard is shown for the coherence of the original architecture. Yet this is not the natural result of a new central heating installation in an old house. Like any other craft, plumbing can be carried out well or badly, and if the householder is not confident about achieving the right result, there is no substitute for employing a skilful plumber who will respect the views of his client on the proper location of pipes and so on, in relation to prized interior features. Easily worked, small-bore copper pipes and their matching 'solder-ring' connections facilitate neat and unobtrusive central heating pipework if installed by skilled hands.

Under the general classification of gas-fired, low-pressure, hot-water central heating, two options exist for the form of the system; it may be the classical 'indirect cylinder' type or it is possible to adopt a 'sealed system' served by a combination boiler. In the first place, hot water storage is achieved in a calorifier (storage cistern), through which passes a pipe coil carrying hot water from the boiler; the system must also include a high-level *feed and expansion tank* as a 'safety valve' against a defective boiler/control mechanism. The latter system, by contrast, has no water storage other than the small amount of water contained in the combination boiler, which is fed from the rising main. In this sealed system, sophisticated controls prevent a dangerous situation from arising. There is a useful saving of space, as neither a feed and expansion tank nor a hot-water, storage cylinder are required. The combination boiler will heat a small circuit of panel radiators very quickly and efficiently, but performance in the 'instant' supply of hot water is less impressive, owed to the small amount of water stored in the boiler and the time taken for water flowing through to heat to washing temperature. Also, if hot water is called for simultaneously at two points (for example, bath and kitchen sink) it is likely that one of these fittings will be starved of hot water. In summary, although the sealed system may prove satisfactory for a small,

single-person dwelling, installation of efficient gas-fired central heating in a family house is likely to require the indirect-cylinder arrangement with the its consequent requirement for space to house a high-level feed and expansion tank and a large hot-water storage cylinder.

If gas cannot be obtained, the adoption of an oil- or solid-fuel-fired boiler is conditioned only by the ready availability of the particular fuel. Additional to the space requirements of the gas-fired system is the need to store the fuel consumed by either type of boiler. Heating oil is conventionally stored in a tank of 500–600 gallons (2,273–2,727 litres) capacity which is always sited outside the house, the oil being supplied to the boiler's burner through connecting pipework either by gravity or under the pressure provided by an electric pump. Solid-fuel boilers are now much more compact and lightweight than the colossal cast-iron devices that occupied part of many an Edwardian basement. Coke is no longer the favoured fuel. Instead, the solid fuel is obtained in the form of pulverised coal 'pellets' which are fed into a hopper at the top of the boiler. This fuel guarantees a consistent temperature and efficient burning reduces it to a small amount of ash, which must be removed periodically from the pan at the foot of the boiler. Unlike oil, the storage space needed for the solid fuel need not be sited outside, although it must be covered so that the fuel remains dry.

Gas-fired boilers create no waste apart from the combustion gases, which must be expelled to the outside air. If an existing and otherwise unused chimney flue that is nearby and which continues to issue into the outside air, the fumes from the boiler may be ducted into it, but in the absence of such a flue, no limitations are placed on the siting of a gas-fired boiler. If it can be located on an external wall, the flue gases can be ducted into the open air via a *balanced flue* which is fitted on to the side or rear of a wall- or floor-mounted boiler to discharge outwards rather than upwards. Householders are encouraged to consider carefully the impact of such a feature on the architecture, the ideal being a location for the flue terminal that is inconspicuous in the context of the elevation. The balanced-flue option is not open for the venting of oil- and solid-fuel-fired boilers because the sulphur contained in the fumes they produce cannot be diluted, and this demands the boiler's direct connection to, and exclusive use of, an existing or newly constructed chimney flue.

The radiators of a typical low-pressure, hot-water central heating system are features of most modern interiors as familiar as the washing machine or refrigerator. Their pressed-metal construction attempts to maximise the radiant area. The cheapest types exhibit a continuous welded flange along the top of the radiator. This profile collects dust and dirt and is very difficult to keep clean. At least one manufacturer produces an otherwise conventional panel radiator that incorporates a 'roll' profile for this detail, giving a neat and easily cleaned top surface. In addition to this basic type, a very wide range of radiators is available, from patterns presenting a completely flat vertical surface to 'dwarf' fittings whose radiant area is formed from continuously corrugated thin steel sheet.

Radiators should be sited in positions where heat loss is greatest – this often means below the windows. In this respect it is possible that no model from a range of standard radiators will suit exactly the size and shape of an under-sill location. In this condition, householders should not rule out the possibility of manufacture of a bespoke radiator to suit any particular circumstance. Providing an adequate manufacturing period is available in advance of the installation, even the largest manufacturers will produce individual radiators to integrate into 'difficult' locations. Thus, cranked or curved panels can be obtained top fit snugly into splayed or segmental bays. Because they will combat cold radiation from local window surfaces far more efficiently than standard flat panels necessarily located elsewhere, these 'specials' may be well worth waiting for.

Something should be said about the scope for installing 'central heating' fuelled from the other major source – namely, electricity. The electricity companies have sought to take a share of the market for central heating by promoting the use of night storage heaters. These units store heat built up from the consumption of cheap-rate, night-time electricity in a dense concrete core and emit this heat when it is wanted during the day. Yet they are not 'central heating' in the true sense as each unit is effectively independent of the other heaters in the system.

Except in dwellings that are extremely well insulated, the running costs of this type of system may be found to be high. Underfloor heating by buried elements is another main type of electric central heating, but, as with piped hot-water underfloor heating, it requires radical modifications to be made to the existing construction and is probably best restricted to new houses where there is the opportunity to integrate it into the building form from the time of the designer's first sketches.

Double Glazing and Secondary Glazing

High on the list of energy conservation measures familiar to every householder comes double-glazing. Widespread awareness of this technique and the general good opinion of its qualities must be due very largely to the extensive advertising devoted to it over the past two or three decades. Yet in the league of cost-effective energy conservation measures it ranks fairly low. The saving on energy costs made by installing double glazing in a formerly single-glazed window is not nearly so marked as the saving which results from installing insulation in a previously uninsulated roof space. Many Edwardian houses, and a significant number of those from the inter-war years, were built with 225mm (9in) thick external walls which offer poor thermal insulation, so that double-glazing the small proportion of these surfaces that is occupied by the windows may save only 5–10 per cent of the heat lost through the fabric. In these terms, leaving the windows single-glazed and adding insulation to the walls is much more worthwhile.

A large number of companies offer the service of installing double-glazed replacement windows and the quality of the products marketed varies widely. Some of the larger companies abide by a good specification for this work, requiring the installation of anodized aluminium window frames in hardwood sub-frames. Often an overly heavy appearance results from this combination of materials, but the hardwood can be painted so that it harmonises with the colour of adjacent surfaces and it is virtually rot-proof. For the installer this arrangement is advantageous because it gives a 'tolerance zone' around the standard-section aluminium frames, allowing neat reconciliation of the inflexible metalwork with window apertures that are likely to be out-of-square.

Also, the hardwood can be machined in the joinery works to the general profile of the jambs, head and sill of an individual window. This option is particularly helpful where, for instance, a rectangular aluminium frame has to be fitted into an opening spanned by a segmental brickwork arch.

Use of hardwood in association with aluminium-framed replacement glazing, naturally provokes the thought that the metal frames might be dispensed with altogether. Purpose-made hardwood windows can easily be fabricated to accommodate pre-manufactured, sealed double-glazed units and they do not require sub-frames. Even if they are entirely unprotected by paint or varnish, many types of hardwood will endure at least as long as the aluminium alloys used in most commercially available replacement windows, and wood, unlike metal, is a good insulator. The possibly short-lived 'thermal break' included in many aluminium frames to ensure that condensation is prevented from forming on the internal frame surfaces is unnecessary in a timber window. Mass-produced, softwood-framed windows are much less durable than any hardwood frame and it is certain that they are unlikely to last as long as aluminium windows, even if their external paint protection is quite carefully maintained. Although 'off-the-shelf' softwood-frame windows that will accommodate sealed double-glazed units are produced, householders are not obliged to replace existing frames with such catalogue items where installation of double-glazing is thought to be essential. Clearly, bespoke replacement frames fabricated from either hardwood or one of the more durable softwoods (for example, Douglas Fir) can incorporate a frame section which will accommodate the thicker double-glazed units. If the considerable cost of this policy is neither manageable nor appropriate, bespoke double-glazed units incorporating a stepped profile at edges can be ordered, allowing the replacement glazing to be housed in the zone formerly occupied by the single glazing. The most readily reversible treatment of existing windows to achieve an improved standard of thermal insulation is the use of *secondary glazing* where independent panes of glass or clear polycarbonate, contained in their own frames, are installed behind the original windows. Many different 'kits' for home assembly of this treatment

are available through the DIY stores and most make a modest impact on the existing construction; frames of small-section PVCu or aluminium, containing the lightweight sheet glazing, being hung on small 'pin' hinges and secured with inconspicuous clips, screwed to the retained wooden frames. In this way, both faces of the secondary glazing remain readily accessible for cleaning and mopping up condensation (a natural shortcoming in a form of double glazing that is not sealed).

NEW FITTINGS AND FURNISHINGS

The diversity of architectural styles seen in Edwardian and inter-war houses means that it is difficult to set down any general rule for furnishing these dwellings in an 'authentic' manner. The only meaningful general point that can be made concerns the materials used in any furnishing item. Other than 'Bakelite', a pioneering plastic of the 1930s, the pre-war generations knew nothing of the plastics familiar today; nylon, polyurethane, polystyrene or PVC. Any carpets or rugs were woollen; door and window ironmongery might be of enamelled pressed mild steel, 'black iron' (wrought iron or forged steel with an eggshell black paint finish) or BMA ('bronze metal antique') – rarely of polished brass. Where ceilings were not of the rare, light-gauge pressed steel panels, or embellished with profiled wood mouldings, the plain and profiled plasterwork was painted with a water-bound distemper. Wall and floor tiling was carried out in fireclay products, fitted joinery was almost invariably 'grained' to simulate woods of superior quality. Fittings, furnishings and finishes in synthetic materials proclaim their modernity when they are seen juxtaposed with the original features.

The introductory chapters to this book contain an account of changing stylistic preferences during the inter-war years and their impact on the form of speculative houses, but for the sake of authenticity of restoration it may be appropriate to add a few words of guidance here on detailing as a reflection of stylistic enthusiasms ruling at the time of construction of your house. The interest of the late nineteenth-century 'domestic revival' architects in the unselfconscious traditional buildings of the countryside engendered the picturesque domestic architecture of simple format practised by the Arts and Crafts Movement architects, which quickly popularized visually dominating roofs, small windows and rough-cast render or pebbledash as external wall finishes. These staple features continued to appear even in the last examples of suburban housing commenced before the outbreak of World War II. Yet the format of the speculative suburban house of the two inter-war decades also continued to feel the somewhat weaker influence of continental *art nouveau*. On its introduction to the UK in the Edwardian years, this mode seems to have been viewed as a sophisticated urban style, causing it to have greater impact upon city-centre houses than rural or suburban dwellings, but the sympathy of the sinuous forms of the style with the potential of certain building crafts – particularly stained glass and ornamental metalwork – soon caused it to have some influence on the detailing of more modest dwellings. Therefore, we find that after about 1905, leaded lights incorporating swirling patterns of coloured glass representing plant and flower forms are as much a feature of the front entrance doors of pebble-dashed villas of the suburbs as they are of the entrance glazing of red-brick Edwardian mansion blocks of the inner city. Whilst the mansion blocks of the inter-war years were to turn to *art deco* as the inspiration for decorative details, despite some simplification of the designs, many conservative speculative builders remained loyal to the spirit of *art nouveau* in the stained-glass panels they installed in the front entrance doors and fanlights of countless suburban houses as late as 1939.

From the outline of stylistic changes and references to the age of specific details made throughout this book, it should be easy to identify the period and 'pattern' of your house, which will establish the standards for the fittings and furnishings you may seek to harmonise with the architecture. The salerooms of most towns continue to be crowded with the commonplace 'brown' furniture of the late nineteenth and early twentieth centuries, and good pieces can often be bought at prices lower than those asked for new mass-produced furniture. Similarly, rugs and carpets (commonly of oriental origin), which nicely complement this period furniture, are sometimes offered for sale in the same auction rooms.

Finding authentic fittings may present a greater problem because few original light fittings and sanitary ware are likely to have survived *in situ*. Several manufacturers of period-pattern light fittings may be found in the UK and although brass is almost invariably used for the bodies of these products, it was by no means the only metal employed for this purpose throughout the Edwardian and inter-war years. However, the opal, coloured, frosted and etched glass shades characteristic of Edwardian pendant and bracket lights are faithfully reproduced in many 'period' fittings and a good range of wall lights of *art deco* style is available.

The sanitary ware original to most Edwardian and all inter-war houses broadly resembles the staple models of the modern ranges. Greater disparities are noticed between the design of the antique and the modern bright-metal fittings. Fortunately, several manufacturers offer plated 'crosshead-type' bath, shower and basin taps, which closely resemble the Edwardian and 'thirties prototypes. For the purist, some vaguely *art deco* patterns of pedestal WCs, bidets and wash-hand basins (all in white china) have recently been reintroduced.

Several wallpaper manufacturers offer a limited range of papers in designs by noteworthy Edwardian designers such as C. F. A. Voysey and Archibald Knox (the latter's work being strongly influenced by *art nouveau*) but these fabrics may be hand-printed, only available to order, and therefore very expensive. Something like the same conditions apply to carpets and textiles suitable for curtains and loose covers, although some recent enthusiasm among modern designers for the autumnal tones and jagged geometry of 'thirties' furnishing fabrics has introduced sympathetic colours and patterns into the ranges of contemporary mass-produced fabrics, allowing the creation of an authentic 'look' without the expense of commissioning bespoke reproduction material.

The introduction of a 'paint mixing' service at the large DIY stores has greatly extended the range of paint colours. This enlargement of the basic 'British Standard range' has made it more possible to obtain colours reproducing those of the original painted surfaces of Edwardian or inter-war joinery and plasterwork. However, it is necessary to stress that the high gloss paints employed everywhere today were unknown to the pre-war generations. The surface of the oil paint used on woodwork and smooth plaster was more similar to the modern 'silk' finishes than to the sheen of current gloss paints. Also, in continuation of the Victorian tradition, those who occupied most pre-war houses thought that where oak or mahogany could not be afforded, it was perfectly legitimate to imitate the patterns of these and more exotic woods by graining. Highly-figured painted surfaces were therefore more usual than a plain paint treatment of joinery in speculative houses, even into the 1930s. To achieve a glossy and durable surface to graining, it would be coated over with clear varnish; a treatment not applied to plain-colour paintwork (which therefore retained its 'eggshell' sheen) for fear that the decoration would be marred by early yellowing of the varnish.

At present, there is little guidance on authentic furnishing to be gained from study of surviving examples of Edwardian or inter-war dwellings because representative interiors have either not survived or it has not been thought important to protect a commonplace interior from this period. So the main source of information on appropriate patterns of furniture and furnishings is the museums of applied art and domestic design. In London, the Victoria and Albert Museum has an impressive collection of bespoke Arts and Crafts Movement and *art nouveau* furniture, though these items could not be said to be the possessions of everyman. Also in London, at Shoreditch, The Geffrye Museum displays a fascinating series of reconstructed 'room settings' from mediaeval times to the post-war period, including 'tableaux' containing representative items of the Edwardian and inter-war interior. To date, the sole exception to this museum-based interpretation of early twentieth-century domestic design in England is a recent initiative of the National Trust; 'Mr Straw's House' at Worksop, Nottinghamshire, an Edwardian semi-detached house of conservative design which was completely redecorated and refurnished to suit the local family who moved there in 1923. Due to the family's circumstances and the frugal habits of the occupants (a family member continuing to occupy the house until the 1980s) the house has survived as a remarkable 'time capsule' of middle-class popular taste of the Edwardian and immediate post-World War I years and readers are thoroughly recommended to visit the house to obtain a more realistic view of the values and preferences of the time than may be gained, for example, from close study of seemingly relevant film and TV presentations.

Glossary of Terms

Architrave Moulded trim covering joint between the frame within a door or window opening and the wall finish.

Area Space separating basement of a house from surrounding earth, to keep the structure dry.

Arris Sharp edge at the meeting of two flat surfaces.

Ashlar Large square-cut stones in fine-jointed masonry.

Asphalt Dark bituminous pitch occurring naturally or made from petroleum.

Backfill Earth, broken brick or stone used to fill excavations after foundations have been laid in them.

Ball valve Automatic water supply operated by a floating ball in a cistern, connected by a lever to a valve closing the water supply when the cistern is full.

Balloon frame Timber house construction in which the studs extend from soleplate to eaves, the floor joists being nailed to them.

Baluster A post in a balustrade.

Balustrade The whole infilling from handrail down to tread or floor level at the edge of a stair, balcony or verandah.

Bargeboard Sloping board along a gable protecting the ends of horizontal roof timbers.

Batten Length of small-section square-sawn softwood to which roof tiles or slates are fixed.

Bay window Angular or curved projection, incorporating windows, from an elevation.

Bearing Structure supporting a beam, joist, plate, purlin or rafter.

Benching Concrete cast in a manhole both sides of a half-round drainage channel, to ensure that no solids are left behind as the chamber drains following a flood.

Bevel Surface meeting another at an angle of less than 90 degrees (a *chamfer* is a 45-degree bevel).

Birdsmouth V-shaped cut in the end of a timber to fit it over a cross-timber.

Bituminous felt Flax, hemp or other fibre matted into sheets of felt, treated with bitumen, for roof covering or underlays.

B.M.A. Bronze metal antique: a finish on door and window ironmongery.

Bond Method of interlocking bricks or stone blocks to create a stable structure *or* layout of roofing tiles or slates for weather tightness.

Bonnet tile Hip tile with a rounded top.

Bossing Forming sheet lead or copper with boxwood shapes and a mallet.

Braced frame Timber building frame with widely spaced heavy corner posts into which horizontal interties supporting upper floors are cut. The studs between posts carry no floor load.

Bressummer Long, heavy timber lintel carrying high-level brickwork or masonry.

Brick nogging Brickwork infill between the studs of a timber frame.

Butt hinge The commonest hinge for doors and casement windows: when the door is shut, its two halves are folded together, one half on the door frame, the other on the door's hanging stile.

Butt joint Joint between two pieces of a building material that meet at their ends without overlapping.

Calorifier A heat exchanger in which water is heated by a submerged coil of pipe with hotter water passing through it (indirect cylinder in central heating).

Came H-section strip of lead or soft copper holding glass quarries in leaded lights.

Cantilever Projecting beam, balcony, roof or floor slab fixed only at one end.

Casement window Window in which one or more lights are hinged to open.

Cavity wall External wall built of two leaves separated by a continuous air gap.

Centre nailing The commonest method of fixing fibre-cement and natural roofing slates.

Cheek The side of a dormer window.

Chemical anchor Metallic fixing secured in brickwork or masonry in an epoxy-mortar sleeve.

Clay plain tile A roofing tile.

Cleat Small piece of wood or metal fixed to a wall to carry a shelf.

Cockspur fastener Metal fastener for casement windows.

Collar Horizontal tie-beam joining rafters halfway up their length.

Common brick The locally cheapest brick, not normally used for the facing of the principal elevation.

Concrete A mixture of water, sand, crushed stone and cement that hardens to a stone-like mass.

Coping A stone, brick, tile or concrete projection, usually overhanging, for weathering the top of an external wall.

Corbel Brick, masonry or concrete projecting from a wall face, usually as support for a beam or truss.

Cornice Moulding close to top of an external wall, over-hanging to shield the wall from rain *or*, a decorative moulding forming the junction between an internal wall and ceiling.

Couple-close roof Pitched-roof structure in which the feet of the common rafters are nailed to horizontal tie beams also acting as ceiling joists.

Creasing tiles Clay tiles laid under the brick-on-edge coping of an external wall to throw rainwater clear of the wall surface.

Dado Decorative or protective panelling applied over the lower part of an internal wall.

Damp-proof course Layer of impervious material preventing moisture rising from the ground into the walls.

Dentil One of a row of small tooth-like blocks forming part of a classical cornice.

Diapering External wall decoration of square or diamond shapes formed in flint work or header bricks contrasting with the rest of the wall surface.

Distemper Matt-finish, water-based paint with whiting as the pigment and bound with glue size; largely super-seded by vinyl emulsion paint.

Dormer Vertical window through a pitched roof, commonly capped with its own pitched roof.

Doubling course Double thickness of slates or tiles ending such roof coverings at the eaves.

Drip Stepped joint formed in a flexible sheet-metal flat roof at right angles to direction of fall.

Drip groove (or **throating**) Groove in the underside of an overhanging projection, designed to stop rainwater flowing back into the house and to throw it off the projection's outer edge.

Dry rot A destructive wood fungus: *serpula lachrymans*.

Eaves The lowest, overhanging part of a pitched roof or the area under it.

Elevation Side view of a building.

Emulsion A water-based paint based on polyvinyl acetate (PVA) emulsion that dries by evaporation.

Enamel Hard gloss paint whose high gloss is obtained by a high proportion of varnish and reduced pigment content; as, therefore, it is not opaque, it requires a matching undercoat.

Encaustic tiles Fireclay decorated and glazed tiles used for paving.

Engineering bricks Bricks of uniform size and shape, high crushing strength and low water absorption.

Espagnolette bolt Vertical bolt on a casement door; turning a handle at mid-height retracts or projects the bolt into keeps housed in the sill and head frame.

Fanlight Window over an entrance door; originally semi-circular, latterly most often rectangular, within the main door frame.

Fascia Horizontal board set on edge and fixed to the rafter ends or external wall face to carry the eaves gutter.

Featheredge boarding Overlapping boards, tapered in cross section, used as external weatherboarding or (verti-cally) in fencing.

Finial An ornament (usually pointed) at the apex of a gable or roof of a turret.

Flashing Strip of flexible metal that excludes water from the junction of a roof covering and a wall or chimney, or between one part of a roof and another.

Flat roof A roof that slopes at less than 12 degrees to the horizontal.

Flaunching Cement mortar fillet surrounding chimney pots on top of a chimney stack to throw off rain.

Fletton A type of common brick, mass-produced close to the eponymous village near Peterborough.

Flint work External walls built with flints, showing their dark-grey broken faces.

Flue Passage for smoke either in a chimney or leading to it.

Footing Alternative term for a foundation.

Foul drain Carries sewage (alternative: *soil drain*).

Foundation Solid base on which a building rests.

French window A casement door.

Furniture beetle Woodworm.

Gable Triangular part of the end wall of a building capped by a pitched roof.

Galvanized steel Steel coated with zinc as a protection against rusting.

Glazing bar T-section bar of wood or metal to hold glass and subdivide a window.

Granolithic Jointless floor finish formed from a mixture of cement, sand and granite chippings, floated over a concrete slab to create a smooth, hardwearing surface.

Half-timbering A decorative treatment of flimsy wooden posts and rails applied to the outside face of an external wall to simulate timber framing.

Hardwood Wood from broadleaved – usually deciduous – trees (angiosperms).

Header brick Brick laid so its end is visible.

Head nailing An alternative, though rarer method of fixing roofing slates (see *centre nailing*)

Hearth The floor of a fireplace and the area in front of it.

Herringbone strutting Stiffening floor joists at mid-span by fixing a light timber strut from the bottom of one to the top of its neighbour and *vice versa.*

Hip Junction of two roof surfaces near the end of a roof that does not finish with a gable.

Hip roll Round timber with a v-cut in its underside, covering the hip and protected with a flexible metal capping.

Holderbat Fixing for holding a pipe to, and clear of, an external wall surface.

Intertie Intermediate horizontal member in a braced-frame timber structure, supporting upper floor joists.

Jamb Vertical side of a door or window frame or opening.

Joist Small-section timber or steel beam directly supporting a floor.

Kentish rag Random rubble walling in a grey limestone of irregular shapes and sizes that is indigenous to Kent.

Kerb Timber upstand, as used to trim a rooflight aperture.

Keyed joint Concave pointing of a mortar joint.

Kingpost truss A timber truss, consisting of principal rafters and a horizontal tie beam in which a vertical kingpost connects the ridge board to the mid-point of the tie beam.

Knapped flint Flints shaped to a roughly square section, flakes having been chipped from their faces before they are built up as a wall facing.

Lap The amount by which the tails of slates or tiles in one course overlap the heads of slates or tiles in the course next-but-one below them.

Lath The base for plastering; formerly split softwood slats, more recently metal-mesh lathing or plasterboard.

Leaded light A lattice of lead *cames* holding clear, translucent, coloured or painted glass forming a picture or geometrical pattern.

Ledge One of two or three horizontal timbers on the back of a ledged and braced door.

Lime mortar Mortar containing only lime, sand and water.

Lime plaster A mixture of lime, sand and water.

Lime putty Wet hydrated lime that has been soaked to grant it plasticity.

Limewash Slightly germicidal distemper, primarily used on external wall surfaces; made by soaking quicklime in water and adding size or other binders.

Linseed oil Traditionally the most valuable oil in the paint and varnish trades; obtained by crushing flax seed.

Lintel Small beam supporting masonry above a door or window opening.

Loft Storage space under a roof.

Loggia Open-sided extension of a house.

Mansard roof Roof, which has on each side a shallow-pitch upper slope and steeper lower slope, usually incorporating dormers, for efficient use of the attic space.

Margin The exposed depth of a roofing tile or slate.

Masonry Stonework and the craft of building stone walls. In Scotland, masonry includes brickwork and laying floor tiles.

Milled lead Lead rolled into sheets from cast slabs.

Mitre Joint made between two members at right angles by cutting each at 45 degrees to its axis so that the line of the joint is seen to cut the corner.

Mortar Mixture of sand with water and Portland cement or lime putty for laying bricks, blocks or stones.

Moulding Continuous projection or groove, used as a decoration, to throw shade and sometimes to throw water away from an external wall surface. In old buildings it may be of stone, brick, plaster, render, terracotta, joinery or cast iron.

Mullion Vertical dividing member of a frame between the lights of a window or door.

Nail sickness Severance by slates of rusted iron fixing nails securing a slate pitched-roof covering.

Newel Post in a flight of stairs carrying the ends of the outer string and handrail and supporting these at an end or corner.

Nib Downward-projecting lug at the head of a roof tile for hooking over the tiling batten.

Nosing Half-round, overhanging front edge of a stair tread or wooden window sill.

Ogee S-shaped line, profile or moulding.

Oriel An overhanging window carried on corbels.

Pallets Short sections of batten built into brickwork bed-joints each side of a door or window opening to provide fixing points for the frame *or*, slatted softwood platforms on which new bricks or tiles are stacked for delivery.

Pantile Wave-section clay roofing tile.

Parapet Low wall at the edge of a roof.

Parting bead Narrow, vertical strip of wood fixed to the pulley stile of a sash window to separate the upper and lower sashes.

Partition Non-load-bearing wall between rooms.

Party wall A wall common to two adjoining houses.

Parging Rendering on the inside of a brick flue.

Parquet A floor of tongued and grooved hardwood blocks, glued to a wooden or concrete sub-floor.

Pebbledash External wall finish in which pebbles are thrown on to a fresh render coat, pushed in and left exposed.

Peg stay Perforated metal-bar stay that holds a casement in place by engaging on a peg installed on the fixed frame.

Perpend Visible part of a vertical joint in brickwork or masonry.

Picture rail Horizontal timber moulding separating the frieze from the lower panels of a plastered internal wall.

Pier Loadbearing brickwork between openings in a wall *or* a shallow buttress bonded to a wall to increase its stability.

Pintle Pin of a hinge for a gate or heavy external door.

Pitched roof Roof with two slopes, the apex of which is at a central ridge.

Place bricks Soft, underburnt bricks used in partitions.

Plastic repair Repair of stone or terracotta with matching mortars.

Pointing Completing mortar joints in brickwork with a surface mortar differing in ingredients and/or colour from the bedding mortar.

Portland cement Artificial cement, formed from burning limestone at high temperature in a rotary kiln, so called because when hard it was thought to resemble Portland stone.

Portland stone A pale grey limestone from the Isle of Portland on England's south coast.

Pressed brick Bricks with sharp arrises formed by moulding under high pressure.

Pulley stile Vertical board flanking the sashes at each side of a sash window. The pulleys over which the sash cords pass are fixed near the top of the pulley stile.

Purlin Horizontal beam in a roof structure at right angles to the trusses and carried on them. It carries the common rafters.

Putty A plastic material used for bedding glass in wood and steel-framed windows and for making a waterproof fillet outside the glass which holds it to the frame; a mixture of whiting and linseed oil.

Quadrant stay A curving, metal, flat-bar casement stay.

Quarry Small pane of glass in a leaded light.

Quarry tile Unglazed but impervious black, brown, buff or red square fireclay flooring tile.

Queenpost truss Roof truss differing from the kingpost truss in omitting the central kingpost in favour of two queenposts, which rise from the tie beam to either side of a central void.

Rafter Sloping timber member extending from the eaves to the ridge of a roof.

Rail Horizontal member with tenons formed at its ends, framed into vertical stiles, as in a panelled door.

Relieving arch Arch built over and clear of a timber lintel or bressummer to deflect load away from it.

Repointing Raking out and refilling brickwork joints with mortar.

Retaining wall Wall supporting and confining a mass of earth.

Ridge Horizontal joint line of roofslopes at the apex of a pitched roof.

Ridge board A horizontal board set on edge at the apex of a pitched roof to which the top ends of the rafters are fixed.

Roll Loaf-section length of wood over which flexible-metal roofing sheets are lapped and folded.

Roughcast External rendering in which the final coat of mortar slurry, containing pebbles, is thrown on and left rough for subsequent painting.

R.S.J. Rolled steel joist.

Rubber Soft, smooth brick suitable for rubbing to shape for gauged brickwork.

Saddleback coping Coping with a sharp apex: i.e. miniature-gable profile in cross-section.

Saddle bar Horizontal metal bar used to stiffen a leaded light.

Sanitaryware Porcelain lavatory basins and WCs.

Sarking Continuous timber boarding underneath roof slating or tiling.

Sarking felt Bituminous felt underneath tile or slate roof coverings.

Sash window A window in which two opening lights (*sashes*) slide up and down in a cased frame, balanced by sash weights connected to the sashes by sash cords passing over sash pulleys.

Scotia A small, concave quadrant moulding.

Scrim Open-weave fabric used to reinforce plasterwork.

Secret gutter A virtually hidden gutter in which the flexible metal gutter lining is covered by the roofing slates, tiles or shingles.

Sheet glass Transparent window glass, less smooth than float or plate glass.

Shingles Thin, rectangular pieces of timber used, in a technique similar to slating, to cover walls or roofs.

Shoring Giving temporary support with shores to a building being repaired, altered or underpinned.

Shuttering Temporary structure, usually of timber, to hold concrete during setting (a.k.a. *formwork*)

Sill The lowest horizontal member of a framed partition, or of a frame for a window or door. A wooden door or window sill may be fixed on top of a stone, concrete or brick sill.

Size A liquid sealer with which plaster is coated so that paint applied over it will not be too much absorbed.

Skylight A rooflight.

Slate hanging Vertical slating covering a wall.

Sleeper wall Thin, honeycomb, brick wall supporting joists of a timber suspended ground floor.

Snap header A half-brick.

Soaker Small, flexible, metal flashing, roughly of slate size, cut to shape by the plumber and laid by the slater, to interlock with slates or tiles and make a watertight joint at hip, valley or abutment.

Soffit The under-surface of a cornice, stair, beam, arch, vault or overhang.

Softwood Timbers of the botanical group gymnosperms

(generally from coniferous trees such as pine, larch, fir and spruce).

Soil and vent pipe (s.v.p.) Vertical pipe conveying sewage from the parts of the house above ground into the soil drain. Its upper end projects above the eaves and is left open to vent the drain.

Soldier course A course of bricks laid on vertically on end, forming a horizontal band in the facing brickwork or a flat arch.

Soleplate Timber member, laid on a low masonry plinth, off which a timber-framed external wall is raised.

Sprig Small headless nail, used for securing glass in wood-frame windows.

Stile Vertical end-framing member of a timber door or window, mortised to enclose the tenon of a rail.

Stooling Upper surface of the end of a stone or concrete lug sill. It is horizontal, to form a bed for the masonry above it.

Stopcock Valve that turns off the water or gas supply.

Strap hinge A band-and-hook hinge.

Stretcher A brick or stone laid with its length in the plane of the face of the wall.

String Sloping board at each end of the treads, housed or cut to carry the treads and risers of a stair flight.

String course Decorative, usually projecting, thin, horizontal strip of stone, brick or stucco that extends across an elevation.

Struck joint Horizontal mortar joint smoothed off by pressing the trowel in at the upper edge so as to throw rainwater out to the face of the brickwork.

Strut Short, diagonal timber, forming part of a truss or frame, included to resist compression.

Stucco Hard, smooth render, often imitating stone, incorporating details such as mouldings, cornices and string courses.

Stud Vertical wooden post within a timber-framed wall or partition.

Substrate A construction layer over-painted, tiled or plastered.

Suspended floor A floor supported only at its ends or, in the case of ground floors, also on intermediate piers or sleeper walls.

Swept valley A roof valley formed from stone slates, clay plain tiles or shingles, cut or made tapered so as to eliminate the need for a flexible-metal gutter.

Terracotta Fine-grained earthernware, fired in moulds to produce plain and moulded building blocks for walling, cornices, string courses and balustrades.

Terrazzo Coloured stones, laid in cement mortar on concrete and ground off to a smooth, level finish.

Tessellated Of, or resembling mosaic.

Thatch A thick roof covering of reed or straw laced with *withies* (flexible sticks cut from willow trees).

Throat A narrowing at the bottom of a flue just above the fireplace that improves the draught from an open fire.

Tile hanging Clay plain tiles fixed vertically to an external wall face to weatherproof it.

Tilting fillet Horizontal board, triangular in cross-section, nailed across rafters or sarking under the eaves doubling-course to tilt that course slightly less steeply than the rest of the roof covering and to ensure that the tails of the lowest tiles or slates bed tightly on each other.

Tingle Thin, flexible metal clip to secure the tail of a replacement slate.

Tongue and groove joint Joint between the edges of boards to form a smooth wall, floor or ceiling which is virtually airtight. The tongue in one board fits in the groove in its neighbour.

Trap U-shape bend in a waste or soil pipe containing enough water to seal the air downstream of the U from that above it.

Trimmer arch Brick arch carrying the concrete slab under the fireplace in an otherwise timber floor: it spans from the chimney-back to the trimming joist in front of the hearth.

Underpinning Installing new foundations to support masonry.

Valley Intersection of two sloping roof surfaces, towards which water flows (the opposite of a hip).

Vault Suspended floor construction showing smooth arched masonry on its underside.

Verandah External gallery, usually with a roof, along the side of a house.

Verge The edge of a pitched roof that overhangs a gable.

Vitreous enamel A glossy and durable glass surface, attached by firing, to cast iron or pressed steel.

Wainscoting Wall panelling made of oak or painted soft-wood.

Wallplate A horizontal timber along the top of a wall at eaves level; it carries the rafters and ceiling joists.

Weephole Small drain hole for water; some perpends in the outer leaf of a cavity wall are left without mortar to act as weepholes.

Weights box The construction surrounding the counter-weights in the jamb of a sash window.

Welt A seam in a flexible-metal roof covering.

Further Reading

Barrett, Helena; Phillips, John, *Suburban Style: The British Home 1840–1960*, Macdonald Orbis, 1987

Jackson, Alan A., *Semi-detached London*, Wild Swan Publications, 1991

Jackson, Albert; Day, David, *Period House*, HarperCollins, 2005

Jeremiah, David. *Architecture and Design for the Family in Britain 1900–70*, Manchester University Press, 2000

Long, Helen C., *The Edwardian House*, Manchester University Press, 1993

Mills, Edward (ed.), *Building Maintenance & Preservation*, Butterworth-Heinemann, 1994

Muthesius, Stefan, *The English Terraced House*, Yale University Press, 1982

Oliver, Paul; Davis, Ian; Bentley, Ian, *Dunroamin: The Suburban Semi and its Enemies*, Pimlico, 1994

Index